CONTINENTAL DEFENSE IN THE EISENHOWER ERA

PALGRAVE STUDIES IN THE HISTORY OF
SCIENCE AND TECHNOLOGY

James Rodger Fleming (Colby College) and Roger D. Launius (National Air and Space Museum), Series Editors

This series presents original, high-quality, and accessible works at the cutting edge of scholarship within the history of science and technology. Books in the series aim to disseminate new knowledge and new perspectives about the history of science and technology, enhance and extend education, foster public understanding, and enrich cultural life. Collectively, these books will break down conventional lines of demarcation by incorporating historical perspectives into issues of current and ongoing concern, offering international and global perspectives on a variety of issues, and bridging the gap between historians and practicing scientists. In this way they advance scholarly conversation within and across traditional disciplines but also help define new areas of intellectual endeavor.

Published by Palgrave Macmillan:

Continental Defense in the Eisenhower Era: Nuclear Antiaircraft Arms and the Cold War
By Christopher J. Bright

Confronting the Climate: British Airs and the Making of Environmental Medicine
By Vladimir Jankovic´

Globalizing Polar Science: Reconsidering the International Polar and Geophysical Years
Edited by Roger D. Launius, James Rodger Fleming, and David H. DeVorkin

Eugenics and the Nature-Nurture Debate in the Twentieth Century
By Aaron Gillette

John F. Kennedy and the Race to the Moon
By John M. Logsdon

A Vision of Modern Science: John Tyndall and the Role of the Scientist in Victorian Culture
By Ursula DeYoung

Searching for Sasquatch: Crackpots, Eggheads, and Cryptozoology
By Brian Regal

Continental Defense in the Eisenhower Era

Nuclear Antiaircraft Arms and the Cold War

Christopher J. Bright

CONTINENTAL DEFENSE IN THE EISENHOWER ERA
Copyright © Christopher J. Bright, 2010.

All rights reserved.

First published in hardcover in 2010 by
PALGRAVE MACMILLAN®
in the United States—a division of St. Martin's Press LLC,
175 Fifth Avenue, New York, NY 10010.

Where this book is distributed in the UK, Europe and the rest of the world, this is by Palgrave Macmillan, a division of Macmillan Publishers Limited, registered in England, company number 785998, of Houndmills, Basingstoke, Hampshire RG21 6XS.

Palgrave Macmillan is the global academic imprint of the above companies and has companies and representatives throughout the world.

Palgrave® and Macmillan® are registered trademarks in the United States, the United Kingdom, Europe and other countries.

ISBN: 978–1–137–02238–7

Library of Congress Cataloging-in-Publication Data is available from the Library of Congress.

A catalogue record of the book is available from the British Library.

Design by Newgen Imaging Systems (P) Ltd., Chennai, India.

First PALGRAVE MACMILLAN paperback edition: August 2012

D 10 9 8 7 6 5 4 3 2

Printed in the United States of America.

For
Sarah Ann and Henry Campbell

Contents

Acknowledgments	ix
Introduction	1
Chapter 1 The Origins of Nuclear Air Defense Arms	5
Chapter 2 Robert Sprague's "Adequate Defense"	23
Chapter 3 Testing, Predelegating, and Announcing	41
Chapter 4 Genie	65
Chapter 5 Nike-Hercules	95
Chapter 6 BOMARC and Falcon	127
Conclusion	151
Notes	161
Bibliography	255
Index	267

Acknowledgments

This manuscript was derived from a dissertation directed in the Department of History at George Washington University by Leo P. Ribuffo. The dissertation benefited from further guidance provided by William Burr, James G. Hershberg, David Alan Rosenberg, and William H. Becker. I appreciate their commitment to and enthusiasm for that endeavor.

I thank Paul Ceruzzi, Warren I. Cikins, John Haskell, Nelson Lankford, and Donald Sweig for encouraging me in my studies. I extend my appreciation to those who provided important information, background details, or comments on this work, especially: William Arkin, Brien Beattie, Michael Binder, Michael Dobbs, Tom Graham, David Haight, Stephen Haller, the late Chuck Hansen, Robert Holden, Linda Hunt, Joseph Jockel, David Krugler, Mark Morgan, Robert S. "Stan" Norris, John Pike, Jeffrey T. Richelson, Stephen I. Schwartz, Rick Sturdevant, and Rick Wilhelm. In addition, the George Washington Cold War Program, an important collaboration of individuals and programs at the university, the National Security Archive, and the Cold War International History Project provided a conducive intellectual and institutional environment for the dissertation.

I am grateful to various institutions, organizations, and offices that provided source material for this project. Several were especially solicitous of my requests, particularly the U.S. Army's Redstone Arsenal, the Air Force Space Command, the Sandia National Laboratories, the Dwight D. Eisenhower Presidential Library, the Air Force Association, the National Security Archive at George Washington University, the Interlibrary Loan Office at George Washington's Melvin Gelman Library, the National Museum of the United States Air Force, the Archives Division of the Smithsonian Institution's National Air and Space Museum, and the National Park Service's Golden Gate National Recreation Area.

I also acknowledge the following scholars, of various ideological persuasions and academic specialties, who helped shape my understanding of American history and politics and the broader scholarly enterprise while at William and Mary, the University of Virginia, and The George Washington University: Tyler Anbinder, Edward P. Crapol, Judith Ewell, the late S.G. Whittle Johnston, David C. Jordan, Morris McCain, and Kenneth W. Thompson.

I am grateful to Sydney and Gloria Albrittain (my in-laws) and Judith and J. Edward Bright (my parents) for support, financial and otherwise. I also received the following awards, which provided critical funds to help underwrite my dissertation: a Daniel and Florence Guggenheim Fellowship from the National Air and Space Museum, a dissertation fellowship from the Department of the Army's Center for Military History, a Grant-in-Aid from the Cosmos Club Foundation in partnership with the Consortium of Universities of the Washington Metropolitan Area, The George Washington University History Department's Elizabeth Earle Heckmann Fellowship, two travel awards from its Columbian College of Arts and Sciences, and a Dwight D. Eisenhower Presidential Library Abilene Travel Grant.

I appreciate the assistance of the fine staff at Palgrave Macmillan, including Chris Chappell and Samantha Hasey.

For her very special role in this endeavor, I recognize my wife, Nancy.

Lastly, I dedicate this work to Sarah Ann and Henry Campbell, whose arrival roughly coincided with the formal inception of this project. In many ways their presence eased this effort, and made the publication of this work all the more special.

Introduction

When Dwight D. Eisenhower entered the White House in 1953, there were 841 nuclear weapons in the American arsenal. When he left office eight years later, the number had grown twenty-two times larger. By January 1961, the United States fielded 18,686 atomic arms.[1] While a considerable portion of this expansion is attributed to warheads carried by long-range bombers or missiles, about one-fifth of the 1961 total was allocated for defensive use over or near the United States to counter an attack by Soviet aircraft.[2]

The development of nuclear antiaircraft weapons and their deployment to more than one hundred locations in the United States made sense to American policy makers at the time. Technological limitations made it difficult to counter high-flying, fast-moving airplanes—a problem compounded by the fact that raiders were expected to carry atomic bombs. It was discovered that nuclear warheads could greatly increase the chance of destroying attacking aircraft and the munitions they carried without endangering friendly forces or nearby noncombatants. Various tests and operational simulations subsequently seemed to demonstrate that such arms, detonated at high altitudes with relatively low nuclear yields, could offer a formidable defense while minimizing the risk of collateral damage. Arrangements to field the arms then proceeded apace.

Although atomic warheads for ground-launched antiaircraft missiles and air-to-air arms were initially contemplated in the final years of Harry Truman's presidency, decisions to make them an integral component of American defenses occurred during the Eisenhower administration. The Army's Nike-Hercules missile, and the Air Force's BOMARC and nuclear Falcon missiles and the Genie rocket were discussed by Ike, his senior aides, civilian consultants, and uniformed advisors at National Security Council meetings, Oval Office conferences, and many staff gatherings throughout Eisenhower's term. The Atomic Energy Commission, the Defense Department, and several corporations and allied organizations cooperated in designing, testing, producing, and fielding these weapons; constructing the facilities they required; and instituting the procedures and policies necessary for their integration into American defenses. These were significant, high-profile endeavors, involving many in and out of government over the course of nearly a decade.

The public, too, was involved. Americans were informed of the development and deployment of nuclear antiaircraft arms. In an effort to facilitate popular acceptance of these weapons, details about their purpose, operation, and safety were broadly disseminated. The arms were touted in news releases, featured in films and television episodes, and made visible in many other ways. The publicly available information about the purpose, operation, and safety of these weapons largely approximated that which was available to policy makers. The need for atomic antiaircraft weapons was readily accepted by most Americans, and few objected to their existence or ubiquity.

This book traces the development of atomic antiaircraft weapons, and recounts related official actions, doctrinal decisions, and public policies. It also discusses their manifestation in popular culture. The central emphasis is on the nuclear aspect of this armament: how and why atomic charges came to be fitted to antiaircraft weapons, who knew about this development, and what they thought about it. There is no similar extant work.

There are several official histories that recount the institutional details of the design and construction of these arms and their various parts. Some make only passing references to the nuclear components in the course of extended discussions of other features and subsystems.[3] A few nonofficial assessments of these weapons and their introduction to the American arsenal exist, although these treatments are brief and do not situate the events within a broader political or cultural context.[4] In addition, several scholarly evaluations of related topics also provide an overview of this armament and the policies that gave rise to it, but essentially only as an aside to other analyses.[5]

This work is neither a weapons system history that traces every aspect of the advent of particular arms, nor an institutional history that details all of the activities of the organizations that brought them about. Similarly, this study does not address the entire panoply of continental defense preparations during Dwight Eisenhower's term, nor does it focus on military units and their leaders, movements, and activities.

Chapter 1 provides an overview of the background and circumstances surrounding the development of nuclear air defense weapons.

The next chapter covers the formulation of the Eisenhower administration's continental defense policy and provides background on Robert Sprague, a particularly influential presidential advisor who did much to spur the development of the first atomic anti-bomber arms. Chapter 3 recounts significant design and test activities, details the initial public announcement of the deployment of these weapons, and discusses the advance authority granted to the Pentagon for their use in the event of an attack. The specific arms are addressed in each of the next three chapters, a task made easier by the fact that the varying types were introduced several months apart over the course of five years. The conclusion describes the withdrawal of these weapons, a process that began only a few years after they first entered the inventory, because fears of an intercontinental ballistic missile attack had come to supplant concerns about a bomber raid.

While some nuclear anti-bomber arms remained in the arsenal for nearly thirty years, the heyday of these weapons lasted only a few years. This may explain why, despite their numbers and the public and official attention they received, their existence has largely been forgotten or overlooked by scholars and analysts. There is considerable literature about the development of the American strategic nuclear arsenal during the Eisenhower administration.[6] Fewer works address tactical nuclear weapons—those arms that were intended for prospective use on (or over) foreign battlefields or the high seas.[7] These evaluations posit varying (and sometimes conflicting) assessments of the president's role in deciding the size of the nation's nuclear arsenal, the types of arms that would comprise it, and the defense strategy that the weapons required.

This study, however, stands apart from these other interpretations. It is difficult to relate the actions, attitudes, and outcomes surrounding strategic weapons during Ike's term to the nation's atomic anti-bomber defenses. During Eisenhower's administration, the president and many officials shared a fear of a surprise Soviet bomber raid on the continental United States. They believed it was necessary to prepare for the possibility of a strike and to consider how to counter it. Eisenhower agreed that these preparations required the advent of nuclear air defense weapons, and he assented to policies that brought this about. Support for this type of nuclear armament, however, reveals little about what he thought or did to encourage or retard the expansion of the balance of the nation's nuclear arsenal.

There is little evidence that Eisenhower and his advisors considered how atomic antiaircraft defenses might fit into a broader nuclear strategy. Intentional or not, this perspective is apt. It means that regardless of almost any alternative decision that might have been made during the Eisenhower years about American strategic forces or other tactical arms, the general outlines of atomic air defense preparations would likely have remained the same. The president and his military and civilian aides believed that weapons that could help protect the nation from a devastating bomber raid were commonsensical necessities. Understanding this perception is necessary in order to fully comprehend the administration's approach to these nuclear arms.

* * *

Two stylistic notes are in order. First, "nuclear" and "atomic" are used interchangeably in the following pages. Second, the official names and designations of the various subject weapons changed in the years under discussion (and since). For simplicity's sake, however, except where noted, the most common are used throughout. This is true regardless of the name or designation that prevailed at a particular time.

Chapter 1

The Origins of Nuclear Air Defense Arms

To those who considered such things in the late 1940s, destroying an aircraft in flight seemed a daunting task. It was also one that was sure to get even more challenging. Owing to technological improvements honed in World War II, airplanes flew higher and faster than their predecessors. In the years following the war's end, for example, average bomber speeds nearly doubled and cruising altitudes increased from 35,000 to 40,000 feet. "[N]o equipment has been devised which is satisfactory against jet-propelled aircraft," lamented an Army general to a congressional committee in 1949, "[t]hree hundred and fifty m.p.h. seems to be the point at which we cease being fully effective."[1] Steadily improving performance meant that planes could outmaneuver or outclimb antiaircraft projectiles, or they could avoid being within lethal range of ground guns altogether. Similarly, aerial engagement of modern bombers required high-performance interceptor aircraft that could locate a target, fly sufficiently high and fast to overtake it, and then sustain an extended fight against a heavily armed opposite prepared to counter, evade, or withstand the attack.[2]

As a result of efforts to improve American air defense weapons, in 1949 the Defense Department granted the Air Force the responsibility for the development of arms intended to substitute for planes. Missiles taking the place of antiaircraft guns were assigned to the Army.[3] Both services sought high-speed "surface-to-air" missiles that could fly dozens of miles and be maneuvered (or "guided") as they approached their targets. The Navy and Air Force also turned to similar, but smaller, lighter, and shorter-ranged "air-to-air" projectiles. Range, speed, and the ability to respond to evasive moves made surface-to-air and air-to-air missiles more lethal than guns and cannons, which shot shells on a ballistic trajectory. These new weapons, however, posed complex design challenges and required advancements in computation, electronics, and fabrication. Work on them proceeded slowly.[4] However, after the USSR detonated a nuclear fission bomb in August 1949, antiaircraft armament research assumed greater urgency. American leaders were increasingly concerned about the prospect of a surprise Soviet bomber attack on the United States, and the perceived need for better American defenses grew.

While an air raid on American cities or defense facilities would have been damaging in any case, a nuclear-armed foe raised the possibility of even greater destruction and larger numbers of casualties. Although the Central Intelligence Agency estimated that the Soviet Union possessed only twenty-two nuclear bombs in 1950, that stockpile was projected to increase by ten times within four years.[5] The Soviets were also assumed to be making many of the same aircraft design advances as the United States, despite efforts to retard the transfer of relevant western technology to the USSR.[6] The Soviet Union was thought to have swept-wing, longer-ranged jet bombers under development to replace the several hundred propeller-driven TU-4 "Bull" bombers in their inventory, which had been copied from American World War II B-29s but were incapable of making round-trip missions to the United States.[7]

In April 1950, President Harry Truman received a national security strategy paper, NSC-68, calling for renewed American efforts to counter the USSR.[8] When the Soviet-allied North Korean government invaded South Korea shortly thereafter, the USSR's hostility to the noncommunist world seemed confirmed, and further attention was focused on the possibility of an unexpected assault on the United States. "[A] Soviet first strike could not be considered any more improbable or irrational than Japan's attack on Pearl Harbor," one analyst observes about the period, "so the enhancement of air defense since the outbreak of fighting in Korea seemed logical."[9]

The term "continental defense" came to describe those programs primarily (but not only) meant to counter a bomber raid.[10] The Air Force had a key role in these preparations.[11] By the end of 1952, the service had established the Air Defense Command (ADC) and organized a civilian Ground Observer Corps to keep watch for planes along the nation's borders. To better monitor airspace, construction was also started on eighty-five radar stations across the country, and arrangements were made to build prototypes of others in Canada, which eventually formed a "Distant Early Warning" line.[12] In addition, the Air Force had commissioned a study to determine if computers could be used to ease air defense decision-making by helping to process and present the large volume of data produced by this network.[13]

While work on the warning net proceeded, the Air Force expedited the acquisition of the Northrop F-89 "Scorpion" interceptor, a poorly performing aircraft that had nonetheless been identified by the service three years before as the best then available.[14] Crews manning these planes were to remain on alert around the clock and be prepared to fly, under the direction of ground controllers, to the vicinity of incoming bombers. Once close, radar on the F-89 would allow a crew to track and fire upon the foes. Hughes Aircraft Corporation was developing a guided air-to-air missile, called "Falcon," for this purpose.[15] With Falcon, the interceptor's radar was to be used to locate a prospective target and determine when it came into the missile's range. A simple computer (termed the "fire control" system) was then to calculate the most advantageous point at which to launch the Falcon. Radar in the missile's nose was to take control thereafter, guiding the weapon to an explosive interception.[16]

While the Falcon offered potentially great improvement over the existing interception technique (maneuvering interceptors into a position that allowed them to shoot machine gun or cannon rounds at bombers), it was a complex weapon program and increasingly beset by delays.[17] Accordingly, the Air Force decided to use "Folding Fin Air-to-Air Rockets" (abbreviated "FFAR") on the F-89 once the Scorpion was fielded.[18] (Projectiles without guidance are typically termed "rockets." Those that can be directed to change course are identified as "missiles.") The Scorpion could carry fifty-two of the short, three-inch diameter FFARs in pods on each wing tip.[19] They could be fired in one, two, or three volleys on a straight trajectory into an aerial zone the size of a football field up to two thousand yards away.[20] Although the rockets required a close approach and could not compensate for last-minute evasive action by the target, with their rudimentary propulsion and lack of guidance mechanism, they offered a technologically simple, readily available interim solution to the dilemma of targeting relatively high-speed aircraft. The need for precision and complexity was minimized with a large lethal destructive area.

A late 1951 Air Defense Command evaluation of the possibility of using atomic weapons against aircraft was predicated upon similar reasoning. Based upon what is probably a well-informed contemporary account of the classified study, it seems the ADC argued that the sizeable blast zone of a nuclear warhead would allow relaxation of exacting fire control and guidance system performance standards. Since atomic arms would succeed when other weapons would not, they were projected to be capable of destroying as much as ninety-five percent of incoming bombers, compared to twenty-five percent assumed to be halted by conventional alternatives.[21] By obliterating munitions along with the bombers carrying them, atomic warheads also prevented the possibility (not foreclosed with conventional defenses) of nuclear stores surviving the destruction of the delivery aircraft. The ADC evaluation theorized that an adversary, faced with such a resulting low likelihood of success, would be deterred from initiating a raid. Thus, the study concluded that nuclear weapons decreased the chance of an attack and provided a lethal recourse in the event any occurred.[22]

An *Air Force Magazine* story, which generated an Associated Press item summarizing the analysis, suggested that either "pilotless aircraft" or "large patrol planes" might eventually carry "atomic-antiaircraft" arms.[23] This latter reference was an acknowledgement of the fact that only the biggest planes in the Air Force inventory could accommodate the size and weight of contemporary nuclear designs. This assessment was confirmed in late 1952 when the Air Force Special Weapons Center, the unit responsible for developing and overseeing the service's atomic armament, concluded "Project Heavenbound." This study doubted the possibility of equipping interceptors with nuclear weapons, because the smallest existing atomic armament was twenty-three feet long and weighed more than five thousand pounds. It did, however, declare that a nuclear warhead for an antiaircraft missile was feasible.[24]

Since 1950, an Air Force surface-to-air missile was under design by Boeing and the University of Michigan Aeronautical Research Center.[25] Initially given a fighter plane's alphanumeric designation and frequently referred to as a "pilotless aircraft," it was tagged with the awkward name "BOMARC," which combined the first letters of one originating organization with an acronym for the other. Despite its stubby eighteen-foot wings (providing some resemblance to an airplane), BOMARC was a missile, launched vertically by a rocket booster, then propelled by two ramjet engines. Eventually designated "IM-99A" (for "interceptor missile") and slated to fly as far as 250 miles up to an 80,000-foot altitude, BOMARC weighed more than 15,000 pounds, was forty-six feet long and had a ten-foot diameter. It was designed to receive guidance information transmitted from various ground points during most of its flight time, until a small onboard radar began to track the target in the final moments and concluded the interception.[26] Since early 1951, a nuclear warhead had been considered for BOMARC, and the ADC report later that year probably encouraged the effort.[27] As armament choices were being evaluated, BOMARC's development proceeded. However, the missile's ramjet engines, radar target seeker, and other features made it a complicated project at the cutting edge of its time. Initial plans to deploy it by 1954 soon proved impossibly ambitious.[28]

While the Air Force made organizational changes and designed new weapons for continental defense, so too did the Army. The Army Antiaircraft Command (ARAACOM) became operational in 1950, and it deployed gun batteries around eight locations, including several cities and Air Force bases; the Atomic Energy Commission installation in Hanford, Washington; and the Sault Ste. Marie, Michigan, canal locks on the Great Lakes.[29] By November 1951, the Army's design of an antiaircraft missile system had been accelerated and a series of final tests initiated.[30] Underway for six years, this program yielded a thirty-four-foot-long surface-to-air missile that flew at 1,500 miles per hour and had a thirty-mile range.[31] Dubbed "Nike" for the Greek goddess of victory, the missile operated in concert with three radars located a mile from the launchers. One radar identified an approaching aircraft, a second tracked the plane once it was targeted, and a third followed the course of a Nike launched in response. A rudimentary computer calibrated the target and missile data and transmitted necessary commands to the missile, guiding it to an interception. Beginning in 1954, the Army supplanted its outmoded antiaircraft guns with the new Nikes at more than two hundred sites around two dozen areas across the United States.[32]

Before this deployment started, the design of a replacement missile began. The original Nike carried three high explosives containing thousands of cubical metal fragments, which were intended to perforate metal aircraft wings or tails, damage or destroy engines, or kill or injure crews. The Nike tracking radar, however, had difficulty discerning multiple distant targets, such as aircraft flying together. In such a case the interceptor missile could be directed to a point between targets and detonate without inflicting lethal damage on any of them. Because warheads had a blast radius of sixty feet, planes flying in feared World War II–style bomber formations, which involved greater separation, might escape harm.[33] As a result, an Army Ordnance Corps official suggested in March 1952 that a study be conducted to determine if substituting a nuclear warhead, with the attendant larger blast area, would address this circumstance.

The Army, Douglas Aircraft Corporation (manufacturer of the missile), Bell Telephone Laboratories (designer of the associated radar, computer, and other electronic gear), and Sandia Corporation (the federal organization responsible for the weaponization of atomic devices developed under the AEC's auspices) evaluated the possibility in July 1952. The group concluded there were two feasible scenarios. On the one hand, the Nike's relatively small diameter could accommodate an existing type of nuclear warhead, provided the device was modified to fit. On the other hand, a larger diameter warhead, designated the "W-7" because of its position in the sequence of American nuclear weapon designs, could be used without change, but would require the development of a new missile. The first option would take approximately eighteen months; the second needed about three years. The W-7, however, was an implosion weapon, which used one-third less plutonium. Given the potentially large numbers of new Nikes that might be obtained, the study noted that the second alternative would minimize the use of this limited-supply critical component, and this could justify the longer development period. The Army agreed and tentatively chose the new missile option in December 1952.[34]

The next month, the Joint Air Defense Board completed a study requested by the service chiefs on nuclear antiaircraft arms. Presumably because it agreed with the perceived advantages of atomic weapons, the board "unequivocally recommended" that reliably deliverable, low-cost, two-to-four-kiloton-yield nuclear warheads be deployed for air defense purposes. (Each kiloton of nuclear yield has the force of a thousand tons of explosives.) The Joint Chiefs of Staff concurred with the JADB, and they informed the Atomic Energy Commission, the entity responsible for designing and building the nation's atomic arms, that the military's "immediate objectives" included modifying existing bombs to serve as warheads for the Army's proposed new Nike and BOMARC.[35] The Air Force subsequently chose the 600-pound, twenty-two-inch diameter "W-12" warhead for its missile, in addition to four different types of conventional warheads.[36] After the JCS ratified the Army's December selection of the W-7 and the new Nike version, by late March 1953, Douglas, Bell, and Sandia were at work on that service's follow-up missile.[37]

The Army's new weapon was first designated "Nike B." In keeping with the service's decision to name its missile's after mythological Greek figures, it was eventually named "Nike-Hercules" to distinguish it from the predecessor, which was rechristened "Nike-Ajax." Thirteen important characteristics were specified for Hercules; effectiveness, reliability, and nuclear safety topped the list.[38] Nike-Hercules was a forty-one-foot-long, 10,000-pound missile that flew at 4,000 miles per hour, and had a seventy-five-mile range and 80,000-foot maximum altitude.[39] To save money and time, it was to use the same launch sites and guidance equipment as Nike-Ajax, because facilities were being built for the earlier version.[40]

The advent of the Nike's W-7 warhead, the W-12 proposed for the BOMARC, and other nuclear explosives intended for purposes other than strategic bombing of terrestrial targets was partly the result of increased American production of fissile material. An expansion of Atomic Energy Commission capacity, previously authorized by President Harry Truman, meant that bomb-grade plutonium and uranium was far more plentiful and no longer needed to be rationed to the Strategic Air Command for offensive purposes.[41] New atomic devices also reflected design and fabrication techniques that had come about since the first such arms were developed in the Manhattan Project.

In "implosion" weapons, which included most of the new designs, a sphere of conventional explosives is arranged around an amount of plutonium or uranium. If the explosives are detonated, the resulting blast compresses (or "implodes") the fissile material with such force that the atoms in the material split. This releases the tremendous heat, energy, and radiation characteristic of a nuclear explosion. Lighter metal bomb cases and subassemblies, and changes that used less fissile material and heavy high explosives yet produced the same blast, allowed for smaller spheres (and hence smaller devices) and lighter weapons.[42]

The W-7, an example of a relatively lighter warhead, weighed about one thousand pounds, was fifty-six inches long, and had a thirty-inch diameter.[43] At a predetermined altitude and speed the warhead armed itself using an "in-flight insertion" process in which the plutonium core was mechanically moved into the center of the conventional charges.[44] It could probably yield two kilotons.[45] (For comparison, the nuclear bomb dropped on Hiroshima, Japan, is estimated at fifteen kilotons, although damage comparisons with antiaircraft arms are difficult, since the World War II weapon was detonated near the ground rather than high in the air.[46])

Atomic antiaircraft weapons were intended to create tremendous atmospheric blast pressures to tear planes apart. However, the precise effects at typical altitudes were not well understood in the early stages of arms development, although some studies of this topic had been done in 1951.[47] Thus, the AEC made plans to evaluate detonations in future nuclear tests in order to learn more about the gust, heat, and radiation produced.[48] An April 1953 technical report, however, theorized that airborne radiation, not blast, would be more lethal to attackers. It posited that radiation from a twenty-kiloton warhead might be so great as to cause "physiological effects" aboard bombers "severe enough to prevent the crew from carrying out their duties."[49] Later analysis, however, made blast damage predominant.

Studies of the effects of nuclear antiaircraft warheads and development of weapons to carry them continued as a new American administration came to office. Advocates of continental defenses believed the American effort remained relatively poorly funded, undermanned, and ill-equipped at the time, partly because it was disfavored by military services that saw it as a distracting adjunct to more important and prestigious responsibilities.[50] The Air Force's preferred focus was on the Strategic Air Command, while the Army favored traditional ground units, especially the infantry.

On February 11, 1953, three weeks after Dwight D. Eisenhower was inaugurated as the thirty-fourth president of the United States, he first considered continental defense plans.[51] At a National Security Council (NSC) meeting that day, the discussion turned to a report meant to focus attention on continental defense weaknesses. Received by Harry S. Truman from top aides the day before Ike succeeded him, the document concluded that the nation's assemblage of guns, interceptor planes, and radar "will not provide an effective defense against mass atomic attack." Signed by Defense Secretary Robert Lovett, Secretary of State Dean Acheson, and Mutual Security Agency director Averell Harriman, NSC 141 said that "[a]s of mid-1952, probably 65–85% of the atomic bombs launched by the U.S.S.R. could be delivered on target." It suggested a more robust, and more costly, defense posture.[52] The new president dismissed the evaluation, telling his NSC that it was "a legacy from three important members of the previous administration who had no personal interest in having its proposals adopted." He had little interest in an eleventh-hour policy proposal from representatives of a political party and governing ideology he had just defeated.

Eisenhower argued instead for a "preparedness program that will give us a respectable position without bankrupting the nation."[53] On April 29, the NSC adopted NSC 149/2, a broad paper setting out U.S. national security goals. It declared that "the U.S. should... [i]ncrease [the] emphasis on...protection of the continental United States from enemy attack," but noted that security was inextricably linked to the health of the domestic economy and the maintenance of a balanced federal budget.[54] Cost was a paramount concern in the

Eisenhower administration's early continental defense deliberations, and something that Ike thought distinguished his term from that of his predecessor.[55]

In May, the NSC received a second report that originated in the Truman administration. NSC 140/1, evaluating "the USSR's net capability to inflict injury on the United States," was produced by a council subcommittee established on the last day of the Missourian's presidency. Led by recently retired Air Force lieutenant General Idwall H. Edwards, the panel determined that in the event of a Soviet attack, the United States could destroy only about seven percent of incoming bombers. Once Nike-Ajax missiles were deployed and other defense improvements were made, the number was predicted to increase to twenty-seven percent in 1955.[56] The JCS, however, expressed skepticism to the NSC about the scenario. They suggested that an all-out strike against the United States might not be how the Soviet Union would initiate war, and thus American defenses should not be predicated upon it.[57] The military leaders were probably reluctant to endorse an evaluation that might spur competition for limited defense dollars. The president apparently agreed with the JCS critique. When the report was presented to the NSC in June, he questioned some key assertions, including presumed Soviet strike tactics and the skill of Soviet bomber pilots, which seemed to indicate he had some doubts about the dangers of a raid.[58]

Earlier the same month, in order to provide the Eisenhower administration with its own comprehensive overview of continental defense, the NSC established a Continental Defense Committee of its Planning Board, the group of council designees that conducted much of the body's analytical work. The committee was charged with evaluating NSC 140/1 and other prior assessments, including a report commissioned by Truman's Defense Department (named after panel chairman and Bell Laboratories president Mervin Kelly) and the Summer Study (a review from the previous season of the computerized radar network proposal).[59] The new NSC committee was to recommend prioritized changes to continental defenses, estimate the cost of a revamped effort, and determine its likely effectiveness. Retired Army lieutenant General Harold "Pinky" Bull, the CIA's representative for the Edwards study and a World War II assistant to Eisenhower, was asked to lead the new committee.[60]

If Eisenhower's national security team expected a review that differed from what came before, they must have been disappointed. Bull's report, presented to the National Security Council on August 6, 1953, echoed, rather than dissented from, much of what the council considered previously. More than eighty pages long, NSC 159 concluded that current protections were inadequate, and recommended many specific measures that could "provide the nation with a reasonable assurance of defense."⁶¹ An enclosure asserted that "[a]s the Soviet capability increases, so must the number and effectiveness of the weapons" deployed in response. Among the "critical" research and development programs requiring continued funding and attention according to this report were Nike and BOMARC, and "atomic warheads for these missiles."⁶² After the JCS expressed some concerns about the costs entailed in the Bull recommendations, the council delayed action on the document. Eisenhower had named replacement service chiefs who were about to assume office. Because NSC 159 was intended as a fundamental statement of administration policy, he apparently believed it was necessary to have it evaluated by the incoming military leaders.⁶³

As the new chiefs were getting settled, the USSR tested a thermonuclear device. This further confirmed the position of those government officials supporting a vigorous continental defense. They saw the United States as facing an extraordinary threat, because nuclear fusion weapons (which cause atoms to join together or "fuse") were even more lethal than their fission predecessors. In an especially well-attended NSC meeting on September 24, these worries were readily apparent.⁶⁴ After the director of Central Intelligence, Allen Dulles, reported the agency's belief that "the USSR is now capable of producing air delivery hydrogen weapons," the NSC considered a revised version of the Bull report.⁶⁵ The new draft incorporated amendments that the Planning Board had composed after the Soviet detonation.⁶⁶ In light of the new danger, NSC 159/3 specifically emphasized that it was "essential" that "within the next two years the capability to destroy attacking aircraft...should be substantially augmented." "[A]ll possible efforts," it continued, "should be made to expedite the equipping of adequate forces with aircraft and missiles which will achieve a high 'kill ratio' before attacking forces can reach our borders."⁶⁷

A group of civilian consultants that the NSC had impaneled earlier to advise on the cost of national defense programs agreed about the danger, but expressed some reluctance to embrace an expansive defense effort. In a written statement distributed at the NSC meeting, historian and Williams College president James Phinney Baxter III and four others, including the head of Pacific Gas and Electric and a steelworkers union leader, declared, "[i]t is our belief that we should depend more upon the increased quality of our killing power than upon increased numbers." The "over-all objective of reducing federal expenditures" should be maintained, they concluded.[68]

The newly installed JCS had a similar take. On an early August cruise aboard the Navy yacht *Sequoia* to discuss defense strategy, they agreed that continental defense needed to be improved but that strategic offensive forces should continue to predominate.[69] When they provided written comments on NSC 159 a month later, they argued it was difficult to settle on the defensive portion of American strategy before broader policies and funding limits had been determined.[70] At the September NSC briefing on NSC 159/3, Navy admiral Arthur W. Radford, the new chairman, also conceded that some defense improvements were "urgent," but expressed the sentiment that the revised paper, like the earlier draft, overemphasized Soviet capabilities. Radford said there was "great anxiety" among the uniformed leaders that an overly ambitious continental defense regime would sap funds better spent on other military functions. The president responded with some sympathy for Radford's view, and again reiterated the need to secure the United States affordably.[71]

Nonetheless, at the conclusion of the meeting, NSC 159/3 was formally submitted to Eisenhower, with only relatively minor modifications. The Defense Department was instructed to report specific plans and cost estimates for the "fighter interceptor" and "anti-aircraft forces," which were among the top tier of recommendations. These programs should, the report said, be "developed to a high state of readiness over the next two years" and "be further strengthened and kept effective" after that. Eisenhower accepted the NSC recommendations. The resulting NSC 159/4 was promulgated on September 25.[72]

As the JCS worked to compile the required details, they confronted budgetary realities. On October 16, after the chiefs proposed a fiscal year 1955 spending plan that was an increase over the current level and $3 billion more than the goal, Defense Secretary Charles Wilson rejected it and asked them to outline instead an "adequate" continental defense that was kept within "feasible" spending limits.[73] The JCS was coincidentally aided in this task by the NSC's near-simultaneous adoption of a new statement of national policy goals.[74]

For many preceding months, a broad, crosscutting "Basic National Security Policy" had been debated. On October 7, the NSC considered a lengthy draft and the president selected his preferred course in those areas in which there was disagreement.[75] Although the paper, NSC 162, mentioned continental defense in only three brief references, in another section it most famously identified nuclear weapons as an integral part of the American arsenal, "available for use as other munitions."[76] The JCS endorsed this language because it allowed them to reduce ground troop strength, eliminate some ships, and draw down overseas commitments. Since nuclear weapons would be used readily in a future war, the need for more extensive (and expensive) military forces and conventional arms was minimized. In addition to emphasizing the cost-saving approach, the JCS also hoped to economize by extending the date by which continental defenses would be ready, and to deploy somewhat smaller antiaircraft and interceptor forces than had been intended previously.[77]

When Admiral Radford returned to the NSC on November 23 to brief members on interceptor and antiaircraft plans as mandated by NSC 159/4, Special Assistant for National Security Affairs Robert Cutler seized upon the delay and reduction in these programs. He argued these changes ran counter to instructions in NSC 159/4. Radford assured him that the Joint Chiefs were trying to advance the identified programs "with all possible speed," but cautioned that "technical problems" and "appreciably lower" defense appropriations nonetheless forced changes. Radford pleaded for flexibility, asked that defensive measures not be given precedence over offensive means, and expressed hope that an "iron-clad directive" would not be issued in connection with the continental defense initiatives.

The president seemed receptive, and a clarification of program priorities was postponed until after the forthcoming approval of the DoD fiscal plan. However, the president did use the occasion to express skepticism about the effectiveness of antiaircraft artillery. "Would ack-ack guns," Eisenhower asked Radford, using military slang for the weapons, "be of any real use in countering aircraft which could now fly at such tremendous heights...?" Radford revealed his doubts, but said that "there was as yet no suitable alternative." The president also expressed concern about nuclear explosives and "the danger of bringing down an enemy aircraft carrying these new weapons...when they might explode over a target area," although he was almost certainly not aware that the Army and Air Force had been considering the same point.[78]

Ike's queries about the particulars of the military response to a Soviet attack on the United States demonstrate a continued interest in the subject. A little more than two weeks earlier, he and First Lady Mamie Eisenhower, along with 170 White House employees, retreated to basement air-raid shelters as part of a drill conducted at the president's behest. Elsewhere in Washington, hundreds of thousands of federal employees and public school students trouped to designated safe zones as some of them had done in two other practice efforts in the past year. The difficulties encountered in these limited rehearsals led to the decision to stage larger, more extensive exercises, some of which also included the president.[79]

While those plans were being contemplated, a $37.6 billion defense budget for fiscal year 1955 was approved in December 1953, down from the current allocation of more than $44 billion.[80] As a result of savings estimated to accrue as a result of NSC 162 and by the continental defense slowdown and force reductions, the budget allowed modest increased funding for anti-bomber programs and allocated more personnel to the Air Force. Army and Navy manpower strength was cut.[81]

In January 1954, the NSC considered the next interceptor and antiaircraft progress report. Although the briefing presented by Air Force chief of staff General Nathan Twining is not available, the tenor of his assessment can be deduced from other documents. Twining likely discussed the BOMARC development and antiaircraft artillery, because the president responded that "the pilotless aircraft" seemed to be one of the "sounder contributions to continental defense," and again said he was "very skeptical" about "any contribution" to be made by antiaircraft guns.[82] Most of the ensuing discussion, however, was still about the pace and cost of implementing an improved defense posture. With the approval of the reduced budget, the JCS and Defense Department civilian leaders were concerned about the continuing priority placed on thwarting a bomber attack. Consequently, they sought to amend the language of NSC 159/4 to specify that continental defense programs would be readied "as rapidly as possible" rather than with "all possible speed." This was meant to avoid hurried initiatives with few budgetary or manpower restraints from consuming limited funds.

Arthur S. Flemming, the director of the Office of Defense Mobilization (charged with coordinating defense production and stockpiling) disagreed. He argued that continental defense needs were so acute that every effort should be made to address them, and believed the change sought by DoD undercut the urgency otherwise apparent in NSC 159/4. Eisenhower sided with Defense, however, expressing doubt that "crash" programs would be beneficial. The NSC approved the proposed language, but instructed the DoD to continue to evaluate defense schedules and costs, and asked that a revised version of NSC 159/4 reflecting these changes be submitted to the council.[83]

The requested revision was approved by the National Security Council on February 17, 1954.[84] Originally designated NSC 159/5, then changed to NSC 5408 with the advent of a new numbering system, it was the administration's comprehensive continental defense statement.[85] In the absence of dramatic changes in the international situation, it was expected to be applicable indefinitely. NSC 5408 combined the amended Bull report's call for top-priority "high kill" antiaircraft forces with the more modest timing phraseology mandated weeks before.[86] The JCS's concerns were satisfied. Admiral Radford considered NSC 5408 "quite satisfactory"—so much so that he did not even refer a draft to the other service chiefs.[87]

Before the next continental defense progress report was conveyed to the NSC in June 1954 pursuant to NSC 5408, the JCS authorized the development of another nuclear antiaircraft weapon: an Air Force air-to-air rocket. In part, the decision to proceed with this armament was related to delays in the technologically complex Falcon program that were apparent by mid-1953.[88] In addition, there were new concerns that Falcon could be foiled if the target emitted signals (termed "electronic countermeasures," or "ECM") that jammed either (or both) of the radars carried by the interceptor and missile.[89] ADC leaders also believed that the January 1953 Joint Air Defense Board report, which urged the design of small air-defense atomic warheads for Nike and BOMARC, provided justification for developing airborne antiaircraft weapons.[90] In holding this view, ADC officials were expressing disagreement with Project Heavenbound's December 1952 conclusion that it was infeasible for interceptors to carry nuclear arms.[91]

As a result of ADC's urging, in July 1953, the Air Force agreed to investigate further the possibility of modifying the Navy's two-thousand-pound, twenty-foot-long Bombardment Aircraft Rocket (known as "BOAR") from an antiship to an antiaircraft weapon to carry either the W-7 or W-12.[92] At the same time, the service also decided to study a new small-diameter rocket and associated nuclear warhead to supplant the FFAR on the F-89. This had been encouraged by a Rand Corporation analysis recently conducted for the Air Force.[93] The Santa Monica think tank argued that design and production advances allowed physically small nuclear bombs with relatively low yields to be created; mating them to a ballistic case and rocket motor would result in a rudimentary air-to-air weapon.[94] In December 1953, another Rand evaluation concluded that such a nuclear rocket, without a guidance mechanism, would be impervious to ECM. Its large blast zone would also compensate for any fire control imprecision. Consequently, Rand declared that an atomic weapon of this nature offered "a very attractive interceptor armament...permitting even small interceptor aircraft to have a very effective multiple firing pass capability," and that it should be "vigorously pursued."[95] An atomic rocket was estimated to take three to five years to enter the Air Force inventory, and the use of FFARs was endorsed in the meantime.[96]

Shortly after the December 1953 Rand report was circulated, the Air Force finished the rocket study mandated in July. A rocket was found to be technically achievable, and a joint Defense Department and AEC study group soon concluded that the associated small atomic warhead was also feasible.[97] Accordingly, on April 2, 1954, the JCS approved the development of the weapon, asking the AEC and Air Force to coordinate the work.[98] Initially codenamed "Ding Dong," and then "High Card" and "Thunderbird," it was eventually designated the "MB-1" and, for no apparent reason, given the nickname "Genie."[99] The MB-1 was nine and one-half feet long, seventeen inches around, and weighed eight hundred pounds.[100] At first, it was to be carried by the F-89D, renamed the F-89J once the FFAR fire control system was modified and changes were made to accommodate one rocket on the underside of each wing in a program code named "Bellboy."[101]

Douglas Aircraft ultimately won the contract to design the rocket casing and integrate the components.[102] When the AEC's General Advisory Committee of scientists was briefed on the project in mid-July 1954, they were told the "interrelated problems of the aircraft, rocket, warhead, fuze, and fire control" necessitated a "very tight program for the next two years." In addition, the Genie's yield was said to have been determined after considering rocket performance, kill probabilities, and safety requirements. While a rocket with a short flight time was difficult to outmaneuver and a large yield was lethal by virtue of a large blast, both characteristics also posed hazards to a launching interceptor by reducing the time it had to avoid the weapon's effects. Conversely, an armament with a relatively long flight time and a low yield increased the safety margin for an interceptor, but could more easily be evaded and thus limited the weapon's lethality. "[T]here is a region, defined by yield and time of flight," the GAC's briefer stated, "in which the attacking plane can kill the enemy and escape."[103] As a result, given Genie's estimated velocity, the AEC's Los Alamos Scientific Laboratory eventually designed a two-kiloton warhead, dubbed "W-25," for the new rocket.[104] It was twenty-six inches long and weighed 220 pounds.[105]

When the W-25 was deployed in 1957, it became the first American "sealed pit" implosion weapon.[106] As the name implies, the fissile core was not removable; the components were manufactured into a single unit.[107] This eased assembly, eliminated the possibility of environmental contamination, reduced maintenance requirements, and increased reliability. Because of the large numbers of W-25 warheads anticipated and the extent to which they would be distributed to Air Force units, designers sought a weapon that could be stored for long periods with minimal upkeep and little concern. This was part of a broader effort to develop so-called "wooden bombs," nuclear arms that were completely inert until properly detonated.[108] An inadvertent nuclear reaction was made impossible in an IFI weapon by extracting essential components; a sealed-pit device required all of the high explosives surrounding the core to be detonated with such exacting precision and simultaneity that it was extraordinarily unlikely to occur accidentally.

Ultimately, all air-defense nuclear warheads were of the sealed-pit variety. In this and other ways, nuclear weapon designers accommodated the military by developing arms with specified characteristics. More generally, in the case of the Nike-Hercules, BOMARC, and Genie warheads, the military perceived inadequacies in existing anti-aircraft weapons and sought to ameliorate these difficulties through the use of nuclear explosives tailored to the task. High-flying, fast-moving, nuclear-laden planes and their payloads were difficult to assuredly destroy using available technology in the early 1950s. A missile or aircraft that could cause a relatively large aerial explosion upon being guided to the target vicinity overcame these limitations. As complex and complicated as nuclear weapon design was (and remains), in the case of the Army and Air Force, the development of small-sized, mechanically reliable air-defense warheads was *relatively easier* than the balance of the tasks involved in fielding technologically sophisticated guided missiles or jet interceptors. Thus, to those who believed an airborne attack was possible and that existing weapons were incapable of countering it, the advent of defensive atomic weapons appeared to make sense. To them, it was a straightforward technological resolution to a critical and persistent defense challenge.

By the time that NSC 162 was adopted in October 1953, development of nuclear armaments for Nike and BOMARC were underway, and the Rand studies and ADC efforts were about to result in the initiation of the Genie and the W-25 efforts. Although NSC 162 specified that atomic arms would henceforth be "available for use as other munitions," there is no evidence of a direct connection between the paper's expression of national policy and the design of atomic antiaircraft arms, despite the phrase's literal meaning.[109] NSC 162 allowed nuclear offensive weapons to supplant conventional forces and freed money, which was then allocated to nuclear defenses. But in the available debates and deliberations surrounding NSC 162, there is no reference or allusion to atomic antiaircraft weapons. The record suggests that proponents of the document's nuclear clause sought only an expression of American willingness to use offensive strategic arms or tactical atomic weapons on a distant battlefield. The design and acquisition of nuclear antiaircraft arms resulted from another process. Indeed, even if NSC 162 had *not* been approved, and assuming continental defense funding problems were otherwise resolved, the deployment of Nike, BOMARC, and Genie would still almost certainly have proceeded precisely in the manner it did.[110]

The fielding of the first of these weapons, however, was still several years away. As a partial stopgap measure, the first FFAR-equipped F-89 entered the Air Force inventory in Minneapolis-St. Paul in January 1954.[111] Shortly thereafter, the AEC reported to the NSC that Nike's W-7 was "in development" and that the W-12 for BOMARC remained "under study."[112] Over the next two and a half years, considerable effort was required to provide the first versions of the Genie to the Air Force. Among other things, this weapon influenced the AEC's communication with the public and was the subject of a high-profile test. Indeed, in coming months, policy-makers heard much about the rocket being developed to carry the W-25, and debated how soon it could be made available.

Chapter 2

Robert Sprague's "Adequate Defense"

Robert C. Sprague was a significant figure in American continental defense efforts during the Eisenhower administration.[1] No one, however, including Sprague, probably anticipated the scope and extent of his involvement when he began the assignment. Soon after first considering initiatives to protect the United States from a surprise Soviet bomber attack, the Massachusetts engineer and industrialist learned about the possibility of nuclear antiaircraft weapons, helped to bring them to the attention of senior policy-makers, and assisted in securing a place for these arms in the American arsenal. Robert Sprague was certain that the defense measures he urged were appropriate, necessary, and urgent. Government leaders agreed.

Sprague, known as "RC," was chief executive of the Sprague Electric Company, which he founded in 1926 to manufacture electronic devices.[2] This sort of work was a family vocation. His father, Frank J. Sprague, had built a sizeable similarly named corporation that designed the nation's first electric streetcar system, in Richmond, Virginia, in 1888, before merging with Edison General Electric a few years later.[3] The younger Sprague graduated from the U.S. Naval Academy in 1921 and subsequently received engineering degrees from the Naval Postgraduate School and the Massachusetts Institute of Technology. He decided to forsake a career in the seagoing service, turned to business even before resigning his commission, and later patented a device that improved radio sound quality. Sprague's corporation, based in North Adams, Massachusetts, became a large and successful producer of specialized electrical components, many of which had military applications.[4] The company even provided parts for the first atomic bombs, although it was probably unaware of the use of the electrical condensers it sold to the Army Corps of Engineers' Manhattan District.[5]

By 1953, Sprague was a Republican of some stature. A few weeks before the presidential inauguration, Dwight D. Eisenhower selected him to become the Air Force's Under Secretary, the service's second-highest civilian spot. Sprague withdrew his name in early February when there was some doubt about the prospect of his confirmation because of controversy in the Senate about Pentagon officials with ties to defense contractors.[6] Shortly thereafter, one source also maintains that Sprague was influential in getting the Air Force to select a proposal advanced by MIT researchers, rather than a competing University of Michigan effort, to develop the computerized system to identify and track air traffic for continental defense purposes. Eventually deployed under the peculiar moniker "Semi-Automatic Ground Environment," SAGE offered tremendous economic advantages and spin-off technologies to the jurisdictions in which it was developed, circumstances certainly understood by proponents.[7]

Through these or other activities, Sprague enjoyed a rapport with the Bay State's senior senator, Republican Leverett Saltonstall. When the August 1953 Soviet thermonuclear detonation sparked public angst in the United States, information about the administration's continental defense deliberations and budgetary limitations was leaked to the press.[8] Senate Democrats took exception to Eisenhower's defense strategy, either because they genuinely disagreed or sought to score partisan points. In October, when Ike warned an Atlantic City gathering of churchwomen that the security of American homes had "almost totally disappeared before the long-range bomber and the destructive power of a single bomb," Tennessee Democratic senator Estes Kefauver chided the president for not promising enhanced protection.[9] A member of the Senate Armed Services Committee, Kefauver asked a panel, chaired by Saltonstall, to investigate.[10] In an effort to undercut what he likely saw as partisan criticism and upstage Kefauver, Saltonstall ordered the committee's preparedness subcommittee to study American continental defenses. The Massachusetts senator announced that Sprague had agreed to direct this "highly technical" review, and stated that Sprague's background made him "uniquely qualified" for this work. "I have great confidence in his ability, energy, and thoroughness," stated Saltonstall, "and I know he will do a fine job."[11]

Between mid-October and mid-February, Sprague received briefings from military and CIA representatives and others, amid his ongoing corporate responsibilities. He also met with Eisenhower's trusted special assistant for national security affairs, Robert "Bobby" Cutler, a Boston Brahmin lawyer, novelist, Army reserve general, and banker whom Sprague may have known in Massachusetts.[12] In conducting his work for Saltonstall, Sprague claimed to have had "access to all classified material which was important to the study."[13]

The administration, however, was initially uncomfortable with the project. There was the perception that the subcommittee's undertaking was an undue usurpation of executive authority. In addition, officials worried about the prospect that information that revealed shortcomings in the nation's defense preparations (including analysis from the Edward and Bull studies and other reports) might become public, resulting in political damage or an intelligence windfall for the Soviets. At the time, estimates of the American defenses and the Soviet ability to inflict damage by way of a surprise bomber attack were among the most closely guarded and sensitive national security details. Nonetheless, Eisenhower and his aides ultimately facilitated Sprague's endeavor.[14]

By mid-February 1954, Sprague had produced a lengthy report. The draft was circulated to various executive departments for "minor comments on accuracy and clarity."[15] Deputy Defense Secretary Roger M. Kyes reported to the NSC that Sprague substantially supported the existing defense program, and provided "a welcome endorsement" of the administration's efforts.[16] On March 25, Sprague presented his findings in a two- to three-hour oral briefing to the full Senate Armed Services Committee.[17] Members were prohibited from circulating the abbreviated version of the written report they received, and note taking was prohibited. These restrictions were intended to limit the possibility of a leak of classified material, and were developed at the president's request by Cutler, who believed they mimicked the process used to inform congressional leaders about the Manhattan Project a decade before.[18] Saltonstall did not object. He observed it was probably the most classified session in the committee's history and released a statement praising Sprague and his work, arguing that the assessment shows "that the specific programs now under way combine to constitute a sound over-all continental defense program."[19] Kefauver was also impressed. He termed the review a "most excellent report" and said he hoped the administration would take heed.[20]

Just before the arrangements for this briefing were finalized, New York Republican representative W. Sterling Cole, the chairman of the Joint Committee on Atomic Energy (JCAE), which had oversight of the nation's nuclear weapon activities, asked that the JCAE and its own recently appointed continental defense consultant receive a companion presentation. A day or so after meeting with Saltonstall's group, it seems Sprague spoke for more than eight hours to a select

JCAE subcommittee, the committee's staff director, and retired Air Force general Elwood "Pete" Quesada, the committee consultant. Presumably, because JCAE members and associates more routinely had access to highly classified data, it was deemed possible to provide them a fuller presentation, although they operated under similar note-taking and report-distribution limitations.[21]

On March 30, Sprague and Saltonstall met with the president and Cutler and presented them with the only written copy of Sprague's full evaluation, which ran more than one hundred and twenty pages.[22] This report, the basis for the earlier briefing to the JCAE, addressed estimated Soviet capabilities, the destructive potential of atomic bombs, civil defense requirements, and antiaircraft weapon needs. A substantial portion was devoted to Sprague's support for various antibomber arms "with high single pass 'kill' probabilities."[23] After describing British success in destroying attacking German planes during the Battle of Britain (it estimated the attrition rate at "about 10%"), the report argued that "[w]ith the enormously increased destructive power of high yield 'A' Bombs, and the even much greater destructive power of multi-megaton 'H' Bombs to come," such a figure was "entirely inadequate and unacceptable...."[24] Accordingly, Sprague strongly endorsed continued Falcon development and the impending introduction of the FFARs and Nike-Ajax. While portions of the report remain classified, it appears that it does not mention nuclear antiaircraft weapons, even though Ajax is referred to as "Nike 1," implying a follow-on version. In addition, BOMARC is identified as a forthcoming weapon carrying "a large high explosive warhead."[25] Thus, notwithstanding his claims of having been privy to *all* defense information, it seems Sprague was not told about the nascent nuclear antiaircraft programs. The emphasis on "high kill probabilities" in his report, and his later actions, demonstrate he would likely have explicitly endorsed this impending capability had he been informed of it.

It is not clear why the information about the development of atomic anti-bomber arms was not conveyed to Sprague. Assuming the services would have been pleased with his support for programs they had underway, perhaps he was not advised about the Nike-Hercules, BOMARC, and Genie activity because it was too prospective or considered insufficiently significant to bring to his attention. The omission did not bother Kyes, based upon his comments to the NSC, and the president was apparently impressed by Sprague's assessment as presented. Eisenhower instructed affected departments to provide their evaluations of relevant recommendations in conjunction with the NSC 5408 status reports due to the National Security Council in June. In transmitting the recommendations, Cutler recounted that "[t]he president evidenced a great interest in the work done by Mr. Sprague."[26]

Sometime soon after the meeting with Eisenhower, Sprague's understanding of the danger, his assessment of defense preparations, and knowledge of forthcoming weapons changed. In a later oral history, he said in the period following the audience with the president, he was alerted by a government contact to the results of the American nuclear test series then ongoing in the Pacific.[27] In the "Castle" tests, the United States detonated early examples of the thermonuclear weapons it was racing to deploy. Besides the accidental irradiation of a Japanese fishing boat, which was widely publicized, Castle revealed to those privy to the information the enormous destructive power of a fusion bomb and the extent of radiation that was produced.[28] Because the Soviets in August had demonstrated the ability to build such an explosive, Sprague said his awareness of the outcome of the American test series meant "it became immediately apparent that this was a new game entirely...a defense against atomic weapons, was not in any sense...an adequate defense against thermonuclear weapons."[29]

Even worse from Sprague's perspective, around this time, the USSR began to display the M-4, a new four-engine, swept-wing jet bomber design, designated "Bison" by the United States. Developed indigenously, it was considered to be far better performing than the existing Soviet Tu-4 copied from the Americans. With almost no intelligence on Soviet force deployment, and worried that Bisons might be staging on the Kola Peninsula above the Arctic Circle in northwestern USSR, Eisenhower approved an Air Force reconnaissance mission to take aerial photographs of airfields in the region. While the pictures produced by the modified American jet bomber on its May 8 overflight revealed no Bisons, foreign diplomats invited to observe a flyby in conjunction with the 1954 May Day festivities in Moscow saw one the week before. The Air Force subsequently estimated that the Bison was capable of intercontinental flight and would be in full-scale production around 1956, based upon the time that U.S. airplane manufacturers calculated it would take for them to conclude a similar project.[30] Air Force chief of staff General Nathan Twining reportedly suggested at the time that this was more significant than the earlier knowledge of a Soviet atomic bomb.[31] At a time when intercontinental jet travel is commonplace, it is perhaps difficult to understand the significant technological achievement represented by the development of aluminum-skinned, swept-wing aircraft with powerful and efficient propulsion sufficient to carry a large payload and ample fuel at relatively high altitude and speed a great distance. The apparent Soviet success in marshaling the necessary design resources and manufacturing techniques was sobering to Americans aware of the relevant intelligence.

Although Sprague probably did not know the Bison details, he probably knew of the general concern about it within the government. This, coupled with his alarm over thermonuclear arms, caused him to prepare an unsolicited "supplementary study" for Saltonstall's subcommittee on June 7. When he summarized it for the group on June 22, he told members that events had "dramatically altered the situation" upon which his first evaluation was based, thus confirming his opinion that weapons with the greatest likelihood of destroying incoming bombers should be a top priority. By this time, however, Sprague had been apprised of the Nike-Hercules efforts. Using the missile's early designation, the supplemental study expressed support for "atomic warheads as planned for the Nike B," a recommendation that Sprague probably repeated orally when appearing before Saltonstall's committee the second time. Still not informed about Genie, which had been authorized two months earlier, Sprague's summary also declared prospectively that "for our interceptors we need rockets and missiles, probably with atomic warheads, to achieve as high single pass kill probabilities as 90%."[32]

Admiral Radford, who attended the presentation, considered the report unduly alarming. He may have merely disagreed with the assessment or feared such musings would lead to higher spending on anti-bomber defenses and sap money from other projects. The JCS chairman reported to Defense Secretary Charles E. Wilson the next day that Sprague "had painted the picture as black as it could be painted at this time." Radford recounted that Sprague asserted that antiaircraft preparations should be considered anew. The chairman said this would likely result in expedited programs and "an increase in the quantity and quality of defense weapons."[33]

The same day that Radford wrote to Wilson, however, Radford attended an NSC meeting where the president expressed his concern about a Soviet strike and Atomic Energy Commission chairman Lewis L. Strauss alluded to armaments intended to blunt a bomber raid. Eisenhower told the council that the nation was "frightened at the prospect of atomic war." "[T]he advantage of surprise almost seemed the decisive factor" in such a conflict, he said, and "we should do anything we could to remove this factor."

In a related colloquy about Strauss's concurrence with a memorandum circulated to the council opposing a nuclear test moratorium, the AEC official said a ban would interfere with arms development. Strauss asserted that the JCS believed nuclear antiaircraft weapons were "almost indispensable," yet research on them was "still in a primitive stage." Because new armaments required testing, the United States could not endorse a moratorium beyond January 1956. This spurred the president to inquire of Strauss, "[I]f and when we succeed" in developing these arms, "how high would such a weapon have to be exploded in order to destroy the hostile aircraft but not the city beneath?" Strauss replied, "[A]t a distance of ten miles or more above the city, the city would not be seriously damaged, even by the fall-out from the explosion." Eisenhower also asked Radford if "attacking Soviet aircraft would fly in formation in an atomic attack" or whether the USSR would allocate a single plane to each target. The JCS chairman answered that groups of bombers would probably be dispatched to "confuse" the defenders.[34] Although Strauss greatly overestimated the altitude for which air defense weapons were being contemplated, it is not apparent if the responses that Radford and Strauss proffered to Eisenhower were extemporaneous answers to unanticipated questions, or if they reflected prior consideration of the topics. Regardless, even in an indirect fashion, this is the first time that the president took note of these arms. It was not the last.

A few days before that June 23 meeting, Eisenhower appointed Robert Sprague as a consultant to the National Security Council, charged with evaluating the progress reports periodically required by NSC 5408.[35] This was officially a part-time job. Sprague ostensibly continued his work in North Adams and traveled to Washington to review documents or make or receive briefings.

The possibility of engaging Sprague in this capacity was broached at least by May 13, when Cutler suggested it to the NSC, and noted Sprague's continuing assignment with Saltonstall. Cutler also said he wanted to "discuss" the appointment with the Defense Department before proceeding.[36] Pentagon officials apparently did not object, either because they concurred or they did they did not want to oppose the president's national security assistant, who was known to have a very favorable impression of Sprague. Indeed, when the industrialist had first accepted the senate work, Culter told Defense Secretary Wilson that "Bob is a very intelligent, perceptive, thoughtful, and able man."[37] Ike agreed. Of the prospect of securing Sprague's services for the NSC, the president told the council that Sprague was "top-flight," a "hard worker," and someone who "had already acquainted himself with the problems of continental defense."[38]

Sprague readily accepted Eisenhower's invitation. On June 21, the day before Sprague's final Senate briefing, he and members of the NSC Planning Board reviewed DoD's draft report on continental defense progress, submitted to the council pursuant to NSC 5408. Sprague and the others suggested minor revisions. It was reworked and returned on June 25 in advance of the next week's NSC meeting.[39] A copy of the June 25 report, bearing Sprague's handwritten marginalia, has a modest amount of redactions for "restricted data," the euphemistic phrase for nuclear weapon information. While the Defense report putatively addressed the situation as of June 1, based upon Sprague's notes and context of the redactions, it appears to outline the defense posture from several months earlier.[40] Of the nuclear antiaircraft weapons, only the Nike-Hercules is mentioned. As with the earlier omissions in the information provided to Sprague for his senate assignment, the report's silence on the other two nascent atomic air defense programs is not significant. The DoD document was undoubtedly a lengthy staff-written assessment first drafted months before, when Hercules work had just begun, Genie had not yet been authorized, and BOMARC's W-12 selection had not been finalized.

Sometime after reviewing the Defense update on continental defenses, Sprague wrote an assessment for the NSC and summarized the impressions of the defense dangers that he had recently shared with Saltonstall's committee. Sprague said later that he believed this report was the first time that Eisenhower, Secretary Wilson, and other NSC members learned of the enormous amount of fallout produced by thermonuclear arms.[41] Sprague's evaluation urged the NSC's newly formed Net Capabilities Evaluation Subcommittee, a body that assumed the responsibilities of Bull's ad hoc group from the year before, to calculate what percentage of an attacking force would have to be destroyed to prevent the United States from suffering so many casualties and so much destruction that it ceased to be a functioning nation. This would then allow the Pentagon to assess the number and composition of forces necessary to inflict the required attrition on the attackers. In making its determination, Sprague suggested that the subcommittee assume that by July 1957 the USSR would possess "as many as 80 ten-megaton and 400 sixty-kiloton bombs," which could be carried by "a fleet" of Tu-4s, Bisons, and another bomber type. Until the preferred defenses were prepared based upon this evaluation, Sprague recommended expediting the construction of certain warning systems, acquisition of FFAR armament for interceptors, and Nike-Ajax deployment. But given the infirmities inherent in those weapons, the report said that "it is probable that an adequate defense cannot be obtained by July 1, 1957, without the use of nuclear warheads on air-to-air and ground-to-air defense missiles." Therefore, Sprague concluded, "[T]he NSC may wish to direct the Defense Department to provide for the development of such warheads," aiming to have them ready by that time.[42] Aware only of the Nike-Hercules project, Sprague was advocating a development program that was already in progress, although the operational date he selected was earlier than that projected by those knowledgeable about the W-7, W-12, and W-25 work and the technological complexities of their delivery systems.

Sprague presented his report to the NSC on a typically hot and humid first day of July 1954. The setting that Thursday was the same as for nearly every council meeting in Eisenhower's first term. At ten a.m., Cutler escorted the president from the Oval Office into the Cabinet Room, announcing the chief executive's arrival as they passed through the workspace of Ann C. Whitman, Eisenhower's personal secretary. As Cutler and two deputies took positions at the end of the ornate oblong table that filled the room, Eisenhower offered greetings to the assemblage and then sat at the middle of the group, his back to the large French windows that offered a view of the Rose Garden. The president was flanked by Secretary of State John Foster Dulles and Defense Secretary Wilson, and across from Vice President Richard M. Nixon, Treasury Secretary George Humphrey, and the Foreign Operations Administration director. Admiral Radford, Lewis Strauss, Central Intelligence director Allen Dulles, and the Attorney General were also in attendance. Sprague, the civilian and uniformed service leaders, and at least twenty-eight additional senior officials and staffers gathered on chairs around the room's perimeter.[43]

After formally introducing Sprague to the attendees and summarizing again the consultant's responsibilities, Cutler highlighted certain elements of the DoD report, and called upon several Pentagon representatives to brief the council on important points. But these oral presentations included more recent information than the June 25 written report reviewed earlier by Sprague and submitted to the council. When Donald A. Quarles, the assistant Defense secretary charged with overseeing research and development activities, addressed the group, he mentioned the atomic air-to-air rocket program. Neither Strauss, nor Radford, nor any other attendee clarified whether this was the weapon that the AEC chairman told the president a week before precluded a nuclear test moratorium, and the possible connection did not seem apparent to anyone. Quarles declared that the rocket (not yet named Genie) was expected to be tested in a year and operational by 1958. It would have a "kill probability" of two, meaning that, on average, for every Genie expended, two bombers would be downed.[44]

Sprague had persistently advocated a defense regime that would yield fifty to ninety percent lethality.[45] Now he learned of an armament that putatively offered many times that, and the Air Force was confident that it would be available in the near term, albeit later than the date on which Sprague's report suggested American defenses should be readied. Sprague's evaluation recommended that the NSC instruct DoD to *initiate* atomic rocket research; Quarles revealed that such was already underway. This was apparently astounding news to the NSC's continental defense advisor. When Quarles concluded, Sprague took the opportunity to "emphasize" the "significance and great importance" he placed on this weapon. He was "very much impressed by the Air Force report" on the rocket, he said, and especially the "kill probability."

Sprague urged the service to "push forward" with design so that U.S. interceptors could be equipped with the new arms "at the earliest possible date." Wanting to receive first the findings of the Net Capabilities Evaluation Subcommittee, the NSC deferred action on the portion of Sprague's report calling for the development of nuclear defenses and a July 1957 operational date.[46] Members probably took this action because they were inclined to take their lead from their Defense Department colleagues rather than an outsider, despite the consultant's apparent credentials and association with the president.

Sprague was not deterred. After the NSC adjourned and the president left for a meeting with Nevada senator Eva Bowring, Sprague drafted a memorandum to Cutler arguing "in the strongest terms" that "the air-to-air defense rocket with atomic warhead" be given "the highest priority." The potential benefits of the proposed weapon were such that Sprague pushed to have "a high percentage" of interceptors armed with it "by January 1, 1957, at the latest." This was six months earlier than he had previously suggested for such defenses. Cutler forwarded the note to Wilson.[47]

On July 19, Wilson replied by conveying a memorandum from the Joint Chiefs of Staff on the topic and a one-page report about the Genie's development status, which had been composed by Quarles.[48] The service leaders declared Sprague's priorities "valid," because they said there was "an urgent requirement" to obtain "high kill capability."

They noted that the development of the necessary nuclear warhead was "not expected to delay" the program, provided that the AEC gave it sufficient emphasis. Rather, it was the design of the rocket vehicle as well as the "adaption [sic] of a delivery aircraft and production of a suitable fire control system" that could pose challenges to the effort. The JCS stipulated, however, that they did not want this program expedited at the expense of other continental defense arms, and pointed out that it was difficult to predict the logistical, management, and fiscal burden that an accelerated effort might impose. Quarles reported much the same.[49]

When the National Security Council met the following week, it considered the JCS correspondence and Sprague's suggestions to expedite the Genie and other continental defense efforts. Quarles, formerly the Sandia president and previously a Republican mayor in New Jersey during his tenure as a Bell Labs executive, provided his evaluation of the Genie recommendation.[50] While the full extent of his remarks are not known, it is clear that he reported that the rocket was "proceeding as rapidly as feasible" and that proposals from five contractors were presently being considered to supply the motor and rocket case. He was agreeable to designating an early readiness date as an "objective," but said, "[I]t cannot be taken as being too firm at this point."[51] Eisenhower remarked "that no one could disagree with Mr. Sprague's objective," in seeking to speed the programs, but "wondered just what could be done in a way of further accelerating" them. Presidential aide and former Minnesota governor Harold E. Stassen responded that "the important question" was not the status of the additional initiatives, but whether "the air to air atomic rocket" should be placed "on a crash basis now." Ike rejoined that "there was a point beyond which one could not go," implying that the weapon could not be hurried regardless of the emphasis which the NSC might place on it. The president was obviously reluctant to mandate a schedule for Genie deployment. It is probable that he feared the high cost and other difficulties that might result from a rushed deployment effort. Consequently, a formal decision about the schedule for continental defense programs was tabled until the next NSC meeting.[52] At that time, the council was slated to approve NSC 5422, a description of the national security situation that was meant to provide guidance to defense agencies as they prepared their budgets for fiscal year 1956.[53]

At the start of the August 5 council meeting, Cutler presented the Planning Board's first draft of NSC 5422. He reviewed the federal revenue predictions upon which it was based. He also called attention to the fact that it included new intelligence estimates predicting that the Soviets would have between one hundred and three hundred Bison bombers by 1959 (each capable of carrying one or two bombs) and a larger nuclear arsenal than had been projected earlier.[54]

Cutler then led the council on a paragraph-by-paragraph assessment of the draft. "The U.S. should accelerate its military and nonmilitary programs for continental defense set forth in NSC 5408 to the fullest extent deemed feasible and operationally desirable," read one portion. Cutler noted that the Defense and State departments, the JCS, and the Budget bureau opposed the phrase "with a view to bringing them to a high state of readiness by July 1957," which was appended to the statement.[55] This objection was undoubtedly rooted in concern about the statement's budgetary implications. In presenting the case for the proposed paragraph, however, Cutler argued that it should be amended to specify "the air-to-air rocket program" as one of the initiatives to be expedited.[56]

The president, maintaining his earlier reticence, responded that he considered the mention of a particular weapon to be an inappropriately precise instruction for a document intended to give broad budget guidance. He argued that such details were better included in NSC 5408, the continental defense guidance. Cutler rejoined that NSC 5408 was silent on the rocket program because it was unknown to the council when the paper was adopted in February. This spurred Stassen, the presidential advisor who supported the rocket previously, to reemphasize his belief that the Genie especially warranted immediate NSC action mandating a "crash approach" to its development. The president countered that while "he had no objection to an NSC recommendation as to the high priority of this program, he did object to deadlines." Although the NSC "could say that the air-to-air rocket program was so important to be almost vital" setting an operational date might "concentrate too much effort on merely meeting the deadline instead of the best solution," he argued. Cutler explained that the paper proffered a readiness date "because of intelligence estimates which seemed to indicate that the time of greatest danger of a Soviet nuclear attack on the United States would be mid-1957." Eisenhower was not persuaded. He said he "had no objection" to NSC 5422 referencing such an "estimate," implying that his concern focused only on the possibility of stipulating a deadline, but actually revealing that he did not share the understanding of the threat. (If he did, why would he not favor having all possible defenses in place by the time of the most acute danger?) Stassen missed this. Apparently unconcerned with expressing pressing a line of argument contrary to the president, he reiterated his position, saying, "[P]riorities might be upsetting," but "they often get results."

Not surprisingly, the NSC eventually acceded to the president's wishes. It elected to conclude the continental defense statement in NSC 5422 with the somewhat more cautious clause "and give to these programs very high priority, having in mind that it is estimated the Soviets will reach a high capability for strategic nuclear attacks by July 1957."[57] Based upon other remarks and records, it was apparently understood that this phraseology included Genie, despite the fact it was not literally covered by an instruction covering items "set forth in NSC 5408."[58]

Left to determine its own development timetable for continental defense, the Pentagon nonetheless embraced Robert Sprague's proposal to field the nuclear air defense rocket by January 1, 1957.[59] Despite not being specifically endorsed by the NSC, Sprague's July memorandum to Cutler shaped the defense effort. This was the first of several instances in which Sprague proved influential in plotting the scope and timing of American nuclear antiaircraft defenses.

The AEC, Douglas Aircraft, the Air Force, and many other organizations expedited the Genie program in late 1954. One month after NSC 5422/2 was approved, congressional leaders were apprised of work on the new weapon and when it was "expected" to be in service.[60] The circumstances that resulted in the congressional notification originated in an August 9 letter from JCAE chairman Cole to Secretary Wilson. Cole wrote that his committee had established another panel. This one was to advise it "on the ways and means of maximizing the role which atomic energy can play in continental defense." Apparently not satisfied with the information received in April from Sprague, the committee had asked retired Army general Albert C. Wedemeyer to chair the group, aided by Quesada (the previous JCAE consultant), famed flier Charles Lindbergh, former AEC chairman Gordon Dean, nuclear strategist Bernard Brodie, and several nuclear weapon scientists, including Herbert York, who later held several key government posts.[61] Eisenhower was "very much distressed" when he learned from Cutler about the new JCAE effort. As with the Saltonstall investigation, the president was concerned about leaks, the possibility that the panel would intrude on his prerogative as chief executive, and the fact that Sprague's earlier presentation was considered insufficient. AEC chairman Strauss, who was acquainted with Cole as a result of his professional responsibilities, was tasked with offering the JCAE an updated oral report from Sprague in exchange for canceling the new study. Cole declined the offer.[62]

The Wedemeyer panel subsequently received a series of presentations, including on the emerging understanding of the danger of thermonuclear fallout. Once Wilson reiterated the classified strictures, Pentagon representatives also met with the group.[63] It was likely that on September 1 an Air Defense Command representative noted that "in January 1957," an "air-to-air rocket with atomic warhead will be available for use in air defense." The presenter also mentioned BOMARC. This missile, it was explained, will "provide a longer range surface-to-air capability." Probably because the W-12 arrangements had still not been finalized, the panel was told that BOMARC "can" (rather than "will") "be armed with an atomic warhead."[64] Because it addressed only those programs within the Air Force's purview, the briefing did not mention the Army's Nike-Hercules.

A few weeks later, at a National Security Council meeting on the eve of Thanksgiving, Robert Sprague assessed the DoD's quarterly NSC 5408 status report. He was pleased that the Air Force finally shared his sense of urgency about Genie and was taking steps to ensure its prompt introduction. The Pentagon document, he told the NSC, "contains very encouraging information," including "indications" that by early 1957 planes "armed with high-kill atomic air-to-air rockets may begin to be phased into our fighter-interceptor forces."[65] When Sprague concluded, Eisenhower said that, "as usual," he "was very grateful for the excellent services" provided by Sprague in a "highly important field."[66]

In this period, the president was especially vocal in his support for measures to protect against a Soviet attack. On December 13, he told Republican congressional leaders (including Saltonstall) and aides that "as a result of the long-range bomber" deployed by the USSR, "only recently had the United States ever had to fear a serious attack on its own lands." This required an emphasis on "retaliatory forces" and "continental defenses."[67] A week later, he reiterated to another group that the military's primary purpose was to "blunt the enemy's initial threat" by way of "a continental defense system of major capability" in addition to staging offensive strikes.[68] Obviously attempting to assuage growing concern about the adequacy of anti-bomber preparations, on January 5, Eisenhower made public a letter to Defense Secretary Wilson that used nearly identical language.[69] Days later, Wilson addressed the Armed Services Committee in the House of Representatives. He explained the high priority the administration was placing on protecting the United States from bomber attack. He noted, among other points, that the "future air defense system" would include "nuclear weapons applications to continental defense."[70]

Not long afterward, Eisenhower received the report produced by the Wedemeyer panel.[71] It concluded that the USSR was rapidly fielding atomic weapons. "[C]rippling damage" to the United States was possible, the study maintained, because the advent of thermonuclear weapons meant that current rates of attrition were "no longer adequate." Among others steps, the report recommended that nuclear warheads be adapted to additional missile types.[72]

Eisenhower conveyed perfunctory appreciation to the JCAE for the study, and Cutler referred copies to agencies, making optional any evaluation or response.[73] The JCS elected to comment, saying that "the atomic warhead is not suitable for universal employment," but antiaircraft applications were exceptions "because of the promise which such programs hold for increased effectiveness in continental defense."[74] Later, an aide to the Defense Secretary wrote to the JCAE to update the committee on missiles scheduled to receive nuclear warheads. The Genie, Nike-Hercules, and BOMARC were all specified.[75]

Two months after Ike received the JCAE document, another panel produced a report expressing a similar assessment. This latter evaluation, however, bore the imprimatur of the administration. In March 1954, a group of scientists who served on an advisory panel to the Office of Defense mobilization met with the president to learn more about his fear of surprise attack. Eisenhower shared with them his distress over the advent of the Bison bombers and urged them to consider how scientific advancements might help preclude a Soviet raid. As a result, the Science Advisory Committee recommended a few months later that a group of scientists and engineers be impaneled to examine technological applications that could improve the nation's offensive forces, intelligence collection, and continental defense efforts.[76] Eisenhower concurred, and in August 1954, committee member and Massachusetts Institute of Technology president James R. Killian, Jr., agreed to lead the effort.[77] Between then and February 1955, forty-two outside experts on the Technological Capabilities Panel met 307 times for meetings, briefings, and field trips, aided by a small staff.[78] In addition to Killian, nine others guided the study. The steering committee included Polaroid camera inventor Edwin H. Land, Williams College president and previous NSC consultant James Phinney Baxter III, and retired General James H. Doolittle, the World War II hero who held an MIT aeronautical engineering doctorate. Killian believed it was "extremely important" for Robert Sprague to play a role in the study in light of his work on continental defense for the NSC. Consequently, Sprague was a full-fledged participant on the steering committee, although inexplicably he was titled "consultant" rather than "member."[79]

Land led the intelligence subgroup. When his team learned that Lockheed had developed a conceptual design for a very high-flying airplane that could be equipped with reconnaissance cameras, he and the others realized it could be used to gather specifics about the number and disposition of the Soviet Bisons. In November 1954, he secured Eisenhower's approval for the development, under CIA auspices, of what became known as the U-2. The Killian panel's final report contained only a vague reference to this activity, because U-2 details were even more highly classified than the "top secret" designation applied to the balance of the group's work.[80] With the exception of the U-2 information, the steering committee, with Cutler's active assistance, presented the highlights of the group's two-volume 190-page assessment, entitled "Meeting the Threat of Surprise Attack," to the National Security Council in a four-hour meeting in the White House Broadcast Room on March 17, 1955. Following discussion, the NSC ordered the report conveyed to executive branch agencies for comments and an estimate of the cost of the items put forth.[81]

The danger posed by a thermonuclear-equipped adversary and the consequent requirement for effective air defenses was a significant theme of the Killian study. The report recommended that nuclear warheads become "the major armament" for American air defense arms.[82]

> Nuclear weapons are the most effective armament with which we can equip our air defense forces. They provide the most direct and reliable method of achieving the high kill probability against single aircraft that modern air defense demands, of creating a potent defense against saturation type attacks, and of actually destroying the enemy nuclear weapons,

the report declared.[83] It specifically called for the "expeditious development, procurement, and deployment" of Nike-Hercules and Genie (about which it said, "[r]ecent studies had shown that the air-to-air atomic rocket can be made compatible with existing and programmed interceptors).[84] The evaluation also urged that "every effort" be made to address growing BOMARC delays.[85] In making this recommendation, the report acknowledged that more such weapons would likely be acquired than would probably be needed. In the event of a raid, some defensive nuclear arms would not be used. The lethality of those that were detonated made the remainder superfluous. In addition, others would not be employed because they were inaptly located as a result of a deployment regime that had to consider various attack scenarios.[86]

For those weapons that could be brought to bear on incoming planes, the Killian panel maintained that it was necessary to do so as soon as attackers were identified and when the bombers were at the greatest distance from their targets. The group thus recommended "the establishment of realistic rules of engagement," and called for granting the military "advance authority for the instant use of atomic warheads," since defense imperatives made it difficult to secure permission in the midst of an attack. Because bombers were likely to be engaged by American forces as they traversed Canadian airspace, the panel also urged negotiations with the nation's northern neighbor to allow the use of defensive atomic arms in this circumstance.[87]

In addition, the Killian committee also called for the development of a two-prong effort meant to assuage public concern about American air defenses and related nuclear tests about to begin in Nevada. It was recommended that one particular "high altitude" exercise in that operation be used prospectively to address angst about the dangers of deploying or using atomic antiaircraft weapons. The panel also said the operation offered an opportunity to demonstrate to an international audience the extent to which American nuclear technology was being directed toward protective purposes.[88]

The Killian group believed that the relatively low yield of atomic antiaircraft arms, and the altitude at which they would be detonated, meant that if used, they would pose little harm to those on the ground below. Even "[i]f all the air defense weapons were actually fired, the total kilotonage would approximate that of a single strategic weapon," the evaluation declared. "Thus, the radioactivity which would be added to the atmosphere by the use of the warheads is of no consequence at all," it concluded.[89] Panel participants probably thought this observation was buttressed by the fact that contemporary nuclear tests by the Soviet Union, United States, and Great Britain regularly involved large surface bursts, which were believed by those involved to pose minimal dangers outside a delineated area. While this assessment may be wrong (radiation risks are still not precisely understood), the remark in a classified document not intended for broad distribution demonstrates the genuine beliefs of proponents of defensive atomic arms.

The members of the Killian committee, probably encouraged by Robert Sprague, forcefully recommended atomic anti-bomber defenses because they thought such were beneficial to the nation's security. As preposterous as it seems fifty years later, to military officials, political leaders, and policy advisors during the Eisenhower years, this effort seemed to be a logical step in light of the perceived threat and the limitations of alternative weapons. In the seventeen months between Robert Sprague's first work for Leverett Saltonstall's subcommittee and the report of the Technological Capabilities Panel, nuclear antiaircraft arms had become a regular topic of discussion at the highest levels of the national security decision-making in the executive branch and in Congress. At times, Robert Sprague, Dwight Eisenhower, NSC members, and the military services disagreed about the priority that should be accorded them and the resources to be allocated to their development. However, no one questioned their utility. No person advocated delaying their deployment. The exigencies of the nation's Cold War circumstances seemed to require defensive atomic weapons. In the coming years, the public would learn about these armaments. Most would react as did their leaders.

Chapter 3

Testing, Predelegating, and Announcing

Preparations for fielding nuclear air-defense weapons proceeded in the two years following the Killian committee's report. The new armaments were developed amid continuing concerns about the Soviet bomber force, occasional publicity about the protective measures being readied in response, and policy changes that seemed essential. Testing was also necessary, both to resolve significant design challenges and to demonstrate the safety of the forthcoming weapons.

At the start of 1955, development concepts for nuclear antiaircraft arms remained tentative, because neither sealed-pit arrangements nor the engineering techniques proposed for the smaller-dimension warheads had yet been proven sound. In addition, because previous atomic tests involved detonations on or near the earth's surface, not much was known about aerial nuclear effects. Without a better understanding of atmospheric blasts, decisions could not be made on weapon yield and other characteristics.[1] To address these issues, seven nuclear tests took place in the spring at the Nevada Test Site, a portion (initially 350 square miles) of the Los Vegas-Tonopah Bombing and Gunnery Range set aside four years earlier by the federal government for the Atomic Energy Commission's use.[2] These detonations (or "shots") comprised half of a test series dubbed "Teapot."[3]

When AEC chairman Lewis Strauss wrote President Eisenhower to obtain the chief executive's authorization for the operation in August 1954, he explained that the test series was necessary, in part, because of the need to verify "ideas which are highly important" to the "air-defense application."[4] Eisenhower gave his consent, Strauss notified the Joint Committee on Atomic Energy, and the AEC issued a terse press release announcing the operation. When Robert Cutler conveyed Eisenhower's approval to Strauss, however, the national security advisor mandated that the NSC oversee the drafting and dissemination of other statements related to this and future tests. This task was to be undertaken by the Operations Coordinating Board (OCB), a body of senior agency representatives that monitored the implementation of NSC policies. Direction from the OCB would allow "coordination of Executive Branch views," including input from other cabinet departments and executive agencies.[5]

Although Cutler did not specify the reason for this new procedure, it had probably been sparked by the growing discontent over nuclear testing, combined with the advent of thermonuclear arms, which threatened to spur further opposition. In 1953, the last time tests had been conducted at the NTS, relatively high levels of radiation reached southern Utah as a result of an error in wind prediction at the time of the blast. Although residents were advised to remain indoors for several hours and the AEC did not believe the incident posed a danger, it nonetheless concerned the commission and the public.[6]

In addition, since shortly after 1954's Castle series in the Pacific, the AEC, the White House, State Department, and others had been debating how to reveal details of the radiation hazards of fusion detonations. These agencies were especially concerned about doing so without harming the prospects for further testing. When the AEC prepared to issue a report about thermonuclear blasts and radiation effects just days before the start of Teapot, for example, Strauss apparently worried that the public might conflate the two events and incorrectly assume the upcoming NTS series involved fusion weapons. Consequently, he appended a statement to the report emphasizing that the commission believed the upcoming Teapot fission test series posed no off-site dangers. To emphasize this point, arrangements were made during Teapot for the U.S. Public Health Service to collect and publicize radiation measurements from outside the NTS property.[7] This was intended to demonstrate the AEC's sincerity and facilitate future tests. If it had doubts about the results, the commission reasoned, it presumably would never have solicited an outside entity to monitor and report on the situation.

To help ease public concern, Teapot also included a more extensive publicity effort than had been the case with previous AEC operations. Regular news briefings were held for each shot to describe the test's purpose, explain any delays, and suggest safe vantage points for the press or other observers.[8] This publicity was generally meant to soothe concerns about testing and undercut opposition, partly by demonstrating the safeguards implemented for such operations. But it also dovetailed with a separate recommendation of the Killian committee and sentiment within the AEC to promote activities related to antiaircraft defenses as a sound component of national security strategy.

It seems the fact that the United States was developing defensive weapons might well have been publicized even in the absence of other efforts to address public concerns about testing.

In August 1954, W.H. Rowen, a junior officer in the AEC's Division of Military Application, the commission component responsible for weapon development, raised the possibility of touting the forthcoming tests of relatively small air-defense devices. Because the tests were associated with "the development of atomic warheads which would be used over our own cities to protect against enemy attack," Rowen suggested, the experiments "should be sold as 'friendly blasts' offering comforting protection."[9] This idea apparently came to the forefront as the OCB's role in coordinating press activities was being settled and as Killian's Technological Capabilities Panel (TCP) was preparing its report calling for "the high altitude shot" at Teapot to be used "as a springboard for a public information program."[10] Because Cutler later wrote that he "discussed with Killian the form, manner and substance of his TCP report" before it was presented to the council, the NSC assistant may have been the conduit that allowed this AEC publicity proposal to become a committee recommendation.[11]

Regardless of the origins of the idea, it was acted upon. Ten days after the Killian panel presented its findings to the NSC, the AEC and Defense Department issued a statement declaring that "certain tests during the current series at the Nevada Test Site are of a nuclear device designed to augment our air defense system."[12] The release further declared that one test apparatus "will be detonated at a point many thousands of feet above the ground." It explained:

> [t]he purpose of the test will be to supplement the data needed by the Continental Air Defense Command and other interested agencies regarding the effects of atomic explosions at high altitudes. Because of their great power, atomic air defense weapons will greatly increase our ability to repel an enemy air attack. The employment of such weapons for air defense purposes will enhance the effectiveness of interceptor aircraft squadrons and ground based air defense units in stopping enemy bombers short of our cities and strategic targets. By providing this added effectiveness to our defenses, atomic weapons produce a further deterrent to aggression against the free world.[13]

The announcement also proffered that

> [a]lthough such a weapon exploded at these altitudes can destroy aircraft within a considerable distance from the point of burst, no damage or injury from blast, heat, or nuclear radiation is anticipated to

properties or individuals from this test. The nuclear radiation on the ground even directly beneath the point of detonation of this defensive weapon could be measured only with the most sensitive of scientific instruments, and a person exposed would receive less than a hundredth of a dose received in a standard x-ray.[14]

As a result of the AEC statement, many news stories appeared that emphasized the announcement's key points.[15]

On April 6, the anticipated shot was undertaken. After several Air Force jets created a contrail grid used to aid blast measurement, a plane released a rudimentary three-kiloton device that detonated at 36,620 feet.[16] This height was well within the performance parameters of typical bombers; the fact that the AEC dubbed the shot the "high altitude" test illustrates that seven miles above the earth's surface was nonetheless seen as a considerable distance at the time. The test was the culmination of a yearlong effort to evaluate nuclear blast and thermal characteristics in connection with antiaircraft weapon design. The physicist who oversaw the experiment later recounted that he and others involved were motivated by a "real threat of a Soviet H-bomb attack on the U.S.," and they saw their activities as central to efforts "to counter that attack with an adequate air defense system."[17] The Associated Press seemed satisfied with their work. The wire service's story said a "dazzling atomic antiaircraft device," had been tested; "a portent of flaming doom for enemy sky invaders."[18] The weapon produced "a huge multi-colored burst," according to the United Press, although it mischaracterized some details, including identifying the weapon as a fully developed air-to-air missile, rather than a specially constructed test mechanism.[19]

Six other experimental detonations intended to evaluate specific antiaircraft warhead designs or their destructive effects took place before or after the April 6 "high altitude" event.[20] In one operation, the Defense Department measured the blast load on three drone aircraft flown past the explosive point.[21] Another involved a device that had tritium gas injected into the fissile core at the time of detonation.[22] This process, termed "boosting," magnified the resulting blast and facilitated the design of a sealed-pit successor to the Nike-Hercules W-7, which had minimal space for the implosion apparatus and fissile material.[23] This shot had probably been alluded to the previous January when a wire story reported that a nuclear Nike missile warhead "capable of destroying with one blast all planes in a path a half mile or more wide" had been "completed" and would be tested during Teapot.[24] Although this account was imprecise and inaccurate on several points (only a rudimentary test device, not a finished warhead, was ready), it was probably the result of an Army leak intended to ensure that the service's air-defense preparations received ample news play.

No matter what the Army's intent, the AEC's press efforts succeeded. When Teapot concluded, the *New York Times* declared that "the feasibility of constructing atomic weapons of very small size" had been proven, and announced that "a warhead for an anti-aircraft or air-to-air guided missile" was now possible. Another story maintained that the work showed "the chances of 'killing'... aircraft have been increased greatly."[25]

The need for this defense capability seemed evident to those privy to new evidence of increased Soviet bomber production. Western observers of the preparations for Moscow's 1955 May Day festivities counted ten M-4 Bison bombers participating in a practice flyover.[26] A few months later, a U.S. Air Force attaché saw a total of twenty-eight M-4s in three waves (along with a new type of swept-wing turboprop Tu-95 "Bear" bomber) at another air show. Because this was more than had been seen months earlier, more than official U.S. estimates predicted were available, and more than three times the amount of equivalent (but troubled) B-52 bombers just entering U.S. Air Force service, it caused a stir. The relatively large number of Soviet planes meant that either the one observed the year before was a production model and not a prototype, or that the Soviets had a faster than anticipated development cycle. Either case cast doubt on the American estimates of the Bison deployment schedule and the number of planes in existence. Years later, both sightings were determined to be deceptions (the Soviets may have flown every existing Bison past observers several times in a way that made it appear as if these were different airplanes), but few suspected it then.[27]

These eyewitness accounts and other intelligence (such as information on the size of the Bison factory and a favorable assessment of Soviet manufacturing capabilities) sparked an upward revision of the official bomber estimates.[28] The difference—or "gap"—between the presumed number of Soviet and U.S. bombers was seen as significant evidence of American vulnerability.

The Soviet Union's capacity to attack the United States was at the forefront of public and official consciousness in the summer of 1955. At five minutes after noon on June 15, klaxons sounded at the White House. This was the signal for an impending bomber raid, and it sent officials and visitors scurrying. They were participating in what they knew was a drill. Pursuant to plan, some senior aides convened at the

South Portico, where they met up with the president and his Secret Service escort.[29] (The First Lady was with her mother at the Eisenhower family farm in Gettysburg, Pennsylvania.[30]) The president, resplendent in a tan suit and brown felt hat, was whisked away by a Cadillac limousine, while his entourage followed in private cars. Eisenhower and most others were destined for a location in the Shenandoah Mountains, forty-eight miles to the west, on the border of Virginia's Clarke and Loudoun counties. There, a small tent city—the "White House Relocation Site"—had been established. Nearby, the Army Corps of Engineers was supervising "Operation High Point," the construction of a permanent underground emergency government facility mandated by NSC 5408.[31] Fifteen thousand employees from other federal agencies in and around the District of Columbia, including six cabinet secretaries, also evacuated the nation's capital at the same time. They decamped to thirty-one other rudimentary facilities, some as far as three hundred miles distant.[32] The Defense Department's civilian and military chiefs helicoptered to "Raven Rock," an underground command post for the Pentagon built during the Truman administration in a mountain in northeastern Maryland, near the Pennsylvania border.[33]

Civil defense warnings sounded in fifty-five other cities in the continental United States that day. Citizens took shelter or evacuated homes, businesses, schools, and hospitals in New York, Los Angeles, Pittsburgh, and St. Louis, as well as Fort Wayne, Utica, and Trenton.[34] This nationwide drill was the second annual nationwide "Operation Alert," a massive preplanned and much-publicized effort meant to test federal, state, and local response to a Soviet air attack. During the seventy-two hours that federal leaders participated, journalists eagerly covered the events, operating out of an "emergency press headquarters" on the third floor of an old Army warehouse in an industrial district near downtown Richmond, Virginia.[35] One account said that "the nation was far from being ready to withstand a hydrogen bomb attack," but reported that Operation Alert allowed leaders to "plan for emergencies the nation would face in an actual raid."[36] There are many reasons why the drill was an inapt exercise (a real emergency would be far more chaotic), and several officials acknowledged it at the time. But the fact that senior government leaders, including the president, took part in such an elaborate program indicates much about their perception of the threat.

On Operation Alert's second day, Ike was driven to Raven Rock from Camp David (where he had gone after conducting business at the relocation site) for an NSC meeting. It was an unconventional location, but otherwise at the usual time and day of the week, with the standard participants, and, except for an initial discussion on Operation Alert's ongoing conduct, featured a typical agenda.[37] One item discussed was the Pentagon's third NSC 5408 progress report.[38] In it, the service leaders maintained that the "U.S. air defense system cannot be expected to counter effectively an all-out attack of the magnitude which the Soviet Union is capable of launching against the continental United States."[39] This was probably a continuation of the efforts by the Joint Chiefs to downplay continental defense possibilities in order to undercut the drive for extensive—and expensive—attack preparations. But the NSC's continental defense consultant, present to assess the DoD report, was not disturbed by this assessment.

Robert Sprague and like-minded NSC members and staffers labored under no illusions that a perfect defense was possible. Rather, they sought substantial improvement over current preparations. For this reason, Sprague was pleased with what he learned from the Pentagon report, saying that DoD had provided "very encouraging information" about "continuing progress" on important continental defense initiatives. Sprague noted, however, that by mid-1957, based on current trends, the USSR would field 350 long-range planes capable of reaching the United States, an increase from the fifty previously predicted. Therefore, he urged the "further acceleration" of programs recommended in the Killian report to achieve "an adequate" antiaircraft defense within two years, the point at which he believed the Soviet bomber force would become formidable. When elaborating on this recommendation, Sprague specifically referenced the Genie and Nike-Hercules (using the names by which they were known at the time), arguing that their entry into the inventory would "vastly increase kill probabilities."[40]

When Eisenhower reacted skeptically to some of Sprague's assessments, the president emphasized that the consultant should "not be apologetic in advancing differing views."[41] It is not clear if Ike's remark is sincere or merely polite. A few months earlier, Dillon Anderson, Robert Cutler's NSC successor, wrote the industrialist to report that the president recently "had some things to say about your work that you would have liked."[42] This suggests that Eisenhower valued, rather than simply tolerated, Sprague's assessments.

The favorable impression was mutual. In September, after Eisenhower suffered a heart attack, Sprague sent a note to the president by way of Anderson, asking if the aide would forward the get-well message in a manner that would ensure it would not get bogged down with communications from less well-connected correspondents. Anderson obligingly complied.[43]

Two months before Ike was stricken, the NSC convened in Washington to consider NSC 5522, the executive branch response to the Killian committee's report.[44] Although there was lengthy debate in July on some portions of the NSC document, the recommendations related to nuclear antiaircraft defenses were among the points that agencies substantially or wholly supported.[45] About the recommendation that nuclear warheads become the "major armament" for air defense, for example, NSC 5522 said the Defense Secretary and JCS "concur" and agreed that "[i]t seems likely that any new air defense weapons systems planned for future development will incorporate a capability for atomic armament."[46] As for arranging for the use of nuclear antiaircraft armament over Canadian airspace, NSC 5522 reported "[a]ction is being expedited" for this through Pentagon channels and noted that the State Department suggested that it might also use diplomatic contacts.[47] NSC 5522 noted that the recommendation for a press statement about Teapot's "high altitude" shot had been "fully implemented."[48]

NSC 5522 reiterated the Defense Department's commitment to having some Genies ready by the first day of 1957. In June, the rocket's W-25 warhead had been designated an "emergency capability" program by the AEC, giving it a high priority and authorizing the stockpiling of an early version before all manufacturing, engineering, and production details had been finalized for the mass-produced types.[49] With the Genie program proceeding, the Pentagon sought assurances that the weapon and other sealed-pit warheads were safely designed. Because high explosives had to detonate with precision and simultaneity in order to compress a fissile core in a way that produced a nuclear yield, it was nearly impossible to occur inadvertently. Defense officials, however, worried that an aircraft crash, fire, or rough ground handling (such as a weapon falling from the wheeled dolly used to move arms about) might cause a single portion, or "one point" of the high explosive to react. If properly designed, this would not cause an atomic detonation, although the conventional blast, like any other such explosion, would be very dangerous.[50] The Pentagon's liaison to the AEC asked for tests to confirm the one-point design theory. In the case of air defense warheads, this was particularly necessary, one Pentagon official explained, because the arms would "remain in a constant state of readiness" and were likely to be "in close proximity to densely populated areas."[51]

In August 1955, the AEC agreed to conduct safety tests for the W-25 and certain other warheads.[52] The president granted permission for the operation on September 5, the AEC then notified the Joint Committee on Atomic Energy, and a vague news release was issued for what was named "Project 56."[53] The AEC undertook the W-25 component of Project 56 in early November, an effort "simulating what is believed to be the severest result to be expected from impact or fire-induced accidental detonation."[54] The weapon behaved as theorized, demonstrating that a one-point detonation of the W-25 or another of the forthcoming new sealed-pit types would not cause a nuclear explosion.[55]

Sandia learned about Project 56 before it took place. The organization's Weapons Effects Department asked permission to participate in order to study an aspect that had thus far been overlooked: the possibility of plutonium contamination as a result of a one-point detonation. The request was granted. Sandia's commitment to a sound and thorough testing regime was consequently validated.[56] In at least one shot, when the one-point blast blew a weapon to bits, minute particles of plutonium from the fissile core were spread in a five hundred–foot radius around the site, and to two smaller areas farther away.[57] Because plutonium is especially dangerous if inhaled or ingested, this contaminated the immediate area. Thus, it was learned that a one-point accident, while free from hazards of a nuclear blast, might cause localized plutonium poisoning. Crews attempting to rescue a pilot from a plane crash that had caused a one-point detonation, for example, could be endangered.

The findings of Project 56 especially concerned the Air Force, because the Genie warhead contained plutonium (in addition to less toxic enriched uranium, nicknamed "oralloy").[58] While only a fraction of weapon mishaps were predicted to result in a one-point explosion, and the service obviously endeavored to minimize accidents of any sort, the risk was present nonetheless. This spurred the consideration of alternatives, including a W-25 version dubbed "Fleegle," which contained only the less dangerous oralloy. The AEC determined, however, that an all-oralloy W-25 would not be safe in the event of a one-point detonation (probably because enriched uranium reacts more readily than plutonium). Because a low-order nuclear reaction would have been worse than plutonium dispersion caused by a one-point explosion, and because of the money and time required, the Air Force eventually decided not to have an alternative weapon designed.[59] Instead, it chose to cope with the potential dangers of the composite plutonium-uranium Genie rocket by imposing stringent handling and flight restrictions once the weapon reached the inventory.[60]

The International News Service apparently had a well-placed source familiar with the Genie rocket during this period. Two months after Project 56, the wire service ran a story that revealed for the first time efforts to "arm jet fighters with atomic anti-aircraft missiles," in a project named "Ding Dong." It also reported that tests "showed the atomic weapons would not go off if the plane crashed," but conceded "[t]here is the possibility that in a crash, a 'low order' explosion—distinguished from a true atomic explosion—might scatter radioactive material over the immediate vicinity."[61] This, too, is the result of an unofficial leak and not an effort by senior policy-makers to disseminate air defense specifics.

One important point was not mentioned in the International News Service story. On December 2, the JCS wrote Defense Secretary Charles E. Wilson asking that he secure advance authority from the president for the use of nuclear antiaircraft arms in continental defense.[62] At the time, any expenditure of atomic weapons required explicit presidential permission. Nuclear air-defense weapons were becoming central to U.S. defense strategy, but as the Killian committee had asserted in its report the previous February, in the brief and hectic period following the detection of a bomber attack, it would be difficult if not impossible to secure the necessary authority while still allowing ample time to react.[63] The memorandum from the JCS was an effort to redress this problem. Wilson sent the correspondence to the Atomic Energy Commission, asking for comments. It languished until early February 1956, when the commission communicated its support.[64]

Coincidentally, the NSC's Planning Board was in the midst of drafting NSC 5602, an updated Basic National Security Plan to supersede NSC 5501, which, in turn, had taken the place of NSC 5422 and NSC 162/2 from 1953. Ever since NSC 162's description of nuclear arms as being "available for use as other munitions," the JCS had been uncertain what this meant in practice, how it ought to influence force structure and doctrine, and how the defense budget was affected.[65] With this confusion probably in mind, the JCS wrote Wilson again on February 15. On this occasion, they reiterated their December request but now urged him also to ask the president to "predelegate" nuclear-use authority in certain additional circumstances.[66] By clarifying the conditions under which atomic arms would be used by the United States, the JCS presumably hoped to ease budgetary, planning, training, and other preparations.

A few days later, the JCS suggested wording for the NSC 5602 draft that more explicitly outlined the role of atomic weapons in American defense policy, although it did not propose any sort of advance authority.[67] When the NSC met on February 27 and again on March 1, much of the debate centered on what language should be included in the policy paper. The NSC adjourned without consensus on the text.[68]

Two weeks later, it fell to the president to decide the issue. Having heard the NSC debate the centrality of nuclear weapons to the U.S. defense posture and cognizant of the JCS' support for predelegation, the president acted.[69] He approved NSC 5602, including the language that had been discussed inconclusively days before.[70] This section declared:

> [i]t is the policy of the United States to integrate nuclear weapons with other weapons in the arsenal of the United States. Nuclear weapons will be used in general war and in military operations short of general war as authorized by the president.[71]

Eisenhower, however, added a final sentence as a result of the Pentagon's request for predelegated permission to use nuclear arms. It stipulated: "[s]uch authorization as may be given in advance will be determined by the president."[72] Presumably at Eisenhower's direction, NSC executive secretary James Lay sent a memorandum on March 15 to Wilson, Secretary of State John Foster Dulles, and AEC chairman Lewis Strauss. Lay explained that the final text was the result of the JCS communication from February 15, and asked the addressees to collectively determine how best to proceed, now that the policy document made predelegated authority possible.[73]

The same day, apparently not aware that Lay's memorandum was en route to him, Wilson wrote to the president. He reminded Eisenhower that "a high velocity air-to-air rocket with [a] nuclear warhead" was under development, that the Killian commission recommended "that nuclear warheads be adopted as a major air defense armament" for other weapons and that "active programs" were underway to bring this about. The Defense Secretary also noted that Project 56 had demonstrated that the W-25 was one-point safe and that Air Force intended to have the first aircraft equipped with the Genie readied in less than nine months. But, "to be effective," Wilson wrote, "they must be expended under the same conditions as the present policy permits expenditure of non-nuclear air defense weapons." He declared he had "consulted with" the Secretary of State and

Lewis Strauss and that the three agreed that the president should approve a basic delegation of nuclear-use authority.[74]

When Eisenhower received Wilson's communication, he declined to act immediately. Apparently, Ike was not satisfied that the secretary had sufficiently collaborated with Dulles and Strauss. He also sought to obtain the trio's recommendations about the possibility of preauthorizing nuclear use for additional purposes. Accordingly, he instructed Wilson to discuss the matter further with his colleagues and then convey a broader set of predelegation options that met with the group's approval.[75]

The Defense Secretary understood. However, Wilson believed that the impending deployment of the Genie rocket and the requirement to obtain Canadian consent for nuclear use in some circumstances meant there could be no delay. He thought nuclear antiaircraft authorization was needed before the other predelegation discussions could be concluded.[76] On April 5, Wilson expressed this point to Dillon Anderson at the National Security Council. He wrote that he had "reconsidered" the issue and that Dulles and Strauss "concurred" with the Pentagon's recommendation.[77] Five days later, NSC Planning Board representatives convened to debate the specific authorization language to be forwarded to Eisenhower.[78] Afterward, Wilson and his two cabinet colleagues were asked to approve the Planning Board's work.[79]

On April 18, the president executed the "Authorization for the Expenditure of Atomic Weapons in Air Defense." "[T]he defense capability of the United States will be greatly increased through the addition of air defense weapons incorporating atomic warheads," the document declared. Eisenhower affixed his signature to the statement, which said, "I deem it necessary...that the use of these weapons in air defense be authorized and their use is hereby authorized in accordance with policy established by the President."[80]

This predelegated authority took effect only after "rules of engagement" had been developed and agreed to by the departments of State and Defense.[81] These regulations delineated the particular circumstances in which antiaircraft nuclear use was permitted. The State Department was involved because of the potential ramifications of U.S. weapons being detonated over or near Canada. State and the Pentagon dickered about the engagement policy for several months, despite the fact that the foreign aspects were limited. But, because the Air Force was preparing for a January 1 operational date for Genie, the delay threatened efforts to be ready by that time. Thus, in early October, Radford wrote to Secretary Wilson asking that he approve rules of engagement applicable only to sovereign American territory, since the State Department's consent was not necessary in this instance and it would allow the authorization to be in place by the time the first Genie-equipped interceptors were deployed. Within a month of Radford's letter, however, the two departments came to agree on the interception guidelines and Radford's request became moot.[82]

The policy stipulated that an interception could be ordered against any aircraft that "[c]ommits a hostile act," or that is "manifestly hostile in intent," such as when "[t]he pattern or actions of incoming unidentified planes indicate beyond a reasonable doubt that a hostile raid is in progress." Aircraft bearing Soviet military markings in American airspace without either permission or indications of distress were also to be targeted.[83] These "Interception and Engagement Instructions and Procedures" were issued December 7, 1956, on the eve of Genie's availability.[84] This finalized the policy authorizing the use of nuclear antiaircraft weapons. It continued in force even after broader predelegated nuclear authority was granted a few years later as the ultimate result of NSC 5602. The policy was deemed "top secret," and a 1959 document specified that "the existence of these instructions will be limited to a highly restricted group of people."[85]

Peter Roman, one of the foremost students of this subject, has argued that the granting of advance nuclear permission demonstrated Eisenhower's confidence in his military subordinates since it reduced civilian control over atomic arms. Roman has also written that predelegation increased the possibility of a nuclear antiaircraft weapon being used accidentally against a nonhostile plane or as a result of a relatively minor provocation, such as a reconnaissance overflight.[86] These are all apt observations. However, Roman misjudges the extent to which nuclear antiaircraft weapons were deployed outside the United States, and thus he might overstate the number of situations that were conducive to a mishap. Roman also acknowledges the low probability of accidents, and notes that Eisenhower and others judged the hazards of such to be acceptable in light of the perceived necessity to prepare for a Soviet attack.[87] In sum, says Roman, Ike and his aides dismissed "[w]hatever risks" they thought existed because "[t]he disasters that could befall the United States if a commander could not act immediately were far greater than any of the dangers."[88]

There is little doubt that the president perceived defensive weapons differently than the much larger strategic arms intended for use against Soviet territory. In a meeting with Admiral Radford just before granting the air defense authorization, Eisenhower told him that, while the use of atomic arms was a topic that "calls for great care," he "would certainly" use "air defense atomic weapons," once available, "against any aircraft attacking the United States."[89] At least one later administration understood this attitude. In 1964, Lyndon Johnson's national security advisor McGeorge Bundy summarized the policy (then still in effect) as "essentially defensive," because it permitted nuclear use "against military targets in the air." He reported that this was "in line with a belief that Eisenhower had that when the destructive force of nuclear weapons would only hit military forces, the decision on their use was a much less serious matter."[90]

Circumstances forced Canadian officials to consider this topic as well at the time. Geography, strong and longstanding bilateral ties, and many practical considerations made it logical to integrate Canada into American bomber defense arrangements, a fact recognized by the Killian committee. In 1956, as the American predelegation authority was being finalized, negotiations were proceeding to allow Genie-equipped interceptors to land, take off from, and overfly southern Canada and the Great Lakes region in the course of responding to a Soviet raid directed at the United States or its northern neighbor. In these instances, the American aircraft were governed by the same "rules of interception and engagement" set for Royal Canadian Air Force interceptors, which probably resembled the U.S. policies. The agreement concluded in February 1957, however, only allowed nuclear-armed U.S. interceptors to enter portions of Canadian airspace in the event of a confirmed attack.[91] U.S. forces could not exercise the predelegated authority in these situations, although (provided time permitted) the president and Canadian prime minister could consult and grant nuclear release authority through normal channels.

When Eisenhower assented to advance use of defensive nuclear weapons in early 1956, he remained discomfited by the possibility of surprise attack and the prospect of countering it. On January 23, the president received a briefing from the NSC's Net Evaluation Subcommittee, charged, like its similarly named predecessors, with determining the Soviet Union's overall (or "net") ability to inflict damage on the United States.[92] It offered a dire assessment, arguing that by 1958 the United States could not avoid catastrophic damage, even with some warning of a Soviet attack.[93] Although this was a controversial conclusion from which Admiral Radford vigorously dissented, the president lamented in his diary that the presentation showed "there was little we could do."[94] Two and a half weeks later, Eisenhower mentioned his distress to Radford. Later in the same meeting, the admiral raised the possibility about conferring with the president about the number and type of each nuclear weapon to be added to the arsenal. Radford said the current arrangements provided little "flexibility," implying that the services were saddled with an unsatisfactory mix or number of weapons. This might have shocked Eisenhower, who responded that he believed that plutonium and uranium "production is now so vast that it may be possible to have everything that is needed." Radford apparently disagreed. He rejoined that "the numbers of weapons needed for anti-aircraft purposes would be very great," as if to suggest that the magnitude of atomic material required for continental defense might deprive the military of ingredients necessary for strategic arms. Perhaps conscious of the size of the growing arsenal, the chairman also added that "it might be possible to redistribute, and even refabricate" some of the air-defense atomic arms after a raid, because they "must be very widely dispersed in anticipation of the first attack."[95] In this, Radford was probably unwittingly reiterating two interrelated points the Killian group made a year before and were apparently widely accepted by officials at the time: More antiaircraft weapons had to be acquired than actually would be used, and warfare, if it came, would not be cataclysmic. Upon conclusion of hostilities, it was presumed that the United States would dismantle unused atomic arms.

The next month, in another meeting with the president, Radford provided additional details about the effort to defend against Soviet bombers. He reported to Eisenhower that "things were really moving very fast" in the continental defense realm, because of "very firm directives" and "a lot of expenditures" that were the "result of the Killian report and the report by Mr. Sprague."[96] Eisenhower took the comments to heart. A few weeks later, in a press conference, the president remarked publicly on the nation's continuing air defense efforts. In response to a query about a proposal by former Illinois governor Adlai Stevenson (the once and future Democratic presidential nominee) to halt nuclear tests, the president said the United States was endeavoring to make atomic arms "useful in defensive purposes," such as "shooting against a fleet of airplanes." In such cases, a nuclear device was "more of a military weapon" rather than "one just of mass destruction" (although he confused thermonuclear and fission arms in his full reply).[97] Later, with the election campaign well underway, Eisenhower issued a written statement on nuclear testing that echoed this point. He asserted that recent exercises "have helped us to develop— not primarily weapons for vaster destruction—but weapons for defense of our people against possible enemy attack."[98]

The testing Eisenhower alluded to in 1956 was a seventeen-shot series that the United States conducted between May 5 and July 22 at the Eniwetok Proving Grounds, which consisted of several atolls in the Marshall Islands in the Pacific.[99] Eisenhower had approved the operation, designated "Redwing," in December 1955.[100] Official correspondence exchanged by government leaders beforehand noted that "[i]n addition to testing weapons for strategic and tactical employment, this program will proof test a prototype warhead for air-to-air rockets and will continue research and development of small designs suitable for use in air-to-air and surface-to-air missiles."[101] The first reference is to a W-25 that was detonated on June 16. This was the final test for the Genie warhead design before production began.[102] Since October, this warhead had been the Defense Department's top nuclear-development priority.[103]

Redwing also involved tests of warheads proposed for the Nike-Hercules. When development of the Hercules was first contemplated, the W-7 was an attractive choice for the prospective missile because it was an existing design and could be modified fairly easily for the new application. The W-7 featured a mechanism that physically inserted the fissile material into the high-explosive core in flight, which was a typical of the weapons of its era. However, once sealed-pit warheads were proven feasible, the Army sought to develop a version for the Nike-Hercules, provided it offered approximately the same two-kiloton yield and had the maintenance and storage conveniences inherent in the later design.[104] Teapot tested one concept, and Redwing offered an opportunity to further the development of the warhead, designated "W-31."[105] In addition, in 1955, the Sandia Corporation had raised the possibility of a second, higher-yield sealed-pit Nike-Hercules warhead that could be used for situations requiring a greater blast radius.[106] The Defense Department agreed with the concept, and the resulting device (initially called "W-37," then "W-31 yield 2" or "W-31Y2") was also evaluated in Redwing.[107] Although the explosive power of the larger warhead has never been revealed, it was probably around twenty-two kilotons.[108] Both W-31 versions were projected to be available in October 1958.[109] Since the Nike-Hercules was scheduled to become operational just a few months before, this meant that the W-7 would be fielded for a relatively short period and at a handful of locations.[110]

Amid the Redwing test series, the Army and Air Force were feuding. The topic was whether the Nike-Hercules or "Talos," a modified Navy nuclear antiaircraft missile, was best suited for defense of Strategic Air Command bases in the United States and which service should operate whatever was selected.[111] At the end of May, in order to trumpet its preferred choice, Army officials revealed details of the

Nike-Hercules to obliging reporters. While the *Washington Post and Times-Herald* said only that it had "an amazing lethal radius," the *New York Times* was more specific, declaring that "[a]nonymous sources" specified that Nike-Hercules "would have an atomic bomb for a warhead" that "would destroy whole groups of planes."[112] The paper said also that officials "acknowledged" that, if detonated, "the radioactive fallout from the comparatively small warhead would not be serious enough to endanger the American public."[113]

Warhead configurations for BOMARC were evaluated during the 1956 Pacific test series as well. The W-12 and then other types of atomic warheads had been contemplated for the Air Force missile since at least 1953.[114] Some required design changes and others affected performance because of the warhead's weight or other characteristics.[115] However, primarily because of problems associated with BOMARC's cutting-edge ramjet propulsion, the program had been repeatedly delayed, which meant that the final warhead decision was also postponed.[116] The sealed-pit concept came about around the time that many of the missile design problems seemed to be overcome. As a result, the 350-pound, three-foot-long "W-40" was proposed for BOMARC early in 1956, and Redwing provided an opportunity to confirm the concept.[117] When the test was successful, the W-40, which yielded about six and one-half kilotons, was selected as the BOMARC armament.[118] The warhead was expected to be ready by July 1959, around the time production of the missile was anticipated to be underway.[119]

The selection of a BOMARC warhead eased some of the design challenges that were delaying the missile program. In the last minutes of flight, for example, control of the BOMARC was to be assumed by a small, onboard radar capable of tracking the target and determining course corrections necessary to achieve an interception. Precision proved difficult, especially given the closing speed of the target and missile. However, once a nuclear warhead with a demonstrated lethal radius greater than the radar system's miss distance was chosen, the need for greater accuracy was obviated.[120]

In advance of Redwing, the NSC's Operations Coordinating Board became involved in the related publicity activities, following the procedure established for Teapot.[121] In early January 1956, Theodore Streibert, director of the U.S. Information Agency, wrote AEC chairman Lewis Strauss about the announcement of Redwing, suggesting that it would be poorly received by international audiences regardless of the details because of growing global discontent with nuclear testing. Streibert, however, said that a statement should nonetheless "provide the maximum possible reassurance to overseas populations." He said among the points to be considered was the fact that

> [t]he 1956 nuclear tests will be concerned with defensive weapons. It would help to mention at least one example of what will be tested, e.g. air-to-air rockets. The reason for this is that public awareness of nuclear testing is centered on high-yield weapons, particularly in connection with Pacific tests. Therefore the "defensive" concept, preferably with concrete examples, would be extremely helpful.[122]

The AEC accepted the suggestion. Since government officials had for months considered the antiaircraft component of the Redwing to be vital, emphasizing this in public statements mostly reiterated what many already thought.[123] The release issued January 12 declared, "[o]ne of the important purposes of this series will be the further development of methods of defense against nuclear attack."[124] The language was picked up in press coverage, and Strauss repeated similar sentiments on CBS's *Face the Nation* a month later and on July 19, when Redwing concluded.[125]

The *New York Times* suggested that Strauss's July statement was related to that year's Operation Alert, which started the next day, since his remarks also tried to minimize concern about fusion fallout. Regardless of any connection (which cannot be confirmed), the 1956 civil defense drill took place without the president, who was on the verge of leaving for a trip to South America. On the day it began, however, Eisenhower held a regular NSC meeting in which he declared, "[W]e can thank the Lord those sirens were part of an exercise and not a real attack," and the council adjourned in time to allow some cabinet members to head to their emergency sites.[126] Three days later, as the drill concluded, the Interior Secretary told a reporter that the exercise showed that some locations might require additional antiaircraft protection.[127]

Whether they would get it depended, in part, on the American understanding of the USSR's ability to stage an attack. At a celebrated four-power summit meeting in Geneva in July 1955, Eisenhower proposed to Soviet leaders that the United States and USSR permit each other to conduct reconnaissance overflights and share information about defense installations. The Soviet leadership, still experiencing post-Stalin leadership tumult, rejected this "Open Skies" initiative.[128] The rebuff, coupled with the uncertainty about Soviet bombers, confirmed Ike's resolve to obtain better intelligence on the USSR's military. In December of that year, he authorized a project to launch camera-laden balloons over the Soviet Union. The effort was halted in February 1956 after 516 were dispatched but only thirty-four produced any useful pictures.[129] From March to May, also with the president's permission, specially fitted reconnaissance versions of American B-47 bombers undertook a total of 156 flights over the Soviet Union near the Kola Peninsula and Bering Straight, including one mission of six planes flying abreast above Siberia. Although these missions found no evidence that planes were based in the region (and earned unpublicized protests from the Soviets), they left unsettled questions about Soviet aircraft stationed elsewhere.[130] Based on this and other information on hand at the time, a mid-1956 National Intelligence Estimate credited the Soviets with sixty-five long-range Bison and Bear bombers. The NIE also predicted that in three years the number would increase to seven hundred.[131]

On July 4, however, a U-2, one of the photographic reconnaissance planes produced by the secret program recommended by Edwin Land's Killian panel subcommittee, conducted its first mission over the USSR. The aircraft's task was to photograph suspected M-4 bomber airfields in the nation's interior. The next day, a second sortie also sought out Bison locations, including the factory where the plane was manufactured. Three more flights took place before July 10, gathering additional information.[132] These efforts were a success. They yielded top-quality stills.

When CIA analysts examined the photographs of the nine air bases and other facilities, they saw few bombers. The photo interpreters concluded that previous observers had been duped into believing the Soviet bomber force was larger than was the case. As a result of the U-2 flights, the government lowered its estimate of the growth rate of the USSR's air arm beginning in early 1957, although the reconnaissance program's classification meant that only those with the highest clearances could learn the reason for the revisions.[133] (The July pictures seemed so dispositive that, of the nineteen other U-2 overflights between November 1956 and May 1960, when the final mission was piloted by Francis Gary Powers, none were intended to gain intelligence on Soviet bomber capabilities.[134]) Significantly, however, the U-2 photography reduced, but did not obviate, American concern about the possibility of a surprise air raid. Even after considering the results of the U-2 effort, policy makers believed that the USSR might still eventually field a substantial strategic air force, but at a more distant date than originally anticipated. A year and a half after the bomber-base missions, for example, an intelligence evaluation estimated that the Soviet Union fielded between ninety and 150 heavy bombers (rather than the 220 originally predicted for this period), but noted that four to six hundred were expected to be available by mid-1960.[135]

As the new intelligence was being gathered and considered in late 1956, the deployment of the first Genie-equipped interceptors loomed. This raised the issue of what should be revealed officially about the new arms. In September, the president was reminded about Genie's forthcoming "initial operational capability date" and told that "[w]ork is underway on a proposed information plan" meant to counter "some anticipated public relations problems."[136] Three months later, Herbert Loper, an aide to Defense Secretary Charles Wilson, wrote Lewis Strauss outlining the need for "a public announcement" of the nation's "new capability."[137] Strauss was involved because the NSC had just adopted a policy that made the AEC chairman responsible for coordinating the approval of government statements about atomic arms with the Operations Coordinating Board and other entities.[138]

Loper's letter outlined the Pentagon's approach, which had been broadened by that time to encompass the Nike-Hercules in addition to the Genie, since the Army missile was expected to be deployed in about eighteen months after the Air Force weapon. A release about these arms was desirable, the letter said, because "widespread deployment" that was "in close proximity to the civil populace" makes "public knowledge and understanding" a "matter of major importance." He argued that the arms "should have a positive effect on national morale" because they "provide a more effective defense against enemy nuclear attack and can be safely deployed on a nationwide scale."[139] Furthermore, wrote Loper,

> [u]nofficial disclosure of the deployment of air defense weapons in American communities and uninformed speculation as to their possible effects upon such communities would seriously undermine public confidence and understanding. Lack of such public confidence and understanding could easily result in lack of public support and undue restrictions on the employment of these weapons to the detriment of national defense.[140]

The government needed to take the initiative, the Defense aide claimed, because the details about the deployment would likely leak in any event. In addition, he said that statements about certain nuclear tests had referenced atomic air defense weapons, there had already been some journalistic "speculation" about them, and visible security changes at some defense installations as a result of their arrival would only pique further curiosity. Finally, Loper explained to Strauss that, "[a] ground accident or air crash involving these weapons is always possible," implying that such a situation would offer a poor opportunity to publicly outline the specifics of the arms for the first time. These were all good points. To his letter, Loper attached a draft press release and background information proposed to accompany the statement. He noted that "[p]rior to the public announcement, the Canadians will be consulted on the information plan and its attachments."[141]

As evidenced by the stories that had leaked in the past two years, fears of "unofficial disclosure" (or at least of announcements not managed by the Pentagon officialdom) were justified. Even as a press statement was contemplated, unauthorized statements continued. In August, an aide to the Army Secretary told a California audience of an Army weapon due within two years "able to destroy an entire fleet of planes in one shot."[142] Days after Loper sent his December letter, a Navy officer spoke in Chicago about Nike-Hercules missiles to be deployed "soon" with "warheads with sufficient power to sweep entire close formations of airplanes from the sky." This led the United Press to conclude the new weapon would be "atomic-armed."[143]

On January 2, one day after the first interceptors with Genie rockets went on alert in the United States, the Defense correspondence was forwarded to the OCB for evaluation.[144] A special committee considered the draft statement and supporting information and incorporated changes suggested by affected agencies. The group worried, apparently for naught, that Western European allies would complain that the arms were being deployed only in the United States. It also recommended that the AEC not cosponsor the announcement (because of the "current identification" of the commission abroad "with 'atoms for peace' rather than weapons programs") and added language proffered by the United States Information Agency ("[d]eployment of these weapons does not mean that the Government has any specific expectation of air attacks").[145] Ultimately, the Working Group on Nuclear Energy concluded that it had "no objection" to the release "from the standpoint of overseas climate of opinion or current international developments," and the OCB approved the plan as amended.[146]

The news release and accompanying briefing materials were submitted to the president on January 22. The papers summarized the Genie's current and future deployment plans, as well as the rocket's yield, safety protocols, and other characteristics. An accompanying memorandum from Defense Secretary Charles Wilson endorsed the need for the announcement, using much of the same language used in Loper's correspondence to Strauss from a month earlier.[147] Eisenhower approved the press statement on January 24 (four days after being inaugurated for the second time), but deleted one sentence and stipulated that Canada must agree to the "proposed action and texts."[148]

The Canadians subsequently hesitated to concur. Various sources suggest this is because of concern that the release would lead to disclosure of an agreement to allow overflights in some circumstances or because it would make Canadian defense preparations appear overly reliant on America or paltry in comparison.[149] However, available documentary evidence suggests the reluctance was due to the reference to surface-to-air nuclear arms, which might have been opposed because this raised possibilities not yet considered, such as U.S. Nike-Hercules missiles being fired into Canadian airspace from near Detroit or other border locations.[150] As the delay dragged into February, the State Department emphasized the urgency of the situation to the nation's northern neighbors. Finally, on February 15, State reported to the OCB that the Canadians "had withdrawn their objection" to the discussion of the "future capabilities of Nike-Hercules and Talos."[151] The Joint Committee on Atomic Energy and the president were notified, with Eisenhower aide Andrew Goodpaster providing a handwritten notation to Eisenhower assuring him that the Pentagon's statement "will not announce any locations" for the new arms.[152]

"The Department of Defense has begun deployment of nuclear weapons within the United States for air defense purposes," the announcement noted on February 20. "Nuclear air defense weapons now have been developed which provide by far the most effective form of defense against air attack. It is essential to our national security that we incorporate these new weapons into our air defense system." They "can destroy aircraft within a considerable distance from the point of burst," and "the employment of such weapons for air defense purposes will greatly enhance the effectiveness of interceptor squadrons and ground based air defense units," it continued. Alluding to the sealed-pit design and one-point characteristic, the statement declared

> [E]laborate precautions have been taken in the design and handling of these air defense weapons to minimize harmful effects resulting from

accidents either on the ground or in the air. Atomic weapons tests conducted by the Atomic Energy Commission have confirmed the possibility of any nuclear explosion occurring as a result of an accident involving either impact or fire is virtually non-existent.[153]

In specifying that "[t]hese weapons generally would be employed at altitudes where the effect of blast, heat, and radiation on the ground would be negligible," the attached "fact sheet" repeated much of the language used in the press release from Teapot's "High Altitude" shot issued two years earlier to comply with the Killian panel recommendation. The handout also noted that the "description and size" of the subject armaments "cannot be released" or photographs of them permitted.[154]

The next day, one newspaper touted the deployment of "[a]tomic rockets for blasting enemy bombers out of the skies," another termed the release "a historic announcement," and a third suggested that it made official what some news stories had speculated about for some time.[155] The *Washington Evening Star* noted that the president determined when nuclear arms were to be used. "Asked if President Eisenhower had delegated such authority in advance," the paper reported, "officials refused to comment, saying that such information was highly classified."[156] All the articles reported the Pentagon's safety assurances. The *Washington Post and Times-Herald*, while expressing concern about the possibility of an accident, editorialized that "[f]rom a defense standpoint the plan makes sense."[157]

With the release of the Defense Department's statement, the Army lost no time in officially confirming the ongoing development of its new missile, although there was not much about it that remained secret. On February 26, the service formally revealed the existence of the Nike-Hercules because it "was undergoing final tests and soon would be ready for use."[158] One newspaper declared that the Army "dropped the veil from the newest anti-aircraft missile," and credited Defense Secretary Charles Wilson as forecasting "more certain kills" because of the weapon's "nuclear capabilities."[159]

While the Army's statement clearly served its institutional interests (it prevented the Air Force's already-deployed Genie from garnering all the attention), it was straightforward and factual. Neither the Army's announcement nor the Pentagon's release from a week before was a cynical exercise meant to mislead an unwitting public. Indeed, in the years since atomic air-defense weapons had been approved, almost every item specified in the Pentagon release had been discussed and accepted by senior government officials and military leaders. Some details were withheld, of course. But, in general, the American public was being asked to accept these weapons for the same reasons that policy makers sought their development. In addition, with Nike-Hercules, BOMARC, and other nuclear antiaircraft arms to follow, there was much yet to do.

Chapter 4

Genie

On December 17, 1956, several MB-1 Genie rockets were moved by train from the Army Ordnance Plant in Burlington, Iowa, to Wurtsmith Air Force Base in northern Michigan and Hamilton Air Force Base outside San Francisco.[1] These were the nation's first nuclear antiaircraft weapons. They were being hurried into position in order to be available by January 1.

The deadline was met. Seven weeks before the Pentagon formally announced the Genie's introduction, a handful of rockets and fifteen interceptors capable of carrying them were ready at the two locations. Ever since the Defense Department had acceded to the timetable originally advocated by Robert Sprague, the Pentagon and Atomic Energy Commission had worked to ensure that this would come about. By July 1957, however, plans to increase the number of aircraft, arms, and bases were delayed because of difficulties in constructing Genie storage facilities at the airfields to which the rockets were to be distributed.[2] The resolution of these problems and continuing work to publicize Genie meant that considerable official and public attention was devoted to the new rocket throughout the year. The rocket remained an important component of American defenses and a part of the cultural lexicon for the remainder of the Eisenhower administration and beyond.

Preparing the Genie for the Air Force inventory involved designing and testing the rocket vehicle and its nuclear warhead, producing both in volume, mating the two elements, and distributing the completed weapons to units ready to receive them. The Air Force and Northrop began project "Bellboy" in March 1956 to rework F-89D "Scorpion" interceptors to carry the new armament.[3] The two-place planes, which were the best type available despite being underpowered and poorly engineered, were sent to an Air Force maintenance depot in Utah, where pylons and wiring were changed to allow one rocket to be fastened beneath each wing.[4]

A new fire control system to enable the plane crews to operate the rockets was installed in each aircraft. The system was comprised of a rudimentary computer linked to an onboard radar. Operated by the weaponeer (a crewman who sat behind the pilot in the cockpit), it was based upon the "lead collision" interception technique. This procedure involved approaching the target perpendicularly so that a large surface area was presented to ease the radar's tracking ability.[5] Based upon the speed and direction of the target and the MB-1's performance characteristics, the fire control apparatus then calculated the ideal time to launch a Genie. The system aimed the rocket ahead of the target (on a "lead course") so that the two would arrive (or "collide") at the same point simultaneously.

The addition of the fire control equipment and the other alterations encountered few difficulties. By December 1956, nine modified Scorpions (redesignated "F-89J") were available at Hamilton and six at Wurtsmith.[6] In the ensuing months, the conversions continued apace. By June 1958, 268 F-89Js were produced, enough for eleven squadrons.[7]

As the first planes were being prepared, Douglas Aircraft and its subcontractors were building Genie rocket bodies in Santa Monica.[8] The agreement to design and produce the vehicles, known then as "Ding Dong," had been finalized in late 1954.[9] Within a year, early versions were test-launched and minor motor and stability problems were resolved.[10] The fusing system was also favorably evaluated at this time, causing the Sandia Corporation to issue a report that affirmatively answered the query posed by its title: "Will Ding Dong Ring the Bell?"[11] Once completed, rockets were sent to the Army's Burlington plant, codenamed "Sugar" by the AEC, to be mated to their nuclear components. Sugar assembled and fitted most U.S. nuclear warheads, using high explosives and other parts it produced, fissile cores from the AEC's Rocky Flats facility near Denver, and pieces supplied by additional sources.[12] The first completed rockets were shipped to the receiving units by rail, probably because ground transportation was believed to pose a lesser chance of a one-point detonation in the event of a crash during transit.

The warheads on the earliest weapons sent to Wurtsmith and Hamilton were specially built. After Teapot demonstrated the feasibility of the W-25 in 1955, it had been placed on an expedited development timetable. However, because the W-25 was not projected to be available until after the desired Genie deployment date, the AEC declared the project an "emergency capability" effort.[13] This designation (given to select other development programs as well) allowed the first few warheads (dubbed "EC-25") to be assembled using preproduction or prototypical parts and techniques in advance of the finalization of the full-scale manufacturing process.[14] Twenty EC-25s were made, and they were fitted to the first few rockets in December 1956.[15] It is likely that four emergency capability Genies were mounted initially to two interceptors at both Wurtsmith and Hamilton, and the rest stowed at temporary storage areas adjacent to the aircraft.[16]

Defense Department regulations prescribed the characteristics of the secure compounds in which various types of nuclear weapons were kept.[17] Genies were to be stored in individual compartments in special buildings built on fifteen-acre parcels proximate to where the interceptors were kept readied. The nonnuclear components of the arms were to be inspected and serviced in another structure erected for this purpose. These facilities were usually to be surrounded by earthen berms (to contain damage from a high-explosive blast, fuel fire, or similar mishap) along with guard posts, fencing, lights, and intrusion alarms. Each complex was expected to cost one million dollars.[18]

The Pentagon elected to build most of these facilities on military bases. Many interceptor squadrons occupied portions of civil airports. The prospect that these units would store and handle nuclear antiaircraft arms forced most to relocate.[19] In mid-1955, the Army Corps of Engineers (responsible for overseeing military construction) awarded a contract for the design of the required storage compounds to Black and Veatch, a Kansas City engineering firm. Although the company submitted drawings for standardized complexes in March 1956, the planning, situating, funding, and erection of these facilities took longer than anticipated.[20]

When it became apparent that the emergency capability Genies would arrive at Wurtsmith and Hamilton before the mandated areas were completed, the ADC obtained a temporary waiver of the storage requirements.[21] The command apparently convinced Pentagon officials that accommodating the few weapons on an interim basis was acceptable. This is probably because of the program's urgency and because security arrangements differed little from those already in place for other munitions.

The cost of the Genie facilities, however, contributed to budgetary angst in spring 1957. For more than a year, the DoD had battled the president and some aides about the amount to be appropriated for national security during Eisenhower's second term. Defense leaders had reluctantly agreed to accept about thirty-eight billion dollars annually. This was less than preferred, but a figure that most thought was manageable. When a few administration officials and legislative leaders intimated that the Fiscal Year 1958 proposal would drop below this amount, the Pentagon objected.[22]

The protests were for naught. The budget was reduced. For the balance of Eisenhower's tenure, the demand for a larger and increasingly expensive defense establishment existed simultaneously with a persistent push for economy. This tension affected the entire panoply of continental defense programs, including the deployment of Genie and other nuclear antiaircraft arms.[23]

In a time of limited budgets, anti-bomber initiatives were attractive targets for spending reductions, especially when proponents conceded that a well-funded and vigorous defense network would never be foolproof. Treasury Secretary George M. Humphrey and his allies, for example, were hostile to a continental defense effort they saw as a futile extravagance. To them, it was projected to cost billions yet still be incapable of preventing huge casualties and enormous destruction. These objections were buttressed by some proponents of the Strategic Air Command who implied that most continental defense funds (save those necessary to maintain an attack warning capability or to enable retaliation) should be reallocated to underwrite more and improved offensive weapons. An expanded offensive arsenal was said to be more likely to deter a Soviet strike than a more modest one resulting from an imperfect defense network completed with limited funds. Of course, continental defense advocates, typified by Robert Sprague, rejected all these arguments. They maintained that the danger of an attack justified an expansive defense effort, and believed that the cost was both necessary and affordable.[24]

Although neither argument prevailed and continental defense expenditures were eventually not as high as some favored or cut as much as others preferred, the number of anti-bomber weapons funded in Eisenhower's second term was less than originally anticipated by the Pentagon. This was entirely a financial decision, rooted primarily in the high cost of constructing the necessary storage and launching infrastructure that the MB-1 and other arms necessitated. There is no evidence that the reduction was motivated by any doubt about the utility of these weapons.

The president was among those who favored atomic antiaircraft arms and understood the costs they entailed. At a cabinet meeting called to discuss agency spending proposals in early June 1957,

Eisenhower wondered aloud why the Atomic Energy Commission sought to expand its production capabilities. "You've been giving us a pretty darn fine arsenal of atomic weapons," he told AEC chairman Lewis Strauss. "[W]hy," he inquired, was an increase (with the attendant expense) necessary "now?" Because the "[b]ulk of the effort is now on small weapons," explained Strauss, such "as for air defense," for which "great numbers" of nuclear warheads "are required."[25] The president was satisfied with this explanation.[26] Indeed, two days later, in a press conference in which he was asked about objections to nuclear testing, Eisenhower argued that these exercises were meant to address the dangers of a raid. "[I]n recent years," he said, American nuclear tests "have been largely" intended to perfect the "defensive type of armament" necessary "to defend against attack from the air."[27]

Early the next month, the Defense Department briefed the president and National Security Council on various weapons, including the MB-1, Nike-Hercules, and BOMARC. The presentation reiterated many of the Genie performance characteristics (including range and blast size) that had previously been conveyed to Eisenhower, and it outlined the tactics for the rocket's use.[28] Ike wrote Defense Secretary Wilson a week later with his impressions of the briefing and mentioned arms that he thought could be considered for reduction. By not commenting on the Genie plans, his assent to them was implied.[29]

Others were also impressed with the capability of the new weapon and pleased with its introduction. Around the same time, a report transmitted to Joint Chiefs of Staff chairman Arthur Radford about the prospect of achieving an "adequate air defense" described the Genie's presence in the arsenal as "a decided step forward."[30]

Days later, Eisenhower participated in 1957's annual Operation Alert. He was flown from the White House to the since-completed emergency presidential facility in Virginia, coincidentally marking the first-ever helicopter flight for a chief executive. At "High Point," Ike consulted with staffers and was briefed on the mock damage suffered in the faux raid.[31] Five thousand other federal officials continued at various shelters for nearly a week, although the president and aides ended their participation the next day.[32]

By the time of the July exercise, manufacture of the W-25 warhead for the Genie began, and the emergency capability weapons in Michigan and California were withdrawn, probably replaced by rockets with production warheads.[33] The EC-25 arms were dismantled; they were never intended as permanent additions to the arsenal because their nonstandard components and assembly made routine diagnostic evaluations difficult and parts replacement impossible.[34] However, the planned distribution of the MB-1 to four other Air Force bases was then suspended, because compounds at those locations were still being built and the Defense Department was reluctant to grant additional storage exceptions beyond what had already been permitted for Wurtsmith and Hamilton.[35] Although the Pentagon was eager to deploy the Genie, it remained conscious of safety considerations.

While some in the Air Force scrambled to prepare installations to accommodate the rocket, others planned to evaluate the MB-1's performance. Various iterations of the warhead, the rocket, and the F-89 fire control computer had all been tested, but a Scorpion had never launched a complete weapon. In January 1956, the congressional Joint Committee on Atomic Energy asked the AEC for a study of this possibility, although it is not clear if members originated the request or if they solicited it on behalf of the Air Force.[36] The AEC, however, believed its function was the design and manufacture of nuclear components. Although testing was a necessary part of these activities, the commission had little interest in funding, supporting, or organizing what it considered to be practice firings or demonstrations of completed arms.

After a May 1955 test of a nuclear antisubmarine device several hundred miles off the U.S. Pacific coast, the AEC's general manager had been advised by the commission's observer at that operation to "strictly limit" the agency's role in any similar activities in the future. Army lieutenant colonel N.D. Greenberg believed the AEC's "interest in weapons effects is very limited" and recommended that if the Pentagon sought further "tests of this nature," the arms should "be turned over to the DOD and the tests be conducted as a completely military matter."[37] General manager Kenneth Field considered this advice when he responded to the JCAE's request. Field explained the development process for the W-25 (and the warhead for the Nike-Hercules). Possibly because the AEC was sensitive to the institutional interests of the Air Force and the wishes of the congressional committee, the correspondence does not explicitly declare the AEC's opposition to a live fire test. Rather, the letter notes that in the course of creating every new armament, "the weapon is tested in various stages of development" in order "to insure that it will operate reliably upon completion." Although arms were "capable of being stockpiled even without a true proof test," Fields pledged nonetheless that the AEC "shall coordinate" with the Pentagon "as to the necessity" of a test "of a complete version of the Ding Dong and the Nike B."[38]

If the AEC hoped to quash the idea, it failed. As preparations were made for the next nuclear test series, the AEC's Division of Military Application (DMA), the commission component responsible for weapon development, reported in a November 1956 memorandum that the Defense Department was planning a "systems test" of the Genie at the Nevada Test Site. The memo noted that this would include the "air burst" of a rocket fired from an Air Force plane (referenced as a "USAF interceptor," using the standard abbreviation for the service). It further explained that the Joint Chiefs of Staff had "recently approved" this exercise, the purpose of which was to confirm "safe delivery maneuvers," "aircraft response," and the radiation dosage received by the crew. DMA officials declared that the test would be conducted only if an analysis by the AEC and DoD of "operational safety problems" demonstrated that "the test can be conducted at NTS without hazard to personnel on or off-site."[39] A later memorandum announced that the "systems test" should henceforth be referenced as a "weapons effects test," possibly because of AEC objections to a designation that implied that the operation's purpose was to demonstrate the W-25's basic functionality.[40]

The AEC did not readily approve the test series (eventually named "Plumbbob") proposed for Nevada in 1957, although the delay had nothing to do with concern over the Genie operation. Rather, Lewis Strauss and at least one other commissioner believed that Plumbbob included more and larger shots than were appropriate for a stateside series, and they argued that it should be undertaken in the Pacific instead. By mid-December, however, an agreement had been reached on a slightly reduced program for the NTS.[41] Three days after Christmas, President Eisenhower approved the twenty-six-shot proposal. Among the points the AEC chairman specified in his letter requesting authorization for the effort was "a Department of Defense test involving an air-burst of the nuclear warhead in the new USAF air-to-air rocket following its launching from an interceptor aircraft."[42]

A month later, the AEC issued a press release announcing the "series of low-yield nuclear tests," describing the "extensive radiation monitoring network," which would again be in place in cooperation with the Public Health Service, and noting that details about shot dates and media accessibility would be forthcoming.[43] The Operations Coordinating Board approved the release with little difficulty, although before Canadian objections delayed the Genie deployment announcement, it appeared that both statements would be distributed simultaneously.[44] One OCB staffer reported that the United States

Information Agency "was not too pleased" with the confluence because "there will be a heavier news emphasis on nuclear weapons" than normal. However, he said agency officials "feel they can make positive use of this since the deployment of the defensive weapon and the testing of defensive weapons can be related and lumped together...."[45] When the Genie deployment announcement was postponed until February, the Plumbbob release was issued alone on January 24, 1957.[46]

Amid this activity, the AEC was considering the operation's safety aspects. When DMA director Alfred Dodd Starbird asked the Los Alamos laboratory to advise him on the possibility of a mishap, the lab chief asked his staff for help in understanding the origins of the inquiry and for assistance in crafting a reply. "I don't know who originated [the] idea of a test," physicist Alvin C. Graves wrote to his superior in response, "but I guess I am guilty of telling Starbird this test could present a safety problem. I became concerned when I heard the DoD was considering using a B-47 as a target. I did not like the thought of a crew bailing out of a B-47 and leaving it on autopilot." Forgetting (or ignorant of) the change in nomenclature, Graves concluded, "I must admit to a great reluctance to a systems test" taking place in Nevada "particularly during the E.C. period."[47] The reason for concern about the emergency capability weapons is not clear, and in any event, one was probably not used. In addition, while the Air Force proposed using a drone in the exercise, no record has been found to substantiate Graves's understanding that an American jet bomber with a full crew complement could have been involved. What Graves "heard" may have been incorrect on several specifics.[48]

The plan as actually codified involved three F-89s. One would fly with a single Genie from an Air Force base at the Nevada Test Site to a predetermined point nearby, where the rocket would be fired at an imaginary aerial target. Instruments on all three planes and the ground would measure the MB-1's performance, the blast, and the radiation produced.[49] A drone was rejected for safety reasons. A precise stationary target point also eased the effects calculations by eliminating any uncertainty about the detonation's exact location.[50] Similarly, it is likely that the Genie to be used in the operation was fitted with a W-25 in order to eliminate any performance variability attributable to the preproduction components and because the EC-25 versions would probably be eliminated from inventory by the time of the test.[51]

The Sandia Corporation produced a study to "review all conditions, however remote," in which the Genie test could result in a rocket exploding on the ground, either because it was prematurely released from the interceptor or properly launched but subsequently malfunctioned. The analysis concluded the chances of either occurring was one in 500,000 (rendered as "2.3×10^{-6}"), a figure "so small" that the "probability should not be a factor in scheduling the test." This estimation was based on the likelihood that a combination of human errors and electrical and mechanical malfunctions would defeat the various fuses, switches, and mechanisms that alternatively prevented power from reaching the warhead before launch, and armed it only after the proper acceleration had been achieved. To protect against a fire control computer malfunction and to account for the possibility that officials monitoring the operation at a distance might perceive a problem not apparent to the fliers, provisions were also made for the Genie to be launched by a signal transmitted from the ground directly to the rocket.[52] Thus, the aircrew could halt the firing, but they could not initiate it.

As the safety of the operation was being evaluated, the publicity benefits of the test were also being considered. The Genie shot offered the opportunity to promote the rocket's deployment and to demonstrate that it could be detonated as intended without danger to those on the ground. Colonel Arthur B. "Barney" Oldfield, the public information officer for the Continental Air Defense Command (CONAD), recounted later that a senior officer instructed him at the time to consider how to trumpet the Genie's introduction. "[E]ven though high classification" meant there was "limited room for sensible discussion" and "public reassurance" about Genie, recalled Oldfield, General Earle E. Partridge "wanted the weapons 'out in the open.'"[53] According to Oldfield, five ADC officers heard about this assignment, and volunteered to stand beneath the MB-1 blast at Plumbbob. They were confident that the rocket would perform as designed, knew that Teapot's High Altitude test in 1955 resulted in little radiation below, and were eager to support the public relations effort. Oldfield accepted the offer, Partridge and the Joint Chiefs of Staff chairman approved, and the necessary arrangements were made.[54]

The AEC facilitated news coverage of the Genie operation (named "Shot John") as it did for other Plumbbob tests.[55] For the MB-1 event, accredited television, radio, and print journalists were advised a week in advance that they would be given access to an on-site vantage point (known as "News Nob"). They were also offered pre- and post-shot briefings.[56] The first session was held the day before the operation, and included ADC commander Joseph H. Atkinson

(Partridge's Air Force deputy) and test advisor Alvin Graves (who did not mention his earlier skepticism or the initial rumor about the way the effort was to be conducted).[57] The journalists knew the purpose of the test was to fire a Genie, but at the briefing Atkinson announced the participation of the Air Force volunteers. He also noted that he would be flying a nearby observation aircraft. In addition, in his presentation, Atkinson summarized the test procedures, the safety measures (including the fact that the rocket would be fired by ground command), and the chances of an accident, which he characterized as "substantially less than one per cent."[58]

Atkinson also emphasized points made previously by the AEC and Pentagon about atomic antiaircraft arms. While "our concept of atomic weapons has been primarily oriented toward mass destruction of ground targets," he said, it was now possible to use nuclear arms "to protect our lives, homes, cities, factories and military installations." Given the "destruction capability" of modern bombers, the journalists were told that "*nuclear* weapons may well be the most *important* concept yet devised for air defense"; they were an "efficient and effective means of stopping a ruthless and determined enemy." The general also reiterated that such arms "will be detonated at relatively high altitudes" and accordingly "the actual fall-out of radioactive particles from these weapons will be negligible...."[59]

Similar observations were included in a briefing prepared for senior Royal Canadian Air Force officers who observed the shot from about ten miles away. The presentation made to them, however, also included secret specifics about the MB-1, since the neighboring military representatives could be provided with classified information not conveyed to reporters. Among other items, the briefing described the Genie's mechanical and electrical safety devices, clarified that it was not intended for use below five thousand feet, and explained that firing distances in the event of actual use were a function of flight time and radiation: Launching the rocket too near the target would irradiate the friendly aircraft; firing the Genie too far away could provide the intercepted plane time to veer away. The presentation also noted that the rocket's lethality was primarily due to the tremendous aerial gust it produced within a one-half to one-mile area. Depending upon the target, the MB-1 kill probability was estimated between ninety-two and one hundred percent.[60]

The RCAF briefing also specified that the rocket "provides some measure of kill probability against the enemy bomb itself."[61] The prospect of destroying attacking aircraft and the munitions they carried was a significant impetus behind the deployment of nuclear antiaircraft weapons. The Killian committee argued this point in its 1955 report, and in subsequent years this justification was mentioned frequently to official or public audiences.

In addition to preparations for the press and other guests, the safety procedures, security requirements, and logistical arrangements for Shot John necessitated considerable coordination among many participants. Like the other tests in the Plumbbob series, the operation was guided by an elaborate plan that detailed all activities, including convoy movements, instrument preparations, loudspeaker announcements, and even personal behavior. The use of electric razors, for example, was prohibited within fifteen minutes of Shot John to prevent electromagnetic emissions from the small motors from possibly interfering with radio transmissions.[62] A process for gathering meteorological and radiological data was also put in place, both to confirm that weather conditions were appropriate for the test to be conducted and to track radioactive dispersion after it occurred.[63]

Figure 4.1 Ground crews prepare to attach a U.S. Air Force Genie MB-1 nuclear air-to-air rocket to the wing of a specially decorated F-89 Scorpion interceptor preparing to conduct Shot John in Operation Plumbbob at the Nevada Test Site on July 19, 1957. For Shot John, five Force officers volunteered to stand beneath a Genie detonated in the air 18,000 feet above them.

Source: Still image taken from official U.S. Air Force movie "Project Genie" in the collection of National Archives and Records Administration.

At 7:00 a.m. on July 19, the shot took place precisely as intended. The Air Force pilots, having conducted thirty practice runs in prior days, including five which resulted in the launch of rockets without nuclear warheads, flew the Scorpions over the "Yucca Flat" portion of the NTS. The Genie was launched. As the planes banked, the rocket flew two and one-half miles in four and one-half seconds, and detonated at a designated "air zero" 18,000 feet above Nevada. By that time, the planes were more than a mile away from the 1.73-kiloton blast.[64]

The crews and planes were examined as soon as possible. Earlier tests had demonstrated that Scorpions would not be impaired by the heat, gust loads, and shock of such a nuclear blast, and analysis after Shot John confirmed this conclusion.[65] It was also determined that the aircraft provided greater shielding than anticipated, and the fliers received less radiation than predicted. The pilot of the Scorpion rigged with sensors to measure the blast effects received the most of the

Figure 4.2 Five Air Force officers recoil as a U.S. Air Force MB-1 Genie nuclear antiaircraft rocket is detonated above them in Operation Plumbbob's Shot John. The placard reading "Ground Zero; Population Five" was fashioned by Colonel Arthur B. "Barney" Oldfield, the Public Information Officer for the Continental Air Defense Command who arranged for the volunteers to participate as part of the Air Force's effort to get the deployment of the nuclear weapon "out in the open."

Source: Still image taken from official U.S. Air Force movie "Project Genie" in the collection of National Archives and Records Administration.

six crewmen involved: 2.73 rem. This was well within the amount that was thought could be safely received in each shot (five rem) or cumulatively in the whole operation (thirty-five rem).[66] From the perspective of nearly fifty years later, when current studies show *any* radiation exposure is dangerous, this seems preposterous.[67] There is no evidence, however, that the Defense Department, the AEC, or the participants themselves believed that the operation posed much danger, at least beyond the risk associated with flying a temperamental fuel-filled jet aircraft laden with a weapon containing conventional explosives. Indeed, even the perception of danger at the time undoubtedly differed from the current understanding. The crews likely traveled in cars without seatbelts on the day of the operation, for example, perhaps while smoking cigarettes. Regardless, based upon the radiological measurements and the F-89's performance in Shot John, one report affirmed the Air Force's assessment by concluding that the "MB-1 air-to-air rocket can be successfully delivered in an operational situation...."[68]

The five Air Force volunteers (and one photographer) standing below the Genie burst also seemed to fare well.[69] While it may have made good theater, measured against the prevailing standards, being positioned three and one-half miles away from a low-kilotonage explosion was not particularly exceptional at the time. Others had previously been closer to similarly sized (or larger) shots, although typically with greater physical protection.[70] Nonetheless, many film and audio recordings were made of the officers astride a hand-lettered "ground zero—population five" sign that Barney Oldfield had fashioned from shirt cardboard earlier that morning in his Las Vegas hotel room. Major Norman Bodinger, whose cousin, magazine editor Norman Cousins, was coincidentally helping to form the National Committee for a Sane Nuclear Policy, radioed a narration to the operation's command center. "The colors are brilliant," he declared before being interrupted temporarily by the shock wave. After the observers recoiled slightly, they excitedly shook hands and extended congratulations all around.[71]

"They said all they experienced was 'a sudden rush of air and a clap like thunder,'" reported the *New York Times* the next day. The volunteers "remained on the spot an hour after the detonation, with Geiger counters, and said radioactive fallout was almost undetectable."[72] *Time* described a "fireball" that gave way to a "rosy, doughnut-shaped cloud," and noted the Genie's ability to "destroy a whole flight of enemy bombers with the smash of its shock wave." A wire service story explained that the volunteers wore "only their regulation summer uniforms" to "prove that civilian populations could survive an overhead nuclear blast."[73] Many other news outlets carried photographs or a story, based on an AEC press release or eyewitness observations from News Nob.[74] Curiously, however, despite (or perhaps because of) this coverage and the details provided previously to the president, Shot John was not mentioned at the next week's National Security Council meeting or, as far as can be determined, in any other forum with Eisenhower.[75]

Not long after the July blast, with W-25-equipped Genies becoming available in quantity but permitted only at Wurtsmith and Hamilton, the Air Defense Command appealed again for further relief from the storage requirements. The Defense Department responded by allowing four other Air Force units with "adequate" interim facilities to receive four Genies (enough to equip two planes) each. There was an additional proviso that in the event of an attack warning, more rockets would be airlifted to those locations.[76]

For some reason, the Air Force changed the way it transported the newly permitted rockets to bases with temporary facilities. On August 31, President Eisenhower was told that "a certain number" of Genies would be moved the next week "by air," according a memorandum from aide Andrew J. Goodpaster. Alluding to the dangers of a one-point detonation, the memo specified that "a crash might result in scattering of radioactive material." Goodpaster wrote that the Pentagon official who advised him about the shipment confided that the "AEC is worried" about the transit method, but had relented because of the military's insistence about "the need to take the risk."[77] Eisenhower was not alarmed. No evidence has been found that he objected to the distribution method. It appears that by the end of 1957, additional permanent storage sites had been completed at some locations and larger numbers of rockets were then distributed.[78]

Around November 1957, the Air Force had informed state-level civil defense authorities of radiological hazards that could be associated with military airplane crashes. Although this warning was applicable to many nuclear weapons, it is possible that the impetus for the contact was the ongoing airborne distribution of Genies. In February 1958 the OCB approved a joint AEC and Pentagon press release about accident hazards. Although the announcement was apparently already being developed, it was spurred by a December telegram to the president from California's Republican governor, who had become alarmed when briefed on the topic by the Golden State's civil defense office.[79] "Many nuclear weapons," the federal government's statement said,

> contain some amount of conventional explosives.... An accident such as the crash of an aircraft or severe wreck of a train carrying a nuclear weapon may cause this conventional explosive to detonate by impact or fire. In most cases, the detonation of a conventional explosive represents the maximum danger that can happen and, of course, its effect is limited to the vicinity of the accident.[80]

However, an accident, the announcement continued, "might possibly cause local scattering of nuclear materials in the form of dust.... Such materials could be hazardous only if taken internally, as by breathing.... [I]t is unlikely that any person inadvertently exposed would inhale dangerous amounts of the unfissioned materials." The release, which added more specifics to the generic assurances included in the air defense announcement from a year before, concluded by urging individuals not to approach crash sites. It also noted that military units were trained in cleanup procedures.[81] The announcement garnered news coverage the next day, and California's chief executive was satisfied.[82]

As the Genies were allocated to additional locations, Barney Oldfield continued, as ordered earlier by Partridge, to manage the concerted and coordinated public relations effort about the defense benefits they putatively offered. The rocket also entered the cultural discourse apart from the Air Force officer's initiative. Throughout, however, many of the themes from the Pentagon's 1957 press release and the briefing for the Shot John journalists were repeated and emphasized.

Oldfield was a native Nebraskan named after a distant relative who was a famous racecar driver. He attended the University of Nebraska on an Army ROTC scholarship, graduating in 1932. Heading to Hollywood (in the interwar years, active-duty commissions were scarce), Oldfield leveraged his journalism degree to become an entertainment-industry reporter and columnist. He earned a spot in Ripley's "Believe It or Not" by setting a record for viewing the most movies (more than five hundred annually) for five straight years. Called up by the Army on the eve of World War II, Oldfield eventually attended paratroop school (the first Army journalist to do so) and after D-Day helped manage war correspondents in Europe, which was the subject of his 1956 book, *Never a Shot in Anger*. After victory in the Pacific, Oldfield joined the Warner Brothers publicity department, where he promoted Ronald Reagan (with whom he developed a lasting friendship), Errol Flynn, and Elizabeth Taylor, among others. He was recalled to active duty by the Air Force before the Korean War, aided press coverage of that conflict, and then transferred to Europe and then to the fledgling Air Defense Command. At least one initiative he started there remains: The Air Force still issues periodic statements on Christmas Eve about the progress of Santa Claus's flight from the North Pole.[83]

Given Oldfield's responsibilities for press relations at the ADC, he probably was closely involved with an extended interview that *U.S. News and World Report* conducted with Partridge in September 1957. While the general was frank about the ability to detect and destroy attacking bombers ("I don't think we'll ever have an overwhelming advantage in defense"), he used the opportunity to tout the Genie (and the forthcoming nuclear-armed Nike-Hercules). Partridge declared the MB-1 "a tremendous advance" and said "[i]t's as important to the air-defense business as radar was in World War II." "Formation flying, in the face of an atomic-warhead-equipped air-defense force is just out of the question," he surmised, because with the new arms, "you don't have to get a direct hit." Partridge also recounted Shot John ("[w]e had some observers on the ground.... They were jolted but not damaged in any way at all") and he explained that "the design of the rocket—the speed at which it leaves the airplane and the distance it goes before it explodes—is such that the attacking airplane is perfectly safe."[84]

In the course of the interview, the magazine also inquired, "[D]o you have to get the President's permission before using one of these atomic rockets?" "Yes," replied the general. "However, the President has given his approval to use, without reference to anybody, any weapon at our disposal if there is a hostile aircraft in the system." *U.S. News and World Report*'s transcription of the discussion also included this exchange:

Q: You don't have to wire Washington?
A: No. We probably would be on the phone talking to people when the thing went off.[85]

Notwithstanding the presumed sensitivity of this subject, the Pentagon, AEC, and the State Department (in consultation with Canada) approved this text before it was published.[86] This caused problems a year later.

Another noteworthy element of Oldfield's work was a proposed television show, which he probably facilitated by drawing upon Hollywood ties. In late 1957, Joseph M. Schenck Enterprises (a Beverly Hills firm named for one of the founders of the motion picture industry), developed a television script about Shot John for *Survival*, a proposed series about NORAD, the joint Canadian-U.S. military unit then being organized. Air Force Reserve colonel Jimmy Stewart, the motivating force behind (and star of) Paramount's *Strategic Air Command* two years before, was to appear as himself in the episode, narrating the program and acting as if he had observed the Genie test while on active duty.[87] "If this baby works," Stewart was to have been told by an officer organizing the shot, "it could mean the difference between destruction and survival for the United States." Later in the script, "General Atkinson" (it is not clear if this is a reference to the actual person or an actor portraying the Air Force general) explains that "Genie is the first air-to-air missile with a nuclear warhead. It'll be used purely for defensive purposes, perhaps in the vicinity of, or even directly over, one or more of our major cities."[88]

Entitled "The Weaponeer," after the functional title bestowed on those in the Air Force responsible for arming and launching nuclear weapons, the program's central dramatic focus was on the F-89 crewman who performed that duty during Shot John. Except for Stewart's fictional role, the script accurately reflected Plumbbob details, including the names of the weaponeer and other participants, and myriad operational specifics. (The depiction of the crew enjoying cigarettes after a late breakfast on a training day is plausible, if unverifiable.[89]) In some cases, too many details were provided. When the script underwent Defense Department review, for example, officials deleted a proposed close-up of a Genie model, as well as a description of the rocket's lethal blast radius. The dimensions, shape, and effects data were classified.[90]

While Oldfield's precise role in the proposed episode is not known, the screenplay demonstrates thorough knowledge of the MB-1, Shot John, and the language and purpose of CONAD's public relations initiative. This strongly suggests his intimate involvement.[91] Despite Oldfield's presumed efforts, however, and a December 1957 *New York Times* article announcing the episode's forthcoming production, there is no indication that it was ever filmed.[92] It appears to have been supplanted by another Paramount and Schenck collaboration, which also was never completed.[93]

Although General Atkinson and the others were not immortalized in celluloid, the F-89 that fired the Genie in Shot John did make it into the movies. Aircraft 53-2547 was ultimately sent to the Montana Air National Guard. Once it was retired from service, it was mounted for display on the unit's property at the Great Falls International Airport. It was there when the 1977 Charles Bronson movie *Telefon* was filmed, and the aircraft can be seen in at least one scene. In 2010, the Scorpion remained exhibited there.[94]

Twenty years before *Telefon*, as the fate of "The Weaponeer" was being decided, Oldfield hit the stump. He addressed a Montana church group in December 1957 about Shot John participant Cliff Barbee, who hailed from Wild Rice, North Dakota. Taking some liberty (by discounting the ground signal that launched the Genie in that operation), Oldfield described Barbee as the person who became "the first to fire a live atomic-warheaded rocket from a manned aircraft." As the weaponeer, Barbee sat "closest to its fiery tail as he cast it out ahead of his plane," knowing that there were individuals below prepared "to take whatever the blast would offer." The shot demonstrated, Oldfield argued, that "the civilian populace of this or any town would be in no danger" if a Genie were "used tactically overhead."[95]

How the Presbyterian Men's Club reacted to this maudlin performance is not known. But, at a dinner meeting of the Junior Chamber of Commerce in Clinton, Iowa, two months later, Oldfield kept to the same theme, this time extolling the professionalism and performance of the native Iowan who had piloted the Shot John aircraft. Thirty-two-year-old Cliff "Hutch" Hutchison, father of four and World War II veteran, had rehearsed the operation with Barbee for months, according to Oldfield. The fact that "five of their friends" stood "bareheaded under the atomic blast" emphasized the seriousness of their task. They were motivated by recognition of "some public disquiet" about the "smaller air defense variety" of nuclear weapons. But Shot John's successful conclusion demonstrated that fears of the weapon were "groundless." "This model of rocket, in numbers, now rests on many of our air defense bases," Oldfield declared, probably exaggerating the extent of deployment on that date, "and more are getting it."[96]

In addition to addressing the putative effectiveness and safety of the MB-1 in his Iowa remarks, Oldfield was eager to justify the cost of the new weapon. The rocket vehicle was worth seven thousand dollars, he explained. Once the "atomic load" was inserted, the price reached "a quarter of a million dollars." Lest this be considered too expensive, Oldfield cautioned, "all things are relative." The value of the buildings and other property in Clinton greatly exceeded this amount, and he said, "[T]here are things which cannot be price-tagged," including "your families," "your homes," and "a way of living." With this in mind, the Genie cost was reasonable, since "[o]ne of these newly acquired atomic rockets could be exchanged for Clinton if war came" or "fear of its being expended...could possibly keep the enemy on his own bases."[97]

This was not the first time that Oldfield discussed the Genie's cost. Nor was it the last. He issued a press release on the subject in 1959 in conjunction with a Las Vegas air fair that attracted an international military and aerospace industry audience.[98] The announcement garnered a front-page article in the *Washington Post and Times-Herald*.[99] However, the disclosure of weapon expenses was prohibited because it was thought that this could allow the size of the U.S. arsenal to be estimated, based upon the total AEC budget. The Air Force investigated and learned of Oldfield's earlier statements as well. An investigative document determined that the colonel

> released or caused to be released to the general public the estimated cost of the GENIE warhead and MB-1 Missile on several occasions between October 1957 and April 1959 without having received authority to do so.[100]

This was a violation of NSC 1706, the prevailing iteration of the policy that required the OCB to approve the dissemination of any nuclear information.[101] Oldfield was "administratively reprimanded" as a result. A letter specifying this was placed in his record, although it noted that "the entire facts of this case" (whatever they may have been) meant that the description of the punishment would be removed from the file when he was transferred. Oldfield's personal papers do not explicitly explain his version of the events, but imply that he consciously violated policy in order to ensure broad public understanding of the Genie and its putative defense benefits. Although the reprimand does not mention it, Oldfield also believed the punishment was related to his other efforts "to use inert models of the 'Genie'" (possibly including in the deleted scene from the Schenck screenplay). Years later, he wrote, "there are times when breaking classification solves more than hardened artery adherence to it."[102] Oldfield's disclosure of the Genie cost was the first time in which an official source acknowledged the figures for a specific American nuclear weapon. In the entire Cold War and ensuing years, the cost of only one or two other warheads has been officially confirmed.[103]

Of course, Oldfield did far more than publicize the Genie's size and shape. He also helped the Shot John participants to tell their stories. A few weeks after the Plumbbob operation, the flight crew and all but one of the ground-zero group were feted in Washington at the annual convention of the Air Force Association, a private group that promoted the service's interests. Before an appreciative audience, Partridge presented each with a commemorative plaque.[104]

Figure 4.3 A U.S. Air Force F-101B Voodoo interceptor carrying two presumably non-nuclear training versions of the Genie MB-1 nuclear air-to-air rocket. The Genie was fitted with a W-25 warhead which yielded two kilotons. With the exception of some flights during the Cuban Missile Crisis, interceptors were allowed to be airborne with the nuclear MB-1 only if responding to a confirmed bomber attack on the United States. In January 1958, six months after Air Force Col. Sidney Bruce stood below an aerial detonation of an MB-1 in Nevada, he touted the F-101 and its armament to a St. Louis audience. Bruce recounted that "four of my friends and I stood directly underneath the burst" in July 1957, and experienced "absolutely no ill effects." "Thus," Bruce asserted, "we feel that the public need have no fear" of this weapon, and he exhorted audience members to convey this assurance to others.

Source: Official U.S. Air Force photograph courtesy of the National Museum of the U.S. Air Force.

Four months later, one of the officer volunteers delivered an address (drafted by Oldfield) at a St Louis press event touting the McDonald F-101B "Voodoo," the F-89's successor. The new interceptor, said Colonel Sidney Bruce in January 1958, will be equipped with an "air-to-air rocket...which carries an atomic warhead." Such a weapon meant that "it is no longer necessary to attain a direct hit in order to achieve a kill," he explained. Bruce also declared that while design features made it "*virtually* impossible" to "have an accidental atomic detonation, either in storage or in flight," the rocket could "be effectively employed in war against airborne targets without affecting personnel on the ground." He recounted Shot John and explained that "four of my friends and I stood directly underneath the burst" with "absolutely no ill effects." "Thus," Bruce asserted, "we feel that the public need have no fear" of this weapon, and he exhorted audience members to convey this assurance to others.[105] When the Air Force subsequently awarded McDonnell Aircraft a contract for eighty-four F-101s, the *Washington Post and Times-Herald* noted the plane carried "an atomic rocket" that was "capable of destroying an entire enemy bomber formation with its nuclear detonation."[106]

As the Genies were distributed across the country, they continued to receive attention. One evening in early February 1958, the nationally broadcast CBS radio news included an interview with an ADC officer who reported that "[a]ir-to air missiles with nuclear warheads" were "being stocked near New York and other major cities." Colonel Frank Ball said it was "relatively impossible" for the arms to explode accidentally. The *New York Times* noted the colonel's remarks the next day. However, the paper did not mention (perhaps because the reporter did not know) that Ball had been one of the Plumbbob–Shot John ground-zero volunteers.[107]

The next week, *Life* magazine excerpted sections of a forthcoming book (*Our Nuclear Future*) by famed nuclear physicist Edward Teller and colleague Albert L. Latter. The pair argued against mounting pressure for a nuclear test ban, citing, in part, the need to develop atomic air-defense arms.[108] "Our main purpose in further experimentation with nuclear bombs is not, of course, to make city-busters more horrible. It is to prepare to make defensive use of nuclear weapons," they wrote.[109]

> For instance, a nuclear weapon may be carried by a fighter plane and used to shoot down an attacking bomber. Since the carrying capacity of the fighter plane is severely limited, the weapon used for this purpose must be both small and light. A major objective of the U.S. nuclear test program is to develop such purely defensive, mobile weapons.[110]

The AEC had been saying much the same for years. Teller and Latter noted that Shot John was an integral component of the defense effort they favored. While participants measured "no significant rise in the radiation level" as a result of the air defense blast, lethal effects did occur elsewhere. "[H]igh in the air an enemy plane could have been demolished," they argued, "even if the nuclear explosion had missed by a considerable distance."[111] Both the magazine article and book were illustrated with several photos of the Shot John Genie launch and of the volunteers.

The *Life* article and subsequent book engendered considerable angst among test ban proponents. Nobel Prize–winning chemist Linus Pauling, a vocal supporter of a ban, subsequently exchanged correspondence about the publications with many like-minded individuals. He also debated Teller on the topic on San Francisco public television. However, nuclear air-defense weapons or the Plumbbob test were not mentioned in any of the written communications or in the face-to-face meeting.[112] Certainly this does not imply that Pauling or his colleagues assented to the deployment of atomic antiaircraft arms, but the obvious absence of any overt objection suggests preoccupation with other topics.

Indeed, the antinuclear movement was still in a formative stage in this period. Its tactics and priorities were in flux. Two and a half weeks after Shot John, on the twelfth anniversary of the Hiroshima bombing, a "radical" offshoot of the "pacifist" Committee on Non-Violent Action trespassed onto NTS property to protest the AEC's activities. Not until a year later, however, did the group stage its first event at a location associated with operational nuclear weapons. In this case, a handful of members leafleted an intercontinental ballistic missile construction site near Cheyenne, Wyoming. Following the voluntary suspension of nuclear testing that year, CNVA and SANE increasingly directed their action at deployed arms, rather than the AEC's facilities.[113] Despite publicity about nuclear air defense weapons and their relative ubiquity, however, these armaments were apparently considered either inconsequential or insufficiently exciting to be the locus of protests during the Eisenhower administration.

Similarly, testing opponent and self-described liberal U.S. representative Charles O. Porter wrote to the AEC in May 1958 to express disagreement with a proposed Pacific shot in which observers were to be invited to measure the low level of radiation produced. "Most people remember the picture in *Life*," complained the first-term congressman from Eugene, Oregon. It featured "Air Force officers standing directly under an air burst and doing so in perfect safety." Porter therefore contended that the forthcoming test was unnecessary because it duplicated this previous activity. As a way of illustrating the presumed redundancy, he asked rhetorically, "Is it not true and rather well known that a high altitude burst...has no local fallout?"[114] Porter did not express objections to Shot John, the weapon it tested, or the defense doctrine associated with both, despite having well-established antinuclear credentials. In the month before penning the letter to the AEC, Porter joined Norman Cousins in addressing a SANE rally in Manhattan and traveled to Eniwetok to "dramatize his opposition to further nuclear tests."[115]

While the left's distress about atomic antiaircraft arms was limited, the defense industry was enthusiastic. Once the Genie was deployed, Douglas Aircraft purchased advertisements, including in the popular press, touting the rocket's role in the nation's defense, and arguing that the weapon's development demonstrated the firm's ability to undertake technologically demanding projects. Illustrated with an official Shot John photograph showing the Genie streaking away from under the Scorpion's left wing, one ad declared that the MB-1 can "knock out an entire fleet of bombers with a single hit or near miss." "Genie's atomic warhead can be fired without radioactive fallout," assured Douglas, making the weapon "usable against sneak attacks over our own or friendly territory."[116]

This possibility became newsworthy in October 1958. In an interview with the *New York Times* that month, General Partridge repeated much of what he had told *U.S. News and World Report* a year before about nuclear air-defense weapons. Advanced permission to use them had been granted, the paper surmised, because it was "an inherent requirement of the defense mission." "It was assumed," the *Times* explained, "that the intention of an enemy attacker against the home soil could hardly be misinterpreted" and this "required swift, powerful interception."[117] In contrast to the reception accorded the earlier *U.S. News* piece, the article caused a stir. Publicly acknowledging predelegated nuclear-use authority was undesirable to policy makers if another nation was implicated.

In the year since the *U.S. News* story, the nation's military organization had changed. In the earlier article, in which Partridge revealed that authority had been granted to him for the use of defensive nuclear weapons, the general was billed as the chief of the North American Air Defense Command. This was imprecise. That joint U.S. and Canadian unit had been announced that August but did not become operational until a week after the story appeared. Even then, the command's activities were tentative because it required parliamentary ratification in Canada, which did not occur until May 1958. Once formal authorization was granted, however, Partridge continued to lead NORAD as well as CONAD, the subordinate American organization. The Air Force's Genies were assigned to CONAD.[118] Advance permission had been provided to Partridge as CONAD commander, and it applied only to CONAD units operating over U.S. territory and adjacent waterways.[119] Since NORAD had not yet been established when the *U.S. News* article appeared and any predelegated authority applied only to American units, the Canadians had apparently paid little heed to the 1957 story, despite its inaccurate reference to Partridge as the new command's leader.

When the *New York Times* reported in 1958 that NORAD was "authorized to fire a nuclear weapon in combat without the specific approval of President Eisenhower," however, the government of his northern neighbor was displeased.[120] The story failed to appreciate the distinction between two similarly named military organizations with the same leader.[121] Accordingly, a Canadian diplomat contacted the State Department the next day seeking a "full explanation" of the suggestion that the commander of a military unit that included Canadian armed forces was authorized to use nuclear weapons without consultation.

At least one U.S. diplomat understood that Partridge's NORAD deputy was Canadian, and realized that the article's incorrect assertion that Partridge's authority extended to forces within NORAD as well as CONAD had caused angst. He recommended explaining the situation to the Canadians and acknowledged that this might necessitate revealing secret specifics of the predelegated authority granted CONAD.[122] Eventually, a senior American official decided to have subordinates confer with the Canadians, but without commenting on the American predelegation authority that had been all but announced a year earlier by Partridge.[123] Because there appears to have been no further complaints, the meeting probably took place and the Canadians were likely satisfied, although evidence to support this contention is not readily available.

Donald Quarles (by then the deputy defense secretary), who had taken personal charge of the Pentagon's inquiry into the story, also summoned Partridge and the Air Force chief of staff to a meeting. Quarles was concerned about the fact that the advance authority had been mentioned in any fashion; he was not upset that it had been incorrectly attributed to NORAD. Quarles was subsequently reminded of the previous approval of the *U.S. News* article and informed that CONAD had used the earlier journalistic piece for many months as a basis for briefing other journalists. Quarles countered that CONAD had received a broadly worded message in September "countermanding" the prior consent given for that material.[124] In response, Partridge replied that he disregarded this instruction because it was included in a communication primarily addressing a dispute between the People's Republic of China and Taiwan and it was not clear that it was applicable to his command.

Partridge's explanation seems plausible. The circular addressing diplomatic and political sensitivities of "nuclear weapons in any foreign area" mandated that "[n]o questions, hypothetical or otherwise, will be answered regarding use [of] nuclear weapons or authority [to] use them."[125] Quarles outlined this exchange in an October 13 memorandum to President Eisenhower, relayed Partridge's contrition, and also expressed sympathy for the general's confusion about the prevailing policy. In addition, Quarles reported to the president that the Pentagon was distributing more precise regulations to clarify the prohibition on public comment on atomic arms.

Based upon this evidence, it appears that Pentagon officials erred in this situation, but concocted a flimsy excuse in order to dodge responsibility. Despite claims to the contrary, top Defense Department leaders were probably not aware that the air-defense nuclear-use authority was revealed in 1957, or that this revelation had been approved by subordinates. (Despite the significance of the *U.S News* article in hindsight, it was not noteworthy at the time, and sparked no other stories.) After the 1958 *New York Times* article caused a diplomatic row and inquiries brought these circumstances to light, a farfetched scenario was advanced to suggest that the initial approval comported with departmental policy, but that it had subsequently been amended to prohibit further acknowledgement of predelegation. This allowed the Pentagon to excuse the publication of the earlier story while making the second article blameworthy. Partridge probably assented to this explanation because it posed no threat of punishment.

None of this concerned Eisenhower. Aide Andrew Goodpaster appended the remark "President has noted" on a top corner of the Quarles memorandum, and there is no indication that Ike did anything more than just that. Despite the Defense Department's concern, it is probable that many attentive citizens assumed that arrangements had been made to permit ready use of nuclear air-defense arms. The existence of atomic antiaircraft weapons, the general attack scenario (Soviet bombers approaching from the north) and approximate response times were known. The earliest use of all available munitions in case of a raid was probably expected. Eisenhower likely understood this, which explains his lack of concern about the related publicity.

In contrast, political scientist Peter Roman, who has studied air defense predelegation, suggests that Partridge's 1958 comments might have been directed at the Soviet Union.[126] According to this reading, a full (if incorrect) understanding of NORAD's ability to use nuclear arms could help to deter an attack. This interpretation is difficult to support with the available evidence; the explanation seems far more prosaic.

While the circumstances and significance of Partridge's remarks to the press were being settled in late 1958, the Air Force was reducing the funding and aircraft allocated to the Continental Air Defense Command. At the end of 1956, for example, there were sixty-five interceptor squadrons. When Dwight Eisenhower left office four years later, the number had decreased to forty-one. Although by that time many of the remaining units had replaced their Scorpions with far better performing, Genie-equipped F-101B and F-106 "Delta Dart" interceptors, the number ultimately fielded was much less than originally anticipated.[127]

In addition to reducing the number of squadrons and aircraft, the locations of many air defense units were also shifted. The Air Force had initially situated interceptors to protect urban areas. Defense doctrine changed in the later Eisenhower term to shield Strategic Air Command bomber bases. It was assumed that deterrence was strengthened if the nation's retaliatory force was protected.[128]

All of this came amid efforts to construct the required Genie storage facilities. Eventually, when the service resolved the force level and basing questions, thirty-one Genie compounds were built at Air Force installations (and on the service's property at Duluth International Airport) in twenty states during the Eisenhower administration.[129] These facilities were erected near the "alert barns," where interceptors were kept fueled, armed, and ready for takeoff, and close to a lounge or dormitory building built for duty crews.[130] If notified of the possible approach of hostile planes, the fliers were to be airborne within five minutes to investigate. Scorpion pilots were to be directed to the vicinity of the unknown craft by air traffic controllers. Once the interlocking network of radars and computers was established (the awkwardly named Semi-Automatic Ground Environment system reportedly partially patroned by Robert Sprague before his NSC consultancy) in later years, interceptors such as the F-106 could be guided automatically by commands transmitted directly to onboard computers.[131]

Because of the small but real possibility of plutonium contamination from a one-point detonation caused by an interceptor crash or some other accident and the unknown consequences of an aerial lightening strike, the Air Force did not allow planes to be airborne while carrying Genies. The only exception was in the event that a bomber attack was positively confirmed. This meant typically four aircraft were on alert at all times: two armed with conventional weapons to make the initial interception, and two that could be fitted with MB-1s and take to the air within thirty minutes if a raid was confirmed to be underway.

It was because of this restriction that the Air Defense Command considered an all-oralloy replacement rocket. Because it would be devoid of plutonium and would not pose the same dangers of a one-point detonation, it presumably would not face the same limitations.[132] When such a weapon proved to be time-consuming, expensive, and not foolproof, the Air Force dropped the idea.[133] Despite the fact that a second W-25 one-point test undertaken in April 1957 showed the danger from an accident involving the existing weapon type to be "an order of magnitude less severe than originally believed," the flight restrictions on the Genie remained throughout the time the rocket was operational.[134] There was one exception. The prohibition was lifted only during the Cuban Missile Crisis.[135]

The Air Force ensured, however, that servicemen knew how to use the Genie in the event of conflict. Pilots and weaponeers practiced on simulators and by firing training versions that did not carry a nuclear warhead or associated subassemblies. Ground crews learned to retrieve weapons from storage "bins," using trailers designed for this purpose, and load them on large numbers of planes in a short period.[136] When the Genie initially entered the Air Force inventory, the Air Force mandated that every twenty-four-plane F-89 squadron be capable of arming at least eighteen aircraft with one hour's notice. This placed a great burden on the interceptor units because this requirement could be invoked at any time and it necessitated a large crew contingent. In order to ensure enough manpower to accomplish the task, only a few loaders could be far from the interceptor compound at any time, including when they were ostensibly off duty. By June 1958, this limitation had become apparent and the order was modified to allow "all operationally ready" planes to be readied within sixty minutes during normal work hours, and at least five aircraft at other times.[137]

Arming some aircraft was an arduous task. With the F-89, Genies could be relatively easily fastened to the pylons on the underside of each wing. The Voodoo and Delta Dart carried the MB-1 internally in the fuselage. Fitting the rocket into the tight space took peculiar physical contortions, made more difficult when done during one of the frequent loading exercises.[138]

Strict safety and security procedures, ultimately approved by the president, applied while planes were being armed and after the task was completed. Any aircraft with a Genie on board could not be moved on the ground under its own power (probably to preclude inadvertent or unauthorized operation of the armament electrical system), and the rocket motors were disabled to prevent accidental ignition. Pins securing the Genies to the planes remained in place unless the craft were ordered airborne. If they were, pilots had instructions to arm the weapons only just before engaging the enemy and were prepared to jettison their Genies over water or unpopulated areas in the event an emergency made a safe landing problematic. Ground crews also received training to respond to crashes in which one-point detonations might occur.[139]

In 1958, the development, codification, and implementation of safety and security procedures became the responsibility of an ADC unit established specifically for this purpose. It conducted occasional inspections of Genie squadrons, including observing surprise "mass load" drills.[140] Performance standards were stringent and an unsatisfactory evaluation could lead to discipline or suspension of a squadron's "combat-ready" status.[141] Even an error involving an inert training rocket was considered evidence of a procedural breach because of the presumption that a nuclear "war reserve" Genie would receive the same handling.[142]

The delivery of the F-101B (starting in January 1959) and F-106 (in May 1959) posed difficulties because units were working with unfamiliar airplane types.[143] In 1960, several squadrons faired poorly in inspections for this reason. In one case, loaders forgot to install a disabling pin in a motor. Elsewhere, two safety switches were not properly sealed. These and lesser lapses (such as the use of outdated checklists) led General Atkinson, the ADC commander, to decry as "intolerable" this "utter disregard for the requirements of safety, operational capability and military discipline." Special teams were assembled to aid the offending units and new training and programs instituted. By the close of the Eisenhower administration, inspection results had improved markedly.[144]

While information about these problems and their apparent resolution has been released, it is difficult to determine the number of MB-1s produced. In 1957, a staff member from the NSC's Net Capabilities Evaluation Subcommittee visited Douglas's Genie assembly line and learned that that "production is currently underway on an order of 4800 tactical weapons," distinguishing them from inert versions to be purchased for training purposes.[145] However, storage sites typically included four or five buildings (at least two had eight) divided into thirty compartments.[146] Each bin held one rocket.[147] The establishment of thirty-one storage sites would have provided accommodations for only about 4,400 Genies. Similarly, each F-89 squadron was allocated 112 rockets.[148] If all thirty-one locations could stow this number, about 3,500 were fielded. However, a reliable secondary source, citing unspecified records, notes that precisely 3,155 Genies were made.[149] This figure makes sense. As the number of planes was limited in the late 1950s, munitions were likely cut back as well. While at least 1,601 Genies had been assembled by March 1958, a problem with the design of a component, probably the "x-unit" (the assemblage of fuses, switches, and wiring that caused the detonation), meant that the W-25 production was behind schedule.[150] It is possible that deliveries lagged just as the Air Force was reconsidering the number needed, and this facilitated a contract reduction.

Regardless of the number of MB-1s produced, the Air Force believed only some would be used in the event of a Soviet raid. As the Killian committee pointed out in its 1955 report, defense preparations required the arms to be broadly distributed in anticipation of many different attack scenarios. The lack of warning time meant that there would be little chance to reallocate weapons, although interceptors involved in a fight were expected to be able to return to base, rearm with additional Genies, and stage successive attacks on incoming planes. For this reason, it was assumed that aircrews in wartime could be exposed to as much as twenty-five rem before being barred from further firing.[151]

If Shot John demonstrated that fliers and those on the ground could easily withstand the detonation of a single MB-1 at altitude, what about multiple bursts such as presumably would occur during a raid? The Armed Forces Special Weapons Project (AFSWP), the multiservice organization that coordinated nuclear armament work, examined this possibility in June 1958. Initially, the investigation centered on two questions: Would naturally occurring cobalt used in engines and other components of modern bombers be converted to radioactive cobalt as the result of a proximate defensive nuclear detonation? If so, did this mean that nuclear antiaircraft arms would induce hazardous cobalt fallout if used over "friendly territory"? The AFSWP's study of these issues concluded that while target aircraft subsumed by the fireball could be largely "vaporized," some metal parts would be broken into "shrapnel-sized" radioactive debris. Based upon the amount of cobalt in engine turbines and other components, and the amount of neutrons released by air defense warheads, the amount of radioactive cobalt that would result was deemed "negligible." In explaining this conclusion, however, the AFSWP study noted that the atmospheric detonation of antiaircraft nuclear weapons (like all atomic arms containing uranium or plutonium) would produce microscopic particles of the hazardous metal strontium 90 (abbreviated as Sr^{90}). While the strontium was "much more hazardous" than cobalt, it, too, was "not expected to be dangerous" because it would be dispersed over a broad region at high altitude. "A relatively large number (say 100) of air bursts could produce fairly large amounts of Sr,"[90] said the report,

> but if the air bursts are more or less randomly distributed over a large area, there will not be a significant local fallout of strontium—rather, the strontium deposition will tend to be uniform over very large areas.... In such circumstances, the strontium itself will probably not be a serious hazard—much less will the cobalt....[152]

Of course, the danger posed by bomb-test-induced strontium was increasingly becoming an issue at the time because of the activism of Linus Pauling and others. Although the AFSWP analysis did not compare the dangers with tests already conducted, they offer some measure of the relative hazards of disbursed detonations. Two weeks before Shot John, for example, Plumbbob's Shot Hood, a test of a prototype strategic missile warhead, took place 1,500 feet above the Nevada Test Site. At seventy-four kilotons, it was equivalent to approximately thirty-seven Genie warheads detonating at precisely the same time at the same spot. The largest U.S. test was the fifteen-megaton 1954 Shot Bravo in the Pacific, which roughly equaled 750 MB-1 bursts at one location.[153] Just as American authorities justified nuclear testing and associated hazards as a necessary part of defense preparations, advocates of atomic antiaircraft weapons believed that creating some airborne strontium in wartime was preferable to a successful Soviet thermonuclear assault on the United States.

After mid-1958, the Genie, of course, was not the only nuclear air-defense weapon that would be brought to bear in the event of such an attack. Eighteen months after the EC-25-equipped rockets were sent to the first interceptor bases, the Army's Nike-Hercules became operational. The circumstances of that deployment are discussed next.

Chapter 5

Nike-Hercules

The Nike-Hercules was first publicly displayed on May 18, 1957. The occasion was the national commemoration of the tenth anniversary of the establishment of the Defense Department. The location was downtown Huntsville, Alabama.

The nascent weapon's existence, and the fact that it carried a nuclear warhead, had been announced three months earlier.[1] Because Nike-Hercules development was being managed at Redstone Arsenal, which was the locus of Army missile research, Huntsville's Armed Forces Day festivities offered a logical opportunity to exhibit a prototype. As a result, a Nike-Hercules (undoubtedly unarmed) appeared on the city's historic Courthouse Square for the event and was touted in the local newspaper along with a parade, armory dedication, flyover, and other activities. The missile garnered many eager visitors, including some with children in tow and cameras in hand.[2]

A little more than a year later, the Army fielded the first operational Nike-Hercules. By the end of the Eisenhower administration, the missile had gained a considerable role in U.S. continental-defense efforts. It was deployed across the country and became visible on the nation's physical as well as cultural landscape. Most Americans approved; the reception accorded the Nike-Hercules in Huntsville foreshadowed the response it received from a broader audience in later years.

Although the Nike-Hercules was sufficiently developed to be displayed on Armed Forces Day, the Army and Douglas were still perfecting it in mid 1957. Ten days after the Alabama exhibition, the Plumbbob test series began. In addition to offering an occasion for the Shot John Genie test, the series provided a chance validate the design of the Army weapon and its associated equipment. During the first Plumbbob detonation (of BOMARC's W-40 warhead) on May 28, for example, two Nike-Hercules guidance radars were operated nearby to determine if the nuclear explosion altered their capabilities. The Army and AEC cooperated in conducting similar exercises in conjunction with four subsequent shots, and the tests revealed no significant problems with using radar amid nuclear blasts.[3] Given the Nike-Hercules system's reliance on ground-based radar to track targets and to guide missiles to an interception, this was an important finding.

Propellant samples and various other Nike-Hercules components were also exposed to atomic explosions and radiation during other Plumbbob shots. At Shot Morgan on October 7, two sets of missile electronics were evaluated. One contained vacuum tubes; the other featured newly developed transistors. The experiment showed that the latter was susceptible to damage caused by the radiation and the electromagnetic pulse produced by a nuclear explosion. Largely as a result, the Army elected to use the older technology in the production missile.[4]

The necessary one-point tests on the higher (twenty-two kiloton) yield W-31 warhead slated for the Nike-Hercules were also conducted during Plumbbob. On July 1 and then again on September 6, the conventional explosives surrounding the fissile core of a W-31Y2 were detonated asymmetrically, replicating the possible result of a transit or storage accident. As predicted, the design proved sound.[5]

Two one-point tests were required because the warhead was designed to have tritium gas injected into its core at the precise moment of detonation to increase or "boost" the resulting nuclear yield. The first exercise checked the warhead without tritium. The second test ensured that it was one-point safe even if the gas was inadvertently present at the time of a mishap. The W-7 warhead, which would be fitted to the first production missiles until the two-kiloton W-31-Y1 was readied, required no such one-point tests because the nuclear material was mechanically moved into position in the warhead just before detonation. Since the components would not be properly configured otherwise, it posed a small risk of an inadvertent nuclear detonation.[6]

As these various evaluations were being conducted in Nevada, the Army continued to field its first generation surface-to-air antiaircraft missile. Beginning in 1954, the Army manned what eventually became 206 specially constructed Nike-Ajax installations surrounding nineteen cities in fifteen states.[7] These facilities (or "batteries") accommodated conventionally armed missiles, along with the one hundred officers and enlisted soldiers who maintained and operated the armament, radars, and associated equipment and infrastructure.[8] (There was a short-lived effort to consider a nuclear warhead for the Nike-Ajax, with the hope that it would be ready before the Nike-Hercules and thus provide an interim atomic capability. This work was canceled because of a valid concern that it would delay or complicate the development of the Hercules warheads.[9])

Nike-Ajax batteries were typically located seventeen to twenty-five miles from the center of each defended area, and consisted of at least two discrete parcels. One, about twelve acres, held twenty to sixty missiles horizontally in several concrete magazines (dubbed "boxes" or "pits") just below the ground. A rectangular door allowed the weapons to be brought to the surface on a large elevator. From there, a missile could be erected for launch or pushed along metal rails atop the magazine and fired from one of three adjacent positions. The second parcel, about fifteen acres and located about a mile from the first, contained the radars used to identify targets and guide missiles fired in response. Since the installations were operated around the clock, barracks, mess halls, and other ancillary facilities were also provided at the radar site or on nearby plots.[10]

The Nike-Ajax used a flammable and caustic liquid fuel that required special and cumbersome handling procedures. The danger posed by the propellant and the presence of the high explosive warheads precipitated the decision to store the missiles in the belowground boxes and to construct protective earthen berms around each site. Underground storage also lessened the land required for the facilities, because if missiles were kept topside instead, safety standards would have required each to be separated to such an extent that a battery would have sprawled over a much larger expanse. This was especially important because land for the Nike-Ajax was purchased or condemned by the federal government on the metropolitan fringe of many areas, and some proximate landowners opposed anything that would retard suburbanization or otherwise harm land values. Others, however, were eager to have the installations regardless of the form they took, because of the economic benefits of the construction and operation of the facilities.[11]

Indeed, once Nike-Ajax batteries were in place, the Army undertook a considerable effort to facilitate a good rapport with affected communities. Officials were eager to demonstrate the need for the Nike-Ajax installations and hoped to encourage receptive attitudes. Nike-Ajax sites were regularly open for formal or informal visits by nearby residents, school groups, and business organizations. Soldiers were also encouraged to become involved in local civic activities.[12]

With the Nike-Ajax in place and the Nike-Hercules development well underway in 1957, the Army Corps of Engineers considered the construction modifications necessitated by the newer missile. The Nike-Hercules would replace the Ajax at many of the existing sites, and this required reconfiguring storage pits, replacing the elevators (the new missile was longer, wider, and heavier than its predecessor), erecting additional fencing, lighting, and sentry posts to ensure the security of the nuclear warheads, and making other alterations. This was a hectic, costly, and complex assignment because of tight schedules, construction differences at various locations, and missile design changes that affected the work.[13]

In addition to modifying existing sites, the Corps prepared to build new installations for the Nike-Hercules around six areas (St. Louis, Cincinnati, Minneapolis-St. Paul, Dallas-Fort Worth, and Kansas City) in the continental United States, as well as Anchorage and Fairbanks. All were then without antiaircraft defenses.[14] These batteries were simpler to construct because they were designed at the outset for the Nike-Hercules (which required no fuel facilities because missiles carried a less hazardous solid propellant sealed within them) and because missile storage was in revetted, aboveground buildings. These installations were easily situated in less populated regions and were not as costly as the alternative.[15] (The Alaska batteries had similar features, but the advantages were obviated by the problems posed by construction in a harsh climate.)

The prospect of these new sites was welcomed in many communities. For example, one rural Minnesota newspaper declared "Guided Missile Station to Locate Here" in a banner headline over a page-one story about a component of the forthcoming Minneapolis-St. Paul Nike-Hercules defenses. The article reported the number of soldiers expected, the Army's land and housing requirements, and the local services to be utilized by the installation, while noting the missiles would be "capable of carrying atomic warheads."[16]

In the midst of the planning for the new batteries in Minnesota and elsewhere, Robert Sprague sparked renewed concern about the possibility of Strategic Air Command bombers being destroyed on the ground by a surprise Soviet air attack. The Air Force had worried about SAC's vulnerability for years and the 1955 Killian study, which Sprague led, had also addressed the subject.[17] After the work of the Technological Capabilities Panel ended, Sprague examined the topic further, probably at the behest of Assistant Defense Secretary Donald Quarles. Termed the "TAPE group" by Sprague (the meaning of the name or acronym is unknown), this evaluation seems to have reemphasized the danger to SAC bases. In March 1956, according to an official Pentagon history based, in part, on classified material, Sprague urged "a redirection of effort from the cities-and-industries thrust" of the nation's antiaircraft network, and called instead for "defense of SAC bases and bombers against obliteration in a saturation attack."[18]

Shortly thereafter (but probably too soon to have been spurred by TAPE), the Air Force initiated efforts to emplace "Talos," a modified Navy nuclear-armed antiaircraft missile, near selected SAC installations.[19] Fielding their own missile gave Air Force leaders control over the timing, scope, and locations of the deployment. However, fearing interservice competition for funds and concerned that its antiaircraft responsibilities were being usurped, the Army responded. It wrestled control of Talos from the Air Force, and then, with presidential and congressional encouragement, scrapped the program.[20] Once assured of its dominance in the surface-to-air missile field, however, the Army established Nike-Ajax batteries at four SAC bases between December 1956 and June 1957.[21] In the course of this dispute, the Defense Secretary deemed the Army responsible for "point defense," the antiaircraft protection of "specified geographical areas, cities and vital installations." The Air Force was charged with maintaining "area defense" antiaircraft weapons: those long-range arms meant to "intercept enemy attacks remote from and without reference to individual vital installations, industrial complexes or population centers."[22] This left the service in control of BOMARC, which was still under development.

As the SAC defenses were being readied, Robert Sprague joined yet another high-level national security study group. The Security Resources Panel, established by the president in April 1957, to study "active and passive defense measures for the protection of the civil population," resembled the Killian effort in its size, scope, and involvement of dozens of prominent industrialists, academics, and retired military officers.[23] Sprague played a key role from the onset. In August 1957, the panel's leader, Ford Foundation president H. Rowan Gaither, Jr., withdrew for health reasons. For most of the balance of the endeavors, Sprague and William Foster, an Olin Mathieson Chemical Corporation executive and veteran of the Truman administration, took charge.[24]

Informally known as the Gaither Committee (despite the midcourse leadership change), the panel was originally conceived as a dispassionate study of the steps that could be taken to protect civilians in the case of an attack. Primarily, this meant examining the possibility of constructing bomb shelters nationwide, but it also included considering weaponry or warning systems that might help blunt or a prepare for a raid. Since any of these posed financial, logistical, and practical difficulties, Eisenhower sought the advice of respected experts, in keeping with a belief that most policy conundrums could be redressed once they had been examined rationally by trained experts, especially those capable of considering technological solutions applicable to the dilemma at hand. Soon after getting underway, however, the committee broadened its mandate considerably and evaluated the nation's offensive forces. Deterring an attack by maintaining extensive retaliatory arms, the members argued, was the best way to ensure the security of the American populace.[25] This changed focus meant the Gaither report was received skeptically by Eisenhower and his advisors.

In November 1957, the group reported to the president and the National Security Council. The Gaither group recommended forty-four billion dollars in new spending, including a larger U.S. strategic bomber and long-range ballistic missile force, a federally funded shelter system, and other items. The committee also called for more antiaircraft missile emplacements to protect SAC installations.[26] Unlike the bulk of the report's recommendations, this item buttressed the Pentagon's thinking. At the time, the Joint Chiefs of Staff was considering the number and location of additional Nike-Hercules batteries to be included in the forthcoming fiscal year 1959 budget. The Gaither report encouraged the decision to situate the missiles around Air Force bases, and this position was further confirmed when a Pentagon evaluation agreed that "defense of the U.S. retaliatory forces must be improved."[27]

The eventual construction (there was a delay occasioned by a funding dispute discussed below) of fourteen additional Nike-Hercules sites at seven other SAC airfields (along with the repositioning of some Genie-equipped interceptor units) to defend the nation's offensive force was meant, of course, to allow a sufficient number of American bombers to survive a Soviet first strike.[28] The knowledge that a raid on U.S. forces would not preclude retaliation strengthened deterrence. A secure offensive force was also considered a necessary component of the "counterforce" nuclear doctrine devised in the early 1950s at the RAND Corporation, the Air Force–funded think tank. This strategy contemplated targeting an enemy's military might rather than population centers. If the Soviets attacked but substantial U.S. forces survived, some could respond by striking the USSR's remaining forces. If the Soviet Union's ability to launch subsequent raids was consequently impaired but America's was not, the counterforce strategy postulated that the Soviets would capitulate in light of this vulnerability. Of course, counterforce required protecting offensive forces so that a sizeable portion could weather a Soviet first strike and then be used as dictated.[29]

The development of this strategy and establishment of Nike-Hercules batteries at SAC bases, however, was largely coincidental. There is little evidence that the decision to field these arms was motivated by counterforce thinking or any other nuclear strategy as the term is presently understood. Rather, a straightforward and apparently commonsensical fear that the mainstay of the American military could be destroyed by a surprise attack led Air Force installations to be defended. Analysis that suggests a broader theoretical underpinning to these arrangements is difficult to sustain.

While the Gaither report succeeded in spurring Nike-Hercules defenses at SAC bases, most of its other recommendations were stillborn. To many panel members, however, the successful orbiting of a Soviet satellite a few weeks before the report was finalized demonstrated that the Soviet Union had the technological and industrial capacity to design and field intercontinental ballistic missiles. Eisenhower was not swayed by this argument, probably because his access to U-2 intelligence (which was not available to the study members) gave him a better understanding of the USSR's small missile arsenal.[30] Indeed, the president told the Gaither committee members that "aircraft would continue to be the primary means of carrying out destruction" in the immediate future[31] Although the Soviet bomber force was not growing at the rate projected earlier, a contemporaneous intelligence estimate credited the Soviet Union with ninety to 150 heavy bombers, and predicted that the number would increase to between four hundred and six hundred by mid-1960.[32]

Robert Sprague was disappointed with the reception the Gaither panel report received. He later recounted that he became "quite inactive" as an administration continental-defense consultant in subsequent months, and said his "assignment terminated" at the end of 1958. James Killian, the former leader of the eponymous 1955 committee, was appointed the president's first science advisor in late 1957, and Sprague said afterward that "the functions that I had been performing" were "taken over" by the former MIT president.[33]

By this time Eisenhower looked to Sprague less frequently for advice on continental-defense matters. Despite its classification, information about the Gaither group and its report was leaked in late 1957, probably by one or more supporters who sought to goad the administration into action.³⁴ Sprague conceded to Killian that the unauthorized disclosure was the result of "bad security on our study" and predicted the failure to safeguard it would bother Ike "enormously."³⁵ He was right. Eisenhower was angered.³⁶ Robert Cutler had also come to the conclusion that Sprague's narrow focus on defensive preparations and existing vulnerabilities meant that he downplayed other considerations. Now Cutler believed Sprague had "a single track mind," albeit one "of great capacity."³⁷ Secretary of State John Foster Dulles agreed.³⁸ The views of these two important presidential confidants probably influenced Ike's impressions.

Sprague, for his part, believed the president's aides were making poor use of the national security information available to them. In the case of the Gaither report, he thought the views of the "extraordinarily well informed" panelists were being improperly rejected. Sprague was also probably disappointed that the administration did not accept his suggestion that Eisenhower convene still another study group after the Gaither body disbanded.³⁹ In February 1960, Sprague was able to air his criticism of the administration's management of the defense policy apparatus when he gave testimony to a congressional subcommittee led by Washington senator Henry Jackson.⁴⁰

However, at the start of 1958, the Eisenhower administration continued to deal with the air defense issues with which Robert Sprague was involved. On January 28, the Army announced that the first Nike-Hercules missiles would be fielded at four modified Nike-Ajax batteries near Chicago, New York, Philadelphia, Washington, and Baltimore (considered a single "defense area") by June 30. The service's statement reiterated that the Nike-Hercules was the "first operational surface-to-air missile which can use an atomic warhead," and that it could "destroy whole formations of planes."⁴¹ One newspaper in the District of Columbia emphasized that the nuclear charge "can neutralize a nuclear bomb carried by the enemy plane so it would not explode as the bomber is destroyed."⁴² The publication subsequently editorialized that "it would be a folly to forget that Moscow still commands a formidable long-range bomber fleet." This meant, the editors thought, that "defensive ground-to-air missiles, coordinated with air-to-air defensive rockets and supported by retaliatory capability, can 'raise the price' for any potential enemy...."⁴³ A month later, Douglas Aircraft, the missile's manufacturer, placed print advertisements touting the "U.S. Army's Atomic Nike Hercules." The company assured readers that the weapon, which was to soon "defend populated, strategic and industrial areas," could "destroy enemy bombers with its atomic warhead at safe distances from the areas being guarded."⁴⁴

The week before the ad appeared, the National Security Council updated the nation's continental-defense strategy paper. Until this time, NSC 5408, adopted in February 1954, prevailed. That document outlined the intent of the continental defense effort (including "[p]reventing devastating attack that might threaten our national survival") and the pace ("with all practicable speed") with which protective measures should be instituted.[45] It had been agreed to only after assurances that it did not privilege certain defensive programs and consequently undercut justification of other weapons. NSC 5606, intended to supplant NSC 5408, foundered in June 1956 on the same point. Opponents quashed NSC 5606 because they feared if it was adopted offensive forces would be forced to share limited funds with air defense programs.[46]

The 1958 document (NSC 5802), however, set forth more general guidance than the prevailing NSC 5408 or the failed NSC 5606. NSC 5802 inelegantly asserted that

> [t]he United States should continue to improve, and to maintain at a high state of readiness, an effective, integrated system of air surveillance, weapons, and control elements, providing defense in depth capable of detecting, identifying, engaging, and destroying enemy aircraft or missiles approaching or operating over the North American Continent before they reach vital targets.[47]

Indeed, the lack of more precise performance standards concerned some but comforted others. When the document came before the NSC, science advisor Killian asserted that weaknesses in the current and planned air defense system meant "less than 50%" of attacking planes would be destroyed in a raid. Therefore, he favored amending the paper to declare that the intent was to down "a high percentage" of enemy aircraft in order to force the Pentagon to refocus its efforts to this end.[48]

This, of course, is precisely what worried DoD. Defense Secretary Neil McElroy (who had succeeded Charles Wilson the previous October) said such instructions could be interpreted to "require a doubling of our air defense costs." Air Force general Nathan Twining, Admiral Arthur Radford's replacement as Joint Chiefs chairman, concurred. If accepted, the change might put the military in "the position where it did not have money left to do anything else in other important defense areas," he said. After a long discussion, the NSC agreed to omit Killian's suggested wording, but stipulated that government agencies "do desire and will strive to achieve improved air defense capabilities."⁴⁹ Not entirely coincidentally, around the same time, President Eisenhower authorized a joint Air Force and Central Intelligence Agency project to develop a camera-carrying reconnaissance satellite. He sought a system that was able to gain additional intelligence about the USSR, but without the performance or political limitations of the U-2.⁵⁰

The doubts expressed by Killian in the course of the NSC 5802 debate about anti-bomber effectiveness primarily concerned the ability to identify and monitor attacking planes. It was not a comment about the effectiveness of atomic arms. Detecting and tracking aircraft as they approached and overflew the continent, vectoring weapons from multiple locations to their vicinity, and then bringing firepower to bear upon them was a complex and difficult task. An October 1958 Pentagon status report on NSC 5802 makes this point clear. In discussing the advent of the Nike-Hercules and other air defense armament, the document emphasized that the "operational performance of all these weapons systems will be dependent to a varying degree upon the quality of the warning, acquisition, and tracking systems which support them."⁵¹

Although atomic air defenses were considered necessary, they were simultaneously considered insufficient to completely stop an enemy attack. While the same status report asserted the nation's ability to counter an air attack had been "progressively increased," in part, because of "improved weapons systems" that "include nuclear warheads," it also argued that "any relative U.S. gain" was questionable. "The continental air defense system cannot be expected to counter completely an all-out attack of the magnitude which [the] Soviets are capable of launching," defense planners declared, especially once the USSR fielded intercontinental ballistic missiles.⁵²

Three months after NSC 5802 was adopted in February 1958, an accident threatened to upend efforts to assure the public about the safety of the forthcoming Nike-Hercules. An explosion at a Nike-Ajax battery in Leonardo, New Jersey, part of the New York City defenses, killed six soldiers and four civilian contractors. The men were modifying a missile while it sat on the aboveground launch rails. An investigation later revealed that they performed several procedures improperly, possibly because of imprecise instructions. These mistakes sparked an explosion that ignited the missile's warheads (which had been removed and placed on the ground) as well as six other nearby missiles.⁵³ Such an incident was unlikely to occur with a Nike-Hercules because this type of work would not be undertaken with a nuclear weapon on-site. Of course, even if a similar mishap did take place, the warhead's design would have precluded a nuclear detonation, although a high-explosive blast and the spread of plutonium would have been lethal to bystanders.[54]

Notwithstanding these differences, some used the Leonardo incident to question the impending Nike-Hercules deployment. When the Nike-Ajax was fielded, the Army bragged that each installation was as "safe as a gas station." After the accident, *Time* wryly declared, "Last week the gas-station blew up." "In the wake of Leonardo's explosive afternoon," the magazine argued, "it was going to be hard to convince the neighbors in New Jersey—or around the Nikes guarding 22 other U.S. industrial complexes—that living alongside atomic warheads was still like living beside a gas station."[55]

Time was too pessimistic. After the accident, the Pentagon worked to head off concern. It reemphasized the points made a year earlier in announcing the first Genie deployments: The chances of an accidental nuclear explosion were "virtually non-existent," it declared in a press statement, because of the "elaborate precautions" that would be in place.[56] The effort worked.[57] A New Jersey meeting subsequently attended by senior Army officials and local residents was cordial. "Let's forget the hysteria and have confidence in the U.S. Army and its competent officers," one woman declared. Another person said, "Let's thank God that we have such defenders so we can go to open meetings like this."[58] News reports also credit "one young housewife" with announcing, "We have just bought a home 1,000 yards behind the Nike base, and we are delighted to be that close. We feel it's just that much more protection."[59] Although there were no plans to convert the Leonardo site for the Nike-Hercules, a fact the Army acknowledged, a general in attendance made clear that the nuclear missile's "more specialized" mechanisms meant that a similar accident "could not occur." In contrast, he reminded the audience of the "damage that would be wrought by the dropping of a nuclear weapon in the area" by an attacking bomber.[60]

As some in the Army calmed the public in late spring 1958, others were busy coordinating the activities of Douglas and Western Electric (responsible for the guidance electronics) and subcontractors involved in producing the Nike-Hercules engines and launching equipment.[61] Soldiers were also completing their training at Fort Bliss, Texas, to operate the new arms, and modification of the first four Nike-Ajax sites was concluding. Eisenhower was kept informed of important milestones in this effort.[62]

Although the Nike-Hercules program had proceeded without a major hindrance, as the deadline to field the first missiles approached, problems arose. Only about twenty-five percent of the initial batch of production missiles performed satisfactorily when they were test-launched (without warheads) in Texas. Even for a cutting-edge system still being perfected, this was an abysmal performance. After an intensive effort, the flaws and a warhead malady (described only as a "pressure-drop problem") were resolved, and missiles were shipped to each of the first operational batteries. The W-7 warheads were probably mated to them on-site, having been sent directly from the AEC's plant.[63]

On June 30, at least four Nike-Hercules were ready at a battery at Montrose Beach on Chicago's lakefront. Like all Nike sites, it had an alphanumeric designator that combined an abbreviation for the metropolitan area and the battery's approximate location on an imaginary one-hundred-point circle encompassing the defended zone (for example, "0" was due north, "50" due south, etc.). Dubbed C-03, the Montrose Beach site was deemed the first to be operational. Within two days, a modified Nike-Ajax emplacement became active in Davidsonville, Maryland, twenty-two miles east of Washington, D.C. (W-25), and one at Fort Tilden in Queens, New York (NY-49).[64] (The soldiers, missiles, and equipment originally destined for Philadelphia were diverted to another assignment discussed below.)

The Army secretary announced the deployment of the missiles on July 1 in a speech to five hundred military and civilian guests at Project AMMO (Army Mobile Missile Orientation), held at New Mexico's White Sands Proving Ground, a desolate test range operated as an adjunct to Fort Bliss. That day, a conventionally armed Nike-Hercules was demonstrated for the first time. It was fired at a simulated aerial target at an altitude of 100,000 feet and fifty-five miles distant. It detonated within fifty feet of the intended spot.[65] The Nike-Hercules performed as designed: The missile outclimbed the target and then dove toward it before exploding. An attack from above both maximized the gust load on the airplane wings and made evasion more difficult.[66]

This exercise was a thinly veiled effort to garner congressional and popular support for the Nike-Hercules and other Army missile programs. This was apparent to the press. "A question left unanswered amidst a six-inch pile of twenty different information portfolios given each of 100 newsmen was whom the 'show' was staged primarily to impress," said one article about the events. "Conjectural targets included foreign nations, friendly or unfriendly, the other armed services, Federal budgeters and taxpayers," it concluded.[67]

Nearly two weeks later, James Killian discussed with the president preparations for an international meeting to establish agreements that

Figure 5.1 Members of Battery A, 2nd Missile Battalion of the U.S. Army's 57th Artillery scramble during an alert drill at the Montrose-Belmont Nike-Hercules nuclear antiaircraft missile site on the lakefront in Chicago, Illinois on September 30, 1959. The Nike-Hercules carried the W-31 nuclear warhead which could yield either two or twenty-two kilotons. In June 1958, the Montrose location became the first of about 123 operational Nike-Hercules sites built around twenty-six cities and ten Air Force bases in twenty-five states.

Source: Official U.S. Army photograph by MSgt Joseph S. Moroz, Jr. Reproduced courtesy of Command Historian, U.S. Army Aviation and Missile Command, Redstone Arsenal, Huntsville, Alabama.

would lessen the likelihood of surprise attack. Eisenhower had proposed the conference in January, although Soviet premier Nikita Khrushchev did not agree to send a delegation until July 2. "[F]or the next several years the greatest threat," the president reminded Killian, "continues to be... military aircraft...."[68] The Soviets were estimated to have between one hundred and 125 heavy bombers at the time, and more than seventy-five more expected within two years.[69] Consequently, the president sought an inspection regime to allow observers, cameras, or other technical means to monitor preparations for a sudden strike on the United States and reciprocal arrangements for the USSR. "What we are aiming to determine," Eisenhower explained to Killian, is if enemy airfields showed signs of having "been brought to a state suggesting imminent attack." Although the Surprise

Attack Conference did not conclude an agreement, its origin and purpose further demonstrated the president's persistent fears.[70]

Four days after Killian's meeting with Eisenhower, 4,500 civil servants left Washington, bound for special facilities distributed in a "relocation arc" west of Washington that ran from Chambersburg, Pennsylvania, through Lexington, in Virginia's Shenandoah Valley. The task of the fleeing workers was to activate alternative headquarters for twenty-three federal agencies as part of 1958's Operation Alert. Although the president took an active interest in the exercise, he did not participate, because he and several others scheduled to do so were preoccupied with the Lebanon intervention.[71]

While Operation Alert was underway, the Nike-Hercules soldiers and equipment initially intended for Philadelphia were preparing for a different task. The battery was training to fire two nuclear rounds to demonstrate that the atomic versions of the missiles would function as designed.[72] The possibility of such a test had been first broached by the Joint Committee on Atomic Energy in January 1956.[73] The Army endorsed the exercise later that year. "Since the Nike B system will be employed over friendly territory," an officer explained to planners (using an early designation for the Nike-Hercules)

> the Army feels that a full-scale test of the complete system should be conducted at the earliest practicable date. Such a test will make possible a complete an integrated test of all mechanical, electrical, and nuclear components of the system in an operational environment. It will serve to instill confidence in the minds of the delivery troops, commanders, and the general public.[74]

The Army hoped to conduct the prospective operation at the Nevada Test Site because transporting the radar and launching apparatus to the Eniwetok Proving Grounds in the Pacific or another location outside the United States would be cumbersome and expensive.[75]

The topic was not raised again for nearly a year (interest was probably rekindled by the positive press coverage the Air Force enjoyed as a result of the Shot John Genie test in July 1957), at which point the AEC's Military Liaison Committee inquired about the legality and practicality of using White Sands, rather than the NTS, because the necessary launch facilities already existed in New Mexico.[76] The reply from AEC chairman Lewis Strauss was clear. In abruptly dismissing both locations, he wrote, "I am definitely opposed to the conduct in FY1958 of such a firing within the continental United States." "Such an operation could not help but further augment the already unfortunate clamor against testing," he argued. Although Strauss said the AEC was "not in a position to judge the necessity...of conducting a proof-test of the overall Nike missile-warhead system," he suggested the Pacific as an alternative and outlined the support ("personnel services in connection with the weather, fallout, and blast prediction") that the Army could expect from the AEC in that case.[77]

The military was not deterred. In February 1958, Donald Quarles (by then the deputy defense secretary) reported to Strauss that the Joint Chiefs of Staff endorsed a Nike-Hercules nuclear test at the NTS or elsewhere, noted that he concurred, and expressed hope that the AEC chairman would join him in "presenting the matter to the President." Significantly, however, Quarles now added another element. In addition to the Nike-Hercules, the Pentagon sought to detonate two more Genies in a separate operation conducted at the same time over the Gulf of Mexico near Eglin Air Force Base on the Florida panhandle. The Air Force was apparently pleased with the publicity benefits of Shot John, but was disappointed that the test's careful choreography (the firing signal transmitted from the ground and the use of an imaginary target, for example) did not replicate actual operating conditions. For the proffered exercise, the Pentagon proposed to fire the Nike-Hercules and Genie at drones "under realistic environments."[78]

In early April, the AEC staff evaluated Quarles' proposal. The staff noted that all of the nuclear detonations included in the "Hardtack" test series, which was to begin at Eniwetok in a few weeks, were to be underground. These arrangements had been made in deference to public concern about fallout. Thus, any atmospheric shots, and especially one in the United States, might have "some repercussions," the staff asserted. They conceded, however, that objections might be minimized "in view of the fact that the firings would be of purely defensive, small weapons." AEC commissioners were urged to "recognize that there is a military advantage to testing any such important system," but also to recognize that the "military gain from such a test must be weighed...against the possibility of [the] hazard involved and any unfavorable domestic or international reaction."[79]

Strauss and others at the AEC were increasingly concerned in the spring of 1958 about growing support for a nuclear test ban in and outside the administration. Secretary of State John Foster Dulles was attempting to persuade Eisenhower to disapprove any further test requests, once Hardtack concluded. Dulles thought continued atomic testing was harming the nation's image and making it difficult to sustain an anti-Soviet coalition abroad. Strauss (and Pentagon leaders) vigorously disagreed. They believed capable weapons assured American security and thought new nuclear warheads were necessary, including for equipping the intercontinental ballistic missiles being developed. In a meeting with Eisenhower, Dulles, and Defense Secretary Neil McElroy in March, Strauss argued that "testing does not result in any significant health hazard." Rather, he said, the "real hazard today is nuclear war, which our weapons development helps to prevent."[80]

Thus, the lack of enthusiasm to the Pentagon's Nike-Hercules and Genie proposals shown by Strauss and others at the AEC may have been rooted in the test ban debate underway. Strauss did not want to endorse any action that weakened support by Ike and the public for continued testing of new nuclear devices. Test shots conducted from Florida of warheads already designed offered no benefit to the AEC. Indeed, they had the prospect attracting attention (because of the location, the novelty of the operations, or both) and further fueling antinuclear sentiment.

The AEC was committed to testing nuclear devices in the course of their development, but not necessarily the weapon in which a finished warhead was fitted. Since the May 1955 antisubmarine test in the Pacific, activities that were meant to validate the functioning of stockpiled nuclear warheads mated to delivery systems were largely within the Pentagon's purview. Although willing to advise on safety and operational procedures as well as provide support services, the AEC believed such exercises were expensive distractions from its primary work, and it ceded the responsibility for such operations to the military. This meant that the Defense Department was in a position to make most of the decisions about the conduct of the proposed Nike-Hercules and Genie exercises. By the end of April, the Defense Department decided to combine the missile and rocket tests and conduct all four shots at Eglin before the United States possibly declared a moratorium on surface and atmospheric nuclear detonations.[81]

The Army ordered two Nike-Hercules batteries at Fort Bliss, including the Philadelphia-bound unit, to move by rail to Eglin's Santa Rosa Island by early July. Once there (the island, within the base's boundaries, was at the mouth of the Pensacola Bay, just a few miles from the coast), one battery was to launch a series of missiles carrying conventional warheads; the other Nike-Hercules fitted with instruments used to measure flight performance. After successfully concluding these shots, the plan was to fire two missiles, each with different version of the W-31 nuclear charge, at a formation of three obsolete Air Force F-80 fighters that had been converted into drones. Because neither the W-31-Y1 nor the W-31-Y2 had yet entered production, the warheads to be sent to Florida for mating to the missiles were specially constructed for this exercise, which was named Operation Snodgrass after the brigadier general selected to command it.[82]

The Genie tests, dubbed "Little David" and "Opera Hat," anticipated an F-89 or F-101 firing production weapons at an F-80 drone flying at an altitude of about thirty-five to forty thousand feet. One shot was to take place at dawn, another at nighttime. Both Snodgrass and Little David/Opera Hat were to make use of airspace over the Gulf of Mexico, which had been a military training area for years and was routinely used to test Air Force weapons (albeit never nuclear arms). Planning documents noted that the operations would take place "25 nautical miles horizontal distance from the nearest populated area."[83]

On June 26, the Military Liaison Committee and the AEC held a joint meeting to discuss the proposed operation. An Air Force colonel told those assembled that "Eglin Air Force base was believed to be the ideal location for testing in view of the air defense environment there and safety features and instrumentation available." Meeting attendees were assured that the blast altitude would preclude retina burns or flash blindness of any who witnessed the detonations. They were also told that the airspace and ocean area beneath the exercise area would be searched and secured before the tests, and there would be no fallout unless it rained "immediately after a shot," in which case "levels of exposure would not be significant" (meaning one rem or less off-site). To foreclose even this possibility, weather forecasts would be taken into account before the tests were conducted.[84]

The Air Force (and presumably the Army) also prepared to advertise the exercise, assuming the weapons worked as designed. Although an announcement contemplated for the onset of the operation was to note "increased activity in the test area," but not specify nuclear detonations, an Air Force unit made extensive arrangements to capture Snodgrass and Little David/Opera Hat on film. In addition to a twenty-minute classified production, the 1352nd Motion Picture Squadron, which filmed Shot John the year before, envisioned a fourteen-minute unclassified companion piece. The first was for training purposes. The second film was probably intended for public dissemination as part of a publicity effort akin to what Barney Oldfield orchestrated for Shot John the year before.[85]

The AEC, however, remained unpersuaded about the need for the operation. Commissioner John F. Floberg said that "he was not convinced that the tests were necessary" and thought that "it was a mistake to proceed with them." Lewis Strauss agreed. He continued to argue that the operation should be moved to Eniwetok, and "questioned the possible adverse public reaction" if it went ahead, although he said "he would be less apprehensive" if there was "a prior announcement." Strauss believed that it was necessary for the AEC to remain apprised of the shots, notwithstanding its limited role in approving or managing them. "[T]he president might request an AEC opinion of the desirability of the tests when he considers authorizing the expenditure of the required materials," he argued, making reference to the permission that had to be granted by the chief executive before a nuclear device was detonated.[86]

Strauss soon had an opportunity to share his views with Eisenhower. The next day, Secretary of State John Foster Dulles and others discussed the Eglin operation with the president in the Oval Office. Navy rear admiral Edward N. Parker, the commander of the Armed Forces Special Weapons Project, the joint military unit responsible for the Pentagon's participation in nuclear (i.e., "special") armament activities, made the case for the test. Strauss made it clear that he "was not concerned over the hazards," but expressed disagreement about the "establishment of a third atomic test area."[87] Strauss believed the test offered little radiological danger or chance of mishap. The Shot John aircrew and ground-zero volunteers had safely participated in that test. Little David/Opera Hat interceptor crews would be just as close. Eglin ground observers or nearby civilians would be much farther than the Plumbbob volunteers. In addition, in the event of a dud in Florida, the unexploded weapons would fall into the Gulf of Mexico.[88]

However, the AEC chairman continued to worry about how the exercise would be perceived by the public. Minutes of the meeting report that Strauss declared the operation "may jeopardize our whole test series."[89] Hardtack was underway by this time, and other nuclear tests were contemplated before a ban was put into place. Strauss did not want what he considered unnecessary initiatives to imperil future test activities he thought were central to the AEC's mission.

In the Oval Office meeting, Dulles and his deputy, Christian Herter, used the opportunity to highlight how Snodgrass and Little David/Opera Hat exemplified nuclear test activities that they thought harmed the nation's relationships with allies. They expressed concern to the president that neighboring nations might react poorly to the operation. Hearing this, Eisenhower decided that Cuba and Mexico should be told that "at some time this summer the U.S. might, in the course of its routine air defense tests," detonate "some relatively small-yield nuclear air defense weapons" at Eglin. If there was a "violent reaction" from either of these governments, Eisenhower said, "the matter would have to be reconsidered." When Herter observed that "there has been some intimation" that there would be "quite a promotional campaign over this matter," Eisenhower responded, "nothing like this is to be done." If the exercise proceeded, however, the president instructed that a public announcement be made in compliance with NSC 1706, which required the Operations Coordinating Board to approve the dissemination of nuclear weapons information.[90]

The State Department contacted the Cuban and Mexican governments the next week, and the OCB approved a press release in anticipation of a decision to proceed.[91] The Air Force continued its preparations by dispatching officers to Eglin who had helped to organize Shot John and other nuclear exercises. They gathered the necessary testing and measurement equipment, and planned for contingencies, such as how to handle a drone if it was irradiated but not destroyed by a blast.[92]

Just as in the Nevada tests, the U.S. Public Health Service also became involved, although officials were disappointed with the short time they were given to prepare. The USPHS made arrangements to collect air, rainwater, milk, crop, and seafood samples from Cuba (in cooperation with the U.S. embassy), Puerto Rico, and the southeastern United States. Health departments in Georgia, Florida, Alabama, and Mississippi were briefed on Snodgrass and Little David/Opera Hat, and the USPHS "answered all questions consistent with [the] security aspects of the project." "In all cases we were received most cordially and promised full cooperation," a senior official reported. The Public Health Service intended to measure and document off-site fallout, in part to "build up a record of radiological safety data in the event of pecuniary cases against the government," and to "establish and maintain public confidence that all reasonable steps are being made to protect the public." "There is no substitute for factual statements," read the USPHS safety plan. "We intend to describe and discuss our program to all interested groups and individuals and solicit their active help in carrying out our mission." The plan also noted that, despite the preparations that implied otherwise, "the only true emergency would be on-site," perhaps from plutonium being scattered as a result of a one-point accident.[93]

By July 17, the Nike-Hercules batteries had arrived at Eglin (their trip was delayed until Project AMMO demonstrated that missile deficiencies had been overcome) and fired one conventional and one instrumented round.[94] The first of these sparked an Associated Press story that mentioned an ongoing "joint Air Force-Army project for testing air defense weapons."[95] On July 24, as one more of each missile type was launched, another White House meeting was convened. For this gathering, Lewis Strauss was an observer. On June 30, he had resigned as AEC chairman, been succeed by California industrialist John McCone, and was awarded the Medal of Freedom from the president.[96] Now, however, Dulles reported that "consultations" with Cuba and Mexico led him "to recommend strongly" that the nuclear operation be moved to the Pacific. The Mexicans "would greatly deplore" the test if it proceeded as planned, he said, and it "would have a more adverse impact on world opinion" than it was worth.[97]

Quarles countered that it was necessary to test the Nike-Hercules and Genie to demonstrate their functionality and to prove they could be used as intended. He argued that an Eniwetok exercise would be costly and inapt. When the president asked if the results of conventional shots in Eglin could be combined with nuclear detonations in the Pacific to yield a good understanding of the two complete systems, Quarles explained that the purpose of the proposed shots were specifically to observe weapon performance, rather than estimate how some might function by testing discrete parts.[98]

Hearing these arguments, Eisenhower "approved transfer or cancellation" of the operation, while requesting "some study of some combination of activities to accomplish the same objectives."[99] Four months earlier when discussing Strauss' opposition to a nuclear test ban, Eisenhower had remarked, "[W]orld opinion, even if not well founded, is a fact; world anxiety exists over tests, and causes tension." As aide Andrew Goodpaster summarized, "The President said he recognizes that testing is not evil, but the fact is people have been brought to believe it is."[100] To Ike, halting Snodgrass and Little David/Opera Hat was probably easy. By doing so he was not depriving the military of crucial operational data, but was taking action to not inflame public opinion.

The next day, one week before the first nuclear shot was to be undertaken at Eglin, Quarles formally notified the Joint Chiefs of the president's decision. Word of the cancelation was also transmitted to the AEC and the military units at Eglin. They were instructed "to obtain such operational data as is practicable short of full scale tests using nuclear warheads."[101] Public Health Service officials also contacted their state-level counterparts, informed them of the test halt, expressed appreciation for "complete cooperation," and asked them to "forget our activities in the area."¹⁰² The request was heeded. There is no evidence that the arrangements for Snodgrass and Little David/Opera Hat were well known at the time. Certainly the two hundred Quakers from around the United States who gathered in Washington on August 5 for a "24 hour prayer and meditation meeting" on the thirteenth anniversary of the Hiroshima bombing had no inkling.¹⁰³

The week before, on July 29, the Nike-Hercules batteries at Eglin fired two final missiles (one instrumented and one with a high-explosive warhead). Either these or the earlier launches were fired against three planes flying in a group. "[T]he Hercules picked off the lead F-80 drone," one report recounted. "[W]ith an atomic warhead," it "could have destroyed the entire formation."¹⁰⁴ In his final assessment of the entire operation, Brigadier General John T. Snodgrass wrote that while the "primary mission" of the exercise was aborted, the "firing of six preparatory and rehearsal rounds, all of which were successful," validated the Nike-Hercules design. Another evaluation said the operation showed the missile could "be safely fired over inhabited areas" because of the ability to direct it at "a precise target point."¹⁰⁵

The Air Force concluded its portion of the test by using Eglin's aerial ranges to fire training versions of the Genie, which produced a smoke "spotting charge." In a routine weekly report in late August, Eisenhower was advised that

> [t]he F-101B (Voodoo) interceptor has successfully fired 19 out of 21 MB-1 rockets with an accuracy well within the warhead's lethal radius. This suggests that had Project Little David been conducted, the scheduled atomic warhead tests would have successfully demonstrated the effectiveness of the weapons system.¹⁰⁶

These nonnuclear tests had to suffice. On August 22, the president announced a one-year suspension on American atomic detonations staring October 31. He also invited the Soviets to join negotiations for a formal multilateral test ban.¹⁰⁷

Although the Genie's functionality had been demonstrated again, the future of the Air Force's BOMARC missile, for which the first four launch sites were being built, was less clear at the time.¹⁰⁸ Congress had come to believe that BOMARC and Nike-Hercules were duplicative, and it reduced allocations for both by twenty percent in the annual military construction legislation passed in late summer 1958.¹⁰⁹ Probably in reaction to the Leonardo mishap, or as a partisan slap at the Republican administration's defense policies, the bill also took note of "the heavy deployment of missiles requiring stockpiles of nuclear warheads immediately adjacent to heavy centers of population," and questioned the "publicity implying that the deployment of these weapons...constitutes no hazard and provides complete security from attack."[110] Even more significantly, however, the Defense appropriations bill, passed in August, required the Defense Secretary to evaluate BOMARC and Nike-Hercules and authorized him to redirect funds from one to the other if his review warranted it.[111]

The Army was already deftly promoting its weapon. Groundbreaking ceremonies for the construction of Nike-Hercules facilities around Kansas City attracted the governor and Defense Department officials, and a converted Los Angeles site was open to the public in late August, before becoming operational.[112] Around the same time, "a group of prominent military and civilian dignitaries" were invited to site C-03 by the general who led Chicago's defenses. A photograph of the event shows about forty-five individuals standing at the base of one of the new missiles erected on its launcher.[113]

If the Army thought these activities earned it a public relations advantage, however, the assessment was probably short-lived. Three days after the Montrose Beach gathering, the *Chicago Sun-Times* reported from Washington that "[t]op Air Force missilemen are circulating a highly derogatory analysis of the 75-mile Army missile," and said they were touting instead the longer-ranged BOMARC, which they considered better performing and less expensive. "[T]he atom-tipped Nike-Hercules, already stationed at one site in Chicago, cannot cope with Russia's fast new bombers," the newspaper alleged, citing anonymous "Air Force officials."[114]

The Army responded with an invigorated publicity program, known internally as "Project TRUTH."[115] On September 4, the news media and civic representatives, uniformed and civilian Army leaders, and officials from Douglas Aircraft and Western Electric were invited to visit the Davidsonville Nike-Hercules battery in Maryland. Guests were told the Army weapon "was three times more effective than any other surface-to-air missile."[116] "Hercules is capable of destroying mass formations," the lieutenant colonel in charge of the site told those assembled, and United Press International noted that the Army emphasized it could "kill an atomic carrier and the atomic weapon it carried."[117] These two capabilities were primary reasons the weapon was developed, and they remained recurring themes in discussions about the missiles for years.[118]

While the Davidsonville function was a well-organized event involving top Army leaders, disseminating information about the Nike-Hercules fell to junior officers in other venues in this period. When soldiers at Fort Bliss were given a half-hour of live television time to demonstrate their abilities as amateur entertainers on local CBS affiliate KROD in November 1958, for example, the Army insisted that a young representative of the public information office be given five minutes in the program to describe the new Nike-Hercules system. The lieutenant's presentation was impressive, and unsurprisingly Sam Donaldson embarked on a career in broadcast journalism after leaving the military.[119]

The need to demonstrate the Nike-Hercules capabilities also spurred efforts to publicize the success (but not the original purpose) of Operation Snodgrass. At Davidsonville, the Eglin launches were alluded to as "recent tests" in which "six Hercules knocked out six jet target planes."[120] After a press release was issued which gave more details, the *Chicago Tribune* reported that one exercise (noted as having taken place in Florida) showed that "an entire formation...would have been destroyed had the missile carried a nuclear warhead."[121] Douglas also purchased nearly full-page ads about Snodgrass in the *New York Times* and *Washington Post and Times-Herald*. "A simulated attack on Continental U.S.A." was met successfully by weapons built by "the Armed Services' Partner in Defense," the advertisements argued.[122]

To further communicate its contribution to the nation's security, the next month Douglas organized a tour of its 1.5 million-square-foot plant in Charlotte, North Carolina, to show reporters and civic leaders "how the Nike-Hercules is assembled from start to finish."[123] The sole woman reporter observed that "the heavy work of missile-making is strictly 'a man's job,' " noting that only men toiled on metal fabrication and painting. "[I]t is in all the electronic work connected with the guidance system that women dominate," she reported. Donald W. Douglas, Jr., the president of the company founded by his namesake, concurred: "Women seem to have a natural talent for the fine precision effort required." It was observed that female workers who packed guidance components demonstrated "a very domestic touch" because of that task's similarity with "the familiar kitchen chore of canning."[124]

While women and men used their apparently natural skills to build actual missiles in North Carolina, boys (and perhaps a few girls) nationwide assembled plastic scale-model Nike-Hercules kits. California's Revell, Inc., which was the largest producer of such goods, annually designed fifty to sixty ready-to-build, carefully crafted replicas of military hardware. The company's president said model subjects were selected based upon their "historical" or "news value."[125] Not surprisingly, Revell's Nike-Hercules kit was released amid the considerable attention the real arms were receiving in 1958.[126] Competitors Aurora, KMT, and Monogram followed suit the next year.[127] Revell's box lid was covered with a dramatic full-color painting of a missile being erected for launch. A corporal appears to yell orders to two other crewmen while a Hercules is fired in the background. The missiles bore markings of the Washington-area Army air defense unit, although a cityscape akin to Manhattan is bathed with sunlight in the background and the balance of the landscape resembles the desert Southwest.[128]

Other than this artistic license, these and other Revell products were noted for their detailed accuracy. "To assure the utmost authenticity, blueprints as well as other technical information are obtained from either the prime contractors or from government bureaus as soon as declassified," summarized one account of the company's product development.[129] Some, however, questioned whether model specifics actually revealed a security breach. They asserted that Henry Blankfort, Revell's public relations executive, could be complicit in Soviet espionage. Blankfort, who had written a Paul Robeson script, among other screenplays, began working for Revell after he was blacklisted in 1951 for refusing to comment on testimony before the House Un-American Activities Committee, which identified him (probably accurately) as a Communist Party member.[130] As a result, the FBI reportedly tried but failed to pressure Revell to sever its relationship with Blankfort.[131]

Although no evidence supports the contention that the toy company executive was a spy, the Soviet Union was interested in obtaining details of the Nike-Hercules. It seems in March 1959, Army lieutenant colonel William H. Whalen met with Colonel Sergei Edemski, a Soviet military attaché at a strip mall around the corner from the American's home in Franconia, Virginia, in the District of Columbia suburbs. The two had become acquainted years before when Whalen's previous posting required attendance at many diplomatic functions in Washington. Subsequently assigned to an office in the Joint Chiefs of Staff, Whalen became indebted and alcoholic, and started to suffer heart problems. When Edemski suggested that the Army officer provide documents to the Soviets for cash, the offer was apparently accepted. According to various sources, in about twenty meetings over the next four years with Edemski or another Soviet embassy staffer, Whalen earned in excess of fourteen thousand dollars by handing over more than two dozen Army documents and by briefing his contacts on information to which he had access.[132]

Among other subjects, the Soviets specifically requested data about the Army's new surface-to-air missile (and the soon-to-be-supplanted Nike-Ajax). The United States government believes Whalen passed on at least six relevant publications in response, including an Army field manual supplement (classified "secret") that detailed the operation and capabilities of a Nike-Hercules battery, as well as warhead information, and background on "missile supply and storage."[133] One later damage assessment reported that Whalen's actions "could have seriously degraded the effectiveness of the surface-to-air capability of the United States."[134]

Whalen passed a routine background investigation amid his clandestine meetings, and his activities were not uncovered for several years, when he was implicated when another case unraveled.[135] The lieutenant colonel, who had since retired and taken a job as a parttime groundskeeper for the Fairfax County, Virginia, Park Authority, was given a fifteen-year prison sentence, and remains one of the highest-ranking U.S. military officers suspected of having been involved in espionage.[136]

It is possible that the information gathered by Whalen was provided to Joseph Berg and Philip Staros, leaders of a Soviet research center dedicated to developing radar-guided antiaircraft guns and surface-to-air missiles akin to the Nike-Ajax and Nike-Hercules. Berg and Staros were previously known as Joel Barr and Alfred Sarant. They were American Communists who worked to develop similar technologies for the United States while simultaneously playing a role in the spy network run by Julius Rosenberg. They fled to the East Bloc just as the Federal Bureau of Investigation began to pursue them.[137] Regardless of the factors contributing to the Soviet development effort, it was a success. The U-2 piloted by Francis Gary Powers was destroyed in May 1960 by a Soviet radar-guided missile essentially equivalent to the Nike-Ajax.[138]

By October 1958, five months before Whalen's alleged espionage activities began, the Philadelphia Nike-Hercules battery had been released from its Snodgrass assignment, moved to a converted Nike-Ajax site east of the city in Lumberton, New Jersey, and became operational.[139] The same month, three additional units near Washington, D.C., New York, and Detroit also became active.[140] In addition, the first W-31 warheads were produced at this time, although they were about a month behind schedule because of uncertain "production difficulties."[141] As a result, the new sealed-pit warhead was probably fitted to the missiles at the four new locations and probably replaced the W-7s on the Nike-Hercules at the three batteries that had been operational since the summer. If so, this means that perhaps as few as twelve W-7-equipped Nike-Hercules (four at each initial battery) existed, and only for a few months. They offered essentially an "emergency capability" akin to that provided by the EC-25 Genie rockets.

The president was kept informed of these developments. On December 19, 1958, Eisenhower met with officials to review plans for dispersing nuclear weapons in allied nations. Ike declared that, he "did not have too much reservation" about the procedures affecting "antiaircraft and antisubmarine weapons," but he did worry about the "protective arrangements" to ensure that other nuclear arms could not be used accidentally or without the proper authorization.[142] Notwithstanding his caveat, this brief exchange may have precipitated a memorandum one month later from Defense Secretary Neil McElroy. "The deployment of the NIKE-HERCULES missile with the W-31...atomic warhead has begun," McElroy informed the president. In making reference to Nike-Hercules batteries in the United States, he outlined "the precautions taken to prevent an inadvertent nuclear launch or an inadvertent detonation of the atomic warhead." While only a heavily redacted copy of this correspondence is available, the extant version notes that the warhead included a "safe plug" and that the missiles were secured to their launchers by pins. All had to be removed for a Nike-Hercules to take flight and detonate. In addition, there were other "safety and control features built into the system," wrote McElroy, including devices that ensured that the proper acceleration and altitude had been reached before the warhead would operate. The memorandum bears the president's handwritten initials in the corner, presumably signaling his satisfaction with the explanation.[143]

The eighth Nike-Hercules battery was readied four days before McElroy communicated with Eisenhower in January 1959. Three more followed in February, four in March, and eight in April. From then until October 1961, nearly constant construction or modification work was underway across the country in order to ready additional sites each month. Ultimately, there were 123 Nike-Hercules sites (eighty-six converted from Nike-Ajax and thirty-four newly built) around twenty-six cities and ten Strategic Air Command bases in twenty-five states in the continental United States.[144] Others were later located in Europe, South Korea, and elsewhere.[145] Ike was kept apprised of these developments.[146]

The distribution of Nike-Hercules batteries in the United States was the result of Defense Secretary McElroy's congressionally mandated review of the nation's surface-to-air missiles coupled with budgetary limits that were imposed later. By early 1960, both the Nike-Hercules and BOMARC were being deployed. The Army program was cut modestly by that time, while the Air Force weapon was reduced drastically.[147]

The advent and operation of the stateside Nike-Hercules facilities was covered closely in local newspapers. "Bay Defense Posts to Get Killer Rockets," blared a *San Francisco Chronicle* headline in January 1959.[148] The *Milwaukee Journal* reported in March of that year that "[t]he city's lake front Nike base is now equipped to fire nuclear warhead Hercules missiles, and shipment of the missiles is expected soon...."[149] A few days later, the *Baltimore Sun* carried the news that "[t]he third Nike-Hercules missile site in the Baltimore area will be placed in operation this spring...," and in August, the *Post-Dispatch* announced that "[t]actical equipment for the four Nike-Hercules missile installations which will form a protective network around St. Louis will be received about Sept. 15...."[150] In at least one city there was also an unsuccessful effort to obtain nuclear antiaircraft defenses. "During and since Ed Johnson's term as governor," the *Denver Post* reported in late 1958, "he has repeatedly urged the Defense Department to place Nikes in the Denver area."[151] However, despite a hopeful headline ("Nike Bases for Denver Called Nearly Certain") and a front-page story, no Nike-Hercules batteries were ever stationed anywhere in Colorado.

In areas with installations, the Army, as it had done with its Nike-Ajax, endeavored to communicate information about the missiles to nearby residents. In July 1959, for example, thousands of San Franciscans flocked to a downtown hotel to see a mockup of a control facility and a sample weapon.[152] On the other side of the continent, an inert Nike-Hercules started on a tour which eventually took it to forty "parades," "patriotic days," and "community events" around Long Island and upstate New York. The missile visited a New Hyde Park elementary school, a Boy Scout jamboree, and the state fair, among other venues.[153]

Efforts to acclimate communities to the Army air defenses were largely successful. In December 1959, Washington newspaper articles (one headlined "Cookies Their Target") solicited Christmas baked goods for local Nike soldiers, and in the following spring, Mayor Richard Daley signed a proclamation declaring "Army Air Defense Week" in Chicago. The mayor noted that the city "requires and deserves the most effective defense against enemy attack," proffered that the Army "will continue to provide Chicago with this effective guided missile protection," and urged citizens to attend related educational programs being organized by the service.[154]

One topic remained problematic in some areas. African American soldiers assigned to certain Nike-Hercules installations encountered racism in nearby communities. This prevented or inhibited the soldiers from securing homes during their assignments or patronizing some businesses. The Army refused to contest local practices. In the case of housing, this meant the service was forced to bend its own rules limiting the distance soldiers were allowed to live from the missile sites.[155] Racial attitudes, however, appeared to be more moderate within Nike-Hercules units. An integrated choral group was formed from batteries in the Norfolk, Virginia, area for performing at "civic functions and religious activities." Half of the ten members were African American.[156]

As a component of the effort to publicize the Nike-Hercules, fact sheets developed by the Army and Western Electric were widely disseminated. The handouts noted that the nuclear warhead had a "very high kill probability," which offered the possibility of "kills of targets in formation." Safety, the handout explained, "was one of the prime system design objectives." As a result, "final arming of the warhead takes place after [the] missile reaches safe altitude" and "interlocking circuitry requires [a] given sequence of operations before [a] missile launch is possible."[157] Wallet cards were also distributed to soldiers so they would have information at hand with which to answer queries ("nuclear warheads in defense weapons permit the destruction of a nuclear bomb as well as the carrier of the bomb") or redress concerns ("the storage of nuclear warheads presents no danger to the civilian community or to military personnel, either through radiation or explosion").[158]

In 1959, the Army also had an artful, professionally produced film, *The Nike-Hercules Story*, made for public viewing. It tells the fictional story of Captain Joe Griffith, Elm Street resident and commander of an unnamed but typical Nike-Hercules battery. "This is what it would be like near our great cities...if on some awful day the enemy attacked in earnest," the narrator announces as the crew practices firing a missile. It is a "dress rehearsal of what would happen if an enemy were to unleash the terrible heat and destruction of nuclear war." Griffith and his men "help to turn the shadow of dread which hangs over us all into a shield." Their missiles, the film declares, have an "an atomic punch" and are capable of destroying "a whole fleet of planes at a blow."[159]

In other situations, the Defense Department worked to ensure that privately produced movies that conceivably touched upon

American air defenses addressed the Nike-Hercules. When queried about a Pentagon contribution to a proposed documentary on the United States, an official in the Office of News Services volunteered that the film could conclude with a scene showing a Nike-Hercules battery "with one of our larger cities in the background." This would demonstrate, the official thought, "that we are aware there is the possibility of an enemy attacking our cities and that we are prepared to defend our liberties in our own backyards."[160]

Efforts to promote the Nike-Hercules extended to breakfast time, too. An official Army photograph accompanied a written description ("the most effective surface-to-air weapon in America's Arsenal of air defense") on a Nike-Hercules trading card distributed with cereal as part of a "Defenders of America" series in 1959. Youthful collectors were urged to "[g]et the entire set by eating NABISCO Shredded Wheat regularly and trading with your friends."[161]

Despite excitement possibly generated by cereal or plastic toys, children and adults had fewer opportunities to visit Nike-Hercules sites compared to Nike-Ajax batteries. A reporter who visited Davidsonville was told by the installation's commander that "[w]e're still anxious to remain a part of the community and not be shut off." "But," he explained, "because the Hercules can carry a nuclear warhead, we are under Atomic Energy restrictions which are rigid."[162]

Rather than hosting guests, soldiers were preoccupied with securing the sites, and operating and maintaining the facilities, equipment, and missiles. Some maintenance was performed on the Nike-Hercules (but not the nuclear warheads) at each battery.[163] Two Army installations, the Letterkenny Ordnance Depot in Pennsylvania and Colorado's Pueblo Ordnance Depot, were responsible for more extensive work and for storing additional missiles.[164]

Nike-Hercules batteries in every defense area typically rotated alert status, with some prepared to fire missiles in fifteen minutes and others within thirty or 120 minutes. The longer period accommodated more extensive maintenance or training, which required taking equipment off-line.[165] In the case of an alert, the alarm was communicated to the control portion of a site, which then contacted the launch section with the necessary instructions about the numbers and types of missiles to be prepared. Soldiers practiced selecting and raising missiles from the pits to the launchers, manning the control console, and rehearsing (but not actually undertaking) the final steps of removing the safety plugs and pins and connecting various cables that permitted a launch.[166] In the case of an attack, proper code words had to be exchanged before procedures that allowed the release of a missile could be taken.[167]

Although the precise ratio is not known, most batteries had missiles with both the W-31Y1 and W-31Y2 warheads, as well as at least one with a conventional explosive charge; such a Nike-Hercules could be used against a low-flying target when use of a nuclear round would cause collateral damage on the ground. The warhead on each missile was denoted by a colored band painted on the aft section. Nuclear versions were also obvious because safe plugs had flags that extended from the missile body (allowing a plug's presence to be readily confirmed), as well as peculiar containers, nicknamed "doghouses" or "mailboxes," which covered the arming system's delicate atmospheric probe on the nose while in storage.[168]

Soldiers authorized to be near a Nike-Hercules or the launch apparatus were required to work in pairs. This "two-man" rule was meant to minimize the possibility of one sabotaging or attempting to arm a weapon.[169] In addition, while fencing and guard posts encircled both the launch and control portions of a Nike-Hercules site, the portion of launch areas containing the missiles and firing apparatus were within a second enclosure. A military police detachment at each battery patrolled this zone around the clock. They were accompanied by German shepherd guard dogs capable of discerning "movements in dark or fog for 200 yards, due to their keen sense of smell."[170] The canine "was not trained to kill or injure," explained an Army press release, "but to stop an intruder in his tracks and assist his military police handler in taking the intruder into custody." Sentries and their dogs underwent an extensive training program before being assigned to a Nike site.[171]

These arrangements, and the number of Nike-Hercules batteries to be guarded, posed challenges for the Army. Obtaining a sufficient supply of dogs was a significant difficulty. In 1960, the Army announced its need for "more than 1,000 German shepherd dogs" and urged individuals to contact the Quartermaster General's office if they had puppies to offer.[172] Lassie Television, Inc., apparently learned of this requirement, and obtained Pentagon approval to film a related episode at a Los Angeles–area Nike-Hercules site that year.[173]

In the show, neither America's lovable collie nor his little towheaded owner are placed on sentry duty, but Timmy does visit a Nike emplacement, realize its important role in the nation's defense, and commit to train a stray dog for the Army. Entitled "The Patriot," the episode features Timmy peering through the battery's fence, while "Lassie whines uncertainly." "Maybe they'll have a visitors' day…. then we could get inside and really see what a Nike base is like," the boy tells his canine companion. He gets his wish. Days later, Timmy and Lassie are driven through the site by an enlisted man while a missile is lifted from its underground magazine. "Look down there!...Is that a missile?" Timmy asks. "It's called the Nike Hercules," the sergeant replies. "It's one of the most effective weapons in America's defense arsenal!"[174] Episode 239 aired twenty-three days after Dwight Eisenhower left the White House.[175]

By that point, the planned Nike-Hercules network was eight months from completion.[176] Although the number of batteries constructed is known, the total number of missiles produced and details about their distribution in the United States is more difficult to determine. One 1964 document says the Army was "authorized" to have as many as 2,448 for continental defense on June 30, 1961, peaking at 2,550 within two years. This includes some missiles that were located in Greenland but still assigned a continental defense mission (Soviet bombers approaching the United States from the USSR presumably would pass over that area). In addition, the document does not make clear if the number authorized was met, nor does it provide details on what percentage of missiles carried nuclear warheads.[177] Nonetheless, since most Nike-Hercules were fitted with one of the two types of the W-31, and the Greenland deployment accounted for fewer than fifty missiles, it seems reasonable to estimate that there were about 2,300 nuclear Nike-Hercules in the United States at the peak of the missile system's operation.[178] Based on the number of boxes built or converted and the number of missiles that could be accommodated in each, there was room for between 1,572 and 1,986 Nike-Hercules on-site.[179] Others were in storage at the Letterkenny and Pueblo depots.

Even without details about the exact number of missiles that existed, policy makers and the public were aware of their presence across the country. Together with the Genie rocket, the Nike-Hercules formed a sizeable component of the American nuclear arsenal at the time. Had the BOMARC been deployed as originally planned, the total number of surface-to-air missile warheads would have been far higher. A changed budgetary and strategic climate led to reductions in that Air Force missile program and affected plans for a nuclear version of the service's Falcon air-to-air guided weapons. The fate of those armaments is recounted next.

Chapter 6
BOMARC and Falcon

The waning days of 1957 were an important period for the two additional types of arms slated to join the American nuclear antiaircraft arsenal. In early December, the Air Force announced the construction of the first launching sites for its long-delayed BOMARC surface-to-air missile.[1] Later the same month, the development of an atomic warhead for the Falcon, the air-to-air guided weapon then being carried, in conventional form, by some fighter interceptors, was proposed.[2] The BOMARC and nuclear Falcon, however, came about amid continuing budget stringency, and at a time when policy makers were shifting their attention to the impending threat posed by intercontinental ballistic missiles. These circumstances influenced the deployment plans for both the BOMARC and nuclear Falcon and affected the public's perception of these weapons.[3]

The conventionally armed Falcon missile, which used a small, built-in radar to guide itself toward a target after being launched by an interceptor, first equipped a specially modified squadron of Scorpions (designated "F-89H") in Michigan in March 1956. The Falcon was a complex and sophisticated weapon that had been in development by Hughes Aircraft since the late 1940s. At the time it was fielded, it was nearly two years behind schedule and still beset with performance and reliability problems. These difficulties were not resolved until July 1957.[4] Despite the drawbacks, the Falcon offered some improvement over the guns and the folding-fin aerial rockets then available for interceptor aircraft, and the circumstances of the missile's deployment demonstrated the continuing perception that there was an acute need for effective anti-bomber weapons.

Indeed, not long after the initial group of F-89Hs became operational, the planes began to be supplanted by the F-102 "Delta Dagger," which had been specifically designed as an interceptor and was meant to redress the altitude, speed, and other shortcomings that plagued the modestly capable Scorpion.[5] (The F-102's introduction did not affect the F-89s that were undergoing modification to the "J" version in order to be equipped with the Genie.) Like the F-89H, the F-102 carried six Falcons.[6] On the Delta Dagger, the missiles were nestled in a compartment inside the plane's fuselage. (Doors on the belly of the F-102 swung open to allow missiles to be launched.) This stowage method gave the new interceptor good aerodynamic characteristics, and allowed it to enjoy greater agility and speed than the plane it replaced. Significantly, because the Delta Dagger's development had been finalized before the Genie had been authorized and the rocket's physical dimensions and aircraft mating mechanisms had been determined, the F-102 could not accommodate the MB-1 once it became available.[7] The plane's inability to carry the Genie later posed a dilemma.

Initially the Air Force planned to field the F-102 only for a relatively brief period. Within a few years it hoped to replace the Delta Dagger with an equal number of the F-101 Voodoo and versions of an upgraded F-102 then under development. Both the Voodoo and the improved Delta Dagger could carry the Genie internally.[8] Thus, once the Air Force's contemplated modernization program concluded, all the service's interceptors were to have been equipped with the MB-1. Given the rocket's lethality and reliability, the Air Defense Command believed its collective "kill probability" would be commensurately increased.

Although the modified F-102 closely resembled its predecessor, the engines and fire control system were considered sufficiently distinctive that the plane received a different designation (F-106) and nickname ("Delta Dart").[9] By the time the F-106 was available in the late 1950s, however, budgetary restrictions resulted in the purchase of fewer planes than anticipated. This meant that the F-102 was slated to comprise a larger portion of the inventory for longer than had been intended.[10] This caused concern, because Air Force leaders believed the Delta Dagger's inability to be fitted with nuclear armament threatened to weaken the effectiveness of its interceptor force. Consequently, in December 1957, General Curtis LeMay, then the Air Force vice chief of staff, urged that a nuclear version of the Falcon be fielded so it could be carried by the F-102.[11]

A guided air-to-air missile with an atomic warhead offered not only high lethality, but also the utilization of interception techniques that were not otherwise possible. Conventional radar-guided Falcons were best suited to attacking from the side. A perpendicular approach maximized the size of the target, which aided the missile guidance radar. An approach from the side or from behind also limited the evasive options of the plane being engaged. By contrast, a head-on attack minimized the target's cross-section, and the high speed of an interceptor frontally closing on a bomber complicated the rudimentary computer's calculation of the precise time to fire the missile, and for the missile to track the target and respond to the target's defensive movements. However, a radar-guided nuclear Falcon would not only be effective in a typical side-on attack, but the large blast area provided by the warhead would also compensate for imprecision in aiming and launching in the case of a head-on approach.[12]

By February 1958, an Air Force study supported LeMay's recommendation to develop a nuclear Falcon, Hughes agreed to begin work on the necessary missile alterations the next month, and the Atomic Energy Commission was charged with developing an appropriate warhead.[13] On June 13, President Eisenhower authorized adding several shots to the "Hardtack" atomic test series then underway at Eniwetok, including two related to the Falcon effort.[14] They were fired in the Pacific in early August. However, after two additional devices intended for another purpose were tested in Nevada in September and October as part of a subsequent series timed to conclude before the test moratorium began, one of these designs was selected for the forthcoming weapon. The warhead was designated "W-54"; the missile was dubbed "GAR-11" in late 1958.[15]

The conventional Falcon was six and one-half feet long, six and one-half inches around, and tipped the scale at less than one hundred and fifty pounds.[16] This relatively small size and light weight posed significant challenges for the W-54's designers since it had to fit into the missile airframe with only modest modifications or performance inhibitions. Indeed, when members of the congressional Joint Committee on Atomic Energy visited the AEC's Los Alamos laboratory and the Sandia Corporation in November 1958, they heard (apparently futile) complaints that the precise dimensional limits imposed by Hughes Aircraft on the W-54 threatened to greatly increase the warhead's development costs.[17] Regardless, the warhead, which was ultimately designed by August 1959, was fifteen inches long, nearly eleven inches in diameter, and weighed only fifty pounds. It yielded about one-half kiloton, and accordingly was considered to be lethal between two hundred and four hundred feet.[18] When the Genie's 220-pound W-25 warhead was approved in 1956, it was state of the art. The fact that three years later a nuclear device could be produced that was a fraction of the W-25's size and weight (with a commensurately reduced yield) demonstrates the trajectory and speed of the American nuclear weapon design effort in the period.

While the Falcon missile body and warhead development work was underway in 1958, BOMARC site construction began. Although, like the Nike-Hercules, a BOMARC was first displayed at Armed Forces Day the previous year (the Air Force missile was exhibited at Andrews Air Force Base near Washington, D.C.), it was not until December 1957 that the Air Force announced that its nuclear-armed surface-to-air missile would be located initially in Bangor, Maine; south-central New Jersey; Long Island; and Cape Cod.[19] These and one other early site were to house the IM-99A; by August the Air Force had authorized the development of a second-generation "IM-99B" model that, unlike its predecessor, used a less hazardous solid propellant and thus could enjoy many handling and storage advantages.[20] In either instance, the BOMARC sites were to include concrete-and-steel missile shelters built aboveground in evenly spaced clusters of seven on a fifty-acre plot.

Each garage-size shelter was to hold one BOMARC, affixed to a horizontal launch arm, and associated apparatus. In the event of firing, the shelter roof would part and the arm would lift the missile vertically. Various maintenance and support functions were to be accommodated on another twenty or so acres abutting the missile storage area (including, for those locations with the IM-99A, facilities associated with that version's caustic and dangerous liquid fuel). The entire rectangular parcel was to be surrounded by a seven-foot-high fence, lights, and intrusion alarms. A small separate area would contain communications links, a radio transmitter, and antenna to communicate the guidance information received from the Semi-Autonomous Ground Environment (SAGE) system to the missile in flight.[21] Curiously (and confusingly), while the launch sites in many instances were to be constructed on land at some distance from an Air Force base, they frequently came to share the name of the nearby installation, despite not being particularly proximate.

When the Pentagon offered a briefing on December 13 about the BOMARC launchers to be built near Otis Air Force Base in Massachusetts, the lieutenant governor and many state and local officials and civic leaders attended. (The commonwealth's chief executive was out of the state.) According to a local newspaper accounts, following cocktails and dinner ("roast beef, sole, or turkey") at the Otis Officers Club, guests had an opportunity to view a mock-up of the proposed construction, examine a missile model, and watch a film of an unarmed BOMARC test flight, all amid the "pleasant accompaniment" of a piano played by a sergeant's "attractive wife." Attendees were told that "[d]espite Sputnik, the defense planners consider 'manually operated bombers' the major threat at this moment," and that "Bomarc is the weapon they believe to be the best present answer to the threat...." The base commander (described as "a connoisseur of air weapons") declared that the missile "brings against its target atomic force...." "[I]t does not have to make physical contact with the target," the colonel explained, "[a] near miss is enough to detonate the charge and blow the target to atoms."²²

As a result of the presentation, one guest said, "I feel a hell of a lot safer tonight tha[n] I did last night," although the lieutenant governor sought to clarify that the BOMARC was a "defensive" rather than "destructive weapon." Another attendee wanted assurances that IM-99A's presence would not increase the likelihood that Cape Cod would become a Soviet target. He was told that the USSR probably preferred to destroy cities and Strategic Air Command bases.²³

While the audience hoped that information about the economic benefits of the BOMARC site's construction and operation would have been more readily available, they were pleasantly surprised with the Air Force's candor. Aside from the precise number of missiles to be accommodated on Cape Cod, few queries were deflected on the grounds that a full response would require revealing classified information. The Air Force, too, was pleased with the reception received, but bemused that a widely anticipated question went unasked. It seems the service was unnecessarily prepared to assure local residents that the arrival of the BOMARC missiles would do "[n]othing at all" to television reception in the area.²⁴

Enthusiasm about BOMARC was not limited to Massachusetts. After the Air Force placed a maintenance installation in Ogden, Utah, in charge of logistics and support work for the missile, several individuals found a way to recognize the significance of the new responsibilities. In early 1958, the wives of two Ogden employees elected to assist Frances Frost (a "blonde native missile") in a Salt Lake City hairstyling contest by developing her coiffeur and attire. Frost won top prize for a hairdo described as having been "inspired by the supersonic Bomarc missile," while her "facile frame" was covered by a full-length black sheath dress, the color, cut, and trim of which had been designed to evoke the new armament. An Air Force periodical recounted that Frost's hair "features supersonic action from nape to crown," with "long-range swirls" that appeared to be "intercepted by flowing lines and high altitude sweeps." The style seemed to suggest a "nuclear payload" that had gone "into super action," the paper said, acknowledging, even then, the "press-agentry" implicit in the description.²⁵

Around the same time that Miss BOMARC was gaining attention, Revell, the California toy company, introduced its plastic BOMARC kit.²⁶ In this instance, however, the firm's vaunted (and controversial)

Figure 6.1 "Miss BOMARC," a contestant in a 1958 hair styling competition held in Salt Lake City, wore attire said to be "inspired by the supersonic bomarc missile." It mimicked the coloring and markings of the U.S. Air Force's nuclear antiaircraft weapon during development, as demonstrated by the adjacent miniature model. Miss Bomarc's supporters pointed out her hairstyle suggested the missile's "nuclear payload" had gone "into super action."

Source: Official U.S. Air Force photograph courtesy of the National Museum of the U.S. Air Force.

penchant for accuracy was lacking. Probably because it was finalized before the relevant decisions about the actual missile were made, the box art putatively showed a test launch rather than an operational situation. The illustration depicted a single missile erected on a rudimentary gantry alone on a desolate plain while a second IM-99 took flight from a similar apparatus in the background. Like Miss BOMARC's attire, the plastic missile was black, with broad white bands around the fuselage. In the case of the real IM-99s used in tests, this color scheme aided photographic tracking of the missiles from the ground. When BOMARCs were actually deployed in their concrete shelters, however, they were painted entirely gray-white with Air Force emblems and markings.[27]

Revell likely did not worry about the inaccuracies, however. When competitor Aurora issued its BOMARC kit in 1959, it too bore the wrong color, as did an inert IM-99 dispatched by the Air Force to fairs, festivals, and other events across the county during this period.[28] The display BOMARC had been prepared at Ogden in February 1958 for this purpose, and it was one of the many weapons trucked around the nation by a 254-person Air Force Orientation Group assigned to Ohio's Wright-Patterson Air Force Base.[29]

No doubt the BOMARC exhibit painted a rosy picture of the weapon. In fact, between September 1952 and September 1958, only half the BOMARC test flights were judged at least partially successful. In the fifty-one attempted BOMARC missions in this time frame, the ramjet engines proved to be especially problematic, as did the onboard radar that was meant to guide the missile to the target in the closing minutes of flight. Some missiles failed to fly the intended distance; others veered out of control.[30] None of these difficulties, of course, had anything to do with the nuclear warhead or raised questions about the utility of arming the BOMARC in this manner.

The IM-99's poor test performance was brought to the attention of policy makers. In October 1958, the National Security Council received a briefing on a special Defense Department report that said intelligence estimates showed that over the next two years, the Soviet Union would have between one hundred and two hundred "heavy bombers" and eight hundred others capable of reaching the outer portions of the U.S. air defense zone. However, the study also asserted that the Soviets would likely field intercontinental ballistic missiles in the coming years. Consequently, among other recommendations was the suggestion that every effort be made to resolve the BOMARC difficulties so that it could be deployed as scheduled. The assessment maintained that the missile "will be becoming available late in relation to the threat," and thus, if problems persisted, "serious consideration" should be given to reducing the program.[31] Otherwise there was the risk that it might be perfected too late to be useful.

At the conclusion of the presentation, national security advisor Gordon Gray, a longtime public servant and former university president who had assumed the position in June from the Office of Defense mobilization, responded. He remarked that the BOMARC comment was a "serious statement" that raised the "question for decision" as to whether this or certain other weapons "should be completed." The president agreed.

Most of Gray's audience apparently did not interpret the NSC advisor's comments as a criticism of BOMARC's performance, but rather as a commentary on the threat it was designed to counter. Deputy Defense Secretary Donald Quarles reacted by defending the Pentagon's weapon plans. "[J]ust as we have gone back to the manned bomber as an effective weapon," he said, "the Soviets would too." It was "risky to assume," Quarles argued, that the USSR would "forgo" the use of airplanes to attack the United States. This spurred Central Intelligence director Allen Dulles, who had earlier remarked that the USSR "had recently been cutting back production of heavy bombers," to emphasize that he nonetheless still believed that "the Soviets will keep up a substantial manned bomber force." He was, however, uncertain about the capabilities of the planes and whether the USSR could "get high speed together with the necessary range."[32]

As a result of the report and ensuing discussion, Eisenhower asked the Joint Chiefs of Staff to evaluate existing or proposed weapons and report back on "obsolescent, antithetical or overlapping" systems. Air Defense was to be given particular attention. Two weeks after the NSC meeting, Gordon Gray proffered some specific comments on this topic.[33] The DoD briefing had outlined the tactics to be used against bombers in case of an attack: Planes would first be engaged by interceptors and long-range BOMARC missiles at a distance from the nation's borders. Bombers that survived these efforts to defend a broad "area" would then be targeted by the Nike-Hercules as the aircraft came within the shorter range of the batteries surrounding close-in defended "points." Gray was skeptical of this plan and its origins. "Candor would compel me to suggest," he wrote to the Joint Chiefs chairman, Air Force general Nathan Twining, "that there is room for the impression that the concept is based on weapons systems in being or programmed and serves as much as justification for programs as it does as a basis."[34]

Twining's response has not been found. It is possible, however, that he both conceded Gray's observations about the background of the strategy while also arguing for its validity. While it is true that

Nike-Hercules and BOMARC were independently developed with little thought to the existence of the other, they were, in fact, complementary weapons of varying ranges and differing guidance methods.[35] The "area" and "point" distinction, with the Air Force responsible for the former and the Army the latter, was a result of the interservice dispute in 1956 over the Talos.[36] A layered anti-bomber defense featuring weapons of varying capabilities may not have been planned, but it made sense.

Despite the fact that the president requested the study of obsolete or superfluous weapons, the air defense examination flagged, probably because DoD had become preoccupied with the congressional cutbacks to both Nike-Hercules and BOMARC and the Air Force and Army rivalry that resulted.[37] While Congress had hoped that the Defense Department would select one of the two missiles for deployment, as a result of several Pentagon reviews and debate within the JCS in fall 1958, DoD decided to continue to field both, albeit at lower levels. Many in Congress were skeptical when they learned of this plan early the next year. When Defense Secretary Neil McElroy did a poor job of explaining his rationale before the Senate Armed Services Committee in May 1959, the panel (with encouragement from Mississippi senator John C. Stennis and Henry M. Jackson, who represented Boeing's home state of Washington) voted to delete Nike-Hercules construction funds and the previously granted site spending authority from the fiscal year 1960 budget. Two weeks later, the Appropriations Committee in the House of Representatives did the opposite. It cut BOMARC funding by half. Chastened by the possibility of having an important defense decision made for him in the course of reconciling these two divergent actions, McElroy asked the JCS to prepare a comprehensive "Master Plan" for air defense that outlined the type and number of weapons they favored for through fiscal year 1963.[38]

As a result, both the Air Force and Army increased their efforts on behalf of their preferred armament. This yielded many news stories. Just as was the case of the *Chicago Sun-Times* article the previous August that highlighted the putative advantages of the BOMARC, each was typically sympathetic to one of the competing weapons.[39]

This interservice dispute caught Eisenhower's attention. As the May 28 National Security Council meeting adjourned, the president said he "was increasingly upset by the vehemence of the fight between the advocates of the NIKE missile and the advocates of BOMARC." "Why," he queried, "do we have to have two armed services of the U.S. shooting two different missiles?" He said the situation seemed to indicate poor management.[40] Four days later, in a private meeting with the president, Gordon Gray concurred with the chief executive's view. "[A]ny consideration of this matter should take into account the tremendous pressure exerted by Defense contractors," Gray told the president. A memorandum by Gray that recounts the conversation says, "The president agreed and said that he had been talking about this problem for a long time."[41]

At the Pentagon, McElroy was busy making decisions. The JCS Master Plan, which had been submitted to him on June 2, offered widely divergent recommendations on Nike-Hercules and BOMARC, based upon the opinions of each service chief. Working with his civilian staff, the defense secretary thus reached his own conclusions. He determined that a total of 31.5 Nike-Hercules battalions should be fielded, along with sixteen BOMARC squadrons, about one-third less than the number urged by the proponent of each type on the JCS.[42]

One week later, McElroy met with the president to report his conclusions. Ike was somewhat concerned about the lack of unanimity within the JCS, but otherwise seemed satisfied with the plan. After incoming Army chief of staff General Lyman Lemnitzer noted it was "a cut-back in previously planned programs," but still a "reasonable solution," Eisenhower agreed. He "recalled that the strength of the Soviet Air Forces was apparently greatly overestimated a couple of years ago," and said, "Now we are more certain of our estimates, and they are much lower. The bomber threat is not so serious as had been thought." Later in the discussion, however, the president asked the Air Force Chief of Staff "how much the Soviets are exercising their bomber aircraft at the present time." When General Thomas D. White replied that "they are conducting an extensive training effort," Eisenhower remarked, "[T]here is reason not to get too complacent over the fact that the estimate of Soviet bombers has been cut back."[43]

This was a transition period. American military and intelligence officials increasingly feared the advent of Soviet ICBMs, but were uncertain when or whether these arms would supplant or supplement bombers. This made assessments of Soviet military strength, and the American policies that resulted, especially tentative. Once intercontinental ballistic missiles came to predominate, most existing defense arrangements would no longer be adequate. Antiaircraft weapons were useless against ICBMs, and their high speed meant there would be insufficient time to institute civil defense measures once their approach was detected. On the other hand, until the Soviets deployed a substantial number of strategic missiles, government leaders thought it was necessary to maintain vigorous anti-bomber defenses.

Some assessments at the time asserted that Soviet bombardment capabilities had peaked. The CIA's Allen Dulles reported to the NSC in

June 1959 that the USSR appeared to have between 150 and 160 long-range aircraft. Although some of them were being "improved both as to altitude and range capabilities," Dulles concluded that "for the next year or two Soviet-manned bomber capabilities against the U.S. would remain substantially unchanged." He further noted that "Soviet production of heavy bombers was marked by a very low level of activity."[44]

Throughout 1959, President Eisenhower remained worried about the prospect of a Soviet air attack and the defense effort this necessitated. In February he convened a meeting with Defense officials to complain that the Pentagon was overestimating the number of atomic arms that it needed. Donald Quarles objected, saying stockpiles of "small nuclear warheads for air defense" were a primary impetus for DoD's projections. To this, Eisenhower was sympathetic. He said he "understands the need for small weapons in air defense." The president believed other components of the arsenal should be curbed, such as "small yield weapons for the infantry." In conclusion, Andrew Goodpaster's notes indicate, Ike "reiterated that we should push atomic weapons for air defense but be more moderate in development of tactical atomic weapons."[45]

Concern about a surprise raid was manifest in other ways in this period, too. Nine weeks after Eisenhower's meeting with Pentagon officials to discuss production of defensive arms, the sixth annual Operation Alert took place. Sirens sounded across the nation at 11:30 a.m. Eastern time as if there were "enemy aircraft over far northern Canada."[46] All television and AM radio stations went off the air at that time to allow the national emergency radio system to be tested. In New York City, the mayor and governor broadcast remarks about the exercise, along with Leo A. Hoegh, the director of the federal Office of Civil and Defense Mobilization. At 1:30 p.m., once the imaginary planes "theoretically broke through Nike missile defenses," sirens sounded again, this time emitting the "take cover" warble. For ten minutes, traffic stopped, Wall Street suspended trading, and shoppers were guided to shelters in stores. While the event went smoothly overall, and civil defense officials continued the drill after the ostensible public portion concluded, some New Yorkers refused to participate. Dorothy Day, the Catholic social activist, and sixteen others were arrested in City Hall Park. Similarly, two Quakers were taken into custody in Queens.[47]

About six weeks later, having obtained the president's assent to the air defense Master Plan, Secretary McElroy presented it to the Senate Armed Services Committee. Some members were pleased. Others, especially Democrats, were not. Washington's senator Jackson pejoratively termed it a "master compromise," and he and some colleagues were disappointed that the Pentagon had not decided to proceed with only a single type of antiaircraft missile, although they differed on which that should be. McElroy rejected this logic, declaring he never intended to choose one over the other, and that the tiered antiaircraft arrangement made sense as a defense strategy, not simply as a way to placate the services.[48]

By contrast, some in the House of Representatives thought the activities of military vendors might offer the primary explanation for the nation's air defense strategy. When McElroy's decision was announced, a Republican congressman from Pennsylvania charged that it was, in part, the result of improper corporate influence. He cited a nearly full-page Boeing advertisement placed in the *Washington Post* two weeks earlier that noted the number and geographical distribution of BOMARC subcontractors. He said the ad's purpose was to affect legislation, and as such, it was an example of inappropriate lobbying. Boeing promptly issued a statement claiming that the ad was merely one of a four-part series that had run since October in an effort to correct "erroneous information" about the company's missile that was "being circulated by partisan sources."[49]

The publicity was relatively innocuous. One ad, in the *New York Times*, included a map of North America showing areas prospectively protected by BOMARC. Another, in a Washington newspaper, was illustrated with a photograph of a test launch alongside text declaring, "Each new BOMARC missile base will protect thousands of square miles."[50] The advertisements delineated other important details about the IM-99, as well. A full-page *Newsweek* ad on February 2 noted, "Armed with a nuclear warhead, a single BOMARC can destroy an entire formation of attackers."[51]

In August, a subcommittee of the House Armed Services Committee held hearings on the legislative ramifications of the ad campaign. A senior Boeing executive appeared to explain that the company placed the advertisements because it "wanted to make sure the public and Congress had the 'proper information,'" in the midst of the air defense debate. He also complained about the lack of attention to an ad on behalf of the Nike-Hercules that appeared in the *Post* the week before Boeing's disputed message.[52]

The subcommittee gave the competition its due the next week. The public relations director for Western Electric Company, the Nike-Hercules contractor responsible for the system's radar and electronics, told the Armed Services members that it was a "coincidence" that an advertisement extolling that missile's "8,000 company team" ran when it did.[53] "I can't believe for a minute anything we would do would have any effect on Congress," declared the executive. "We certainly wouldn't want to do anything like that."[54] However, when the executive noted that the Army had "suggested" that the firm "might advertise Nike more than we had," Chairman F. Edward Hebert of Louisiana thought the inquiry was yielding results. "[N]ow we are getting somewhere," he declared.[55]

Days later, the Army secretary testified that the service did not believe that Western Electric's action was "intended to influence Congress or anyone else." Rather, he said, "Army information officers undoubtedly remarked to industry representatives that the Army was proud of Nike development and that the public could be better informed about it."[56] Donald Douglas, Jr., also appeared before Hebert's body to discuss the activities of his firm. He acknowledged, "We discuss with Army public relations officers our public relations program every year," but he denied any improper actions.[57]

As ridiculous as these corporate demurrers seem, the focus of the Armed Services investigation came instead to be directed at retired officers who had become employees of other defense contractors and at entertainment benefits that those companies offered influential service members. Companies involved in air defense work apparently were not noteworthy in either category. Neither Boeing, Douglas, nor Western Electric were caught up in subsequent discussions of that topic.[58]

With the Armed Services Committee's focus shifted elsewhere, the first BOMARC installation was declared operational. Since January 1958, the Corps of Engineers had been overseeing the preparation of the site in a New Jersey scrub-pine forest fourteen miles southeast of Trenton. The site's namesake, McGuire Air Force Base, was six miles west. For some reason, the service had decided early on that this site would lead the rest. Fifty-six reinforced concrete missile shelters were built there, in two groups of four rows of seven, spaced so that a high-explosive detonation in one would not necessary endanger another.[59]

The work, however, ran over budget and behind schedule and sparked litigation that dragged on for years. Even after McGuire was completed, Boeing required ten months to install and prepare ancillary equipment at the site and inspect and ready the first missile.[60] By late summer 1959, only a single BOMARC had been fitted to a launcher and properly calibrated. An official history declares that "by severely straining the concept of operational readiness, it was possible to declare the BOMARC squadron at McGuire operationally ready on 1 September 1959 according to plan." The Air Force feared that any delay in readying the sites, at least on paper, would endanger continued funding for the entire program. Until mid-December, an Air Force and Boeing team struggled to check out and fuel a second missile. Its internal electronic components failed twenty-one consecutive tests at which time it was learned that the effort had worn out certain sensitive parts.[61]

On December 1, however, the installation at Westhampton Beach, New York, two miles from Suffolk Air Force Base on Long Island, was able to prepare an IM-99A and was declared the second operational facility. The Suffolk site also had been built to house fifty-six missiles, and it suffered from many of the same construction delays and missile problems that afflicted McGuire and its armament.[62] Extrapolations from the BOMARC tests at the time showed that about forty-three percent of the missiles in storage would take flight if needed; twenty-three percent of those would hit the target. This meant that overall only about eleven percent of readied missiles (however many that may have been) could function as intended.[63] Obviously, this was a dismal forecast. The cost of the initial BOMARC facilities also demonstrates the difficulties faced by the building program. Although forty-three million dollars was budgeted for the first four BOMARC locations in fiscal year 1958, subsequent estimates projected that $38.5 million would be required for just the first two installations.[64]

Other details about the status of both McGuire and Suffolk in the months after construction was completed are difficult to discern. Despite the "operational" designations and other vague indications that more than one missile at each location was readied by early 1960, it is possible that the Air Force did not permit any BOMARCs to be armed with atomic warheads until May 1960. Nuclear safety rules were not promulgated until the month before, and it was necessary to modify the launchers in response to concern that the IM-99 launch gantry would inadequately restrain a missile in the event a rocket motor was accidentally ignited.[65] Before the W-40 warheads were mated to the missiles, a few BOMARCs may have been capable of taking flight. Without armament, however, they were useless, and the weapon's official status was a charade, meant to suggest a far greater capability than existed. This assessment is buttressed by a June 1960 news account that quotes some officials as describing both McGuire and Suffolk as being in "a quasi-operational state," and saying that neither location was "fully combat ready."[66]

As BOMARC sites were struggling with their armament, several studies were considering the missile's fate. In summer 1959, an ad hoc group assembled by George Kistiakowsky, James Killian's successor as presidential science advisor, had been briefed on the Pentagon's newly developed air defense "Master Plan" and the intelligence upon which it was based. When the group issued its report a few months later, the panel said it believed there was "conclusive evidence that the Soviet [Union] is continually striving to increase the operational effectiveness of its strategic bomber force." This "constitutes a deadly threat-in-being which will continue to be a serious threat of major proportion," it argued. The committee, however, also noted that "as the Soviet ICBM capability increases, the relative importance of the air-breathing threat will decrease with time...." The ad hoc group predicted that "the ICBM and manned-bomber threat will be of comparable significance" until "about 1963," at which time, "the ICBM threat will predominate." According to the panel, because BOMARC was not expected to be completely deployed until after that date, and because the missile's performance was contingent upon the operation of the SAGE radar and computer system (which was vulnerable to attack), this raised "serious questions" about the utility of the weapon and the expenditures proposed for it.[67]

A continental defense study body and a subordinate "weapons group" subsequently organized by the Presidential Science Advisory Committee in late 1959 embraced the ad hoc group's recommendations.[68] In February 1960, an Air Force assessment conducted with assistance from the MITRE Corporation, a research arm of the Massachusetts Institute of Technology, also reached similar conclusions.[69] These evaluations may have been buttressed by a CIA intelligence report estimating that the Soviet Union would field only between 140 and two hundred ICBMs by mid-1961.[70]

With this information in hand, Pentagon officials trooped to Capitol Hill in March 1960 to ask Congress to amend the DoD budget for the coming fiscal year, despite that fact that Defense leaders had endorsed the spending plan in its existing form in January. The Defense Department sought to redirect funds to cover the cost of more ICBMs, radar to detect a Soviet missile attack, and other programs by cutting the allocation for SAGE by more than half and reducing BOMARC monies by ninety percent.[71] Now, only a total of eight installations for the Air Force antiaircraft missile were to be built. Sites in southeastern Virginia; near Lake Superior, twelve miles outside of Duluth, Minnesota; at Kincheloe Air Force Base in Michigan's Upper Peninsula; and at the Niagara Falls Airport were to join the four facilities that had been completed or were nearing completion at the time.[72] This was a far cry from the forty bases (and nearly five thousand missiles) that had been contemplated for placement along the nation's northern border and on both coasts as late as 1957.[73]

By this time, cutting BOMARC was an easy decision for the Department of Defense. It was a complex weapon not expected to be perfected until after the threat it was intended to counter had been supplanted.[74] Previously, as deployment lagged, plans had been reduced accordingly, although the 1960 cutback was the most dramatic.[75]

Congress, however, was conflicted about the Pentagon request. While the House of Representatives voted to eliminate *all* further BOMARC funding after learning of the DoD proposal, the Senate accepted the Defense recommendation, but added funds to finish two additional installations already being built. One was in western Oregon. The second was north of Boeing's headquarters in Seattle, in a state represented by Senator Jackson, and his equally influential colleague, Warren Magnuson.[76] When the two congressional chambers met in July to reconcile the competing versions of the appropriations bill, however, the administration's request was revived. It became law.[77]

One assessment suggests that the House's more drastic reduction may not have been embraced because of the downing of an American U-2 over the USSR in May and the resulting collapse of the planned summit involving Eisenhower and Soviet premier Nikita Khrushchev.[78] With superpower tensions rising, this interpretation holds that legislators considered the lower body's proposal too precipitous. Although that connection between the U-2 crisis and continental defense preparations is speculative, the two subjects definitely share at least one link. Khrushchev first spoke about the shoot-down in a radio address on May 5, the same day that the president, Gordon Gray, George Kistiakowsky, Allen Dulles, and many cabinet secretaries and other officials had been flown by helicopter to High Point for 1960's Operation Alert.[79]

While Eisenhower met with aides, the federal civil defense director convened a meeting at another location of several "Emergency Agency Designees." This was a group of five prominent business leaders, two cabinet secretaries (labor and agriculture), a Harvard college dean, and the Federal Reserve chairman whom Eisenhower had personally selected a year earlier to administer a portion of the federal government in the event a surprise attack disrupted the existing bureaucratic hierarchy. Forty-seven years later, presidential aide Andrew Goodpaster told an interviewer that this group, which he said was "absolutely glittering in terms of its quality," demonstrated the significance that Eisenhower placed on preparing for an attack. That subject "was deeply on his mind," Goodpaster recalled.[80]

As Ike and others rehearsed their roles in the event of a raid, airmen at the McGuire and Suffolk BOMARC installations continued to prepare the missiles and facilities in their charge. By June 3, McGuire passed an Air Force safety and readiness inspection that evaluated the unit's nuclear warhead handling, safety, and security procedures.[81] Despite their favorable evaluation, however, examiners noted that

Figure 6.2 Four of fifty-six U.S. Air Force BOMARC IM-99A nuclear antiaircraft missiles emplaced at a site about fourteen miles southeast of Trenton, NJ, near McGuire Air Force Base. Each missile carried a W-40 nuclear warhead which yielded about six and one half kilotons. Missiles remained horizontal in the shelters shown except when preparing to launch or the erection equipment was being tested. Thirteen months before this photograph was taken in October 1960, McGuire became the first BOMARC site to be declared operational. It also was the location of a June 1960 accident in which fire destroyed a warhead.

Source: Official U.S. Air Force photograph courtesy of the National Museum of the U.S. Air Force.

mandated periodic inspections of the missiles had been postponed. McGuire did not have all of the necessary test equipment, and some that it did possess did not function properly. "[A]lthough there was no way of knowing...what the inspection report portended," says one account, it "foretold what happened at McGuire four days later...."[82]

In the absence of proper diagnostic examinations, McGuire airmen failed to identify substandard components on several BOMARCs. One flawed piece that went unnoticed at the time was a fitting that joined the missile to a tank containing highly pressurized helium used in the fueling process. On June 7, the piece cracked in one of the BOMARC shelters, allowing the tank to burst with explosive force. This sparked an enormous fire.[83] Airmen trained hoses on the conflagration, which kept the flames from spreading beyond the affected building, but the intense heat and flame enveloped the IM-99. The fire consumed the high-explosive components surrounding the warhead's fissile material and most of the weapon's radioactive matter puddled on the shelter floor. Some minute plutonium fragments were swept along by the runoff from the water used to fight the blaze.[84] The fact the high explosives did not detonate was a testament to the warhead design, including the use of explosive material that could withstand such extreme circumstances.

Minutes after the blaze started, an Air Force policeman contacted the local New Jersey State Police barracks for assistance in blocking traffic on public roads near the installation. The trooper taking the call understood the airman to report that "an atomic warhead exploded."[85] The Air Force sergeant later disputed that characterization of his remarks, but not before state police officials notified their Trenton headquarters and the Associated Press learned of the alleged report and distributed a news bulletin repeating that description.[86] The Air Force quickly clarified the nature of the incident, and within thirty minutes of the first news advisory, the AP issued a second that corrected the earlier announcement and noted only that the accident "released a 'small amount' of radioactive material in the immediate area of the explosion." A third bulletin subsequently repeated Pentagon assurances that "there is no radiation danger to the public."[87] The speed with which the erroneous bulletin was righted limited the difficulties posed by the miscommunication, although there were some angst-filled minutes in the interim and a few state officials later faulted the Air Force's emergency notification procedures.[88]

As the fire was brought under control in the following hours, a specially trained seven-person nuclear-response team arrived from a New York Air Force base. They joined state and federal public health officials who had previously been summoned to the site.[89] Spot checks across sixty-six square miles outside the facility's boundaries found no trace of radiation in subsequent days.[90] Once the fire was extinguished, the walls of the affected shelter were painted, and a mixture of concrete and asphalt was spread on the floor and across the apron and adjacent soil where the plutonium-laced water had pooled. This was intended to trap plutonium particles and keep them from being inhaled. According to one contemporary report, "minute amounts" of plutonium oxide ("about 2 to 3 times the normal background count") were found about one hundred yards away, having been carried by the wind before the accident site was sealed. However, the evaluation argued that "[t]his figure is infinitesimal when compared to the allowable tolerance figure, and constitutes no hazard."[91] Other measurements confirmed that the efforts to trap the plutonium at or adjacent to the scene of the mishap had worked. No radiation seeped into the ground or water supply.[92]

New Jersey's governor termed DoD's response to the incident as "super cautious." One official history acknowledges that, while "uninformed rumor created considerable anxiety among the civilian population in the McGuire area," the accident "was in reality a minor one."[93] Nonetheless, it was, according to another history, "perhaps the worst" event involving any of the Air Defense Command's nuclear weapons.[94]

The McGuire site eventually resumed operations, although the destroyed shelter was fenced off and never rebuilt or rearmed. Environmental monitoring continued, and no dangers were identified. Once the initial tumult subsided, there was little public concern about the installation's operation.[95] However, when a subsequent inquiry revealed that the accident originated with the helium tank, pressure in similar vessels at other BOMARC sites was reduced. A modification to render the equipment operational again was not devised and applied until October 1961. In the sixteen months between the accident and the retrofit, BOMARC capabilities were further degraded, because without readily available high-pressure gas, a missile launch required several hours rather than the intended two minutes.[96] For a weapon meant to offer near-immediate response to a surprise attack, this was a crippling alteration to operating procedures.

Another problem also arose in this period that threatened the safety of the BOMARC's atomic charge, although arrangements were made to accommodate this difficulty until it was resolved. In mid-1959, a study showed that some nuclear warheads previously thought to be one-point safe might not be. The evaluation suggested that in some instances, depending upon the specific spot that detonated on the high explosives surrounding the fissile core, a nuclear reaction might occur.[97] While the precise details are impossible to discern because relevant documents remain classified, it appears that the BOMARC's W-40, which was just then beginning production, was among those warheads about which there was some uncertainty. In August the W-40 was apparently "temporarily" modified in some fashion to make it safer, and this problem could have contributed to the delay in arming IM-99s already on site.[98]

In the meantime, AEC chairman John McCone met with the president and others in July 1959 to discuss the study of the one-point situation. McCone sought to convince Eisenhower that more extensive one-point experiments should be conducted on the affected warheads after the test moratorium expired on October 31. The chairman reminded Eisenhower that if a weapon design was flawed, a one-point test could result in an atomic explosion, and a decision to proceed should be predicated on that possibility since it was tantamount to initiating a nuclear test series soon after the moratorium's expiration. The president agreed with the need for the safety experiments, but he took exception to McCone's analysis. Eisenhower said he did not consider the proposed activities to be "nuclear tests," but rather experimental activities not prohibited by the ban.[99]

By November, however, the test moratorium had been extended, and at a White House meeting that month, McCone revealed that a subsequent report concluded that the original estimates of the one-point problem "had been in some respects in error and had exaggerated the probability of a dangerous incident." He said the safety of the questionable designs still needed to the confirmed, but the situation was less urgent that it appeared initially. McCone advocated instituting a test program that involved detonating modified versions of warheads in an underground "containment vessel."[100] The warheads under study would contain fissile material, but far less than they did normally. Thus, if a weapon was not one-point safe, a measurable nuclear reaction (but one with an insignificant yield) would occur, and the radiation would be contained below ground. (Indeed, the high explosives would cause a more powerful blast than that caused by the fissioning of the small amount of nuclear material.)

Eisenhower authorized this work, called "hydro-dynamic" or "hydronuclear experimentation." He assured the AEC that he did not consider it "a nuclear weapon test" of the type prohibited by the moratorium.[101] Until George Kistiakosky, Eisenhower's science advisor, referenced the activities in memoirs published sixteen years later, these activities were not well known.[102]

It is probable that the temporarily modified W-40 underwent a hydro-dynamic evaluation in early 1960. Nuclear weapon researcher Chuck Hansen says this led to the development of a "one-point safe version of the W-40," dubbed "mod 2," which was not available until December 1963.[103] This might incorrectly imply that the earlier type was unsafe. Kistiakowsky termed the hydrodynamic experimentation process "a more severe test system," and it may be more precise to say that the subsequent W-40 design was developed to meet more stringent conditions.[104]

In March 1960, as the warhead issue was being resolved, the BOMARC site on Cape Cod was declared operational. It was followed three months later by the facility at Dow Air Force Base in Maine. In October, the site in Newport News, Virginia, on the peninsula between Williamsburg and Langley Air Force Base, was finished. In 1961, the installations in Michigan (June) and Minnesota (July) were prepared.[105] Niagara Falls followed in early 1962, finally providing the Air Force with the eight BOMARC launch locations in the United States that it ultimately requested.[106]

Earlier Canada had agreed that two IM-99B installations would be located on its territory. The United States eventually provided the missiles to Canada, along with the warheads and a contingent of men to maintain ostensible custody of them. The Canadians paid to build and operate the facilities, each of which accommodated twenty-eight missiles. In addition to whatever other influence the missiles had on politics and culture in Canada, at least one musical quartet took note. Before releasing their international rock and roll hit "Clap Your Hands," the four young Canadian men who comprised the Del Tones decided to rechristen themselves the Beau-Marks in reference to the weapons their nation was adopting.[107]

The first five U.S. sites received the IM-99A, although Suffolk and Dow had room only for twenty-eight rather than fifty-six launchers. The last three installations built accommodated only the B version. Kincheloe and Duluth each had twenty-eight shelters.[108] Niagara held forty-six launchers, probably because, as the last site constructed, the number of shelters was adjusted to match the number of BOMARCs that had been manufactured.[109] Around the time the newest sites became operational, twenty-eight additional launchers each were built at McGuire, Otis, and Langley so they, too, could handle the IM-99B.[110] Thus, accounting for the destroyed shelter at McGuire, it is possible to calculate that there were precisely 409 total BOMARC launchers in the United States.

Determining the exact number of missiles (and warheads) is harder. By the end of 1960, the Air Force intended to purchase 462 BOMARCs.[111] Every group of twenty-eight shelters was to have thirty missiles (to allow some to be out of service for maintenance or other reasons).[112] If this had ratio remained for the number of launchers actually built, there should have been 438 IM-99s (each with one W-40) in the United States at peak deployment. The total was probably less than that because, for the Bomarc B, plans were changed to procure only one additional missile for every twenty-eight launchers.[113] A declassified 1964 document shows that there were only 383 "missiles on launchers" as of the previous June. By that time, however, the IM-99 was in the process of being retired, although it is not possible to determine how this affected the numbers that month. Nonetheless, it appears that about four hundred BOMARC missiles and W-40 warheads were produced for the United States.

A Pentagon air-defense exercise in 1960 simulated the firing of fifty-two IM-99s. Those faux launchings were part of an operation called "Sky Shield I," which took place for six hours in the early morning of September 10. In planning for at least ten months, it involved halting all North American civilian air traffic so that 310 Air Force bombers could stage mock raids against targets in the United States and Canada while radar, interceptors, and missiles practiced their response.[114]

Sky Shield was considered an essential test of the American defense mechanism, conducted in the most realistic environment possible. It originated with a suggestion from General Earle Partridge, the first leader of the North American Air Defense Command. It was approved by the NSC and closely coordinated by the Federal Aviation Agency (as it was then known) and the nation's airlines, which were pleased to do their part for national defense. About 1,300 commercial and three hundred more private flights were canceled or delayed in the United States and Canada for Sky Shield. The exercise had been announced the previous June, presumably giving travelers time to make alternative arrangements.[115]

Overall, more than one thousand fighter interceptor missions were flown (without nuclear armament), and in addition to the mock BOMARC launchings, there were 254 simulated Nike-Hercules firings. Two other Sky Shields were held in succeeding years. The last, in 1962, was the final time all flights in U.S. airspace were grounded until the morning of September 11, 2001, forty-one years and one day later.[116]

Two months after the first Sky Shield, the Air Force began modifying its F-102s to carry the GAR-11.[117] The Falcon's availability, however, was delayed by persistent fuse problems and two blasts (in February and October 1959) at facilities that produced the high explosives for the nuclear warheads. Work could not resume on the W-54 until safety procedures were improved and the repairs were made to the affected installations.[118] In the interim, studies showed that the Falcon warhead might yield less than intended. This caused the high-explosive components to be redesigned. After the Soviets announced the resumption of nuclear tests in August 1961, the United States followed suit, and the reconfigured W-54 was tested in Operation Nougat, which started at the Nevada Test Site the next month. This confirmed that the alterations were satisfactory.[119] Around that time, the GAR-11 finally reached the first Air Force units, although all the fuse difficulties were not resolved until shortly thereafter.[120]

The Pentagon disclosed the existence of the new missile eight months before it was readied. In late April 1960, the Air Force, joined by Hughes Aircraft, announced that the new Falcon version of the "first air-to-air guided missile carrying an atomic warhead" had

Figure 6.3 The U.S. Air Force's Falcon (GAR-11) guided nuclear antiaircraft missile with an interceptor in the background. The nuclear Falcon entered the inventory in 1961 as the result of the Air Force's decision to have a nuclear antiaircraft weapon capable of being carried by the F-102 Delta Dagger interceptor. The Falcon's W-54 warhead yielded about one-half kiloton. Designed in 1959, it was fifteen inches long, nearly eleven inches in diameter, and only weighed fifty pounds. The relative small size of this nuclear device compared to those developed just three years earlier demonstrates the rapid pace of the American nuclear weapon design effort in the period.

Source: Official U.S. Air Force photograph courtesy of the National Museum of the U.S. Air Force.

begun testing. Press coverage noted that it was designed for the F-102, provided its estimated yield, and quoted a Hughes official remarking that it was "particularly valuable for head-on attacks against supersonic bombers."[121] Unlike Barney Oldfield's experience with the Genie, photographs were also released, and appeared with explanatory captions in several publications.[122] On the eve of the delivery of the first GAR-11s, Hughes also ran an advertisement in at least one publication showing the missile and describing its "nuclear punch," which was "particularly effective in high-speed closures against bombers carrying the deadliest of weapons."[123]

Although the GAR-11 was almost two years behind schedule, the Pentagon probably eventually obtained about 1,900 nuclear Falcons.[124] They were stored on interceptor bases in bins built for the Genie, and faced similar handling, safety, and security restrictions—with one important exception. F-102s were routinely allowed to ferry GAR-11s from one location to another, provided their motor ignition systems were disabled. This prevented the missiles from being accidentally fired while an interceptor carried its own armament to a dispersal airfield from which it might operate in time of heightened readiness.[125] Allowing nuclear Falcons to be airborne in these circumstances was probably permitted because the relatively small amount of plutonium in a GAR-11 greatly lessened the hazard from a one-point accident in the event of a plane crash or if the missile was jettisoned for some reason.

Other than news stories resulting from press releases issued by the Pentagon or the Falcon's manufacturer, there was relatively little publicity about the advent and deployment of the GAR-11. The missile was not featured in a Lassie episode, considered as the subject of a Jimmy Stewart movie, nor the inspiration for a beauty queen's hairstyle. In the nearly five years between the Defense Department's announcement of the Genie's deployment and the Falcon entering the Air Force's inventory, nuclear air-defense weapons had become commonplace in the United States. They were no longer noteworthy, nor was the threat they were intended to counter considered to be the most significant. As ICBMs were believed to supplant bombers in the Soviet Union's arsenal, air defense arms were both less important to the Pentagon's war plans and less likely to garner popular attention.

John F. Kennedy inherited the anti-bomber arrangements instituted by Dwight Eisenhower's administration. The development and deployment of nuclear air-defense arms did not conclude until years after Ike left office. Within a few years, however, the changed threat became apparent and elements of the defense network began to be dismantled.

Conclusion

While the fundamental decisions about nuclear antiaircraft arms were made during President Eisenhower's term, his immediate successor agreed with the need for the weapons and accepted the ideas upon which they were predicated. Indeed, it was not until John F. Kennedy's administration that atomic anti-bomber armament reached its peak deployment in the United States. Shortly afterward, however, the nation's defense preparations underwent substantial change. After the advent of Soviet intercontinental ballistic missiles, which were more difficult to counter and which could almost assuredly inflict enormous destruction, policy makers believed it was impractical and illogical to maintain extensive preparations to defend against an aircraft raid that might take place before or after an ICBM barrage. Partly for this reason, and also because atomic air-defense weapons were costly to retain, and because BOMARC never performed as intended, they began to be removed from service. Although a substantial number were dismantled by the end of the 1960s, others remained in the inventory longer.

John Kennedy became president in January 1961. Among other military hardware, his inaugural parade featured four (presumably unarmed) Genie rockets arrayed on a flatbed truck.[1] By this time, the air-to-air rocket was well established in the Air Force stockpile; the Genie was manufactured until sometime between 1962 and 1963.[2] About nine months into the Kennedy presidency, the final thirteen planned Nike-Hercules batteries also became operational.[3] A few months after that, the last U.S. BOMARC site, on the grounds of the Niagara Falls International Airport, opened.[4] Finally, while two hundred nuclear Falcons were available by December 1961, the remaining 1,700 that eventually entered the Air Force probably became ready in early 1965.[5]

In early 1962, once substantial numbers of Genie rockets and nuclear Falcons were in the Air Force inventory, the service apparently sought to conduct a live-fire test of both weapons, similar to the Snodgrass/Opera Hat operation that President Eisenhower had canceled four years earlier. In this instance, rather than Florida, the activity was to take place near Eniwetok in the South Pacific. An official history says the effort was "doomed to frustration" once the United States agreed a treaty banning aboveground nuclear tests.[6] Nothing further is known about "Blue Straw" and whether John Kennedy reviewed the operation's plans to the same extent that Dwight Eisenhower did with the earlier proposal.[7]

By the second half of 1962, as the number of nuclear air-defense weapons was reaching the maximum level, the United States faced one of the gravest episodes of the Cold War. In late summer and early fall of that year, American leaders worried about the possibility of a military buildup in Cuba. Beginning on October 14, U-2 reconnaissance flights began. They yielded aerial photographs showing that launch facilities for Soviet Medium- and Intermediate-Range Ballistic Missiles (MRBMs and IRBMs, respectively) were being prepared on the island and also provided evidence that MiG-21 fighters and forty-two medium-range, jet-powered, nuclear-capable bombers (designated the "IL-28" by the Soviets but known in the west as the "Beagle") had been shipped there as well.[8] The Cuban Missile Crisis was underway.

The presence of the missiles preoccupied most American officials at the time. The sole purpose of both the MRBMs and the IRBMs was to deliver nuclear warheads; once readied, the weapons could reach most of the United States. By contrast, senior political and military leaders were divided on the question of the possibility that the Beagles and MiGs might be equipped with nuclear bombs. They agreed, however, that the arrival of the planes on the island signaled that the USSR might be undertaking preparations for an atomic attack on the United States, perhaps with the forces in Cuba serving as a diversion or component of a larger strike.[9] Because this could involve bombers flying from the Soviet Union, U.S. air defense forces (in addition to other units) assumed a higher state of readiness.

On October 22, pursuant to a plan that was coincidentally in the midst of being developed, 161 interceptors were flown to sixteen alternative bases as part of the alert process. More broadly distributing defending forces was meant to ease the task of responding to possible aerial incursions and also to complicate Soviet efforts to target interceptor bases. There were no weapons stored at the dispersal locations, however, so the planes had to be loaded with Genies and Falcons and the arms carried by the fighters in the course of their move. For the Genie, this was an unprecedented contravention of regulations that prohibited planes from being airborne with the MB-1 unless an attack had been confirmed. It was considered necessary because dispersing the interceptors without armament would have been nonsensical.[10]

In most instances, the weapons were disabled before the flight. While there was still a chance of a one-point accident caused by a crash or similar mishap, the arms were incapable of being launched or producing a nuclear detonation. At least two squadrons, however, did ferry their Genies in an operational configuration, in part because of a concern that qualified airmen would not be available at the dispersal airfields to restore the weapons to firing status. These planes could theoretically have fired a weapon in flight, although other standard mechanical safeguards would have precluded a ground burst. While the interceptors were dispersed without incident, it was difficult to store, guard, and maintain the nuclear weapons properly at the new locations in the absence of the personnel and facilities available at the originating bases. These problems, however, were overcome.[11]

Despite the fact that air defense forces assumed a higher alert, the Joint Chiefs of Staff reiterated that the procedures which governed contact with potentially hostile aircraft remained in place. Fighter planes dispatched to intercept suspicious aircraft could not carry the Genie or nuclear Falcon. Those sent airborne after the initial group could do so if it was determined that the intruders were executing an atomic attack.[12]

There was one exception to this policy. Two F-102s carrying fully readied nuclear Falcons took flight over Alaska during the crisis to meet a wayward U-2 returning from a mission over the Soviet Union. In addition, an error in Wisconsin (the sounding of the wrong signal) led fliers to believe that a Soviet bomber attack had been confirmed and nearly allowed two Genie-equipped F-106s to take off. Political scientist Scott Sagan, who has studied nuclear safety issues presented by these and other cases, has also argued that there was some possibility that American bombers, being staged for missions to the USSR at this time, might have been mistaken for Soviet planes and been fired upon by U.S. interceptors carrying nuclear weapons. He believes that in either case, or in some other "bizarre combination" of events, it is possible that American atomic air-to-air arms could have been detonated. According to this analysis, such an event could have somehow sparked a broader nuclear exchange, especially given international tensions and the attack preparations that were being made. Sagan concedes, however, that this was an "unlikely" prospect.[13] This assessment seems appropriate.

Army Nike-Hercules units around cities and Strategic Air Command bases also made special arrangements during the Cuban

Missile Crisis, although none of the alert steps were particularly noteworthy. For example, a missile battery near Seattle that was out of service for maintenance was rushed back into operation.[14] Sites elsewhere increased the number of missiles that they were prepared to fire in five minutes.[15] Similarly, the BOMARC helium tank problem had been resolved for a year, and most IM-99s had since been returned to their routine two-minute status.[16] When the crisis arose, however, evaluation of the B version was still underway. This involved a SAGE facility in Montgomery, Alabama, that controlled test missiles launched (without warheads) from a facility on the Florida panhandle. These activities were suspended during the Cuban situation to free the SAGE tracking system for potentially more pressing air defense duties.[17]

The military was concerned about protecting Florida from attack by air. When continental defense arrangements were devised during the Eisenhower administration, the possibility of a strike originating from south of the United States was not contemplated. Consequently, there were no antiaircraft missile sites dedicated to defending Florida or the surrounding area, although some fighter interceptors were available.[18] As a result, on October 24, a mobile Nike-Hercules training battalion was ordered to travel by rail from Fort Bliss, Texas, to the Miami area.[19] With other Nike units emplaced at permanent facilities across the country, this was the only one that could easily be organized for shipment elsewhere on relatively short notice.[20]

At this time, General John Gerhart, the NORAD commander, contemplated the defensive preparations he thought should be undertaken. On October 27, he sent a message to the JCS, commenting on the military's "operational plan" (or "OPLAN") being instituted in connection with the Cuban situation. "Rules of engagement for the Florida area prescribe the use of high explosive weapons only," he noted. Gerhart believed this aspect of plan was unsatisfactory. "In the event of an IL-28 raid from Cuba which penetrates U.S. air space," he explained, "I consider it imperative to use weapons with maximum kill capability." He reminded the JCS that NORAD already had the authority to use nuclear weapons in certain instances. Gerhart asked for "clarification" of the OPLAN and inquired if it altered his "authority...to use nuclear weapons...should a raid from Cuba penetrate the Air Defense Identification Zone or sovereign boundaries of the U.S." He concluded by pointing out the distribution of warheads at the permanent Nike-Hercules batteries. Using the two-letter abbreviation for "high-explosive" rounds, Gerhart cabled, "your attention [is] invited to the fact that in most locations Nike-Hercules units have no[,] repeat no[,] HE warheads."[21]

The JCS responded the same day. The service leaders reiterated that "nonnuclear armaments" were prescribed for air defense forces in the Florida area. They emphasized, however, that "nuclear weapons could be used to destroy hostile aircraft" if an attack was indicated by a "pattern of actions elsewhere."[22] Apparently, the JCS wanted to foreclose antiaircraft nuclear use in almost any instance in connection with Cuba, unless it was determined that a broader Soviet nuclear attack was underway.

The next day, Lieutenant General Theodore W. Parker, the Army's deputy chief of staff for military operations who oversaw many activities in the service's situation room at the Pentagon during the crisis, asked subordinates to determine from the Army Air Defense Command if it was "a fact" that the Nike-Hercules sites across the nation had few nonnuclear warheads. The situation room log shows the reply: "For the most part this is true. There are two HE warheads in each of 34 sites." The log says missiles with conventional "[w]arheads are also available at Fort Bliss…[and] 83 are at Pueblo Ord[nance] Depot."[23] Parker also confirmed that the Nike-Hercules unit being shipped to Florida also had only high-explosive warheads on all seventy-two missiles it carried.[24]

Although years before the general had supervised the emplacement of Nike-Ajax missiles around Chicago, he was apparently unfamiliar with the capabilities of the successor nuclear batteries and the number and type of missiles typically available in each magazine across the country.[25] His inquiries seem to evince some concern that the Cuban situation potentially posed a scenario in which the use of nuclear antiaircraft weapons was undesirable. It is possible that Parker feared potential complications, even from the defensive use of atomic armament. Although not commenting on this particular incident, one scholarly assessment takes a contrary view and declares that nuclear antiaircraft weapons are "not of primary interest in considering the question of escalation," especially if they are expended "against aircraft thought to be carrying offensive nuclear weapons."[26]

There is no evidence that there was a change in the type of missiles allocated to any Nike-Hercules unit during the crisis. After tensions subsided, however, a decision was made to make permanent the surface-to-air missile defenses that had been established. Four new sets of aboveground launch and control facilities were constructed in South Florida by 1965.[27] These batteries held the nuclear Nike-Hercules.[28] When BOMARC B testing concluded in December 1962, consideration was also given to converting the single test launcher at Eglin Air Force Base on the Panhandle to an operational site to be used in the defense of the southeastern United States. This idea came to naught and the facility was designated for training instead.[29]

Even that role was limited. In August 1963, the Air Force recommended to the Defense Secretary that the BOMARC A be withdrawn from its five launching locations as a cost-savings measure. The A version, with its liquid fuel and shorter range, was especially cumbersome to maintain and offered no advantages over the later type. The plan was approved and the last IM-99A was taken off alert in July 1964. The warheads were subsequently removed and the missiles provided to the Navy for use as target drones. The two BOMARC sites (at Dow Air Force Base in Maine and at Suffolk Air Force on Long Island) that housed only the IM-99A were closed, less than five years after the first BOMARC A had become operational.[30] The other sites remained active because they held the newer IM-99Bs.

The Air Force, however, did not seem to have much interest in that version either. This attitude was justified. Between November 1963 and the end of 1964, operational units took turns traveling to the Eglin facility to practice launching missiles. In nine tries in that period, six IM-99Bs (without nuclear warheads) managed to take off and five hit their targets. However, in the midst of these exercises, all of the spare missiles were exhausted. Thus, starting in April 1964, operational BOMARCs were taken from Niagara Falls, disarmed, and sent to Eglin for training launches. Since the New York site accommodated forty-six missiles and the other active locations held only twenty-eight, the Air Force apparently thought Niagara Falls had BOMARCs to spare. After that site was reduced to twenty-eight missiles, the service planned for other locations to rotate the responsibility for providing the six IM-99Bs required for the annual practice. At that rate, only a total of 132 BOMARCs would remain in service by mid-1972.[31]

This plan demonstrates what Air Force leaders thought of the BOMARC. Had officials believed it was an important component of anti-bomber defenses, an alternative training method could surely have been devised that did not involve expending a significant portion of the relatively few operational missiles on hand. However, if only about fifty-percent were likely to take flight and find their targets in time of war, Air Force leaders presumably either thought that retaining the full complement was unnecessary or that training was worthwhile, which might improve the performance of a consequently reduced number.

Dissatisfaction with BOMARC reflected concerns about the performance of the vehicle; it did not indicate disagreement with the concept of using nuclear arms for antiaircraft defense. In 1964, a book portraying the Air Force's perspective on the defense situation repeated arguments expressed throughout the previous decade. "Why are nuclear weapons needed for attack against enemy bombers?" a senior general at the Air Defense Command is asked by the author. "Wouldn't conventional high explosives do the job as well, without any radioactive fallout?" Major General Arthur C. Agan responds:

> Not at all. High explosives knock out individual bombers.... But others might get through. Most importantly, the nuclear-tipped defense missiles would not only kill several bombers at once—the weapon carriers—but they would also kill the weapons, the nuclear bombs or nuclear air-to-ground missiles that the enemy is carrying toward our targets.... [T]he fallout from our nuclear weapons would not endanger populations because they are smaller in yield than the big bombs... designed to knock out strategic targets or event cities.

He further explains:

> Suppose we used a high-explosive weapon against an enemy bomber some fifty miles away from a big city. We would knock him out of the sky, but his nuclear bombs, if they were armed, would detonate... and the winds could carry lethal fallout to that city within a few hours. We stopped the bomber, prevented damage to the city's physical structures—and permitted lethal damage to human lives. If our interceptor pilots had used nuclear missiles against the bomber, we would have prevented both because the nuclear missiles would have destroyed its lethal payload as well as the bomber. Only minor contamination of no appreciable significance would result from the explosion of our defensive weapons and the ensuing debris of the enemy's bombs. Hundreds of thousands, perhaps more, casualties would have followed our using high-explosive missiles to kill the enemy bombers.[32]

Here, in one long-winded reply, are most of the points made if favor of nuclear air defense arms in the course of ten years.

A little more than a year after the last BOMARC A was withdrawn, the decision was made to dismantle the first Nike-Hercules sites. As the lasting deployment in Florida demonstrates, the Pentagon was not displeased with the Army missile's performance, but rather believed some locations were superfluous. In November 1965, President Johnson was informed that the eighteen Nike-Hercules batteries around SAC bases would be closed. ICBMs, "which can be launched with little warning, are now the Soviet's [sic] prime offensive weapon against our bomber bases," aide Joseph Califano told the president in a memorandum. "While Nikes were effective against the bomber threat they are not effective against ICBM's, and are thus largely obsolete against the main threat."[33] The Army's nuclear defense of SAC ended in June 1966, six years after the Nike-Hercules was first emplaced around bomber bases.[34]

This was just the beginning. The cost of upkeep of the remaining Nike-Hercules sites continued to drain the Army budget. In 1968 and early 1969, all the batteries around Kansas City, Dallas, and St. Louis closed, in addition to some near Washington, Philadelphia, New York, Pittsburgh, and Hartford. In 1970, defense of Cincinnati and Dayton (a single "defense area"), Buffalo, and Niagara Falls concluded, and the next year the same occurred in Bridgeport, Cleveland, Milwaukee, and Minneapolis-St. Paul, while some batteries in other cities were also shuttered.[35]

Following the Nike-Hercules drawdown, the Air Force announced that it intended to close its five remaining BOMARC bases.[36] This decision, in March 1972, was perhaps spurred by the announcement seven months before by the Canadian authorities that they intended to cease operations at the two IM-99B sites they maintained. "[S]ince the superpowers are now armed with missiles," Canada's Defense minister explained at the time, "an attack by bombers is unlikely."[37] The Canadian action threatened to leave a portion of the U.S. northern border without BOMARC defenses. Coupled with the missile's poor performance and attrition attributable to training, deciding to close the remaining U.S. facilities was a logical response. The last American BOMARC bases, including McGuire, shut down in October 1972.[38]

In this period, the F-102 was also being withdrawn. American interceptor forces were being reduced, and since the F-106 was superior, it made sense to first retire the older plane. Probably because the nuclear Falcon was the Delta Dagger's primary armament, the loss of these aircraft lessened the need for the GAR-11. The atomic air-to-air missile was removed from the Air Force arsenal by April 1972.[39] The defense secretary no doubt approved these and other reductions, and the president was probably informed. But unlike the extensive NSC deliberations that surrounded the deployment of nuclear antiaircraft arms a decade before, it does not seem that any of these actions were especially noteworthy to senior policymakers or sparked much discussion.

Two years later, the Nike-Hercules program practically ended in the continental United States. In late 1973, Defense Secretary James Schlesinger decided to close forty-eight of the fifty-two remaining Nike-Hercules batteries the next year.[40] "Since we cannot defend our cities against strategic missiles," Schlesinger explained shortly thereafter to congress, "there is nothing to be gained by trying to defend them against a relatively small force of Soviet bombers."[41] The *Washington Post* reported that the cuts "reflect the end of an era."[42] By the end of 1974, Schlesinger's order was fulfilled.[43] Had *Lassie*'s Timmy been a real person, he need not have worried about the Army's guard dogs at this time. Many of the nearly two hundred canines were assigned elsewhere or offered to police departments once their work at the antiaircraft facilities ended. The military noted, however, that they "cannot be retrained as pets."[44]

The Miami-area Nike-Hercules sites remained, in part, to provide stateside training opportunities, since the weapon was still fielded in Europe. The Defense Department also either had genuine concern about the threat from Cuba or deferred to powerful lawmakers from Louisiana and Florida who did.[45] The Florida units, along with the final two batteries in Alaska, closed in June 1979.[46]

A few years before, with the number of atomic air-defense weapons drastically reduced, the predelegated permission to use nuclear weapons was apparently rescinded. "Action is under way in the Department of Defense to revoke this authorization in the near future," a retired Navy vice admiral serving as a Pentagon nuclear advisor told the Foreign Affairs committee of the House of Representatives in March 1976.[47] Presumably this took place, because when the Navy contemplated a new shipborne nuclear antiaircraft missile eight years later, press accounts intimated that it would be difficult to use because no provisions existed to allow it to be expended without prior consultation with the president.[48]

As interceptors were retired and the air defense efforts lessened, MB-1s were removed from the inventory. By 1983, two hundred Genie rockets remained in Air Force service.[49] The last were phased out by 1986, presumably in anticipation of the end of the service life of the F-106, the only plane that could then carry the weapon.[50] For nearly thirty years, the United States had fielded one or more types of antiaircraft nuclear weapons. With the Genie gone, that effort came to a close.

Had the deployment of the arms had any effect on the Soviet Union and its military plans? In February 1962, eight months before retiring as the top public relations official at NORAD, Barney Oldfield spoke to a Texas convention of aerospace writers. He summarized recent remarks by Defense Secretary Robert McNamara. Oldfield noted that the secretary had acknowledged that "we cannot provide an absolute defense against unfriendly forces which might approach the North American continent," but had also said "we have a highly effective system against manned bomber attack...particularly since the Soviet Union did not build the large manned bomber force anticipated many years ago by the planners of the system...." Oldfield seized upon this portion of McNamara's statement. "Lest this be interpreted as a planning error," declared the Air Force officer, "let me say that any defensive force formidable enough to discourage a production line is a pretty good expenditure of effort and money."[51]

There is little evidence, however, that the Soviet Union's nuclear strategy was influenced by America's atomic anti-bomber defenses. Available information suggests that the USSR did strive to develop capable, long-range bombers, but encountered difficulties in designing and producing sufficiently powerful and fuel-efficient engines. Once ICBM production seemed feasible, research and manufacturing efforts were redirected to this task instead.[52] U.S. defenses do not appear to have been a factor in the Soviet decisions.

In his memoirs, however, Nikita Khrushchev did suggest that American antiaircraft preparations had been on his mind. The former premier noted that the performance characteristics of the TU-95 bomber meant it would have been "shot down long before it got anywhere near its target."[53] This may reflect his honest impression or it may have been a disingenuous, self-serving declaration offered as a way to explain why more and better bombers had not been deployed during his tenure.

Regardless of Khrushchev's attitude, it seems clear that to Dwight Eisenhower, his aides, and military officials that atomic antiaircraft arms seemed a necessary and logical addition to the nation's arsenal in the 1950s. In the years before the threat of an ICBM attack became the predominant defense dilemma, Ike and those around him sought to field armaments offering the greatest chance to down high-flying, fast-moving Soviet bombers before nuclear weapons could be loosed on the United States. Millions of Americans, including those who lived, worked, and played near where the arms were kept at the ready, seemed to approve. Of course, neither the Genie, Nike-Hercules, BOMARC, nor nuclear Falcon were ever used against attacking planes. The design, development, and deployment of these weapons was an expensive, time-consuming, and fleeting exercise based on honest yet imperfect intelligence about Soviet capabilities and intentions, but driven by a desire to protect the nation.

Notes

Introduction

1. "Restricted Data Classification Decisions, 1946 to the Present (RDD-8)," U.S. Department of Energy, January 1, 2002, p. D-1, in author's possession. This document was declassified and distributed in 2009 at the request of the Federation of American Scientists. Calculations assume the figures provided are those for the last day of each calendar year.
2. The one-fifth estimate is based on 4,186 air defense weapons, assuming the following production and deployment figures as of January 1961: 1,701 Genie rockets (forty-one months of production averaging 48.5 MB-1s each month); 2,188 Nike-Hercules missiles (2,448 missiles eventually authorized before the Cuban Missile Crisis, less 60 estimated missiles not yet provided to the final thirteen launch sites built before the crisis); 297 BOMARC missiles (89 each at McGuire and Otis, 59 at Langley, and 30 each at Suffolk and Dow); and no operational Falcon missiles.
3. For example, Richard F. McMullen, *History of Air Defense Weapons; 1946–1962* A[ir] D[efense] C[ommand] Historical Study 14 (n.p.: Air Defense Command, n.d.); Thomas W. Ray, *Nuclear Armament; Its Acquisition, Control, and Application to Manned Interceptors, 1951–1963*; A[ir] D[efense] C[ommand] Historical Study No. 20 (n.p.: Air Defense Command, n.d.); Mary T. Cagle, *History of the Nike-Hercules Weapon System* (U.S. Army Missile Command: Redstone Arsenal, Alabama), 1973; Margaret C. Bagwell, *History of the BOMARC Weapon System; 1953–1957* (Wright-Patterson Air Force Base, [Ohio]: Air Materiel Command, 1959); and Thomas W. Ray, *BOMARC and Nuclear Armament*, A[ir] D[efense] C[ommand] Historical Study No. 21 (n.p.: Air Defense Command, n.d.).
4. For example, Carl Posey, "The Thin Aluminum Line: Supersonic Airplanes and a Screen of Radar Stood Ready during the Cold War to Avert the End of the World," *Air and Space Smithsonian* (December 2006/January 2007): 60–67 (on Genie, Falcon, and BOMARC); Stephen P. Moeller, "Vigilant and Invincible," *ADA* (May–June 1995): 2–42 (on the Nike-Hercules); and Clayton K.S. Chun, "Winged Interceptor: Politics and Strategy in the Development of the Bomarc Missile," *Airpower History* (Winter 1998): 44–59. For a treatment of the Canadian aspects of nuclear

air defense arms, see John Clearwater, *Canadian Nuclear Weapons: The Untold Story of Canada's Cold War Arsenal* (Toronto: Dundurn Press, 1998); John Clearwater, *U.S. Nuclear Weapons in Canada* (Toronto: Dundurn Press, 1999); and Sean M. Maloney, *Learning to Love the Bomb: Canada's Nuclear Weapons During the Cold War* (Washington: Potomac Books, 2007).

5. For example, Steven I. Schwartz, ed., *Atomic Audit: The Costs and Consequences of U.S. Nuclear Weapons Since 1940* (Washington: Brookings Institution, 1998); Kenneth Schaffel, *The Emerging Shield: The Air Force and the Evolution of Continental Air Defense, 1945–1960* (Washington: Office of Air Force History, 1991); Richard M. Leighton, *Strategy, Money, and the New Look, 1953–1956: History of the Office of the Secretary of Defense, Vol. III* (Washington: Office of the Secretary of Defense, 2001); Robert J. Watson, *Into the Missile Age, 1956–1960: History of the Office of the Secretary of Defense, Vol. IV* (Washington: Office of the Secretary of Defense, 1997); U.S. Army, *History of Strategic Air and Ballistic Missile Defense: Volume I, 1945–1955* and *Volume II, 1956–1972* (Washington: Center of Military History, c. 1975). This last two-part work was written by John Steinbrunner, Ernest May, and others under contract to the BDM Corporation and the U.S. Army. The volumes were declassified in 2005 (volume I) and 2006 (volume II). They were published with minor redactions in 2009 by the U.S. Army Center of Military History.

6. For example, David Alan Rosenberg, "The Origins of Overkill: Nuclear Weapons and American Strategy," in Norman A. Graebner, ed., *The National Security: Its Theory and Practice, 1945–1960* (New York: Oxford University Press, 1986); Fred Kaplan, *The Wizards of Armageddon* (Stanford: Stanford University Press, 1983); Campbell Craig, *Destroying the Village: Eisenhower and Thermonuclear War* (New York: Columbia University Press, 1998); and Andreas Wenger, *Living With Peril: Eisenhower, Kennedy, and Nuclear Weapons* (Lanham, MD: Rowman & Littlefield, 1997).

7. In a 1991 review essay, political scientist Robert Jervis wrote, "Because of their perceived importance, novelty, and menace, strategic nuclear weapons have generally held our attention. There are fewer studies of the confused programs for tactical nuclear weapons.... A more complete picture will require scholars to fill in these large areas." See Robert Jervis, "The Military History of the Cold War," *Diplomatic History* 15, no. 1 (Winter 1991): 91–113 (quotation p. 93).

1 The Origins of Nuclear Air Defense Arms

1. Major General K.F. Cramer, quoted in James Meikle Eglin, *Air Defense in the Nuclear Age: The Post-War Development of American and Soviet Strategic Defense Systems* (New York: Garland Publishing, 1988), p. 54.

2. Mary T. Cagle, *Development, Production, and Deployment of the Nike Ajax Guided Missile System, 1945–1959* (Redstone Arsenal, Alabama: Army Guided Missile Agency), n.d., pp. 2–3; Mary T. Cagle, *History*

of the Nike Hercules Weapon System (U.S. Army Missile Command: Redstone Arsenal, Alabama), 1973, p. 3; Trevor N. Dupuy, *The Evolution of Weapons and Warfare* (Da Capo Press: New York, 1984), pp. 270–271; Kenneth Schaffel, *The Emerging Shield: The Air Force and the Evolution of Continental Air Defense, 1945–1960* (Washington: Office of Air Force History, 1991), p. 99; Walter M. Vann, "Antiaircraft Defense," *Military Review*, vol. 37, January 58: 61–66; U.S. Army, *History of Strategic Air and Ballistic Missile Defense: Volume I, 1945–1955* (Washington: Center of Military History, c. 1975), pp. 119–123; and "Can Wolf Pack Interception Pay Off?" *Air Force Magazine* (March 1954): 37. For a description of early postwar mathematical calculations inherent in situating guns and interceptors to yield the maximum possible target engagement time, see James Randall Larkins, "The International Aspects of Air Defense of the United States Against Attack by Hostile Aircraft," Georgetown University master's thesis, 1959, pp. 31–46.
3. Roy S. Barnard, *The History of ARADCOM, Volume 1, the Gun Era: 1950–1955* (U.S. Army, n.d.) p. 27.
4. Richard F. McMullen, *History of Air Defense Weapons; 1946–1962* A[ir] D[efense] C[ommand] Historical Study no. 14 (n.p.: Air Defense Command, n.d.); and Cagle, *Ajax*.
5. "Soviet Capabilities and Intentions; N[ational] I[ntelligence] E[stimate]-3," *Declassified Documents Reference System* (hereafter *DDRS*), no. CK3100426846, p. 4; and S. Nelson Drew, ed. (with analysis by Paul H. Nitze), *NSC-68: Forging the Strategy of Containment* (Washington: National Defense University Press, 1994). For a discussion of the bomber estimates that were considered in the preparation of NSC 68, see Lawrence Aronsen, "Seeing Red: U.S. Air Force Assessments of the Soviet Union, 1945–1949, *Intelligence and National Security*, vol. 16, no. 2, Summer 2001): 103–132, especially p. 124.
6. Jeffrey A. Engel, "The Surly Bonds: American Cold War Constraints on British Aviation," *Enterprise & Society: The International Journal of Business History* (March 2005, vol. 6 no. 1): 1–44.
7. Schaffel, pp. 130–131; For the details of the TU-4 story, see Von Hardesy, "Made in the USSR," *Air & Space Smithsonian* (February/March 2001): 68–79.
8. S. Nelson Drew, ed., *NSC-68*.
9. Schaffel, p. 131.
10. The U.S. Navy fielded nuclear antiaircraft weapons for defending ships at sea. The service also had unrelated continental defense responsibilities, including operating radar-bearing "picket ships" offshore. For details, see Joseph F. Bouchard, "Guarding the Cold War Ramparts: The U.S. Navy's Role in Continental Air Defense," *Navy War College Review* (Summer 1999, vol. 52, no. 3).
11. Robert J. Watson, *History of the Joint Chiefs of Staff: The Joint Chiefs and National Policy, Vol. V, 1953–1954* (Washington: Historical Division, Joint Chiefs of Staff, 1986), pp. 112–115.
12. Richard M. Leighton, *Strategy, Money, and the New Look, 1953–1956: History of the Office of the Secretary of Defense, Vol. III* (Washington:

Office of the Secretary of Defense, 2001), pp. 116–117; Watson, pp. 118–119.
13. Schaffel, pp. 83–167.
14. Schaffel, p. 100; Jay Miller, "The Scorpion; A Pictorial Report," *Air University Review* (vol. 31, no. 5, July–August 1980).
15. McMullen, *Air Defense Weapons*, p. 88.
16. McMullen, *Air Defense Weapons*, pp. 79–80; and W.H.C. Higgins, B.D. Holbrook, and J.W. Emling, "Electrical Computers for Fire Control," in M.D. Fagan, ed., *A History of Engineering and Science in the Bell System: National Service in War and Peace (1925–1975)*, vol. 2 (New York: Bell Telephone Laboratories, 1975), pp. 133–135.
17. McMullen, *Air Defense Weapons*, pp. 108, 89, 157, 277–280.
18. McMullen, *Air Defense Weapons*, p. 89.
19. Larry Davis and Dave Menard, *F-89 Scorpion in Action* (Carrollton, TX: Squadron/Signal Publications, 1990), p. 18; McMullen, *Air Defense Weapons*, p. 157.
20. Davis and Menard, p. 18. For an account of (unintentionally) being on the receiving end of all 104 FFARs fired by an F-89, see O.H. Billman, "Basic Instinct," *Air and Space Smithsonian*, August/September 2004, pp. 16–17.
21. See "A-Bombs for Air Defense," *Air Force Magazine* (July 1952): 21–24, 53. This periodical is the authoritative publication of the private Air Force Association, and is a reliable source for information. This account of a plan "being considered at the highest levels" to use "atomic warheads for air defense" echoes the summary of the 1951 study provided in *Nuclear Weapons in the Air Defense System: Special Historical Study no. 2*, n.p., [September 1953?], p. 2 (provided by special courtesy of John Pike of globalsecurity.org. This document is also apparently sometimes known as Denys Volan, *The Use of Nuclear Weapons in Air Defense, 1952–1953*.). Over the next eighteen months, there was other public speculation about the possibility of nuclear air-defense weapons. Lloyd Berkner, a famed physicist who led the organization which ran the AEC's Brookhaven Laboratories, told the National Conference of Editorial Writers in October 1953 that defenses against a bomber raid could be improved by, among other steps, undertaking research to "break up formations over the sea or uninhabited land wastes with atomic weapons." (See Allan A. Needell, *Science, Cold War, and the American State: Lloyd V. Berkner and the Balance of Professional Ideals* (Amsterdam: Harwood Academic Publishers, 2000), p. 251. Months later, in a journal article, Berkner approvingly cited a suggestion by Representative W. Sterling Cole "that in our defense we use atomic 'warheads in such profusion that an enemy seeking to penetrate our defenses would be confronted by a barrage of atomic firepower.'" See Lloyd V. Berkner, "Continental Defense," *Current History* 26, no. 153 (May 1954): 257–262.
22. *Nuclear Weapons in the Air Defense System*, p. 2.
23. "A-Bombs for Air Defense," and "Small Atomic Bombs 'Planned' to Smash Enemy Air Attack," *Washington Post*, June 23, 1952, p. 1.

24. Chuck Hansen, *Swords of Armageddon*, CD-ROM (1995), Table 4-11, p.1; *Nuclear Weapons in the Air Defense System*, p. 5; McMullen, *Air Defense Weapons*, pp. 158–159. For Heavenbound's reference to BOMARC, see Thomas W. Ray, *BOMARC and Nuclear Armament*, A[ir] D[efense] C[ommand] Historical Study no. 21 (n.p.: Air Defense Command, n.d.), p. 3.
25. McMullen, *Air Defese Weapons*, pp. 90–91.
26. Margaret C. Bagwell, *History of the BOMARC Weapon System: 1953–1957* (Wright-Patterson Air Force Base, [Ohio]: Air Materiel Command, 1959), pp. 2–7, 12–14.
27. *Nuclear Weapons in the Air Defense System*, pp. 1–3; Richard F. McMullen, *Interceptor Missiles in Air Defense: 1944–1964* (A[ir] D[efense] C[ommand] Historical Study no. 30), February 1965, p. 33.
28. Bagwell, pp. 2–7.
29. Barnard, pp. 53–55, 79–81.
30. For a complete weapon system history, see Cagle, *Ajax*. For the source of the date of the final test series, see Cagle, *Ajax*, p. 81.
31. Stanley Ulanoff, *Illustrated Guide to U.S. Missiles and Rockets* (Garden City, New York: Doubleday & Company, 1959), pp. 20–22.
32. The first Nike missiles were deployed in 1954. For further details about three typical sites, including the first permanent emplacement in the nation and two other batteries near the District of Columbia, see Christopher John Bright, "Nike Defends Washington: Antiaircraft Missiles in Fairfax County, Virginia, During the Cold War, 1954–74," *Virginia Magazine of History and Biography* (vol. 105, no.3, Summer 1997): 317–346.
33. Cagle, *Ajax*, pp. 154–155, Cagle, *Hercules*, pp. 15, 35.
34. Cagle, *Hercules*, pp. 35–37.
35. *Nuclear Weapons in the Air Defense System*, p. 5 and Memorandum, Department of Defense Armed Forces Special Weapons Project, subject: Atomic Weapons Test at High Altitudes, Department of Energy/Nevada Nuclear Testing Archive accession no. NV0061778 (hereafter "DOE/NV no."). According to an informed source, the Joint Air Defense Board was organized by the Air Force Chief of Staff in 1952 to coordinate interservice air-defense activities. The source says this origin makes the "joint" nature of the panel questionable and cites senior Army criticism. See *History of Strategic Air and Ballistic Missile Defense*, p. 146.
36. For W-12 dimensions, Ray, *BOMARC*, p. 4; a heavier weight is specified in Hansen, *Swords of Armageddon*, Table A-2, p. 1. For conventional warhead consideration, see Bagwell, pp. 41–42 and Ray, *BOMARC*, p. 7. For consideration of W-12 for BOMARC, Ray, *BOMARC* pp. 4–5; and "A History of the Air Force Atomic Energy Program, 1943–1953," vol. IV, Nuclear History document collection, item no. NH00014, National Security Archive, unpaginated last page (chart entitled "Appendix to Chapter XIV; Development Status in 1953 of Warheads for Guided Missiles,"); "Semiannual Historical Report; Headquarters, Field Command, the Armed Forces Special Weapons Command, Sandia Base,

Albuquerque, New Mexico, 1 July 1953–31 December 1953," p. 235 (uncataloged collection, National Security Archive); and Bagwell, p. 40.
37. Cagle, *Hercules*, pp. 35–40.
38. Cagle, *Hercules*, pp. 35–40. The renaming occurred in November 1956. For naming conventions, see "List of Ordnance Corps Guided Missile Projects with Type Designation and Popular Names," which is Appendix 9 in Cagle, *Ajax*, pp. 250–254. For ease of identification, "Hercules" is used in this study henceforth to refer to the second missile version, even in references prior to the date of formal redesignation.
39. Ulanoff, pp. 24–25.
40. Cagle, *Hercules*, pp. 35–40.
41. Richard G. Hewlett and Oscar E. Anderson, Jr., *Atomic Shield: A History of the United States Atomic Energy Commission, Vol. II, 1947–1952* (Berkeley: University of California Press, 1990); Doris M. Condit, *History of the Office of the Secretary of Defense, Vol. II: The Test of War, 1950–1953* (Washington: Historical Office, Office of the Secretary of Defense, 1988) pp. 467–473; Walter S. Poole, *History of the Joint Chiefs of Staff: The Joint Chiefs and National Policy, Vol. IV, 1950–1952* (Wilmington, DE: Michael Glazier, Inc., 1980), pp. 142–250.
42. Chuck Hansen, *U.S. Nuclear Weapons: The Secret History* (Arlington, TX: Aerofax, 1988), pp. 20–32, 105. See also document with crossed-out caption "Weapon Program Background Information for Study Relative Effects of a Limitation on Test Operations," p. 49, in Chuck Hansen Collection, Box 22, Folder 4, National Security Archive (hereafter "Hansen Collection"); and "History of the Air Force Atomic Energy Program." Unfortunately, most page numbers of the latter document are missing or illegible, making precise references impossible. In the Hansen Collection, most folders are unnamed but are arranged chronologically. Folder numbers are assigned for each box in ascending order from the oldest date to the most recent.
43. See "United States Atomic Energy Commission, Program Status Report to the Joint Committee on Atomic Energy, Part III—Weapons," December 31, 1958, p. 9, in Hansen Collection, Box 28, Folder 4; "Weapon Program Background Information," p. 49.
44. "Weapon Program Background Information" p. 49; Memorandum to Brigadier General Alfred D. Starbird from K.F. Hertford, Subject: XW-7 X3 Nike-B PROGRAM, February 24, 1954, DOE/NV no. NV0103942. In-flight insertion is described in Necah Stewart Furman, *Sandia National Laboratories: The Postwar Decade* (Albuquerque: University of New Mexico Press, 1990), pp. 410–411.
45. "Summary of Major Events and Problems of the [Army] Ordnance Corps, July 1955–June 1956," p. 44, call no. 40-2.1 AA 1956, in the collection of the U.S. Army Center of Military History (hereafter "USACMH"). This report says two warhead versions, yielding two and twenty-two kilotons, were "under consideration" at the time and that one type was scheduled for operational availability in October 1958. Two years later, an equivalent annual report noted that Nike-Hercules with W-7 warheads had been deployed and that tests were *initiated* on adapting a

twenty-eight-kiloton warhead while W-31 tests *continued*. Since the W-31 supplanted the W-7 shortly thereafter, it's likely that the W-7 and its W-31 replacement both yielded two kilotons and the higher yield W-7 was not fielded. See "Summary of Major Events and Problems of the [Army] Ordnance Corps, July 1957–June 1958," p. 44, call no. 40-2.1 AA 1958, USACMH.
46. John Malik, "The Yields of the Hiroshima and Nagasaki Nuclear Explosions," Los Alamos National Laboratory, September 1985, LA-8819.
47. *Nuclear Weapons in the Air Defense System*, footnote 2, p. 1 lists "USAF OOA Working Paper No. 25, 'A Generalized Study of the Effects of Atomic Bomb Explosions on Aircraft in Flight," July 18, 1951, and "Tech. Memo T-131, 'A Preliminary Study of Aircraft Vulnerability to Atomic Explosions," December 15, 1951. Paul W. Ifland, "The Relative Importance of Nuclear Radiation from Atomic Weapons Detonated at High Altitudes," Technical Analysis Report-A[rmed] F[orces] S[pecial] W[eapons] P[roject] No. 500, April 23, 1953, attached to transmittal memorandum dated May 28, 1953, both of which comprise DOE/NV no. NV017352, bases some of its analysis on 1951 "Buster" nuclear tests. See, for example, p. 23.
48. Frank H. Shelton, *Reflections of a Nuclear Weaponeer* (Colorado Springs: Shelton Enterprises, 1988), pp. 7-3 to 7-8; Luedecke memorandum to Assistant Chief of Staff, G-4, Department of the Army, subject: Atomic Weapons Test at High Altitudes, October 9, 1953, DOE/NV no. NV0061778.
49. Ifland, including pp. 9, 15.
50. Leighton, p. 114–115.
51. The following policy discussions, with slightly different interpretations, are summarized in Leighton, pp. 114–149; Watson, pp. 111–148; and Joseph T. Jockel, "The United States and Canadian Efforts at Continental Air Defense: 1945–1957," unpublished PhD dissertation, Johns Hopkins University, 1978. For an earlier overview of the Eisenhower approach, written before most primary documents were available, see Samuel P. Huntington, *The Common Defense: Strategic Programs in National Politics* (New York: Columbia University Press, 1966) pp. 326–41. This latter study overemphasizes the connection of NSC 162 to continental defense. Also providing a slightly dated overview is Eglin, *Air Defense in the Nuclear Age*.
52. "Report to the National Security Council by the Secretaries of State and Defense and the Director for Mutual Security," (NSC 141), January 19, 1953, in *Foreign Relations of the United States, 1952–1954*, vol. II, part 1, National Security Affairs (Government Printing Office: Washington, 1984), pp. 209–22 (hereafter identified as *FRUS* with year, volume, and page specified).
53. "Memorandum of Discussion at the 131st Meeting of the National Security Council, Wednesday, February 11, 1953," *FRUS, 1952–1954*, vol. II, part 1, pp. 236–237. Two scholars argue that memoranda of discussion of NSC meetings very faithfully reproduce the sentiments

expressed (based upon one scholar's evaluation of memoranda summarizing meetings he attended). Therefore, unless noted otherwise, quotations drawn from such memoranda will be attributed to individuals as if they actually spoke the words. See Robert R. Bowie and Richard H. Immerman, *Waging Peace: How Eisenhower Shaped an Enduring Cold War Strategy* (Oxford: Oxford University Press, 1998), p. 6.

54. "Report to the National Security Council by the Executive Secretary (Lay)," NSC 149/2, *FRUS, 1952–1954*, vol. II, part 1, pp. 305–308. The quotation is on p. 308. For a discussion of this period, see Bowie and Immerman, pp. 99–107.
55. Leighton, pp. 69, 118–119.
56. "Report to the National Security Council by the Executive Secretary (Lay)," NSC 140, *FRUS, 1952–1954*, vol. II, part 1, pp. 205–206; "Report to the National Security Council by the Special Evaluation Subcommittee of the National Security Council," NSC 140/1 in *FRUS, 1952–1954*, vol. II, part 1, pp. 328–49. The president and NSC were briefed by Edwards on his report on June 4, 1953, but they took no formal action.
57. "Memorandum by the Secretary of the Joint Chiefs of Staff (Lalor) to the Executive Secretary of the National Security Council (Lay)," *FRUS, 1952–1954*, vol. II, part 1, pp. 355–356.
58. See "Memorandum of Discussion at the 148th Meeting of the National Security Council, Thursday, June 4, 1953," *FRUS, 1952–1954*, vol. II, part 1, pp. 367–370. For further discussion, see Valerie L. Adams, *Eisenhower's Fine Group of Fellows: Crafting a National Security Policy to Uphold the Great Equation* (Lanham, Maryland: Lexington Books, 2006), p. 90.
59. The Bull group also reviewed continental defense proposals developed by the services pursuant to NSC 139, adopted late in the Truman administration (for NSC 139, see *FRUS, 1952–1954*, vol. VI, pp. 2063–2064). See also Leighton, pp. 116–117, 121; and Watson, pp. 121–123. On the origin and outcome of the Kelly study, see Watson, pp. 119–20. For Planning Board description, see Bowie and Immerman, p. 91, and Adams, pp. 91–92.
60. See "A Report to the National Security Council by the Continental Defense Committee on Continental Defense," NSC 159, 22 July 1953, *DDRS* no. CK2349431349, and *FRUS, 1952–1954*, part 1, II, note 2, p. 465–466. For Bull's background, see "Retired Lt. Gen. Harold Bull Dies at 83, Former National War College Chief," *Washington Post*, November 3, 1976, p. B12. For Bull's nickname, see *History of Strategic Air and Ballistic Missile Defense*, p. 26.
61. NSC 159, p. 4.
62. NSC 159, including pp. 54–55.
63. "Minutes of the 158th Meeting of the National Security Council [August 6, 1953]," Folder "NSC Agenda and Minutes—1953 (7)," Box 1, NSC Series, Administrative Subseries, White House Office [hereafter "WHO"], Office of Special Assistant for National Security Affairs [hereafter "OSANSA"], Records, 1952–61, Dwight D. Eisenhower Presidential Library (hereafter "DDEL"). Leighton, pp. 124–125; Watson, p. 127.

64. Leighton, p. 128.
65. See "Discussion at the 163rd Meeting of the National Security Council, Thursday, September 24, 1953," September 25, 1953, *DDRS* no. CK3100158631.
66. *FRUS, 1952–1954*, vol. II, part 1, note 2, pp. 465–466.
67. "A Report to the National Security Council by the Executive Secretary on Continental Defense," NSC 159/4, September 25, 1953, *DDRS* no. CK3100217465, including p. 20. NSC 159/3 cannot be located but is described in *FRUS, 1952–1954*, vol. II, part 1, notes 2 and 3, pp. 465–466. However, meeting minutes reflect the changes made to NSC 159/3 to yield NSC 159/4. (See "Discussion at the 163rd Meeting of the National Security Council.") Because none of the changes affected quoted portions of NSC 159/4, it can be assumed that those sections were originally reflected in NSC 159/3 and were carried over into the subsequent version.
68. "Views of the NSC Consultants on Continental Defense," September 24, 1953, *DDRS* no. CK3100122235. For the appointment of the consultants, see "Editorial Note," *FRUS, 1952–1954*, vol. II, part 1, p. 244. For further background on each, see Edward T. Folliard, "Ike Security Council Meets Today to Ponder Defense Needs Against Any H-Bomb Blitz," *Washington Post*, September 24, 1953, p. 6. A Republican, Baxter was the historian for the Office of Scientific Research and Development during World War II, and the winner of the 1947 Pulitzer for a book about the OSRD's accomplishments. See Alden Whitman, "James P. Baxter 3d Dies; Ex-President of Williams," *New York Times*, June 19, 1975, p. 38. See also, Adams, p. 92.
69. Watson, pp. 17–18; Bowie and Immerman, p. 184.
70. Jockel, p. 190; Watson, p. 129; JCS comments are in "A Report to the National Security Council by the Joint Chiefs of Staff on Continental Defense," NSC 159/2, September 1, 1953, Folder "Continental Defense 1953 (4)," Box 22, Disaster File Series, WHO, NSC Staff, Papers, 1948–61, DDEL.
71. "Discussion at the 163rd Meeting of the National Security Council."
72. NSC 159/4 and "Discussion at the 163rd Meeting of the National Security Council."
73. Watson, pp. 26–29; and "Discussion at the 176th Meeting of the National Security Council, Wednesday, December 16, 1953," December 17, 1953, *DDRS* no. 3100236231. Quotes are from Bowie and Immerman, pp. 194–195.
74. Watson, pp. 130–; Jockel, pp. 191–192. Leighton, p. 129, argues that the request for financial specifics in 159/4 was intended to force the continental defense document to be reconciled with NSC 162.
75. Bowie and Immerman, p. 146.
76. "Report to the National Security Council by the Executive Secretary (Lay)," NSC 162/2, *FRUS, 1952–1954*, vol II, part 1, pp. 577–597. Quote is p. 593. Continental defense references on pp. 579, 583, 591.
77. Jockel, pp. 192–195; Leighton, pp. 131–135; and Watson, pp. 131–132.
78. "Discussion at the 172nd Meeting of the National Security Council, Monday, November 23, 1953," November 24, 1953, *DDRS* no. CK3100333071.

79. Information in author's possession, provided by very special courtesy of David F. Krugler.
80. "Discussion at the 176th meeting"; Bowie and Immerman, pp. 194–197. Watson, pp. 28–29.
81. "Discussion at the 176th meeting"; Bowie and Immerman, pp. 194–197; Watson, pp. 28–29; Leighton, p. 135; Jockel, pp. 192–195.
82. "Discussion at the 180th Meeting of the National Security Council, Thursday, January 14, 1954," January 15, 1954, *DDRS* no. 3100125868. Twining's presentation also formed the basis of a "Special Annex" to NSC 5408. For this point, see "Memorandum for Colonel Bonesteel," January 21, 1954, in Folder "Continental Defense 1954 (2)," Box 22, Disaster File Series, WHO, NSC Staff, Papers, 1948–61, DDEL; the supplementary document is "Special Annex to NSC 159/5," February 3, 1954, *DDRS* no. CK3100218962.
83. "Discussion at the 180th Meeting."
84. "Memorandum of Discussion at the 185th Meeting of the National Security Council, Wednesday, February 17, 1954," *FRUS, 1952–1954,* vol. II, part 1, pp. 624–628.
85. On December 23, 1953, the president approved a new NSC paper number system, which replaced the protocol that had been in existence since the council's creation. The new system combined the last two digits of the year of a paper's origination with a number representing its sequence among those issued that year. Thus, NSC 5408 was the eighth paper to be circulated by the NSC in 1954. See Memorandum, "Subject: Discussion at the 177th Meeting of the National Security Council, Wednesday, December 23, 1953," December 24, 1953, *DDRS* no. CK3100162429.
86. "Draft Statement of Policy Proposed by the National Security Council," [NSC 5408], February 11, 1953, *FRUS, 1952–1954,* vol. II, part 1, pp. 611–24. Appendices are "Special Annex" cited above and "Financial Appendix," *DDRS* no. CK3100209043.
87. "Memorandum to Brig. General C. H. Bonesteel," January 28, 1954, in Folder "Continental Defense 1954 (2)," Box 22, Disaster File Series, WHO, NSC Staff, Papers, 1948–61, DDEL. Robert Cutler drafted the NSC 5408 "Special Annex" (see citation above). It listed defense details that Cutler thought necessary for the council to have, but that he also wanted to keep out of the main body of the policy paper for stylistic reasons. Among other items, the annex projected the number and location criteria for the deployment of antiaircraft forces. Unlike NSC 159, it did not mention nuclear warheads in connection with either BOMARC or Nike, although this was not a substantive omission. See "Memorandum to Brig. General C. H. Bonesteel"; "Draft Statement of Policy Proposed by the National Security Council," [NSC 5408]; and "Special Annex."
88. McMullen, *Air Defense Weapons,* pp. 108, 89, 157, 277–280.
89. Schaffel, p. 233.
90. McMullen, *Air Defense Weapons,* p. 159.
91. Hansen, *U.S. Nuclear Weapons,* pp. 180–181; *Nuclear Weapons in the Air Defense System,* pp. 6–7, 9.

92. Hansen, *U.S. Nuclear Weapons*, pp. 180–181; *Nuclear Weapons in the Air Defense System*, p. 10.
93. McMullen, *Air Defense Weapons*, p. 160; and *Nuclear Weapons in the Air Defense System*, p. 10. This history says the Air Force sought warheads for "guided air rockets," which is confused terminology as noted in the text above. Based upon the context and the events which followed, this is properly a reference to an unguided rocket.
94. The Rand report, Research Memorandum 1100, remains classified. Based on redactions in another Rand document, it appears that even the study's number and issue date are (were?) classified, but because the redactions were done incautiously, these details are nonetheless discernable. See E.J. Barlow, *Active Air Defense of the United States: 1954–1960*, R-250 (abridged) (Santa Monica, California: Rand Corporation, December 1, 1953). RM-1100 is described on pp. 77–78, although both the number and issue date are redacted in the associated footnote. However, the number is revealed in footnotes to Table 14 on p. 117. In addition, p. 153 contains a chronological listing of Research Memoranda. Because the entries before and after RM-1100 survive intact, it is possible to determine the period in which that report was issued. R-250 was provided by very special courtesy of Professor Joseph Jockel of St. Lawrence University, Canton, New York.
95. Barlow, pp. 77–78.
96. In outlining the best possible American defense network to counter what was assumed to be a typical Soviet "intercontinental manned bomber" attack, the Rand document supported the use of BOAR, Nike-Hercules, and the nuclear BOMARC against groups of planes. Rand claimed they could increase defense effectiveness by twenty-five to one hundred percent, thus compensating for the high development costs of the weapons and their atomic warheads. Probably because RAND was affiliated with the Air Force, and Army information was consequently not readily available, the report is confused about the Nike program. For example, it suggests that equipping the new Nike with a nuclear warhead should be considered, oblivious to the fact that the missile was being developed *specifically* for that purpose. See Barlow, pp. 2–3, 76–77, 81, 84–86.
97. "MB-1 'Genie'" in Folder "Genie Missile Documents," Box 52, Desind Collection, Archives Division, National Air and Space Museum.
98. Robert LeBaron [Chairman, Military Liaison Committee] memorandum to Chairman, Atomic Energy Commission, April 2, 1954, in Hansen Collection, Box 19, Folder 3; "Chronology of Significant Events and Decision Relating to the U.S. Missile and Earth Satellite Development Programs, May 1942 Through October 1957," Historical Section, Joint Chiefs of Staff, November 22, 1957, Nuclear History document collection, item no. NH00006, National Security Archive, p. 37. One source almost certainly erroneously describes the origins of the nuclear rocket by suggesting that an Air Force report dated June 8, 1953 (and almost certainly written weeks before) declared "some" interceptors would be armed with such a weapon "by 1955." (See Watson, pp. 122–123.) Before June 1953, the Air Force had yet to determine if an atomic rocket

was feasible, much less authorize its development and estimate a date of availability.
99. McMullen, *Air Defense Weapons*, p. 291. After 1961, as part of a comprehensive Air Force renumbering effort, the MB-1 was designated AIR-2A. MB-1 and Genie are used interchangeably throughout the text, regardless of date. Some sources erroneously attribute the additional code name "Bird Dog" to Genie. However, Bird Dog was a type of high-explosive rocket with large fragmentation warhead. See Barlow, p. 79.
100. McMullen, *Air Defense Weapons*, p. 291; "Appendix A" in R.A. Kirkman and D.K. Wade, *Armament System Specification, F-106A Weapon System*, [publication no.] ZQ-8-009 (San Diego: Convair, December 1957) in Hansen Collection, Box 25, Folder 2.
101. Thomas W. Ray, *Nuclear Armament: Its Acquisition, Control, and Application to Manned Interceptors, 1951–1963*; A[ir] D[efense] C[ommand] Historical Study No. 20 (n.p.: Air Defense Command, n.d.), pp. 20–21 (also provided by special courtesy of John Pike of globalsecurity.org).
102. Ray, *Nuclear Armament*, pp. 4–5.
103. "Minutes: Forty-first Meeting of the General Advisory Committee to the U.S. Atomic Energy Commission," July 12, 13, 14, 15, 1954, p. 3, Hansen Collection, Box 20, Folder 3. The GAC expressed no opposition to the expedited work plan as outlined. Curiously, just three months earlier, days before the W-25 warhead for the Genie was authorized, members spoke out about "the possible use of large numbers of small bombs for air defense, and the fall-out hazards which this would entail." They suggested that the use of "atomic weapons in defense against airplanes should be thoroughly examined." (See "Minutes: Thirty-ninth Meeting of the General Advisory Committee to the U.S. Atomic Energy Commission," March 31, April 1, 2, 1954, pp. 1–2, Hansen Collection, Box 19, Folder 3.) This attitudinal change is difficult to explain except by suggesting that the initial objections rested on the misinformed or outdated presumption that the yield of the "small bombs" to be used was much larger than that which was actually proposed.
104. For yield, see "MB-1 Atomic Air-to-Air Rocket," Department of Defense fact sheet, *DDRS* no. CK3100213098; and "Memorandum for Admiral Radford, Subject: Report of Field Trip with NESC Staff," p. 5, *DDRS* no. 3100460496. For Los Alamos design responsibility, see Hansen, *U.S. Nuclear Weapons*, p. 176.
105. "Program Status Report to the Joint Committee on Atomic Weapons, Part III—Weapons," United States Atomic Energy Commission, December 31, 1958, p 9, Hansen Collection, Box 28, Folder 4. These figures vary slightly in some sources.
106. Hansen, *Swords of Armageddon*, p. VII-91.
107. Ray, *Nuclear Armament*, p. 5
108. *Recollections for Tomorrow: 1949–1989* (Sandia National Laboratories, 1989), 10–11; Furman, pp. 660–662; "Minutes: Forty-first Meeting of the General Advisory Committee," p. 3.

109. NSC 162/2, p. 593. An alternative assessment which makes NSC 162/2 central to Genie's development is Peter Roman, "Ike's Hair-Trigger: U.S. Nuclear Predelegation, 1953–60," *Security Studies* 7, no. 4 (Summer 1998): 121–64, especially pp. 122–27. The central topic of this essay is engaged in chapter 3.
110. For a discussion of alternative outcomes in the absence of NSC 162, see Jockel, p. 195.
111. Davis and Menard, p. 18.
112. "The Atomic Energy Program: Semiannual Status Report to the President as of December 31, 1953," U.S. Atomic Energy Commission, February 1, 1954, Hansen Collection, Box 19, Folder 1.

2 Robert Sprague's "Adequate Defense"

1. Despite his significance to continental-defense planning in the Eisenhower administration, there is relatively scant coverage of Robert Sprague in the historical literature. One exceptional work, which properly situates him among Ike's influential advisors ("one individual proved enormously helpful") is Valerie L. Adams, *Eisenhower's Fine Group of Fellows: Crafting a National Security Policy to Uphold the Great Equation* (Lanham, Maryland: Lexington Books, 2006), especially pp. 97–100 (quotation p. 97).
2. Frederick Dalzell, *Engineering Invention: Frank J. Sprague and the U.S. Electrical Industry* (Cambridge, MA: MIT Press, 2010), p. 233; "Robert C. Sprague, 91; Began Sprague Electric," *New York Times*, October 1, 1991, p. D23. Sprague's papers are held by the Dwight D. Eisenhower presidential library. As of November 2004, they had not been opened to researchers and no timetable for such existed.
3. Harold C. Passer, *The Electrical Manufacturers, 1875–1900: A Study in Competition, Entrepreneurship, Technical Change, and Economic Growth* (Cambridge: Harvard University Press, 1953), pp. 232–248.
4. "Sprague," *New York Times*; "Robert C. Sprague, [Dies] at 91; Invented Radio Control, Started N. Adams Firm," *Boston Globe*, September 28, 1991, p. 30; Robert C. Duncan, "Robert C. Sprague; 1900–1991," *Memorial Tributes*, vol. 6 (Washington: National Academy of Engineering, 1993), pp. 217–219. For product line, see Sprague Electric advertisement in *Signal*, March 1959, p. 4, in collection of National Air and Space Museum archives, file no. ON-30010-01.
5. B. Bruce-Biggs, *The Shield of Faith: A Chronicle of Strategic Defense from Zepplins to Star Wars* (New York: Simon and Schuster, 1988), pp. 82–83.
6. "Chicago Lawyer is Named Under Secretary of Air," *New York Times*, February 21, 1953, p. 2; Richard D. Challener, interviewer, "A Transcript of a Recorded Interview with Robert Sprague," John Foster Dulles Oral History Project, Princeton University Library, August 1964, pp. 2–3. Sprague planned to take special steps to insulate himself from his business interests in light of objections raised in the nomination of Defense Secretary Charles Wilson, deputy Roger M. Kyes, and others. See

"Sprague Passes Up Air Force Post; Refuses to Sell $5,000,000 Stock," *New York Times*, February 11, 1953, p. 1.
7. Thomas P. Hughes, *Rescuing Prometheus* (New York: Random House, 1998), pp. 43–44. Similarly, Fairfax County, Virginia, can trace the origins of its substantial computer systems integration and telecommunications industrial base to the establishment there of an East Coast branch of the System Development Corporation, the Rand subsidiary given the responsibility of writing the SAGE software. See Claude Baum, *The System Builders: The Story of SDC* (Santa Monica, California: System Development Corporation, 1981) and Paul Ceruzzi, *Internet Alley: High Technology in Tysons Corner, 1945–2005* (Cambridge: MIT Press, 2008).
8. See, for example, Stewart Alsop, "Candor is Not Enough," *Washington Post*, September 18, 1953, p. 23; James Reston, "Atom 'Candor' Lacks It; President Started Out to 'Tell All' on TV, but Budget Battles Clouded the Picture," *New York Times*, September 23, 1953, p. 18; Drew Pearson, "Defense of Economy: Up to Ike," *Washington Post*, September 24, 1953, p. 43; and Edward T. Folliard, "Ike, Security Council Meets Today to Ponder Defense Needs Against Any H-Bomb Blitz," *Washington Post*, September 24, 1953, p. 6. The latter is a reference to the NSC's consideration of NSC 159/3.
9. "Eisenhower Urges Atomic Stockpiles for Defense of U.S.; In Talk Before Church Women, He Cites Need for Protection Against Plans of Russia," *New York Times*, October 7, 1953, p. 1; "The Text of President Eisenhower's Address Before United Church Women," *New York Times*, October 7, 1953, p. 3; Clayton Knowles, "Bomb Statement Praised by Cole; But Congressman Would Have Estimate of Defense, Too—Kefauver for Inquiry," *New York Times*, October 9, 1953, p. 15.
10. Knowles, *New York Times*, October 9, 1953.
11. John D. Morris, "Senators to Study Atomic Defenses; Industrialist is Named to Head Project as Kefauver Calls for 'Complete Review,'" *New York Times*, October 11, 1953, p. 1. The following section is also recounted briefly in David L. Snead, *The Gaither Committee, Eisenhower, and the Cold War* (Columbus: Ohio State University Press, 1999), pp. 52–56.
12. Robert Cutler, *No Time for Rest* (Boston: Little, Brown, 1966); Jean Hardy, "Eisenhower Aide Robert Cutler Dies," *Washington Post*, May 10, 1974, p. B22; "Robert Cutler is Dead at 78; Aided Eisenhower on Security," *New York Times*, May 10, 1974, p. 40; and Adams, p. 40.
13. Challener, "Interview with Robert Sprague," pp. 3–4. In this portion of the oral interview, Sprague also describes what he considers the single exception to unfettered access to classified data. This access and exception are also addressed in "Memorandum for the Secretary of Defense," from Robert Cutler, October 28, 1953, in Folder "Continental Defense, Study of—by Robert C. Sprague (1953–1954)(1)," Box 2, NSC Series, Subject Subseries, White House Office [hereafter "WHO"], Office of the Special Assistant for National Security Affairs [hereafter "OSANSA"], Records, 1952–61, Dwight D. Eisenhower Library (hereafter "DDEL"); and "Memorandum for the Record," by Robert Cutler, December 11, 1955,

Declassified Documents Reference System (hereafter *DDRS*) no. CK3100456612. One record, compiled four years after Sprague's assignment in the course of an informal inquiry into the leak of the Gaither Committee report, inaccurately recounts details of Sprague's work, probably because the details had become muddled in the period since the work concluded. Therefore, limited reliance should be placed upon "Memorandum for the Files," by James S. Lay, Jr., December 9, 1957, in Folder "Sprague Report [re continental defense]," Box 18, Executive Secretary Subject File, WHO, NSC Staff, Papers, 1948–61, DDEL.

14. "Memorandum for the Record," by R[obert] C[utler], March 2, 1954, in Folder "Continental Defense, Study of—by Robert C. Sprague (1953–1954)(3)," Box 2, NSC Series, Subject Subseries, WHO, OSANSA, Records, 1952–61, DDEL; Challener, "Interview with Robert Sprague," p. 3.
15. "Memorandum for the Record," March 2, 1954.
16. "Memorandum of Discussion at the 185th Meeting of the National Security Council, Wednesday, February 17, 1954," in *Foreign Relations of the United States, 1952–1954*, vol. II, part 1, National Security Affairs (Government Printing Office: Washington, 1984), p. 627 (hereafter identified as *FRUS* with year, volume, and page specified).
17. "Conclusions and Recommendations," February 26, 1954, [and] March 30, 1954, [sic] in Folder "Sprague Report (Cont. Defense)," Box 18, NSC staff papers, Executive Secretariat Subject File, DDEL. A heavily redacted version of this document is available as *DDRS* no. CK3100288527; "Memorandum for the Record," March 2, 1954; Robert Cutler letter to Robert C. Sprague, March 27, 1954, DOE/NV no. NV0406976; Robert Cutler letter to W. Sterling Cole (with attachment), March 10, 1954, DOE/NV no. NV0406887; "Report on Continental Defense to the Senate Armed Services Committee by Robert C. Sprague," March 18, 1954, in Folder "Sprague Robert C. Material," Box 33, Ann W. Whitman Files, Administrative Series, Dwight D. Eisenhower Papers as President, 1953–61, DDEL (portions also in *DDRS* no. CK3100263557).
18. "Memorandum for the Record," March 2, 1954; and "Memorandum for the Chairman, Operations Coordinating Board," from Robert Cutler, March 31, 1954, Department of Energy/Nevada Nuclear Testing Archive accession no. NV0311742 (hereafter "DOE/NV no.").
19. Darrell Garwood, *Washington Post and Times-Herald*, March 26, 1954, p. A10.
20. "U.S. Atom Defense is Called 'Sound,'" *New York Times*, March 26, 1954, p. 5. The general outline of the briefing soon became public, probably because Saltonstall sought to demonstrate that he and his Republican colleagues adequately understood the nation's defense challenge. See "Can the H-Bomb Be Stopped? Fantastic Weapons of Defense Are on the Way," *U.S. News & World Report* 36, no. 16, April 16, 1954: 17–19.
21. "Memorandum for the Record," March 2, 1954; Cutler letter to Sprague, March 27, 1954; Cutler letter to Cole, March 10, 1954.
22. "Memorandum for the Chairman," from Robert Cutler, March 31, 1954; Challener, "Interview with Robert Sprague," p. 3; Robert Cutler letter to

Secretary of Defense, March 31, 1954, in Folder "Sprague Report [re continental defense]," Box 18, Executive Secretary Subject File, WHO, NSC Staff Papers, 1948–61, DDEL. On the point that the president received the sole copy (besides fact that cover bears notation "no. 1 copy of 1") see "Memorandum for the Record," April 21, 1954, in Folder "Sprague Report [re continental defense]," Box 18, Executive Secretary Subject File, WHO, NSC Staff Papers, 1948–61, DDEL.

23. The full report is "Study of Continental Defense for the Interim Subcommittee on Preparedness of the Senate Armed Services Committee by Robert C. Sprague," February 26, 1954, 1954, in Folder "Study of Continental Defense by Robert C. Sprague [February 26, 1954]," Box 2, NSC Series, Subject Subseries, WHO, OSANSA, Records, 1952–61, DDEL; (also in *DDRS* no. CK3100280650). Quotation in p. 21.
24. "Study of Continental Defense," p. 36.
25. "Study of Continental Defense," p. 71.
26. Cutler letter to Secretary of Defense, March 31, 1954; "Memorandum for the Chairman," from Robert Cutler, March 31, 1954 (quotation). For an overview of popular understanding of continental defense challenges of the era, see "The Truth About Our Air Defense," *Air Force Magazine* (May 1953): 25–34, 36; James R. Killian Jr. and A.G. Hill, "For a Continental Defense," *Atlantic* 192, no. 5 (November 1953): 37–41; Charles J.V. Murphy, "The U.S. as a Bombing Target," *Fortune* 9 (November 1953): 118–120, 219–228; and "Don't Count Your Missiles Before They Are Hatched," *Air Force Magazine* (February 1954): 23–27.
27. Challener, "Interview with Robert Sprague," p. 7.
28. "Fishing Boat Crew Reports A-Ash Burns," *Washington Post*, March 16, 1954, p. 8; Lindesay Parrott, "Nuclear Downpour Hit Ship During Test at Bikini—U.S. Inquiry Asked," *New York Times*, March 17, 1954, p. 1; "Fish Put on Japanese Market Feared Tainted by Atom Ash," *Washington Post*, March 17, 1954, p. 10; Lindesay Parrott, "Case of Bikini Fishermen Causes a Furor in Japan," *New York Times*, March 28, 1954, p. E5. For an indication of contemporary public understanding of the capability of the Castle device (estimated to be "at least five times as powerful as the Hiroshima bomb") and thermonuclear weapons in general, see Ben Moreell, "What the H-Bomb Can Do to US Industries," *U.S. News and World Report* (May 7, 1954): 58–64.
29. Challener, "Interview with Robert Sprague," pp. 7–8.
30. Richard M. Leighton, *Strategy, Money, and the New Look, 1953–1956: History of the Office of the Secretary of Defense, Vol. III* (Washington: Office of the Secretary of Defense, 2001), p. 267. John Prados, *The Soviet Estimate: U.S. Intelligence Analysis and Soviet Strategic Forces* (Princeton: Princeton University Press, 1986), p. 41; Gregory W. Pedlow and Donald E. Welzenbach, *The CIA and the U-2 Program, 1954–1974* (Washington: Central Intelligence Agency, 1988), p. 20; R. Cargill Hall, "The Truth about Overflights," *MHQ; the Quarterly Journal of Military History* 9, no. 3 (Spring 1997): 25–39. The Bison was mentioned in a May NSC meeting. See "Discussion at the 197th Meeting of the National Security

Council, Thursday, May 13, 1954," *DDRS* no. CK3100162222. For a discussion of Ike's belief in the necessity of the overflights, see Andrew Goodpaster, "Cold War Overflights: A View from the White House," in *Early Cold War Overflights; Symposium Proceedings, Volume I: Memoirs* (Washington: National Reconnaissance Office, 2003), pp. 37–46.
31. James Meikle Eglin, *Air Defense in the Nuclear Age; the Post-War Development of American and Soviet Strategic Defense Systems* (New York: Garland Publishing, 1988), p. 91.
32. "Supplementary Study of Continental Defense for the Interim Subcommittee on Preparedness of the Senate Armed Services Committee," Robert C. Sprague, June 7, 1954, DOE/NV no. NV0331817.
33. "Memorandum for the Secretary of Defense," from Arthur Radford, June 23, 1954.
34. Discussion at the 203rd Meeting of the National Security Council, Wednesday, June 23, 1954," *DDRS* no. CK3100223809. This document recounts that Strauss termed the forthcoming antiaircraft armament as "a small *megaton* [emphasis added] weapon." This phrase is also credited to Eisenhower when he poses his question to Strauss. This is almost certainly either a mistake in transcription or a verbal gaffe by Strauss, which was repeated by the president. There is no record of an antiaircraft weapon with (or nearly) megatonnage yield being contemplated, and the description and timing fit the *multikiloton* arms under development at the time. This exchange is also mentioned in Gregg Herken, *Cardinal Choices: Presidential Science Advising from the Atomic Bomb to SDI* (New York: Oxford University Press, 1992) p. 89. Background is provided in Richard G. Hewlett and Jack M. Holl, *Atoms for Peace and War, 1953–61: Eisenhower and the Atomic Energy Commission* (Berkeley: University of California Press, 1989), pp. 275–276. Strauss's imperious nature helped lead to the Senate later rejecting his nomination as Secretary of Commerce, one of the few times that Congress has not confirmed a cabinet nominee. More recently, he has been criticized for his role in stripping nuclear physicist Robert Oppenheimer of his security clearance. Strauss was a complicated man. A Jewish Republican patrician from Virginia at a time when allegiance to the Democratic Party was commonplace, he developed a close personal relationship with Eisenhower, and as AEC chairman had the chief executive's full confidence. For a letter from Strauss to Eisenhower expressing thanks for birthday wishes, see Folder "Atomic Energy Commission 1955–56 (8)" Box 4, Ann C. Whitman File, Administration Series, Dwight D. Eisenhower Papers as President, 1953–61, DDEL.) A thorough treatment of Strauss is Richard Pfau, *No Sacrifice Too Great: The Life of Lewis L. Strauss* (Charlottesville: University Press of Virginia, 1984). A less sympathetic evaluation portrays Strauss as a "Manichean" Cold Warrior who was driven by "rigid anticommunism." See Benjamin P. Greene, *Eisenhower, Science Advice, and the Nuclear Test Ban Debate, 1945–1963* (Stanford: Stanford University Press, 2007) (quotation p. 31). Greene notes that Strauss supported Robert Taft, not Eisenhower, for the 1952 Republican presidential nomination. After Ike secured the nomination, Strauss was brought into the campaign to

diversify the effort's advisors. Eisenhower and Strauss had met only a few times and were not personally close when the president appointed the Virginian the AEC chairman. See Greene, p. 30.

35. "Discussion at the 205th Meeting of the National Security Council, Thursday, July 1, 1954," *DDRS* no. CK3100072526. Sprague was appointed June 18. That same day, Cutler wrote to Wilson about a recommendation proffered in Sprague's full report. Cutler told the Defense Secretary that the "[t]he president has received the communication" about the suggestion "from a person in whom he places great confidence...." This vague reference to Sprague is in keeping with the president's instruction to circulate Sprague's recommendations without attribution. However, Cutler's description of Eisenhower's impression of Sprague is apt. Sprague may have reminded Cutler of this recommendation when reporting to the NSC on his first day as a consultant. See "Memorandum for Secretary Wilson," from Robert Cutler, June 18, 1954, in Folder "Continental Defense 1954 (7)," Box 22, Disaster File, WHO, NSC Staff Papers, 1948–61, DDEL. For a review of the purpose of NSC engaging consultants, see Adams, p. 42.

36. "Discussion at the 197th Meeting of the National Security Council, Thursday, May 13, 1954," *DDRS* no. CK3100072459 (note differing redactions from identically captioned document, bearing a different number, cited above).

37. "Memorandum for the Secretary of Defense," from Robert Cutler, October 28, 1953.

38. "Discussion at the 197th Meeting," *DDRS* no. CK3100072459.

39. "Discussion at the 205th Meeting," p. 9.

40. See "Department of Defense Progress Report to National Security Council on Status of Military Continental U.S. Defense Programs as of 1 June 1954," June 25, 1954, Office of Secretary of Defense, *DDRS* no. CK3100440635. Adjacent to a deleted part of a paragraph addressing armament for the F-102, a new jet interceptor under development, Sprague has written "BOAR," probably signifying that the missing language pertains to the since-discounted ADC study of using the Navy bomb as an air-to-air weapon. Two other redactions amid descriptions of "Nike I" capabilities are likely brief mentions of the Nike-Hercules nuclear warhead work underway. BOMARC is discussed, but that section is available in full. There is no security deletion, and hence no discussion of the W-12 development. The handwriting can be identified as Sprague's because it matches the signature on the transmittal page of the report "Meeting the Threat of Surprise Attack" cited below. The BOAR air-to-air bombing possibility was investigated by the Air Force until sometime before November 1954. (See Thomas W. Ray, *Nuclear Armament: Its Acquisition, Control, and Application to Manned Interceptors, 1951–1963*; A[ir] D[efense] C[ommand] Historical Study no. 20 (n.p.: Air Defense Command, n.d.), p. 4.) The progress report, with identical redactions, can be found in Folder "Continental Defense, Study of—by Robert C. Sprague (1953–1954)(6)," Box 2, NSC Series, Subject Subseries, WHO, OSANSA, Records, 1952–61,

DDEL. The author has a declassification request pending for the excised portions.
41. Challener, "Interview with Robert Sprague," p. 9.
42. "Report of Mr. Robert C. Sprague to the National Security Council on Continental Defense," July 1, 1954, in Folder "Continental Defense 1954 (8)," Box 23, Disaster File, WHO, NSC Staff Papers, 1948–61, DDEL. This document was declassified for this project. Sprague's conclusions are also noted in "Memorandum for the National Security Council," July 1, 1954, in Folder "Continental Defense 1954 (8)," Box 23, Disaster File, WHO, NSC Staff Papers, 1948–61, DDEL. Other copies are in Folder "NSC 5408-Continental Defense (2)," Box 9, NSC Series, policy papers Subseries, WHO, OSANSA, Records, 1952–61, DDEL; and portions are in *DDRS* no. CK3100441753. For the establishment of the Net Capabilities Evaluation, see "Discussion at the 201st Meeting of the National Security Council, Wednesday, June 9, 1954," *DDRS* no. CK3100214303. Sprague further summarizes his July 1 evaluation in "Report of Mr. Robert C. Sprague to the National Security Council on Continental Defense," July 29, 1954, in Folder "Sprague Report [re continental defense]," Box 18, Executive Secretary Subject File, WHO, NSC Staff Papers, 1948–61, DDEL. (Curiously, this document is withdrawn from another DDEL file on the basis that it remains classified.) Sprague also remarks on the July 1 report in Challener, "Interview with Robert Sprague," pp. 8–9. The report is also discussed in U.S. Army, *History of Strategic Air and Ballistic Missile Defense: Volume II, 1956–1972* (Washington: Center of Military History, c. 1975), pp. 82–83.
43. For the weather on July 1, 1954, see "National Weather Summary," *Washington Post and Times-Herald*, June 30, 1954, p. 16; "National Weather Summary," *Washington Post and Times-Herald*, July 1, 1954, p. 20; and "National Weather Summary," *Washington Post and Times-Herald*, June 2, 1954, p. 26. For meeting procedures and timing, see Cutler, pp. 294–313, especially p. 312; Henry M. Jackson, ed., *The National Security Council: Jackson Subcommittee Papers on Policy-Making at the Presidential Level* (New York: Frederick A. Praeger, 1965), pp. 136–137; and Robert R. Bowie and Richard H. Immerman, *Waging Peace: How Eisenhower Shaped an Enduring Cold War Strategy* (Oxford: Oxford University Press, 1998), pp. 90–91. For meeting attendance, see "Minutes of the 205th Meeting of the National Security Council," *DDRS* no. CK3100226666. This document and most other agendas and minutes list the location as the "conference room." However, Cutler reports that all but two NSC meetings took place in the "cabinet room." Some memoranda of discussion specify individuals coming or going from the "cabinet room," although the associated minutes note the "conference room" as the location. Thus, it appears that meetings in the cabinet room were routinely and inaccurately recorded as having taken place elsewhere. Curiously, July 1 was to be Cutler's last day as an Eisenhower assistant, but the president earlier prevailed upon him to remain beyond the term to which he had originally committed. See Cutler, pp. 327–328.

Eisenhower presided over 329 of the 346 meetings of his National Security Council during his eight years in the White House. Each gathering typically lasted two and a half hours. (See Cole C. Kingseed, *Eisenhower and the Suez Criis of 1956* [Baton Rouge: Louisiana State University Press, 1995], p. 20.) For Whitman's assessment of Eisenhower's opinion of the utility of NSC meetings (he "complains that he knows every word of the presentations as they are to be made"), see Stephen E. Ambrose, *Eisenhower: The President* (New York: Simon and Schuster, 1984), p. 345.

44. "Discussion at the 205th Meeting;" Leighton, pp. 281–282; and Robert J. Watson, *History of the Joint Chiefs of Staff: The Joint Chiefs and National Policy, Vol. V, 1953–1954* (Washington: Historical Division, Joint Chiefs of Staff, 1986), p. 136. Both Watson and Leighton incorrectly describe the rocket discussion. There is some confusion as to whether the Genie program was reviewed in the presentation by Quarles or Air Force lieutenant colonel James Bothwell. In "Discussion at the 205th Meeting," Val Peterson says it is the Air Force briefer. However, Quarles answers the question posed on the topic, and another reference notes that Quarles provided the briefing. See "Report of Mr. Robert C. Sprague."

45. See, for example, "Supplementary Study of Continental Defense."

46. "Discussion at the 205th Meeting."

47. "Memorandum for the Secretary of Defense," July 19, 1954, p. 6, in Folder "Continental Defense 1954 (8)," Box 23, Disaster File, WHO, NSC Staff Papers, 1948–61, DDEL (quoting Sprague's correspondence). This document was declassified for this project. "Discussion at the 206th Meeting of the National Security Council, Thursday, July 29, 1954," *DDRS* no. CK3100217324; "Report of Mr. Robert C. Sprague"; Leighton, p. 282. For Eisenhower's schedule, see Presidential Papers of Dwight David Eisenhower at http://www.eisenhowermemorial.org/presidential-papers/first-term/chronology/1954-07.htm.

48. "Memorandum for the Secretary od [sic] Defense," Donald A. Quarles, July 16, 1954; "Memorandum for the National Security Council," from S. Everett Gleason, July 19, 1954; and "Memorandum for the Executive Secretary[,] National Security Council," from C[harles] E[.] Wilson, July 19, 1954; all in Folder "Continental Defense 1954 (8)," Box 23, Disaster File, WHO, NSC Staff Papers, 1948–61, DDEL. These documents were declassified at the author's request. The Quarles memorandum is characterized in "Memorandum for the Secretary of Defense," July 19, 1954, p. 6; "Report of Mr. Robert C. Sprague"; and in Leighton, p. 283.

49. "Memorandum for the Secretary of Defense," July 19, 1954, p. 6; "Memorandum for the Secretary od [sic] Defense," July 16, 1954.

50. For Quarles's New Jersey activities, see Bruce-Biggs, p. 97; and Jack Raymond, "Quarles Dies in Sleep at 64; McElroy May Now Stay On," *New York Times*, May 9, 1959, pp. 1, 21.

51. "Discussion at the 206th Meeting," p. 3. The record is muddled at this point. Sprague recommended that the rocket be accelerated to be ready by *January 1*. The JCS agreed to this date. Sprague's report to the NSC says this is also the date that Quarles has agreed in writing is an acceptable

"objective." (See "Report of Mr. Robert C. Sprague.") The record of the NSC discussion, however, notes that Quarles remarked on the feasibility of *July 1*. (See "Discussion at the 206th Meeting," p. 3.) Since January was the date ultimately adopted and a July deadline was not raised until the next meeting, it is possible that this is an error in transcription.
52. Discussion at the 206th Meeting," pp. 1–5, 7 (quotations, p. 3).
53. "Discussion at the 209th Meeting of the National Security Council, Thursday, August 5, 1954," *DDRS* no. CK3100224140.
54. "Discussion at the 209th Meeting." NSC 5422/1 is not available. All evidence suggests that NSC 5422/2 contained the same text and charts outlining Soviet strength. For NSC 5422/2, see "Statement of Policy by the National Security Council," *FRUS, 1952–1954*, vol. II, part 1, pp. 715–733. Cited Soviet estimates are p. 725.
55. "Discussion at the 209th Meeting," p. 5; footnote 4, *FRUS, 1952–1954*, vol. II, part 1, p. 703.
56. "Discussion at the 209th Meeting," pp. 1–7, 14 (quotation p. 5). This meeting is also discussed in Leighton, pp. 285–286.
57. "Discussion at the 209th Meeting," pp. 1–7, 14.
58. "Discussion at the 209th Meeting," p. 6. Notes taken by a State Department official shed further light on these discussions and the intent expressed, even if they are less comprehensive. See "Comments on NSC 5422 at Cabinet Meeting on August 5, 1954," August 6, 1954, Nuclear History document collection, item no. NH00483, National Security Archive, p. 2.
59. On November 23, 1954, the Pentagon amended the date by which it anticipated interceptors could be armed with the new weapon. Rather than "in early" 1957, the rocket was expected sometime "during" that year. (See "Summary of Significant Changes to the Draft of the Department of Defense Progress Report to the National Security Council on Status of Military Continental Defense Programs as of November 1, 1954," November 23, 1954, in Folder "Continental Defense 1954 (9)," Box 23, Disaster File, WHO, NSC Staff Papers, 1948–61, DDEL. This document was declassified for this study.) "During" 1957 describes the period in which large quantities of the production weapon would be available; as discussed below, the Defense Department remained committed to ensuring that a handful of hand-built "emergency capability" Genies were ready by January 1.
60. "Presentation on Continental Air Defense System," [probably September 1, 1954], *DDRS* no. CK3100427684. This document is otherwise unidentified and is stamped with "February 18, 1955," although it is not at all clear that is the date of the subject presentation. Indeed, the content makes it likely that this is a September 1, 1954, briefing for the JCAE consultants described as "Air Defense Command presentation by Brig. Gen K.P. Bergquist" in "Memorandum for the General Manager: Subject: Wedemeyer Panel Briefings," from Paul F. Foster, September 2, 1954, DOE/NV no. NV0136964.
61. Sterling Cole letter to Secretary of Defense [Charles E. Wilson], August 9, 1954, in NSC Series, Subject Subseries, WHO, OSANSA, Records,

1952–61, DDEL (author's possession); C.E. Wilson letter to W. Sterling Cole, August 16, 1954, in NSC Series, Subject Subseries, WHO, OSANSA, Records, 1952–61, DDEL (author's possession). The latter names the consultants who were finally selected to participate. See also Leighton, pp. 290–292.

62. "Conference with Admiral Strauss and Asst Secy Quarles," [memorandum for the record], by Robert Cutler, August 11, 1954, in Folder "Atomic Energy-Miscellaneous (4) [1953–54]," Box 1, NSC Series, Subject Subseries, WHO, OSANSA, Records, 1952–61, DDEL; "For the Record," by Robert Cutler, August 11, 1954, and "Memorandum for the Chairman, Joint Chiefs of Staff, Subject: Briefings for Joint Committee on Atomic Energy Panel," from C.E. Wilson, August 13, 1954, both in NSC Series, Subject Subseries, WHO, OSANSA, Records, 1952–61, DDEL (both in author's possession).

63. Wilson letter to Cole, August 16, 1954; "Memorandum for the General Manager"; Hewlett and Holl, p. 277.

64. "Presentation on Continental Air Defense System." Quotations p. 17.

65. "Report of Robert C. Sprague (NSC Consultant) to the National Security Council on Continental Defense," November 24, 1954, DDRS no. CK3100188417. Quote is p. 3. See also Leighton, pp. 287–289.

66. "Discussion at the 225th Meeting of the National Security Council, Wednesday, November 24, 1954," *DDRS* no. CK3100217635, p. 14. The NSC's Net Capabilities Evaluation Subcommittee also reported its findings to the council in November. Ostensibly led by Radford and Allen Dulles but actually conducted by subordinates, the study recommended no changes to continental defenses. (See Watson, pp. 139–141, which notes that the report cannot be located.) "Discussion at the 222nd Meeting of the National Security Council, Thursday, November 4, 1954," *DDRS* no. CK3100282801 is a heavily redacted summary of relevant NSC discussions. For an account of the study by one who actually conducted it, see Ray S. Cline, *Secrets, Spies, and Scholars: Blueprint of the Essential CIA* (Washington: Acropolis Books, 1976), pp. 140–143.

67. "Note by the Assistant Staff Secretary to the President (Minnich) on the Legislative Leadership Meeting, December 13, 1954, in *FRUS, 1952–1954*, vol. II, part 1, p. 823.

68. Quoted in Samuel F. Wells, Jr., "The Origins of Massive Retaliation," *Political Science Quarterly* 96, no. 1 (Spring 1981): 39.

69. See *Defense's Nuclear Agency, 1947–1997* (Washington: Defense Threat Reduction Agency, 2002), pp. 117–118; Kenneth W. Condit, *History of the Joint Chiefs of Staff: The Joint Chiefs and National Policy, Vol. VI, 1955–1956* (Washington: Historical Office, Joint Staff, 1992), p. 9.

70. *History of Strategic Air and Ballistic Missile Defense: Volume II, 1956–1972*, pp. 36–37.

71. The date that the White House received the final report is not clear. However, on January 21, 1955, Eisenhower sent a thank you letter. See Dwight D. Eisenhower letter to Clinton P. Anderson [Chairman, Joint Committee on Atomic Energy], January 21, 1955, in Folder "Continental Defense, Study of-by Robert C. Sprague (1955)(2)," [sic] Box 3, NSC

Series, Subject Subseries, WHO, OSANSA, Records, 1953–61, DDEL. Eisenhower instructed AEC chairman Lewis Strauss to appoint a liaison to monitor the activities of the group. While the AEC representative reported that laws restricting the dissemination of nuclear data were respected ("at no time during the discussions were statutory prohibitions violated"), he also maintained that the group did not exceed its mandate (see "Memorandum for the General Manager," p. 1). The panel members later explained that they interpreted their assignment to include any "measures applied anywhere or in any fashion which could make the country less vulnerable" to attack. See "Report of the Continental Defense Panel, Joint Congressional Committee on Atomic Energy," n.d. in Folder "Continental Defense, Study of—by Robert C. Sprague (1955)(1)," [sic] Box 3, NSC Series, Subject Subseries, WHO, OSANSA, Records, 1953–61, DDEL.

72. "Report of the Continental Defense Panel," pp. 1–2, 4, 10.
73. Eisenhower letter to Anderson, January 21, 1955; "Memorandum for: The Secretary of State [et al]," from Robert Cutler, January 28, 1955, in Folder "Continental Defense, Study of—by Robert C. Sprague (1955)(1)," [sic] Box 3, NSC Series, Subject Subseries, WHO, OSANSA, Records, 1953–61, DDEL.
74. "Appendix" attached to "Memorandum for the Secretary of Defense, Subject: Report of the Continental Defense Panel of the Joint Congressional Committee on Atomic Energy," from N[athan] F. Twining, March 14, 1955, in Folder "Continental Defense, Study of—by Robert C. Sprague (1955)(1)," [sic] Box 3, NSC Series, Subject Subseries, WHO, OSANSA, Records, 1953–61, DDEL, p. 5. Eisenhower subsequently wrote to the JCAE saying the report had been studied and "the views of the Panel are being kept in mind." See Dwight D. Eisenhower letter to Clinton P. Anderson, April 27, 1955 in Folder "Continental Defense, Study of—by Robert C. Sprague (1955)(2)," [sic] Box 3, NSC Series, Subject Subseries, WHO, OSANSA, Records, 1953–61, DDEL.
75. Herbert B. Loper letter to Clinton P. Anderson, March 15, 1955, in Chuck Hansen Collection, Box 21, Folder 1, National Security Archive. (In the Hansen Collection, most folders are unnamed but are arranged chronologically. Folder numbers are assigned for each box in ascending order, from the oldest date to the most recent.)
76. Adams, pp. 115–116; James R. Killian, Jr., *Sputnik, Scientists, and Eisenhower: A Memoir of the First Special Assistant to the President for Science and Technology* (Cambridge: MIT Press, 1977), p. 68; Lee A. DuBridge letter to Arthur S. Flemming, May 24, 1954, *DDRS* no. CK3100268736; and Pedlow and Welzenbach, pp. 26–27. The impetus for the March 27 meeting came from Assistant Air Force Secretary Trevor Gardner, who became alarmed about the vulnerability of the Strategic Air Command to surprise attack after reviewing the RAND study on the topic. He met with the Science Advisory Committee to complain that they were not sufficiently engaged in proposing protective alternatives. The meeting with Eisenhower was an indirect result of this complaint. (See Pedlow and Welzenbach, pp. 26–27.) In addition to works here and

below, the Technological Capabilities Panel is treated in Snead, pp. 35–40; and McGeorge Bundy, *Danger and Survival: Choices about the Bomb in the First Fifty Years* (New York: Random House, 1988), pp. 325–328.

77. "Meeting the Threat of Surprise Attack; Technological Capabilities Panel of the Science Advisory Committee," vol. II, February 14, 1955, p. 185, *DDRS* no. CK3100218088.

78. "Meeting the Threat of Surprise Attack; Technological Capabilities Panel of the Science Advisory Committee," vol. I, February 14, 1955, p. iii, *DDRS* no. CK3100217980; "Meeting the Threat of Surprise Attack," vol II, pp. 187–189; Pedlow and Welzenbach, p. 27.

79. "Meeting the Threat of Surprise Attack," vol. I, p. iii; and Adams, p. 121 (Killian quotation about Sprague). Doolittle had also served on the so-called "Solarium Study," which set to determine the broad contours of Eisenhower's foreign policy at the outset of the presidential term. See Adams, p. 48.

80. Killian, pp. 81–82; Pedlow and Welzenbach, pp. 27–33; "Meeting the Threat of Surprise Attack," vol. I, p. 27; Snead, p. 40; Adams, pp. 109–135; Richard B. Damms, "James Killian, the Technological Capabilities Panel, and the Emergence of President Eisenhower's 'Scientific-Technological Elite,'" *Diplomatic History* 24, no. 1 (Winter 2000): 70.

81. "Memorandum of Discussion at the 241st Meeting of the National Security Council, Washington, March 17, 1954," *FRUS, 1955–1957*, vol. XIX, National Security Policy (Government Printing Office: Washington, 1990), pp. 63–67. Killian, and others who apparently rely on him, give an erroneous date for this meeting. See Killian, p. 70. For Cutler's role in the "form, manner, and substance" of the report and its presentation, see Cutler, p. 350. For the length of the meeting, see Jackson, ed., p. 130.

82. "Meeting the Threat of Surprise Attack," vol. II, p. 108.

83. "Meeting the Threat of Surprise Attack," vol. II, p. 75; *History of Strategic Air and Ballistic Missile Defense: Volume II, 1956–1972*, p. 83.

84. "Meeting the Threat of Surprise Attack," vol. II, pp. 75–76, 108.

85. "Meeting the Threat of Surprise Attack," vol. II, p. 107.

86. "Meeting the Threat of Surprise Attack," vol. II, pp. 105–108.

87. "Meeting the Threat of Surprise Attack," vol. II, pp. 107–108.

88. "Meeting the Threat of Surprise Attack," vol. II, pp. 107–108.

89. "Meeting the Threat of Surprise Attack," vol. II, pp. 76, 107–108. This should not be confused with recommendations to continue "studies directed toward better understanding of the radiological hazards that may result from the detonation of large numbers of nuclear weapons," and that "[p]lans for the military use of nuclear bombs should not at this time be restrained because of the long-term radiological hazard." These points are raised in the report section captioned "Strengthening Our Striking Power," and apply to larger yield offensive arms. See "Meeting the Threat of Surprise Attack," vol. I, pp. 38–39.

3 Testing, Predelegating, and Announcing

1. See Chuck Hansen, *Swords of Armageddon*, CD-ROM (1995), p. VIII-74, and Table A-1; A.R. Luedecke memorandum to Assistant Chief of Staff, G-4, Department of the Army, subject: Atomic Weapons Test at High Altitudes, October 9, 1953, Department of Energy/Nevada Nuclear Testing Archive accession no. (hereafter "DOE/NV no.") NV0061778; Frank H. Shelton, *Reflections of a Nuclear Weaponeer* (Colorado Springs: Shelton Enterprises, 1988), pp. 7-3 to 7-7.
2. A. Constandina Titus, *Bombs in the Backyard: Atomic Testing and American Politics* (Reno and Las Vegas: University of Nevada Press, 2001), pp. 55-56; "The Final Teapot Tests," March 23, 1955–May 15, 1955, DNA 6013F, p. 14, in the files of the Office of Corporate Historian, Sandia National Laboratories.
3. Hansen, *Swords of Armageddon*, Table A-1.
4. Lewis Strauss letter to the President [Dwight D. Eisenhower], August 30, 1954, in Folder "Atomic Energy-Miscellaneous (3)," Box 1, in NSC Series, Subject Subseries, White House Office [hereafter "WHO"], Office of Special Assistant for National Security Affairs [hereafter "OSANSA"], Records, 1952-61, Dwight D. Eisenhower Library [hereafter "DDEL"]. One scholarly interpretation argues that Lewis Strauss "was convinced that the nation's survival depended upon its ability to maintain its nuclear superiority through continuous testing," and that he manipulated his position as AEC chairman and his close rapport with the president to bring this about. (See Benjamin P. Greene, *Eisenhower, Science Advice, and the Nuclear Test Ban Debate, 1945-1963* [Stanford: Stanford University Press, 2007], p. 5.) Another asserts that Strauss's "only mantra seemed to be to build bigger and more destructive weapons." (See Valerie L. Adams, *Eisenhower's Fine Group of Fellows: Crafting a National Security Policy to Uphold the Great Equation* [Lanham, MD: Lexington Books, 2006], p. 133). As shown in this study, to the extent that Strauss's support for testing is considered to have been driven by a simple mechanistic desire for more, higher yielding, and/or more assuredly delivered nuclear arms than the Soviet Union, such an evaluation fails to address adequately the specific arguments Strauss advanced for tests, including those necessary for the development of atomic air-defense weapons.
5. Robert Cutler memorandum to Chairman, Atomic Energy Commission [Lewis L. Strauss], September 7, 1954 in Folder "Atomic Energy Commission-General (3) [January-September 1954]," Box 1, Special Assistant Series, Subject Subseries, WHO, OSANSA, Records, 1952-61, DDEL; Lewis L. Strauss letter to W. Sterling Cole, September 24, 1954, in Chuck Hansen Collection (hereafter "Hansen Collection"), Box 20, Folder 4, National Security Archive. (In the Hansen Collection, most folders are unnamed but are arranged chronologically. Folder numbers are assigned for each box in ascending order from the oldest date to the most recent.) Paul Foster memorandum to G. J. Anderson, September 24, 1954, in DOE/NV no. NV0001326; Strauss implemented Cutler's recommendation. See Lewis L. Strauss letter to Robert Cutler, January 3, 1955, DOE/NV no. NV0000818.

6. Michael Joshua Silverman, "No Immediate Risk: Environmental Safety in Nuclear Weapons Production, 1942–1985," unpublished PhD dissertation, Carnegie Mellon University, 2000, pp. 207–222, 231.
7. Richard G. Hewlett and Jack M. Holl, *Atoms for Peace and War, 1953–61: Eisenhower and the Atomic Energy Commission* (Berkeley: University of California Press, 1989), pp. 280–286, 289; Silverman, pp. 235–236. The announcement of the Teapot series was not convincing to everyone. The executive secretary of the American Free Academy for Cancer Research sent a telegram to the Nevada governor: "Your people of the state of Nevada ought to impeach you.... Nevada rates tops for the biggest suckers of the nation....We in Illinois...believe the H-bomb should be dropped on the enemies and not on America." This sparked a reply from Governor Charles Russell's executive assistant: "You have been grossly misinformed regarding property damage and injury from atom bomb shots in Nevada. Further there have been no H-bomb tests in Nevada....Further, no one in Nevada could prevent the tests, because they are conducted upon Federal domain....There have been no protests from any resident of Nevada concerning the atom bomb tests in this State." See J. Sinclair telegram to Charles Russell, March 30, 1955; Arthur N. Suverkrup letter to J. Sinclair, March 30, 1955, Both in Box 21, Folder 2, Hansen Collection.
8. Silverman, p. 235. See also, for example, Gladwin Hill, "A.E.C. is Lifting Curtain on Tests," *New York Times*, February 24, 1955, p. 12; "The A.E.C. Opens Up," *New York Times*, February 25, 1955, p. 20; "Baby Atom Blast Set Off in Nevada," *Los Angeles Times*, February 20, 1955; "Atomic Blast Jolts Cities for 135 Miles," *Norfolk Virginian-Pilot*, February 23, 1955. Nevada's Operation Upshot-Knothole, conducted in 1953, also had a significant public relations component, most of which was related to the test of a cannon firing a nuclear shell. In Teapot, most shots, not merely exceptional examples, were trumpeted. On Upshot-Knothole, see James Lamont, "The Atomic Cannon: It Was Fired Once, But It Helped End a War," *Invention & Technology* 21, no. 1 (Summer 2005): 53. Some interpretive conclusions of this article, such as Upshot-Knothole's relationship to the end of the Korean War, are questionable.
9. W.H. Rowen memorandum to Wm L. Guthrie, August 20, 1954, Box 20, Folder 4, Hansen Collection; Director, Office of Information, Atomic Energy Commission memorandum to Director, Los Alamos Scientific Laboratory, August 31, 1954, quoted in Hansen, *Swords of Armageddon*, pp. V-63 to V-64.
10. "Meeting the Threat of Surprise Attack, Technological Capabilities Panel of the Science Advisory Committee," vol. II, February 14, 1955, p. 108, *Declassified Documents Reference System* (hereafter *DDRS*) no. CK3100218088.
11. Robert Cutler, *No Time for Rest* (Boston: Little, Brown, 1966), p. 350.
12. Morse Salisbury memorandum [with attached press release] to Lewis L. Strauss et al., March 24, 1955, Box 21, Folder 1, Hansen Collection. The announcement was released soon after the Killian recommendation was officially received, and it gained the necessary approval from the OCB

and State Department in a short period. This is probably further evidence that work on it almost certainly commenced before the report was submitted, demonstrating collaborative efforts between panel members and the administration.
13. Morse Salisbury memorandum.
14. Morse Salisbury memorandum.
15. See, for example, "U.S. Develops Atom Air Defense; Missile Designed to Halt Bombers," *New York Times*, March 28, 1958, p. 1; Darrell Garwood, "Atomic Blast Six Miles Up to Test New Air Defense; Nuclear Warhead For Missiles Use to Be Tried Out Soon in Nevada," *Washington Post and Times-Herald*, March 28, 1955, p. 1.
16. "The Final Teapot Tests," pp. 14, 16; Hansen, *Swords of Armageddon*, Table A-1; "New Blast Believed Test of Air Fleet Destroyer," *Washington Post and Times-Herald*, March 26, 1955, p. 2; "Atom Device Detonated 6 Miles High," *Washington Post and Times-Herald*, April 7, 1955, p. 9. For a letter outlining the proposed "2 kt" blast at "about 40,000 feet" for the "military weapons effects program," see Donald A. Quarles letter to Lewis L. Strauss, June 1, 1954, in Box 20, Folder 2, Hansen Collection.
17. Shelton, p. 7-7.
18. "Atom Device."
19. "Air-Fleet Killer is Tested by A.E.C.," *New York Times*, April 7, 1955, p. 1.
20. Hansen, *Swords of Armageddon*, Table A-1, pp. 6-8.
21. Shelton, pp. 7-7, 7-8, 7-16, 7-17. Originally this was to be a ten-kiloton surface burst. For safety reasons, it was changed. (It was believed that a tower shot produced less fallout.) See Donald A. Quarles letter to Lewis L. Strauss, June 1, 1954, Box 20, Folder 2, Hansen Collection; and Lewis L. Strauss letter to Donald A. Quarles, July 1, 1954, attached to "Note by the Secretary," July 16, 1954, Box 20, Folder 3, Hansen Collection; Robert Bennyhoff, "Army Tests Equipment in Huge A-Blast; Two Pilotless Planes Crash, Third Lands; Flash Melts Tower, *Washington Post and Times-Herald*, April 16, 1954, p. 1.
22. Hansen, *Swords of Armageddon*, Table A-1.
23. Initial work on the "XW-31" warhead is noted in "Semiannual Historical Report; Headquarters, Field Command, The Armed Forces Special Weapons Command, Sandia Base, Albuquerque, New Mexico, 1 July 1954–31 December 1954," pp. 230-1 (uncataloged collection, National Security Archive). Hansen asserts, without elaboration, that Teapot "established design principles for the XW-31"; in Hansen, *Swords of Armageddon*, p. VII-192. See also Hansen, *Swords of Armageddon*, p. VII-191, VII-198; and Chuck Hansen, *U.S. Nuclear Weapons: The Secret History* (Arlington, Texas: Aerofax, 1988), p. 13.
24. Darrell Garwood, "Atomic Head Developed for Nike Missile," *Washington Post and Times-Herald*, January 25, 1955, p. 9.
25. Hanson W. Baldwin, "The Teapot Tests; A Report on Current Nuclear Series Indicating Break-Through Weapons," *New York Times*, April 25, 1955, p. 11; Baldwin, *New York Times*, May 1, 1955.

26. Philip J. Klass, *Secret Sentries in Space* (New York: Random House, 1971), pp. 7-8; "Editorial Note," in *Foreign Relations of the United States, 1955-1957*, vol. XIX, National Security Policy (Government Printing Office: Washington, 1990), p. 78 (hereafter identified as *FRUS* with year, volume, and page specified).
27. John Prados, *The Soviet Estimate: U.S. Intelligence Analysis and Soviet Strategic Forces* (Princeton: Princeton University Press, 1986), pp. 42-43; Lawrence Freedman, *U.S. Intelligence and the Soviet Strategic Threat* (Princeton: Princeton University Press), 2nd edition, 1986, pp. 65-66; Steven J. Zaloga, *Target America: The Soviet Union and the Strategic Arms Race, 1945-1964* (Novato, California: Presidio Press, 1993), pp. 83-85; Richard M. Leighton, *Strategy, Money, and the New Look, 1953-1956: History of the Office of the Secretary of Defense, Vol. III* (Washington: Office of the Secretary of Defense, 2001), pp. 379-386, 393-394; and Fred Kaplan, *The Wizards of Armageddon* (Stanford: Stanford University Press, 1983), pp. 156-160. Kaplan concedes deception but is uncertain that it was a result of repeat overflights (see p. 160). For background on Bear, see Zaloga, pp. 85-88. For a mention of alternator problems in early B-52s, some monthly delivery numbers, and a discussion that holds that the response to bomber intelligence was logical, see Colin S. Gray, " 'Gap' Prediction and America's Defense: Arms Race Behavior in the Eisenhower Years," *Orbis* 16, no. 1 (Spring 1972): 257-274.
28. Prados, pp. 42-43; Freedman, pp. 65-66; Zaloga, pp. 83-85.
29. Edward L. Beach memorandum to Mr. [James] Hagerty, et al., June 14, 1955, *DDRS* no. CK3100461968; "White House Locator List for Federal Civil Defense Drill, June 15-17, 1955, *DDRS* no. 3100258235; "White House Emergency Plan," p. 1, *DDRS* no. CK3100103126. The version is dated August 3, 1955, but there is ample evidence that the process it outlines was closely followed in the course of the 1955 Operation Alert. See David F. Krugler, *This Is Only a Test: How Washington, D.C., Prepared for Nuclear War* (New York: Palgrave Macmillan, 2006), pp. 124-130. This book is the definitive treatment of the subject.
30. W.H. Lawrence, "Eisenhower Cites Limited Test Aim," *New York Times*, June 17, 1955, p. 11; "Official Wives Sit It Out," *Washington Post and Times-Herald*, June 16, 1954, p. 35.
31. Krugler p. 126; "Official Wives Sit It Out"; Guy Oakes, *The Imaginary War: Civil Defense and American Cold War Culture* (New York: Oxford University Press, 1994), pp. 84-86. Ted Gup, "Doomesday Hideaway," *Time*, December 9, 1991, pp. 26-29; Stephen I. Schwartz, *Atomic Audit: The Costs and Consequences of U.S. Nuclear Weapons Since 1940* (Washington: Brookings Institution Press, 1998), pp. 212-213.
32. Alvin Shuster, "President and His Aides Leave Washington Before Mock Hydrogen Bomb Attack," *New York Times*, June 16, 1955, p. 16. This article incorrectly suggests that Secretary of State John Foster Dulles did not participate; for a corrective, see Krugler, p. 127.
33. Schwartz, pp. 210-211; "President and His Aides Leave Washington Before Mock Hydrogen Bomb Attack"; "Texts on Defense Alert," *New York Times*, June 16, 1955, p. 16.

34. Bernard Stengren, "Somber Stillness Blankets City as Traffic Halts During the Air Raid Test," *New York Times*, June 16, 1955, p. 17; "List of Cities Under Air 'Attack,'" *New York Times*, June 16, 1955, p. 16.
35. Krugler, p. 126; "Mrs. Hobby Stops Off for Lunch During Trip," *New York Times*, June 16, 1955; Oakes, pp. 87–88; John D. Morris, "Fleeing Agencies Get News Lesson," *New York Times*, June 16, 1955, p. 16; Russell Baker, "All Is Confusion Newsmen Report," *New York Times*, June 16, 1955, p. 19. Also see e-mail dated January 29, 2005, and January 31, 2005, from Professor David F. Krugler; and *Hill's Richmond City Directory, 1955*, pp. 273–274, courtesy Richmond (Virginia) Public Library, all in author's possession.
36. Damon Stetson, "Center Reports Flaw in Alert," *New York Times*, June 18, 1955, p. 8.
37. Lawrence, *New York Times*; and information in author's possession, provided by very special courtesy of David F. Krugler.
38. "Discussion at the 252nd Meeting of the National Security Council, Thursday, June 16, 1955," *DDRS* no. CK3100102969.
39. "Discussion at the 252nd Meeting."
40. "Report of Robert C. Sprague (NSC Consultant) to the National Security Council on Continental Defense," June 16, 1955, *DDRS* no. CK3100094753; quotations on p. 3–5; Leighton, pp. 427–428.
41. "Discussion at the 252nd Meeting," pp. 2, 3, 9.
42. Dillon Anderson letter to Robert C. Sprague, April 9, 1955, in Folder "Sprague Report [re continental defense]," Box 18, Executive Secretary Subject File, WHO, NSC Staff Papers, 1948–61, DDEL. Anderson, a Texas lawyer and campaign aide, had assumed the position of Special Assistant for National Security Affairs eight days earlier. Robert Cutler returned to his pre-administration position as chairman of Boston's Old Colony Trust Company. See Cutler, p. 333.
43. See Robert C. Sprague letter to Dillon Anderson, September 26, 1955, and Dillon Anderson letter to Robert C. Sprague, September 29, 1955, both in Folder "September 1955 (6)," Box 1, Special Assistant Series, Chronological Subseries, WHO, OSANSA, Records, 1952–61, DDEL. In a brief telephone oral interview nine months before he died, Eisenhower aide Andrew Goodpaster said Sprague "dramatized" the Soviet threat owing to the "particular view" he held. Goodpaster maintains that Sprague attempted to "stampede Ike" into action, but said at the time, "Ike knows this," and was thus able to rebuff Sprague's policy preferences. (Goodpaster had no memory of nuclear antiaircraft weapons and the discussions surrounding them until provided with copies of memoranda and meeting summaries.) See written notes of author's telephone interviews with Andrew Goodpaster, August 13, 2004, and September 23, 2004, in author's possession. Aside from Sprague's relationship with Eisenhower, he maintained a good rapport with others in the administration, notwithstanding his status as a consultant and not a full-time employee. For example, in 1956, Sprague exchanged Christmas cards with Jimmy Lay and others on the NSC staff. See John Prados, *Keepers of the Keys: A History of the National Security Council From Truman to Bush* (New York: William Morrow and Co., 1991), p. 75.

44. "Proposed Council Action on the Recommendations of the Report to the President by the Technological Capabilities Panel of the Science Advisory Committee, Office of Defense Mobilization," July 22, 1955, *DDRS* no. CK3100473687; and "Proposed Council Action on the Recommendations of the Report to the President by the Technological Capabilities Panel of the Science Advisory Committee, Office of Defense Mobilization," July 26, 1955, *DDRS* no. 3100162530.
45. "Discussion at the 257th Meeting of the National Security Council, Thursday, August 4, 1955," *DDRS* no. CK3100496527.
46. "NSC 5522," June 8, 1955, *DDRS* no. CK3100084257, pp. A25, S11. In May 1955, the Joint Chiefs of Staff referred the Killian report and four other studies bearing on various aspects of continental defense to the Weapons Systems Evaluation Group (WSEG), an internal Pentagon research arm. Among other points, the WSEG apparently endorsed the concept of using nuclear weapons to destroy megaton weapons. See U.S. Army, *History of Strategic Air and Ballistic Missile Defense: Volume II, 1956–1972* (Washington: Center of Military History, c. 1975), p. 88. (For WSEG history and date of report, see Paul Ceruzzi, *Internet Alley: High Technology in Tysons Corner, 1945–2005* (Cambridge: MIT Press, 2008), pp. 33–35.) However, the former evaluation also asserts that Defense Department leaders "evidenced some concern for the concept of nuclear warheads for air defense weapons" when considering NSC 5522. No support for this description can be found. The analysis further speculates departmental officials may "implicitly" have been expressing a belief in the primacy of offensive rather than defensive weapons and/or been distressed about prospect of limited nuclear material inefficiently being allocated to a Nike-Ajax warhead. (See *History of Strategic Air and Ballistic Missile Defense*, p. 89.) Even assuming the characterization is apt, the first rationale is plausible. The second is less so. By August 1955, the decision to develop a nuclear Nike-Ajax warhead had been settled for more than two years in favor of a new Nike-Hercules missile and associated warhead. However, perhaps evincing continued discussion of the topic, a senior Army air defense general told an audience of junior officers in September 1956 that "[t]he Department of Army has stated a strong desire for an atomic warhead for Nike I." See briefing captioned "Atomics in Air Defense," September 22, 1956, in Folder "Military Planning, 1956–1957(1)," Box 6, Subject Series, Department of Defense Subseries, WHO, Office of Staff Secretary [hereafter "OSS"], Records, 1952–61, DDEL, p. 4. This briefing paper was declassified for this study.
47. "NSC 5522," p. S11. State's comments are included on this page. They are redacted from pp. S3 and A2.
48. "NSC 5522," p. S11.
49. Hansen, *U.S. Nuclear Weapons: The Secret History*, p. 177; Necah Stewart Furman, *Sandia National Laboratories: The Postwar Decade* (University of New Mexico Press: 1990), pp. 641–2, 647.
50. Thomas W. Ray, *Nuclear Armament: Its Acquisition, Control, and Application to Manned Interceptors, 1951–1963*; A[ir] D[efense] C[ommand] Historical Study No. 20 (n.p.: Air Defense Command, n.d.),

pp. 12–13; Hansen, *Swords of Armageddon*, p. V-66; For "one-point" definition, see Lewis L. Strauss letter to Clinton P. Anderson, September 23, 1955, Box 21, Folder 4, Hansen Collection.
51. Herbert B. Loper letter to Lewis L. Strauss, June 13, 1955 (attached to W.B. McCool memorandum to Atomic Energy Commission, June 20, 1955), Box 21, Folder 3, Hansen Collection.
52. W.B. McCool memorandum to Alfred D. Starbird, August 25, 1955, Box 21, Folder 4, Hansen Collection; Donald J. Leerhey letter to Alvin C. Graves, June 30, 1955; and memorandum captioned "One-Point Tests at Nevada Test Site," July 13, 1955; both Box 21, Folder 3, Hansen Collection.
53. Letter requesting permission is Chairman [Lewis L. Strauss] letter to the president, September 2, 1955, in Folder "Atomic Energy-Miscellaneous (4) [1953–54]," Box 1, NSC Series, Subject Subseries, WHO, OSANSA, Records, 1952–61, DDEL. Permission conveyed by telegram Ann [Whitman] to Art Minnich, September 5, 1955, in Folder "Atomic Energy Commission—1955–56 (6)," Box 4, Ann W. Whitman Files, Administrative Series, Dwight D. Eisenhower Papers as President, 1953–61, DDEL. Joint Committee notification is Lewis L. Strauss letter to Clinton P. Anderson, September 23, 1955. Press release, dated October 10, 1955, Box 21, Folder 4, Hansen Collection. Operation name is in Hansen, *Swords of Armageddon*, p. VII-72.
54. The W-25 was tested between November 1 and November 3; various dates are given. See, for example, W.B. McCool memorandum to Atomic Energy Commission, October 24, 1955 (with attachment, especially p. 2), Box 21, Folder 5, Hansen Collection; and K.E. Fields letter to Carl T. Durham, January 17, 1957, quoted in Hansen, *Swords of Armageddon*, p. VII-92. "One-Point Tests at Nevada Test Site," "Minutes of the Sixteenth Meeting, Technical Advisory Panel on Atomic Energy," February 29, 1956, Box 22, Folder 1, Hansen Collection. Quotation in Lewis L. Strauss letter to Clinton P. Anderson, September 23, 1955.
55. K.F. Hertford telex to Bridg [*sic*] Gen R.G. Butler et al., December 13, 1955, Box 21, Folder 5 in Hansen Collection.
56. "Operation Plumbbob; Summary Report, Test Group 57," October 10, 1958, p. 18, Box 25, Folder 1, Hansen Collection.
57. "Minutes of the Sixteen Meeting, Technical Advisory Panel on Atomic Energy, 17 February 1956, 0930, Room 3C-136, The Pentagon," February 29, 1956, Box 22, Folder 1, Hansen Collection. Another W-25 one-point test was conduced at the NTS in April 1957 to further study plutonium dispersal patterns, develop decontamination techniques, and gather other data. See general manager [AEC] letter to Carl T. Durham, March 12, 1957, in Box 24, Folder 1, Hansen Collection; and Hansen, *Swords of Armageddon*, p. VII-96 and VII 97.
58. "Oralloy" is a contraction of "Oak Ridge alloy," the code name given to enriched uranium during the Manhattan Project for the location in which it was produced. See http://encyclopedia.thefreedictionary.com/Oralloy.
59. "Semiannual Historical Report: Headquarters, Field Command, the Armed Forces Special Weapons Project, Sandia Base, Albuquerque, New

Mexico, Volume I, 1 July 1957–31 December 1957," pp. 207, 224 (uncataloged collection, National Security Archive); Hansen, *Swords of Armageddon*, pp. VII-87, VII-98 to VII-104; N.E. Bradbury letter to Brig. Gen. Alfred D. Starbird, October 11, 1956, Box 23, Folder 1; J.B. Macauley letter to Lewis Strauss, August 5, 1957, Box 24, Folder 4; W.F. Libby letter to Carl T. Durham, August 23, 1957, Box 24, Folder 4; all in Hansen Collection; and Paul Fine memorandum to Harold Knapp, December 13, 1957, DOE/NV no. NV0103944.

60. Ray, *Nuclear Armament: Its Acquisition, Control, and Application to Manned Interceptors*, pp. 27–36. Project 56 also resulted in a recommendation that the AEC construct several buildings for the assembly of plutonium-bearing sealed-pit weapons so that a one-point accident during manufacturing would only halt work in one affected facility. See "Minutes of the Sixteenth Meeting, Technical Advisory Panel"; Hansen, *Swords of Armageddon*, pp. VII-75, VII-83.

61. Darrell Garwood, "Jets to Pack A-Punch Under Tentative Plan," *Washington Post and Times-Herald*, January 7, 1956, p. 15.

62. W.B. McCool memorandum to the Atomic Energy Commission, April 25, 1961, p. 12, Box 31, Folder 3, Hansen Collection.

63. "Meeting the Threat of Surprise Attack," vol. II, p. 108.

64. W.B. McCool memorandum to the Atomic Energy Commission, April 25, 1961, pp. 12–13.

65. "Report to the National Security Council by the Executive Secretary (Lay)," NSC 162/2, *FRUS, 1952–1954*, vol. II, part 1, pp. 577–597. Quote is p. 593. See also Robert R. Bowie and Richard H. Immerman, *Waging Peace: How Eisenhower Shaped an Enduring Cold War Strategy* (Oxford: Oxford University Press, 1998), pp. 190–198.

66. "Memorandum for the Secretary of Defense," from Arthur Radford, February 15, 1956, in Folder "Policy Regarding Use of Nuclear Weapons," Box 11, Record Group 59, Records of the Department of State [hereafter DoS Records], Executive Secretariat, NSC Meeting Files and Reports, National Archives and Records Administration [hereafter NARA]. (This and other NARA documents in this section in author's possession, provided by very special courtesy of William Burr of the National Security Archive); "Memorandum of Discussion at the 278th Meeting of the National Security Council, Washington, March 1, 1956," in *FRUS, 1955–1957*, vol. XIX, p. 229, footnote 9; W.B. McCool memorandum to the Atomic Energy Commission, April 25, 1961, p. 13.

67. Kenneth W. Condit, *History of the Joint Chiefs of Staff: The Joint Chiefs and National Policy, Vol. VI, 1955–1956* (Washington: Historical Office, Joint Staff, 1992), p. 15.

68. "Memorandum of Discussion at the 277th Meeting of the National Security Council, Washington, February 27, 1956," in *FRUS, 1955–1957*, vol. XIX, pp. 201–208; "Memorandum of Discussion at the 278th Meeting of the National Security Council," pp. 218–229. The discussions recounted make it clear that the proposed wording was not motivated by continental defense concerns. That phrase is never used during the NSC meeting, and comments about "forces" and a hypothetical

"military commander in the field" suggest that the language is directed at other circumstances. (See p. 204.)
69. For details of the president's notification of the JCS predelegation request, see "Memorandum for the File"; C.E. Wilson letter to Secretary [John Foster Dulles?], April 5, 1956, from the National Security Archive collection on nuclear predelegation.
70. "Memorandum of Discussion at the 278th Meeting of the National Security Council," p. 229.
71. NSC 5602/1, in *FRUS, 1955–1957*, vol. XIX, p. 246.
72. NSC 5602/1, p. 246.
73. "Memorandum for the Secretary of State, the Secretary of Defense, the Chairman, Atomic Energy Commission" from James S. Lay, Jr., March 15, 1956, in Folder "Policy Regarding Use of Nuclear Weapons," Box 11, Record Group 59, DoS Records, Executive Secretariat, NSC Meeting Files and Reports, NARA; handwritten notes from the meeting with Eisenhower that resulted in this memorandum are in Folder "Secretary of Defense [November 1953–January 1959]," Box 11, Subject Series, Department of Defense Subseries, WHO, OSS, Records, 1952–61, DDEL. It is also discussed in "Memorandum of Discussion at the 278th Meeting of the National Security Council, Washington, March 1, 1956," p. 229, footnote 9; and in Robert J. Watson, *Into the Missile Age, 1956–1960: History of the Office of the Secretary of Defense, Vol. IV* (Washington: Office of the Secretary of Defense, 1997), p. 450.
74. C.E. Wilson letter to president, March 15, 1956 in Folder "Policy Regarding Use of Nuclear Weapons," Box 11, Record Group 59, DoS Records, Executive Secretariat, NSC Meeting Files and Reports, NARA.
75. Andrew Goodpaster memorandum for the Secretary of Defense, March 20, 1956, in Folder "Secretary of Defense," Box 11, Subject Series, Department of Defense Subseries, WHO, OSS, Records, 1952–61, DDEL. (This memorandum was declassified for this study.) Also "Memorandum for the File"; W.B. McCool memorandum to the Atomic Energy Commission, April 25, 1961, pp. 13; and C.E. Wilson letter to Secretary [John Foster Dulles?], April 5, 1956; and [James S. Lay, Jr.] "Memorandum for the President," c. April 26, 1957.
76. C.E. Wilson letter to Secretary [John Foster Dulles?], April 5, 1956"; W.B. McCool memorandum to the Atomic Energy Commission, April 25, 1961, p. 14.
77. C.E. Wilson letter to Mr. [Dillon] Anderson, April 5, 1956 in Folder "Policy Regarding Use of Nuclear Weapons," Box 11, Record Group 59, DoS Records, Executive Secretariat, NSC Meeting Files and Reports, NARA.
78. "Memorandum for the Secretary of State, the Chairman, Atomic Energy Commission," from James S. Lay, Jr., April 9, 1956, in Folder "Policy Regarding Use of Nuclear Weapons," Box 11, Record Group 59, DoS Records, Executive Secretariat, NSC Meeting Files and Reports, NARA.
79. "Memorandum for the Secretary of State, the Secretary of Defense, the Chairman, Atomic Energy Commission" from James S. Lay, Jr., April 10,

1956, in Folder "Policy Regarding Use of Nuclear Weapons," Box 11, Record Group 59, DoS Records, Executive Secretariat, NSC Meeting Files and Reports, NARA.

80. "Memorandum for the Executive Secretary, National Security Council," from John Foster Dulles, April 17, 1956, in Folder "Policy Regarding Use of Nuclear Weapons," Box 11, Record Group 59, DoS Records, Executive Secretariat, NSC Meeting Files and Reports, NARA. The authorization also makes reference to defending against aerial attack in the United States, its "territories and possessions" (Alaska and Hawaii were not yet states), off the coasts, and "in the vicinity of U.S. foreign bases." This last point had no immediate relevance. Nuclear antiaircraft weapons were not contemplated for overseas installations for some time, and by the time they were, supplemental nuclear authorizations addressing these circumstances had come into force. It is possible, however, that the "foreign bases" language was included because establishing it in the policy beforehand was thought to be a way to ease the situation when it came about. (See "Instructions for the Expenditure of Nuclear Weapons in Accordance with the Presidential Authorization Dated May 22, 1957," from Folder "Atomic Weapons, Correspondence and Background for Presidential Approval and Instructions for Use of [1953–1960] (2)," Box 1, NSC Series, Subject Subseries, WHO, OSANSA, Records, 1952–61, DDEL, from the National Security Archive collection on nuclear predelegation.) Some have suggested that a change in atomic weapon custody policy around the same time was related to the antiaircraft predelegation decision. Since the advent of atomic armaments, the Atomic Energy Commission had maintained legal possession of all weapons produced, with provisions for the military to take control in the event of war. In the early Eisenhower administration, because the cumbersome nature of this arrangement was recognized, some warheads were distributed to the military but remained under nominal AEC control. After 1955's Operation Alert, when the Defense Department rehearsed the release procedure, the Pentagon and AEC asked the president in March 1956 to alter the process. He did so two weeks before signing the predelegation order. This expedited (and in some cases made nearly automatic) the transfer of custody in some situations. It does not appear that this change had much to do with the impending deployment of air defense weapons. Decisions to seek and implement custody changes proceeded independently from the antiaircraft issues and the timing was largely coincidental. Had the new process not been instituted, air defense arms would probably have been treated as had some other weapons: They would have been assigned to military units but remained legally under the control of civilians at the AEC. See Peter Roman, "Ike's Hair-Trigger: U.S. Nuclear Predelegation, 1953–60," *Security Studies* 7, no. 4 (Summer 1998): 131–134; and Daniel Shuchman, "Nuclear Strategy and the Problem of Command and Control," *Survival* 29, no. 4: 344; and Lewis Strauss and Reuben Robinson [Deputy Secretary of Defense] letter to the president, March 23, 1956, in Folder "Atomic Energy Matters (AEC, Defense) Presidential Actions (1)," Box 5, Subject Series, Alpha Subseries,

WHO, OSS, 1952–61, DDEL; W.B. McCool memorandum to the Atomic Energy Commission, April 25, 1961, p. 22.
81. "Memorandum for the File," Department of State, April 2, 1956, from the National Security Archive collection on nuclear predelegation.
82. Roman, pp. 135–139.
83. Roman, p. 138 and p. 135, note 46 (text of rules of engagement). These rules originated in continental defense instructions issued soon after the start of the Korean War. See Kenneth Schaffel, *The Emerging Shield: The Air Force and the Evolution of Continental Air Defense, 1945–1960* (Washington: Office of Air Force History), 1991, p. 135.
84. "Instructions for the Expenditure of Nuclear Weapons in Accordance with the Presidential Authorization Dated May 22, 1957," p. 10.
85. The subsequent authority, classification, and dissemination restrictions are noted in "Instructions for the Expenditure of Nuclear Weapons in Accordance with the Presidential Authorization Dated May 22, 1957" (including p. 12). For declaration that the previous air defense permission is "continued in full force and effect," see p. 10. Eisenhower also instructed that before the predelegaged authority became effective, implementing instructions must be codified. This took years. For additional details on the subsequent broader predelegation, see Roman.
86. Eisenhower apparently did not always have strong confidence in those in possession of atomic arms. Days after the 1952 presidential election, AEC official Roy B. Snapp met with Eisenhower for a briefing on commission issues. An AEC history says that in connection with nuclear weapons, the president-elect "expressed to Snapp his concern that some junior officer might decide that they could be used like other weapons." This is an ironic statement in light of nearly identical language allowing such included in later NSC documents and Eisenhower's actions as president. See Richard G. Hewlett and Jack M. Holl, *Atoms for Peace and War, 1953–61: Eisenhower and the Atomic Energy Commission* (Berkeley: University of California Press, 1989), p. 5.
87. Roman, p. 140–145. Few forces assigned outside of the United States were dedicated to continental defense. Predelegation did not apply to Canadian overflights. It is not clear if it applied to American forces in or over Greenland. In 1959, Nike-Hercules missiles were emplaced around Thule, Greenland, because the air base there offered a good spot to defend against Soviet attackers transiting the pole, and it was a staging area for American bombers. Nike-Hercules units eventually located in South Korea and Western Europe did not have continental defense functions and thus are outside the scope of this study. For Nike-Hercules in Greenland, see Mary T. Cagle, *History of the Nike Hercules Weapon System* (U.S. Army Missile Command: Redstone Arsenal, Alabama), 1973, p. 244. There is no evidence that Genie-equipped aircraft operated from foreign sites except at Thule and, after 1965, two bases in Canada. See John Clearwater, *U.S. Nuclear Weapons in Canada* (Toronto: The Dundurn Press, 1999), pp. 152 and 179 for discussion of air defense warheads arriving at Canada's Goose Bay Air Base and Ernest Harmon Air Force Base. For an NSC discussion of the possibility of arming

Canadian planes with nuclear air-defense weapons, see "Memorandum of Discussion at the 325th Meeting of the National Security Council, Washington, May 27, 1957," in *FRUS, 1955–1957*, vol. XIX, pp. 497, 506. For a letter about the "introduction and storage of nuclear weapons" at Thule, see Robert Murphy letter to Mansfield D. Sprague, November 26, 1957, Nuclear History document collection, item no. NH01068, National Security Archive. Roman, p. 139, note 57 cites other documents discussing the introduction of nuclear weapons to Thule. He suggests this is a reference to desired Genie deployment. They could also be related to the Nike-Hercules or antisubmarine or strategic weapons.
88. Roman, p. 145.
89. "Memorandum of a Conference with the President, White House, Washington, March 30, 1956, 3 p.m.," in *FRUS, 1955–1957*, vol. XIX, p. 280–281 (quotation on p. 281).
90. McG[eorge] B[undy], "Memorandum to the President," September 23, 1964, from the National Security Archive collection on nuclear predelegation.
91. Clearwater, pp. 50–53. The overflight agreement is reproduced on pp. 219–220. The best treatment of the subject is Sean M. Maloney, *Learning to Love the Bomb: Canada's Nuclear Weapons During the Cold War* (Washington: Potomac Books, 2007), pp. 64–66.
92. "Memorandum for the Record by the President's Special Assistant for National Security Affairs (Anderson)," January 23, 1956, in *FRUS, 1955–1957*, vol. XIX, pp. 188–191; "Editorial Note," in *FRUS, 1955–1957*, vol. XIX, p. 56.
93. "Diary Entry by the President," January 23, 1956, in *FRUS, 1955–1957*, vol. XIX, pp. 187–188 (erroneously showing 1956, rather than 1958, as the date selected for study); "Memorandum for the Record by the President's Special Assistant for National Security Affairs (Anderson)," January 23, 1956; "Discussion at the 263rd Meeting of the National Security Council, Thursday, October 27, 1956," *DDRS* no. CK3100528571.
94. Radford declared that it was not "altogether factual" and was rooted in "approximations based on certain assumptions," which if changed would result in "different answers." See "Discussion at the 263rd Meeting of the National Security Council, Thursday, October 27, 1956," p. 9; "Diary Entry by the President," January 23, 1956, p. 188.
95. "Memorandum for Record," February 10, 1956, *DDRS* no. CK3100452797. This exchange is also noted in David Alan Rosenberg, "The Origins of Overkill: Nuclear Weapons and American Strategy," in Norman A. Graebner, ed., *The National Security: Its Theory and Practice, 1945–1960* (New York: Oxford University Press, 1986), p. 154.
96. Memorandum captioned "Meeting Held at 2:30 in the President's office," March 29, 1956, *DDRS* no. 3100392692.
97. "Transcript of the President's News Conference on Foreign and Domestic Matters," *New York Times*, April 26, 1956, p. 16.

98. Eisenhower twice issued a statement with essentially this language within two weeks. For the first, see "President's Statement on H-Bomb Tests," *New York Times*, October 6, 1956, p. 11. The quotation is drawn from p. 3 of "Statement by the President," October 24, 1956, in Folder "Atomic Energy Commission 1955–56 (2)," Box 4, Ann W. Whitman Files, Administrative Series, Dwight D. Eisenhower Papers as President, 1953–61, DDEL. Lewis Strauss also echoed the administration line in a speech in Battle Creek, Michigan, in this period. (See "Remarks Prepared by Lewis L. Strauss, Chairman, U.S. Atomic Energy Commission, for Delivery to Joint U.S.-Canada Civil Defense Committee," in Box 9, Lewis L. Strauss Papers, Herbert Hoover Presidential Library (hereafter HHPL).) For a discussion of this period, see Stephen E. Ambrose, *Eisenhower: The President* (New York: Simon and Schuster, 1984), pp. 347–350.
99. "Editorial Note," in *FRUS, 1955–1957*, vol. XX, p. 392.
100. W.F. Libby letter to Clinton P. Anderson, December 29, 1955, Box 21, Folder 5, Hansen Collection.
101. Lewis L. Strauss letter to John Foster Dulles, October 25, 1955, in DOE/NV no. NV0108261.
102. Hansen, *Swords of Armageddon*, pp. VII-84, 85, and 86. The yield for the June 16, 1956, shot is given in official sources as 1.7 kilotons. See "Restricted Data Classification Decisions, 1946 to the Present (RDD-8)," U.S. Department of Energy, January 1, 2002, p. 113, in author's possession. This document was declassified and distributed in 2009 at the request of the Federation of American Scientists.
103. Herbert Loper memorandum to Chairman, U.S. Atomic Energy Commission, October 5, 1955, attached to W.B. McCool memorandum to Atomic Energy Commission, October 17, 1955, in Box 21, Folder 4, Hansen Collection.
104. Hansen, *Swords of Armageddon*, pp. VII-173, VII-198, "Summary of Major Events and Problems of the [Army] Ordnance Corps, July 1958–June 1959," p. 53, call no. 40-2.1 AA 1959, in the collection of the U.S. Army Center of Military History (hereafter "USACMH").
105. Document hand-captioned "B. United States Weapon Progr[am]," c. June 1956, Box 22, Folder 4, Hansen Collection.
106. Hansen, *Swords of Armageddon*, pp. VII-192 and VII-193.
107. Hansen, *Swords of Armageddon*, pp. VII-193 and VII-194; "B. United States Weapon Progr[am]."
108. A 1956 Army document mentions a twenty-two-kiloton Nike-Hercules warhead under consideration. (See "Summary of Major Events and Problems of the [Army] Ordnance Corps, July 1955–June 1956," p. 44, call no. 40-2.1 AA 1956, in USACMH. A subsequent report mentions a twenty-eight-kiloton warhead, which, based upon the context, appears not to have been fielded. (See "Summary of Major Events and Problems of the [Army] Ordnance Corps, July 1957–June 1958," p. 44, call no. 40-2.1 AA 1958, USACMH.) This comports with approximate yields noted in Hansen, *Swords of Armageddon*, p. VII-198. Other secondary sources give a wide variance in Nike-Hercules W-31 yields, in part

because a third, higher-yield version, was developed for the Army's Honest Johns surface-to-surface missile. Some erroneously attribute this third type to Nike-Hercules. For Honest John, see Hansen, *Swords of Armageddon*, p. VII-196.

109. "B. United States Weapon Progr[am]."
110. DCSLOG memorandum to Chief of Engineers, May 3, 1957, captioned "Requirements of Atomic NIKE HERCULES," DOE/NV no. NV0311428.
111. Condit, pp. 62–65. The Talos warhead was also tested during Teapot. See "The Final Teapot Tests," p. 14; Hansen, *Swords of Armageddon*, Table A-1, pp. V-55 to V-56, VII-61, VII-64 to VII-65, VII-187 to VII-188. Although the land-based Talos was eventually canceled, beginning in 1959 the U.S. Navy fielded three hundred maritime versions for defense against air attack at sea. (See Hansen, *Swords of Armageddon*, p. VII-190.) The Talos was developed for the same reasons as land-based nuclear air-defense arms, although the naval aspect is outside the scope of this project.
112. Sanky Trimble, "Secret Nike Most Powerful," *Washington Post and Times-Herald*, May 24, 1956, p. 8; Anthony Leviero, "Defense Aides Back Nike, Call New One Phenomenal," *New York Times*, May 29, 1956, p. 1.
113. Leviero, *New York Times*, May 29, 1956.
114. *Nuclear Weapons in the Air Defense System: Special Historical Study no. 2*, n.p., [September 1953], pp. 1–3; Richard F. McMullen, *Interceptor Missiles in Air Defense: 1944–1964* (A[ir] D[efense] C[ommand] Historical Study no. 30), February 1965, p. 33.
115. Hansen, *Swords of Armageddon*, p. VII-200; Thomas W. Ray, *BOMARC and Nuclear Armament*, and A[ir] D[efense] C[ommand] Historical Study No. 21 (n.p.: Air Defense Command, n.d.), pp. 4–5.
116. Richard F. McMullen, *History of Air Defense Weapons; 1946–1962* A[ir] D[efense] C[ommand] Historical Study 14 (n.p.: Air Defense Command), n.d., pp. 302–304; Margaret C. Bagwell, *History of the BOMARC Weapon System; 1953–1957* (Wright-Patterson Air Force Base, [Ohio]: Air Materiel Command, 1959).
117. Ray, *BOMARC and Nuclear Armament*, p. 6; "B. United States Weapon Progr[am]," p. 4. The relevant test was probably the Erie (May 31) or Seminole (June 6) shots. See Hansen, *Swords of Armageddon*, Table A-1, p. 9, and p. VII-202.
118. This figure is redacted from Ray, *BOMARC and Nuclear Armament*, p. 1. However, it states that "the destruction of Hiroshima in August 1945" was caused by "an atomic blast of twice this magnitude." Since the Hiroshima bomb was estimated at the time this report was written to be about thirteen kilotons, the W-40 yield can easily be calculated. For Hiroshima yield, see John Malik, "The Yields of the Hiroshima and Nagasaki Nuclear Explosions," Los Alamos National Laboratory, September 1985, LA-8819, p. 1.
119. "B. United States Weapon Progr[am]," p. 52.
120. McMullen, *Interceptor Missiles*, pp. 50–51.

121. Paul F. Foster memorandum to Elmer B. Staats, October 21, 1955, Box 21, Folder 5, Hansen Collection.
122. Theodore C. Streibert memorandum for Lewis L. Strauss, January 3, 1956, Box 22, Folder 1, Hansen Collection.
123. Hansen believes Streibert's argument "was far from the whole truth," because only five of seventeen Redwing shots were related to air defense. See Hansen, *Swords of Armageddon*, p. V-158. This does not, however, address the significance that test proponents placed on the antiaircraft program in internal communications, which had little connection with influencing public opinion. See Lewis L. Strauss letter to John Foster Dulles, October 25, 1955, cited above.
124. Everett Holles memorandum to Lewis Strauss, January 6, 1956, in Lewis L. Strauss Papers, Atomic Energy Commission Series, Folder "Red Wing, 1955–56," HHPL. Other drafts in this file show that Strauss actively participated in editing the proposed release and exercised final authority in approving it before seeking concurrence from other government officials.
125. John G. Norris, "New Tests to Stress A-Defenses," *Washington Post and Times-Herald*, January 13, 1956, p. 1; Hanson Baldwin, "Major Atomic Tests Will Start in March," *New York Times*, February 23, 1956, p. 1, "Atomic Tests to Stress Defense; Strauss Notes Gain in Weapons," *New York Times*, February 27, 1956, p. 1; "Statement by Lewis L. Strauss, Chairman, U.S. Atomic Energy Commission," July 19, 1956, DOE/NV no. NV0324187.
126. Anthony Leviero, "Mock Attack Hits 75 Areas in Nation—'State of War' Set," *New York Times*, July 21, 1956, p. 1; "Statement by Lewis L. Strauss, Chairman, U.S. Atomic Energy Commission."
127. Chalmers M. Roberts, "Fatal A-Raid Discounted By Officials After Check," *Washington Post and Times-Herald*, July 24, 1956, p. 25. For Eisenhower's favorable assessment of the 1956 operation and his remark about "how necessary this work is," see "Notes on the Expanded Cabinet Meeting held from 2:30 to 3:45 P.M. on Wednesday, July 25, 1956," *DDRS* no. CK3100117439.
128. W.W. Rostow, *Open Skies: Eisenhower's Proposal of July 21, 1955* (Austin: University of Texas Press, 1982). Some Soviet military leaders argued later that Eisenhower's proposal was intended to provide justification for unilateral overflights once the U-2 was perfected. This supposition is weakened by the fact that, because of the tight classification of the U-2 program, most of the proponents of Open Skies were not aware of the plane's development. Eisenhower, of course, is a significant exception. See Raymond L. Garthoff, *Assessing the Adversary: Estimates by the Eisenhower Administration of Soviet Intentions and Capabilities* (Washington: Brookings Institution, 1991), p. 11.
129. Gregory W. Pedlow and Donald E. Welzenbach, *The CIA and the U-2 Program, 1954–1974* (Washington: Central Intelligence Agency, 1988), pp. 84–85; For Eisenhower's low opinion of the balloon effort, see "Memorandum for Record," February 10, 1956, p. 5.

130. R. Cargill Hall, "The Truth about Overflights," *MHQ: The Quarterly Journal of Military History* 9, no. 3 (Spring 1997): 36–37; Rostow, p. 192. For a discussion of Ike's belief in the necessity of these overflights and his approval of them, see Andrew Goodpaster, "Cold War Overflights: A View from the White House," in *Early Cold War Overflights: Symposium Proceedings, Volume I, Memoirs* (Washington: National Reconnaissance Office, 2003), pp. 37–46. Goodpaster concedes, "[m]y own memory is not clear and detailed" on the topic, but he outlines his extant recollections, which appear well formed.
131. Watson, p. 408.
132. Pedlow and Welzenbach, pp. 104–106.
133. Pedlow and Welzenbach, pp. 111–112.
134. Pedlow and Welzenbach, pp. 124, 140, 316.
135. Watson, pp. 432–433.
136. "Staff Notes No. 16," September 11, 1956, *DDRS* no. CK3100 423663.
137. Herbert B. Loper letter to Lewis L. Strauss, December 18, 1956, in Folder "OCB 000.9 [Atomic Energy] (File #5) (6) [August 1956–January 1957]," Box 11, OCB Central Files Series, WHO, NSC Staff Papers, 1948–61, DDEL.
138. "NSC Action 1631," November 14, 1956, *DDRS* no. CK3100236201.
139. Herbert B. Loper letter to Lewis L. Strauss, December 18, 1956.
140. Herbert B. Loper letter to Lewis L. Strauss, December 18, 1956.
141. Herbert B. Loper letter to Lewis L. Strauss, December 18, 1956.
142. "Nike B Seen Destructive to Air Invaders," *Washington Post and Times-Herald*, August 18, 1956, p. 4.
143. "Army Developing New Atom Missile," *New York Times*, December 24, 1956, p. 24; John W. Finney, "Potent New Nike B Due in 2 Years," *Washington Post and Times-Herald*, December 24, 1956, p. A2.
144. Paul F. Foster memorandum to Elmer B. Staats, January 2, 1957, in Folder "OCB 000.9 [Atomic Energy] (File #5) (6) [August 1956–January 1957]," Box 11, OCB Central Files Series, WHO, NSC Staff Papers, 1948–61, DDEL.
145. "Atoms for Peace" and Allied opinion is addressed in "Draft Outline, Report of the OCB Working Group on Nuclear Energy on Public Information Plan on Air Defense Weapons," January 4, 1957, attached to Paul F. Foster memorandum to Elmer B. Staats, January 2, 1957 (see esp. pp. 1–2). USIA suggestion is in Joseph Henson memorandum to members of OCB Nuclear Energy Working Group, January 11, 1957 in Folder "OCB 000.9 [Atomic Energy] (File #5) (7) [August 1956–January 1957]," Box 11, OCB Central Files Series, WHO, NSC Staff Papers, 1948–61, DDEL. The preceding document provides the offered language. The quotation is from the final release, which amended the wording slightly.
146. "Report of the OCB Working Group on Nuclear Energy on Public Information Plan on Air Defense Weapons," January 7, 1957, p. 4, attached to "Note to Holders of Memo for the Operations Coordinating Board, DTD January 7, 1957," January 8, 1957, in Folder "OCB 000.9

[Atomic Energy] (File #5) (7) [August 1956–January 1957]," Box 11, OCB Central Files Series, WHO, NSC Staff Papers, 1948–61, DDEL; and memorandum captioned "The Board took the following action," January 16, 1957, in Folder "OCB 000.9 [Atomic Energy] (File #5) (8) [August 1956–January 1957]," Box 11, OCB Central Files Series, WHO, NSC Staff Papers, 1948–61, DDEL.

147. C.E. Wilson memorandum to the president, January 22, 1957, *DDRS* no. CK3100212948; attachments "MB-1 Deployment," *DDRS* no. CK3100213100; and "MB-1 Atomic Air-to-Air Rocket," *DDRS* no. CK3100213098.

148. Andrew Goodpaster memorandum for the Deputy Secretary of Defense, January 24, 1957, in Folder "Department of Defense, Vol. I (4) [January–April 1957]," Box 1, Subject Series, Department of Defense Subseries, WHO, OSS, Records, 1952–61, DDEL. The inexplicably deleted sentence read: "[T]he continuous improvement of our air defense system to keep ahead of potential enemy forces is essential to our national survival." See C.E. Wilson memorandum to the president, January 22, 1957. Because the release was issued on February 20, the day after the United States and Canada exchanged notes codifying Genie overflight arrangements, a connection between the two events is suggested. As outlined in the text, however, this timing is probably coincidental.

149. Maloney, pp. 65–66; Clearwater, pp. 50, 52.

150. This topic was specifically considered in 1959. See "Policy Guidance for NORAD Commanders Regarding Use of Nuclear Weapons," May 26, 1959, Nuclear History document collection, item no. NH01359, National Security Archive.

151. R. Hirsch memorandum to Elmer Staats, February 13, 1957, and attachments, all in Folder "OCB 000.9 [Atomic Energy] (File #6) (1) [February–March 1957]," Box 11, OCB Central Files Series, WHO, NSC Staff Papers, 1948–61, DDEL.

152. "Staff Notes No. 74," February 15, 1957, *DDRS* no. CK3100238900 (emphasis in the original); "Staff Notes No. 74," [earlier draft], February 15, 1957, in Folder "Staff Notes 66–80," Box 24, WHO, Staff Research Group, Records, 1956–61, DDEL; Herbert Loper letter to Carl T. Durham, February 19, 1957, Folder 6, Box 23, Hansen Collection.

153. "Deployment of Nuclear Weapons for Air Defense Announced," February 20, 1957, Department of Defense, Office of Public Information, in Folder "Nuclear Energy Matters (2) [Jan 1958]," Box 4, OCB Series, Subject Subseries, WHO, OSANSA, Records, 1952–61, DDEL.

154. "Fact Sheet; Nuclear Weapons for Air Defense," February 20, 1957, Department of Defense, Office of Public Information, in Folder "Nuclear Energy Matters (2) [Jan 1958]," Box 4, OCB Series, Subject Subseries, WHO, OSANSA, Records, 1952–61, DDEL.

155. John C. Norris, "U.S. Bases Getting New A-Rockets for Jet Use; Wilson Says Live Nuclear Warheads Will Be Stored at Each Airfield," *Washington Post and Times-Herald*, February 21, 1957, p. A1; John A. Giles, "Nikes

Ringing Capital to Get A-Arms Soon," *Washington Evening Star*, February 21, 1957, p. A-4; Jack Raymond, "U.S. Air Defense Armed with Nuclear Warheads," *New York Times*, February 21, 1957, p. 1.
156. John A. Giles, "Nikes Ringing Capital to Get A-Arms Soon."
157. "Atomic Defense," *Washington Post and Times-Herald*, February 22, 1957, p. A16.
158. "New Missile Undergoes Final Tests," *New York Times*, February 27, 1957, p. 12.
159. "New Missile Unveiled at White Sands," *Las Cruces* (New Mexico) *Sun News*, February 26, 1957, available in the National Air and Space Museum archives, file number ON-430700-01.

4 Genie

1. Shipping date is in "Report of the OCB Working Group on Nuclear Energy on Public Information Plan on Air Defense Weapons," January 7, 1957, p. 2, attached to "Note to Holders of Memo for the Operations Coordinating Board, DTD January 7, 1957," January 8, 1957, in Folder "OCB 000.9 [Atomic Energy] (File #5) (7) [August 1956–January 1957]," Box 11, OCB Central Files Series, White House Office [hereafter "WHO"], NSC Staff Papers, 1948–61, Dwight D. Eisenhower Library [hereafter "DDEL"]; destination is noted in document provided to the president captioned "MB-1 Deployment" *Declassified Documents Reference System* (hereafter *DDRS*), no. CK3100213100; assembly location and transit method is noted in K.F. Hertford telex to Brig. Gen. Alfred D. Starbird, November 28, 1956, pp. 2, 7, Department of Energy/Nevada Nuclear Testing Archive accession no. NV0103953 (hereafter "DOE/NV no.").
2. Thomas W. Ray, *Nuclear Armament: Its Acquisition, Control, and Application to Manned Interceptors, 1951–1963*; A[ir] D[efense] C[ommand] Historical Study No. 20 (n.p.: Air Defense Command, n.d.), p. 22.
3. Ray, pp. 20–21; Richard F. McMullen, *History of Air Defense Weapons; 1946–1962* A[ir] D[efense] C[ommand] Historical Study 14 (n.p.: Air Defense Command, n.d.), p. 210; Helen Rice, *History of Ogden Air Materiel Area: Hill Air Force Base, Utah, 1934–1960* (n.p.: Air Force Logistics Command, n.d.), pp. 164, 187; Jay Miller, "The Scorpion: A Pictorial Report," *Air University Review* 31, no. 5 (July–August 1980).
4. McMullen, pp. 38–40, 64–66, 103–107; Rice, pp. 164, 187.
5. Ray, pp. 26–27.
6. Ray, p. 21; McMullen, pp. 153, 245–248, 293.
7. McMullen, p. 210.
8. W.B. Rosson memorandum to Admiral Radford, July 3, 1957, *DDRS* no. CK3100460496.
9. Douglas Aircraft Company, Inc., news release, April 14, 1961, in Folder "Genie AIR-2A McDonnell Douglas Astronautics," in the collection of the Air Force Association, Arlington, Virginia (hereafter AFA).

10. Ray, p. 7. Genie motors were provided by a Douglas subcontractor, Aerojet-General Company. See Ray, pp. 10, 43.
11. Frank H. Shelton, *Reflections of a Nuclear Weaponeer* (Colorado Springs: Shelton Enterprises, 1988), p. 8–22.
12. "Sugar" and high-explosive source is noted in United States Atomic Energy Commission, "Program Status Report," December 31, 1954, p. 8, in Chuck Hansen Collection, Box 21, Folder 1, National Security Archive (hereafter "Hansen Collection;" in this collection, most folders are unnamed, but are arranged chronologically. Folder numbers are assigned for each box in ascending order from the oldest date to the most recent.) Pit source ("RF") is in K.F. Hertford telex to Brig. Gen. Alfred D. Starbird, November 28, 1956, p. 4; some component suppliers, including Alcoa, Philway, and Los Angeles Standard Rubber are listed in M.S. Kennedy letter to W.M. Johnson, November 23, 1956, captioned "EC-25 and W-25 Planning Schedule, XCII-576," in DOE/NV no. NV0972182. For other listing of production sources and parts providers, see W.B. McCool memorandum to Atomic Energy Commission, February 24, 1958, pp. 13–14, Box 26, Folder 1, Hansen Collection.
13. Chuck Hansen, *U.S. Nuclear Weapons: The Secret History* (Arlington, Texas: Aerofax, 1988), p. 177. As early as November 1954, the Pentagon understood that only EC-25 Genies would be available by January 1; the production versions were anticipated to be ready by midyear. See "Summary of Significant Changes to the Draft of the Department of Defense Progress Report to the National Security Council on Status of Military Continental Defense Programs as of November 1, 1954," November 23, 1954, in Folder "Continental Defense 1954 (9)," Box 23, Disaster File, WHO, NSC Staff Papers, 1948–61, DDEL. This document was declassified for this study.
14. Necah Stewart Furman, *Sandia National Laboratories: The Postwar Decade* (University of New Mexico Press: 1990), pp. 641–642, 647.
15. Hansen, *U.S. Nuclear Weapons*, p. 177. It is not clear that all twenty EC-25 warheads were mated to vehicles. One document notes a "small number of warheads assembled to rockets," but gives no further details or explanation. See "Notes on Design of 25 Warhead and Genie System," attached to document captioned "Summary of Safety Aspects of Certain Weapons," August 8, 1957, DOE/NV no. NV0318042. Another says the EC-25 weapons were manufactured by December 1956, and "deliveries were made to the Department of Defense in January and February" 1957. (See W.B. McCool memorandum to the Atomic Energy Commission, May 29, 1957, p. 1, in Box 24, Folder 2, Hansen Collection.) While the deliveries may have continued in early 1957, the source cited above clearly establishes the first shipment date.
16. Available records are not explicit about the first storage or armament arrangements. However, from the context of redacted sections of an official Air Force history, it is almost certain that the Wurtsmith and Hamilton facilities were temporary. (See Ray, pp. 14–15, 22, 24). The arming of planes at other bases having only interim storage is specified

(two planes with two rockets each), and it is probable that the same procedure applied at Wurtsmith and Hamilton. (See Ray, p. 22.)
17. Ray, pp. 14–15.
18. Karen J. Weitze, *Cold War Infrastructure for Air Defense: The Fighter and Command Missions* (Langley Air Force Base, Virginia: Headquarters, Air Combat Command, 1999), pp. 76–77; Ray, pp. 14–18. In early 1958, Aerojet General built a California complex to conduct impact and fire tests on the W-25 and Genie. See "Semiannual Historical Report; Headquarters, Field Command, The Armed Forces Special Weapons Command, Sandia Base, Albuquerque, New Mexico, 1 January 1958–30 June 1958," p. 382 (uncataloged collection, National Security Archive).
19. U.S. Army, *History of Strategic Air and Ballistic Missile Defense: Volume II, 1956–1972* (Washington: Center of Military History, c. 1975), p. 153.
20. Weitze, pp. 76–77; Ray, pp. 14–18.
21. Ray, p. 22.
22. See Edward J. Kolodziej, *The Uncommon Defense and Congress, 1945–1963* (Columbus: Ohio State University Press, 1966), pp. 241–245; Stephen E. Ambrose, *Eisenhower: The President* (New York: Simon and Schuster, 1984), pp. 388–389, 394–395; Robert J. Watson, *Into the Missile Age; 1956–1960; History of the Office of the Secretary of Defense, Vol. IV* (Washington: Office of the Secretary of Defense, 1997), pp. 73–95, 310–311.
23. Kolodziej, pp. 241–245; Ambrose, pp. 388–389, 394–395; and Watson, pp. 73–95, 310–311. For a brief discussion of how interservice rivalries and how disputes over service roles had budgetary implications, see Donald R. Baucom, *The Origins of SDI: 1944–1983* (Lawrence: University Press of Kansas, 1992), pp. 8–9.
24. "Memorandum of Discussion at the 288th Meeting of the National Security Council, Washington, June 15, 1956," (pp. 322–323, 327–331), "Memorandum of Discussion at the 293rd and 294th Meetings of the National Security Council, Washington, August 16 and August 17, 1956," (pp. 350–351), "Memorandum of Discussion at the 307th Meeting of the National Security Council, Washington, December 21, 1956," (pp. 384–394) in *Foreign Relations of the United States, 1955–1957*, vol. XIX, National Security Policy (Government Printing Office: Washington, 1990), hereafter identified as *FRUS* with year, volume, and page specified. Also, Memorandum for the President from Director, Bureau of the Budget, [c. December 1956], *Declassified Documents Reference System* (hereafter *DDRS*) no. CK3100392943; Richard M. Leighton, *Strategy, Money, and the New Look, 1953–1956: History of the Office of the Secretary of Defense, Vol. III* (Washington: Office of the Secretary of Defense, 2001), pp. 302–303; Watson, pp. 408–411; and Richard D. Challener, interviewer, "A Transcript of a Recorded Interview with Robert Sprague," John Foster Dulles Oral History Project, Princeton University Library, 11 August 1964, pp. 15–16, 40–44. This source includes Robert Sprague's assessment of Humphrey's view of the continental defense effort ("it was utter nonsense that this country couldn't

afford to do it"). In addition to Sprague, an ad hoc JCS committee also recommended more vigorous defenses, much to Radford's surprise (and consternation). See Memorandum for Admiral Radford from the Chairman's Staff Group, July 17, 1957, *DDRS* no. CK3100460504; and "Chronology of Significant Events and Decisions Relating to the U.S. Missile and Earth Satellite Development Programs, May 1942 through October 1957," pp. 73, 91–92, Nuclear History document collection, item no. NH00006, National Security Archive. Putative continental-defense deficiencies were also identified in connection with partisan critiques of the administration's conduct. See "Senate Report Calls Air Defense Weak," *New York Times*, January 30, 1957, p. 1. For Eisenhower's reaction to this Democratic evaluation, see Ambrose, p. 397. Since at least 1953, SAC had favored a warning network to allow its planes to become airborne before an attack. See Joseph T. Jockel, "The United States and Canadian Efforts at Continental Air Defense: 1945–1957," unpublished PhD dissertation, Johns Hopkins University, 1978, pp. 171–172.

25. Handwritten cabinet minutes, in Folder "C-37 (3) June 3, 1957," Box 4, in Cabinet Series, Records of the White House Staff Secretary; and "Minutes of Cabinet Meeting," in Folder "Cabinet Meeting of June 3, 1957," Box 9, in Ann W. Whitman Files, Cabinet Series, Dwight D. Eisenhower Papers as President, 1953–61; both in DDEL.

26. Several months hence, the president expressed concern about the "tremendous number of enormous weapons" sought by the military, but no objection to the relatively smaller explosives that would soon comprise the nation's nuclear antiaircraft arsenal. See "Memorandum of a Conference with the President, White House, Washington, October 31, 1957," in *FRUS, 1955–1957*, vol. XIX, pp. 617–618.

27. "Transcript of the President's News Conference on Foreign and Domestic Matters," *New York Times*, June 6, 1957, p. 14. The substance of the president's remarks, including on the topic of the development of defense arms, was communicated immediately to AEC officials at the Nevada Test Site. See memorandum captioned "Phone Conversation Between General Starbird and G.W. Johnson," June 5, 1957, in Box 24, Folder 3, in Hansen Collection.

28. For the briefing, see "The Guided Missile Program," Office of the Secretary of Defense, July 1957, *DDRS* no. CK3100285850. For information provided at the time the press release was approved, see "MB-1 Deployment," [January 22, 1957,] *DDRS* no. CK3100213100.

29. Dwight D. Eisenhower letter to Charles E. Wilson, July 8, 1957, *DDRS* no. CK3100252341.

30. Rosson memorandum.

31. "President Leaves Golfer in the Air," *New York Times*, June 15, 1957, p. 6; Robert C. Jensen, "'Attack' Set Friday for Area's Alert," *Washington Post and Times-Herald*, July 11, 1957, p. B1; W.H. Lawrence, "President Leaves Capital," *New York Times*, July 13, 1957, p. 1.

32. W.H. Lawrence, "President to Use 'Copter in Test," *New York Times*, July 12, 1957, p. 2; "President to Lead Exodus From Capital in D.C.

Test" *Washington Post and Times-Herald,* July 2, 1957, p. B2. The Air Force provided the pilots and helicopters for this exercise. Around this time, the service became responsible for helicopter evacuation of the president in event of emergency. For details on the Air Force preparations (including the possibility of burrowing into a White House bunker to retrieve the chief executive if the helicopters arrived after an attack), see Ted Gup, "The Doomsday Blueprints," *Time,* August 10, 1992, p. 32. It appears that other arrangements were made for more routine presidential helicopter travel. In October 1957, the Air Force asked to be "temporarily relieved" of this assignment because "present available craft are inferior in several areas to those of other services." The Marines took over the task permanently. See "Memorandum for Mr. Albert P. Toner," October 24, 1957, in Folder "Defense 186-253," Box 4, White House Office [hereafter WHO], Staff Research Group, Records, 1956-61, DDEL. For a possibly apocryphal story about the origins of the Marine assignment (Ike's annoyance that his slower Air Force helicopter was outpaced by a staff-laden Marine craft), see Virgil Olson, "Flying on Foreign Choppers," *Washington Times,* February 1, 2004, p. B5.

33. Hansen, *Swords of Armageddon,* CD-ROM (1995), p. VII-91; Documents labeled "Table B; Data Date 12/31/84," in Box 1, Folder 2; "Table C; Cumulative History of LANL/DOD and EC Programs Suspended or Cancelled," in Box 2, Folder 2; and W.B. McCool memorandum to the Atomic Energy Commission, May 29, 1957, p. 2; all in Hansen Collection. In a semiannual report on activities, the Development Division of the Armed Forces Special Weapons Project noted it concluded responsibility for the EC-25 sometime between January 1 and June 30, 1958, because the weapon was "[r]etired from stockpile." The discrepancy in dates may reflect some lag between the formal and practical end of responsibilities or an indication that the division had some role in the EC-25 dismantlement, which conceivably stretched into the first days of the reporting period. See "Semiannual Historical Report; Headquarters, Field Command, The Armed Forces Special Weapons Command, Sandia Base, Albuquerque, New Mexico, 1 January 1958-30 June 1958," p. 400.

34. K.F. Hertford telex to Brig. Gen. Alfred D. Starbird, November 28, 1956.

35. Ray, p. 22.

36. Minutes of Executive Session of Meeting No. 1166, Atomic Energy Commission, January 24, 1956, p. 33, Box 22, Folder 1, Hansen Collection.

37. N.D. Greenberg memorandum Vincent G. Huston, May 20, 1955, attached to Vincent Huston memorandum to K.E. Fields, May 24, 1955, Box 21, Folder 3, Hansen Collection. On the "Wigwam" test of the "Lulu" antisubmarine weapon, see Charles Corddry, "U.S. Plans Undersea Atomic Blast off West Coast," *Washington Post and Times-Herald,* May 10, 1955, p. 7; "U.S. Will Test Atom as Submarine Killer," *New York Times,* May 10, 1955, p. 1. For public announcement of Lulu deployment, see Herbert Loper letter to Lewis Strauss, October 10, 1956 (on need to issue a statement), Box 23, Folder 1, Hansen Collection;

John G. Norris, "A-Device Can Destroy Submarines Miles Away," *Washington Post and Times-Herald*, October 26, 1956, p. A-3; and "Navy Using Atom in Depth Charges," *New York Times*, October 26, 1956, p. 14 (resulting press coverage). For internal discussion about questions posed by Norris in writing the above-cited story, see Henry G. Vermillion memorandum to the files, October 26, 1956, in Box 23, Folder 1, Hansen Collection; "Restricted Data Classification Decisions, 1946 to the Present (RDD-8)," U.S. Department of Energy, January 1, 2002, pp. 92, 106, 118 in author's possession. This document was declassified and distributed in 2009 at the request of the Federation of American Scientists. The development of nuclear antisubmarine weapons is outside the scope of this project. However, a cursory examination of the topic shows that their intent and purpose mirrors that of nuclear antiaircraft armament.
38. K.E. Fields letter to Henry M. Jackson, February 24, 1956, DOE/NV no. NV0074039.
39. Quotations in W.B. McCool memorandum to Atomic Energy Commission, November 9, 1956, pp. 2, 21, NV/DOE no. NV0072542. Herbert B. Loper letter to Lewis L. Strauss, November 7, 1956, attached to W.B. McCool memorandum to Atomic Energy Commission, November 19, 1956, DOE/NV no. 0063983.
40. Horacio Rivero memorandum for Chairman, Military Liaison Committee, December 14, 1956, Box 23, Folder 2, Hansen Collection.
41. "Commission Discussion of Operation Pilgrim," DOE/NV no. NV0072541. ("Pilgrim" was an early code name for the operation eventually designated "Plumbbob.")
42. Number of shots is in Hansen, *Swords of Armageddon*, Table A-1, pp. 10–13. Approval is Lewis L. Strauss letter to the President, December 21, 1956, DOE/NV no. NV0108283. Presidential aide Andrew Goodpaster noted beneath Ike's signature that the chief executive's approval was "subject to his understanding that all the tests proposed will be held in Nevada." Eisenhower may have learned of the commission's disagreement over the size and location of the series, and his instructions may demonstrate that he opposed the conduct of the operation outside of the United States because of how this could be perceived by foreign audiences.
43. Atomic Energy Commission press release, January 24, 1957, DOE/NV no. NV0143832. Michael Joshua Silverman, "No Immediate Risk: Environmental Safety in Nuclear Weapons Production, 1942–1985," unpublished PhD dissertation, Carnegie Mellon University, 2000, pp. 247–248.
44. For the submission of the draft release to the OCB, see Paul Foster memorandum to Elmer B. Staats, January 6(?), 1957, in Folder "OCB 000.9 [Atomic Energy] (File #5) (6) [August 1956 January 1957]," Box 11, OCB Central Files Series, WHO, NSC Staff Papers, 1948–61, DDEL.
45. R. Hirsch memorandum to Mr. [Elmer] Staats, January 17, 1957, in Folder "OCB 000.9 [Atomic Energy] (File #5) (8) [August 1956–January 1957]," Box 11, OCB Central Files Series, WHO, NSC Staff Papers, 1948–61, DDEL.

46. Atomic Energy Commission press release, January 24, 1957; "New Bomb Tests Coming in Spring," *New York Times*, January 25, 1957, p. 22; Darrell Garwood, "Another Series of Nuclear Tests to Be Held in Nevada This Spring," *Washington Post and Times-Herald*, January 25, 1957, p. A1.
47. Alfred D. Starbird telex to [Kenner] Hertford, December 27, 1956, and attached "classified routing slip," Box 23, Folder 3, Hansen Collection. Starbird was an interesting and accomplished engineer. The son of an Army general, he held degrees from West Point and Princeton, and competed in the pentathlon in the 1936 Olympics. See press release captioned "Colonel Alfred D. Starbird Named Director of AEC Division of Military Application," June 27, 1955, Box 21, Folder 3, Hansen Collection; Dwight Chapin, "Driven to Succeed; Kate Starbird's Determination Made Her Soar at Stanford." *San Francisco Chronicle*, March 22, 1996.
48. Alfred D. Starbird memorandum for the chairman, September 22, 1957, DOE/NV no. NV0108443.
49. "Remarks by Lieutenant General J.H. Atkinson, USAF, Commander, Air Defense Command," July 18, 1957, in Box 24, Folder 3, Hansen Collection.
50. Starbird memorandum for the chairman, September 22, 1957; "Operation Plumbbob; Nuclear Radiation Received by Crews Firing the MB-1 Rocket, Project 2.9," May 27, 1959, p. 9, Box 25, Folder 1, Hansen Collection.
51. A later briefing references a test of "a stockpiled weapon." This could be interpreted to mean a Genie with a W-25 (rather than an EC-25) warhead. See draft remarks attached to Richard T. Coiner, Jr. memorandum to Chief, Armed Forces Special Weapons Project, June 4, 1957, DOE/NV no. NV0102557.
52. E.H. Draper memorandum to R.A. Rice, February 7, 1957, Box 23, Folder 6, Hansen Collection; and "Final Report, Operation Plumbbob, 4950th Test Group (N)," p. 39, DOE/NV no. NV0039493. Months later, another study evaluated the "probability of [a] nuclear disaster" occurring following an otherwise normal and authorized launch. This probably refers to the possibility that the rocket would detonate prematurely (thus killing the interceptor crew) or fall to the ground. Presumably the study determined that the chance of a "disaster" was low. See "Semiannual Historical Report; Headquarters, Field Command, The Armed Forces Special Weapons Project, Sandia Base, Albuquerque, New Mexico, Volume I, 1 July 1957–31 December 1957," p. 226 (uncataloged collection, National Security Archive).
53. See typewritten notes appended to "Memo from the Office of the Commander-in-Chief CON[tinental]A[ir]D[efense Command]," n.d., in RG3702.AM, "Oldfield, Barney [Arthur Barney]," Series 4 "Personal Papers, 1928–1970s," Box 30, Folder 10 "NORAD, 1954–1962" in collection of Nebraska State Historical Society (hereafter "Oldfield Papers").
54. For familiarity with the high-altitude results, see Richard L. Miller, *Under the Cloud: The Decades of Nuclear Testing* (New York: The Free

Press, 1986), pp. 269–70. For other items, see "Ground Zero: Fact for the Fretful" at http://www.aracnet.com/~pdxavets/genie.htm; and Howard L. Rosenberg, *Atomic Soldiers: American Victims of Nuclear Experiments* (Boston: Beacon Press, 1980), p. 89. This work is clearly based upon discussions with Oldfield because similar details are included in the Oldfield Papers, although records of specific communications between Oldfield and Rosenberg could not be found.

55. "AEC Invites Newsmen to A-Rocket Test," *Washington Post and Times-Herald*, July 13, 1957, p. A3.
56. "Note to Correspondents," July 12, 1957, DOE/NV no. NV0336568. This notice specifies that participants must be U.S. citizens.
57. "Note to Correspondents," July 16, 1957, DOE/NV no. NV0144046.
58. "Remarks by Lieutenant General J.H. Atkinson, USAF, Commander, Air Defense Command."
59. "Remarks by Lieutenant General J.H. Atkinson, USAF, Commander, Air Defense Command." Emphasis in original.
60. Draft remarks attached to Richard T. Coiner, Jr. memorandum to Chief, Armed Forces Special Weapons Project, June 4, 1957. RCAF observers are also noted in Herbert B. Loper memorandum for the OCB Staff Representative, Working Group on Nuclear Energy Matters and Related Projects, March 21, 1957, *DDRS* no. CK3100318111. For details on the RCAF delegation, see Sean M. Maloney, *Learning to Love the Bomb: Canada's Nuclear Weapons During the Cold War* (Washington: Potomac Books, 2007), pp. 93, 96.
61. Draft remarks attached to Richard T. Coiner, Jr., memorandum to Chief, Armed Forces Special Weapons Project, June 4, 1957.
62. "Annex M to Test Director's Operation Plan No. CTDN-22," attached to memorandum "To: distribution, Re: Annex M, CDI, dated July 15, 1957, to Secret-RD Test Director's Operation Plan, CTDN-22 dated April 1, 1957," July 15, 1957, DOE/NV no. NV0077404.
63. For radiological monitoring reports, see "John Event-Survey Meter Monitoring Logs," DOE/NV no. NV0019121. Meteorological data is shown in a document bearing that caption (DOE/NV no. NV0017406). For a discussion of the public relations aspects of meteorological and radiological predictions during tests at the NTS, see Silverman, including pp. 222–224, 235–236.
64. For an initial report, see James E. Reeves telex to A.D. Starbird, July 19, 1957, DOE/NV no. NV0123822. For time and location, see uncaptioned press release, Nevada Test Organization, Office of Test Information, July 19, 1957, DOE/NV no. NV0144063. For number of practice efforts, see "Final Report, Operation Plumbbob, 4950th Test Group (N)," p. 160. For five nonnuclear launches, see "Remarks by Lieutenant General J.H. Atkinson, USAF, Commander, Air Defense Command." For Genie distance and interceptor location, see "Operation Plumbbob; Nuclear Radiation Received by Crews Firing the MB-1 Rocket, Project 2.9," p. 12. For flight time and kilotonage, see "Operation Plumbbob, Project 5.5, In-Flight Structural Response of an F-89D Aircraft to a Nuclear Detonation (U)," [March 22, 1960], pp. 12, 43,

DOE/NV no. NV0173393. The title of this last source indicates that the test aircraft was a Scorpion that had not received the standard modification to fire the Genie or had been retrofitted but not yet been officially designated a "J" version. A secondary source suggests this is incorrect. See Gerald Balzer and Mike Darrio, *Northrop F-89 Scorpion* (Arlington Texas: Aerofax, 1993).

65. "Operation Plumbbob, Project 5.5, In-Flight Structural Response of an F-89D Aircraft to a Nuclear Detonation (U)."

66. Rem is an abbreviation for "Roentgen Equivalent Man," which takes into account the type of radiation received. A Roentgen is a unit of radiation measurement. For Shot John exposure, see "Operation Plumbbob; Nuclear Radiation Received by Crews Firing the MB-1 Rocket, Project 2.9," p. 13. Although initial estimates predicted the airmen received about five rems, there was some earlier understanding that the radiation received by the aircrew might be in excess of this amount. This was allowed, provided the overall thirty-five-rem limit was maintained. See James Reeves telex to Alfred D. Starbird, July 19, 1957, DOE/NV no. NV0077904; and "Operation Plumbbob, Project 5.5, In-Flight Structural Response of an F-89D Aircraft to a Nuclear Detonation (U)," p. 16. For a mention of the possibility of crews receiving thirteen rem, see remarks attached to Richard T. Coiner, Jr., memorandum to Chief, Armed Forces Special Weapons Project, June 4, 1957, p. 12. As late as 1979, the federal government allowed individuals working with radiation, such as x-ray technicians, to receive as much as three rem of radiation per quarter and five rem per year. See "Letter of Notification to Participants," attached to Edwin Still memorandum for Service NTPR Teams, July 31, 1979, DOE/NV no. NV0403134. For a sound overview of the controversy surrounding the government's understanding of the risk of nuclear testing at the NTS, see A. Costandina Titus, *Bombs in the Backyard: Atomic Testing and American Politics* (Reno and Las Vegas: University of Nevada Press, 1989). For a discussion of the "history of risk" in the U.S. nuclear enterprise, see Silverman, pp. 14–19.

67. For a generally positive evaluation of Plumbbob dosimetry practices, see National Research Council, *Film Badge Dosimetry in Atmospheric Nuclear Tests* (Washington: National Academy Press, 1989), pp. 154–159. In 2005, another National Research Council panel concluded that "there is no dose of radiation, however low, that can be deemed completely safe." This includes medical x-rays. See Shankar Vedantam, "Low Radiation Doses Still Pose Risk, Panel Finds," *Washington Post*, June 30, 2005, p. A7. Four years earlier, the *New York Times* reported that "up to now, regulators have typically acted as if every bit of excess exposure is potentially hazardous. But some scientists question this assumption." A 2000 report from the General Accounting Office said that "[t]he standards administered by the E.P.A. and N.R.C. to protect the public from low level radiation exposure do not have a conclusive scientific basis, despite decades of research." The article also reported, "[S]ome scientists even say low radiation doses may be beneficial." See Gina Kolata, "For Radiation, How Much Is Too Much?" *New York Times*, November 27, 2001, p. F1.

68. "Operation Plumbbob; Nuclear Radiation Received by Crews Firing the MB-1 Rocket, Project 2.9," p. 14. Because that report was based upon Shot John, it specified the conclusion applied to the specific altitude of that operation, but said, "Although no definite statements can be made concerning MB-1 delivery at other altitudes, it is considered that theoretical predictions made for other altitudes will hold within a factor of two." Shot John's radioactivity measurements were possible despite the loss of one instrumented balloon tethered near the area of the blast. See "AFSWC Weekly Summary Reports, 1957," p. 2, in Box 24, Folder 5, Hansen Collection. For dangers of operating frontline aircraft of the time (in 1957, twenty-eight B-47 accidents claimed the lives of sixty-three airmen), see Walter J. Boyne, "The Dawn of Discipline: A B-47 pilot Remembers When an Airplane—and Curtis LeMay—Stiffened the Spine of the Strategic Air Command," *Air and Space Smithsonian* (July 2009).
69. See caption on photograph 157302 AC in Folder "Genie AIR-2A McDonnell Douglas Astronautics," AFA. For the photographer's participation, see remarks by George Yoshitake in *The Atomic Filmmakers: Behind the Scenes*, prod. and dir. Peter Kuran, 45 min., Visual Concept Entertainment, 1997, videocassette. In his recollection, Oldfield maintained that his assignment to raise public awareness was the primary purpose of the test. "The key part of all this was to get agreement from the Joint Chiefs of Staff to fire an MB-1 in the 1957 test series...," wrote Oldfield years later. (See typewritten notes appended to "Memo from the Office of the Commander-in-Chief CON[tinental]A[ir]D[efense Command].") The evidence cited above clearly demonstrates other Air Force and JCAE motivations.
70. In 1953, 2,500 Army soldiers witnessed the detonation of a 15-kiloton nuclear cannon round from trenches 2.3 miles away. See James Lamont, "The Atomic Cannon: It Was Fired Once, But It Helped End a War," *Invention & Technology* 21, no. 1 (Summer 2005): 50–54. Miller, p. 271 reports that the ground-zero participants remained on-site an extra hour because of a logistical foul-up. None of the sources cited refer to this situation and no other evidence of this has been found.
71. For details of the morning of the shot, see Rosenberg, p. 89, and Atomic *Filmmakers*. "Ground Zero: Fact for the Fretful" notes the connection between Bodinger and Cousins. For SANE, see advertisement captioned "We Are Facing a Danger Unlike Any Danger That Has Ever Existed..." *New York Times*, November 15, 1957, p.15; "New Group to Seek 'Sane' Atom Policy," *New York Times*, November 15, 1957, p. 54.
72. Gladwin Hill, "First Atomic Rocket Fired by Jet over Nevada Desert," *New York Times*, 20 July 1957, p. A1.
73. "The A-Rocket," *Time*, July 29, 1957, p. 16; "1st Air-to-Air A-Rocket Fired; 5 Stand Beneath," *Washington Post and Times-Herald*, 20 July 1957, p. A8. The six volunteers received exams immediately following and then periodically after the Plumbbob test. The long-term fate of the volunteers cannot be determined. All in their mid-thirties in 1957, they lived at least twenty more years based upon the last newspaper citation to

their activities. By 1997, one remained alive. See Al Stump, "Five Stood under the Bomb and Lived to Talk about It," *Los Angeles Herald-Examiner*, 1977 (in author's possession) and *Atomic Filmmakers*. A "search of more than two dozen books and Web sites on nuclear weapons produced no information that the officers experienced unusual medical problems in later years," according to a 2002 journalistic inquiry. See Robert F. Dorr, "Genie Missile Added Nuclear Punch to Air Defense Fighters," *Air Force Times* 63, no. 15 (November 4, 2002): 40–41.

74. See "Jet Fires Air-to-Air Atomic Rocket While Officers Check Effects Below," *Los Angeles Times*, July 20, 1957; Richard Sweeney, "USAF Fires Atomic Air-to-Air Missile," *Aviation Week*, July 29, 1957, pp. 33–35; and coverage in *Los Angeles Examiner*, *Santa Fe New Mexican*, and *Salt Lake Tribune*. For the press statement, see uncaptioned release, July 19, 1957, DOE/NV no. 0144063. It inexplicably lists the photographer as "Mr. L.C. Yamosopo," possibly indicating that Yoshitake was a last-minute substitution.

75. "Memorandum of Discussion at the 332nd Meeting of the National Security Council, Washington, July 25, 1957," in *FRUS, 1955–1957*, vol. XIX, National Security Policy, pp. 556–565.

76. Otis is noted as the first location under construction in Weitze, p. 76. It is not clear if this means other than the two initial locations with temporary facilities. For the other arrangements, see Ray, pp. 22, 24.

77. Andrew Goodpaster Memorandum for Record, September 3, 1957, *DDRS* no. CK3100165792. A curious deletion in this document (based upon the context) could reference a location outside the United States, possibly Greenland. On July 10, 1957, the military's Committee on Storage and Transportation of Nuclear Components had met to "formulate rules for the shipment of sealed pits," which included discussion of rail transportation. (See "Semiannual Historical Report; Headquarters, Field Command, The Armed Forces Special Weapons Project, Sandia Base, Albuquerque, New Mexico, Volume I, 1 July 1957–31 December 1957," p. 377.) In early 1958, the AEC conducted an informal study of the "transportation of weapons." This may have been engendered by the AEC's unspecified concern about the earlier W-25 shipments. For reference to the study, see Memorandum for General A.D. Starbird from Lewis L. Strauss, March 27, 1958, in Box 25, Folder 5, Hansen Collection.

78. "Semiannual Historical Report; Headquarters, Field Command, The Armed Forces Special Weapons Project, Sandia Base, Albuquerque, New Mexico, Volume I, 1 July 1957–31 December 1957," p. 306.

79. "Joint Statement by Department of Defense and Atomic Energy Commission," February 14, 1958, Box 26, Folder 1, Hansen Collection; Governor Goodwin J. Knight telegram to the President, December 17, 1957, Gov. Goodwin Knight Disaster Council Files, 1957–1958, California State Archives, Office of the Secretary of State, Sacramento. California civil defense officials sought to publicize the warning immediately upon being contacted by the Air Force. Military officials convinced them to delay any announcement until the forthcoming release was

issued. Although Knight misunderstood the topic to be "nuclear-armed" aircraft, he wrote Eisenhower that he believed "that this matter is of such vital importance to the people of California that information should immediately be made available so that protective measures may be instituted without delay." This communication received priority consideration at the White House and the attention of top aide Sherman Anderson. See material in Folders "Nuclear Energy Matters (2) [Jan. 1958]," and "Nuclear Energy Matters (4) [Feb.–Mar. 1958]," both in Box 4, OCB Series, Subject Subseries, WHO, Office of Special Assistant for National Security Affairs [hereafter "OSANSA"], Records, 1952–61, DDEL.

80. "Joint Statement by Department of Defense and Atomic Energy Commission," February 14, 1958.
81. "Joint Statement by Department of Defense and Atomic Energy Commission," February 14, 1958.
82. See Gov. Goodwin Knight Disaster Council Files, 1957–1958, California State Archives, Office of the Secretary of State, Sacramento; Jack Raymond, "U.S. Admits Peril in Atomic Mishaps," *New York Times*, February 15, 1958, p. 9; Arthur W. Arundel, "Decontamination Teams Set Up to Guard Public in A-Accidents," *Washington Post and Times-Herald*, February 15, 1958, p. A9.
83. "Colonel Barney Oldfield," [North American Air Defense Command news release], in Series 4 "Personal Papers, 1928–1970s," Box 30, Folder 10 "NORAD, 1954–1962," Oldfield Papers; and "Biographical Note," for RG3702 "Oldfield, Barney (Arthur Barney)," Oldfield Papers. Barney Oldfield, *Never a Shot in Anger* (New York: Duell, Sloan, and Pearce, 1956). For Santa Claus origins, see "Santa Claus Barney," at http://www.oldfields.org/military/airforcekoreanorad/santaclaus_barney.html. For continuing tradition, see Kortney Stringer, "Click Here for Santa's Lap," *Wall Street Journal*, December 14, 2004, p. B1. Oldfield continued a correspondence with Reagan through the presidency. (See finding aid, Oldfield Papers.)
84. "$61 Billions [sic] for a 2-Hour Warning Against Sneak Attack," *U.S. News and World Report*, September 6, 1957, pp. 72–85. Oldfield probably was not happy with this interview. Partridge is pessimistic despite leading questions from his interviewer clearly meant to elicit confident statements about the state of North America's air defenses.
85. "$61 Billions for a 2-Hour Warning Against Sneak Attack," *U.S. News and World Report*.
86. Donald A. Quarles [Secretary of Defense] memorandum for the president (with attachments), October 13, 1958, in Folder "Department of Defense, Vol. III (3) [October–December 1958]," Box 1, Subject Series, Department of Defense Subseries, WHO, Office of Staff Secretary, Records, 1952–61, DDEL.
87. "The Weaponeer," (screenplay by Joseph W. Parker) in *Department of Defense Film Collection*, Box 28, Folder 3, Georgetown University Library, Special Collections Division, Washington, DC; Oscar Godbout, "Two Pilot Films Being Shot for TV; Series by Schenk [sic] and T.P.A. Set in U.S. and Canada—Jane Russell Signed," *New York Times*, December 18,

1957, p. 71. For details about this collection and the script-approval process, see Lawrence H. Suid, *Guts and Glory: The Making of the American Military Image in Film* (Lexington: University Press of Kentucky, 2002). For a review of DoD participation in movies and television programs extolling the Air Force's contributions to national defense of the era, see Steve Call, *Selling Air Power: Military Aviation and American Popular Culture after World War II* (College Station: Texas A&M University Press, 2009), 116–131. For Stewart's specific role in urging Paramount to produce *Strategic Air Command*, see Marc Eliot, *Jimmy Stewart: A Biography* (New York: Harmony Books, 2006), 279–280. While Stewart's knowledge of "The Weaponeer" or familiarity with Oldfield is unknown, there are some possible connections. Between late 1957 and June 1958, Stewart narrated a film produced and distributed by the U.S. Air Force's 1352nd Motion Picture Squadron, the same unit that made a documentary about Shot John. (See "History of the 1352nd Motion Picture Squadron (Lookout Mountain Air Force Station) 1 January 1958–30 June 1958," call no. K-SQ-MOT-1353-HI, Iris no. 426501, Air Force Historical Research Agency, Maxwell Air Force Base, Alabama; and "Project Genie" film, 2 reels, no. USAF 27976R1 and USAF 27976R2, National Archives and Records Administration.) In September 1958, Stewart flew from California to Texas in an Air Defense Command interceptor to attend the annual Air Force Association convention. The next year, he was promoted to brigadier general in the Air Force Reserve and given a reserve assignment as the service's deputy director of the Office of Information. In 1960, it seems Stewart visited Air Defense Command and Nike-Hercules units at Thule Air Force Base in Greenland. All of these activities may have brought him into contact with Oldfield. (See Eliot, pp. 307, 323, 364; and Starr Smith, *Jimmy Stewart, Bomber Pilot* (St. Paul, Minnesota: Zenith Press, 2005), p. 201.) Oldfield also endeavored to maintain associations with fellow Nebraskans throughout his professional life. This may have led to an acquaintance with Darryl Zanuck, who cofounded Twentieth Century Pictures with Joseph Schenck. For a discussion of support for Eisenhower foreign policy among influential studio officials, including Zanuck and Nicholas Schenck, Joseph's brother, see Frances Stonor Saunders, *The Cultural Cold War: The CIA and the World of Arts and Letters* (New York: The New Press, 1999) pp. 284–290.
88. "The Weaponeer," pp. 2, 43.
89. "The Weaponeer," p. 17.
90. "The Weaponeer," pp. 2, 5.
91. Curiously, the circumstances that begat the ground-zero volunteers were incorrectly explained. When one character declares in the script that "a geiger [sic] counter and other radiation measuring instruments" will be placed beneath the explosion, another responds, "The brass as the Atomic Energy Commission think we need something more dramatic." This is a curious attribution of responsibility given the AEC's actual ambivalence to the operation. See "The Weaponeer," p. 19.
92. Oscar Godbout, "Two Pilot Films Being Shot for TV." It is also possible that either Oldfield or Stewart promoted the screenplay as a way to

burnish Stewart's image. In August 1957, one month after Shot John, the Senate rejected Stewart's nomination to brigadier general. Opposition, led by Maine senator Margaret Chase Smith, focused on the claim that Stewart had been insufficiently attentive to reservist activities and his intended promotion was an effort to revive a flagging career of a prominent Eisenhower supporter. See Eliot, pp. 280, 304–307; and Smith, pp. 197–199.
93. Thomas M. Pryor, "U.S. and Canada to Help in Movie," *New York Times*, October 30, 1958, p. 35.
94. Information in author's possession.
95. "Address by Colonel Barney Oldfield, Director, Information Services, North American Air Defense Command, Before Men's Club, Presbyterian Church, Billings, Montana, December 10, 1957," in Series 6 "Speeches, Addresses, 1950–1995, & Undated," Box 31, Folder 3, Oldfield Papers. Oldfield remained fascinated with the volunteers years later. When the Air Force was compiling an official history of air defense operations in the Cold War (Kenneth Schaffel, *The Emerging Shield: The Air Force and the Evolution of Continental Air Defense, 1945–1960* (Washington: Office of Air Force History, 1991)) Oldfield ensured they were mentioned. See Barney Oldfield letter to Kenneth Schaffel, June 12, 1985, Box 12, Oldfield Papers.
96. "Address by Colonel Barney Oldfield, Director, Information Services, North American Air Defense Command, Before the Clinton Junior Chamber of Commerce Annual 'Bosses Night,'" Clinton, Iowa, February 19, 1958," Oldfield Papers, Series 6, Box 31, Folder 5.
97. "Address by Colonel Barney Oldfield, Director, Information Services, North American Air Defense Command, Before the Clinton Junior Chamber of Commerce Annual 'Bosses Night,'" Clinton, Iowa, February 19, 1958," Oldfield Papers, Series 6, Box 31, Folder 5.
98. John G. Norris, "500 Officials from 47 Countries Get Eyeful of Progress at Air Congress," *Washington Post and Times-Herald*, April 14, 1959, p. A8.
99. John G. Norris, "AF reveals A-Warhead Cost Figure," *Washington Post and Times-Herald*, April 15, 1959, A1.
100. See Laurence S. Kuter memorandum to Colonel Arthur B. Oldfield, n.d., appended to "Memo from the Office of the Commander-in-Chief CON[tinental]A[ir]D[efense Command]."
101. Kuter memorandum to Oldfield attached to "Memo from the Office of the Commander-in-Chief, CON[inental]A[ir]D[efense Command]." For information in NSC 1706, see "Memorandum," April 8, 1957, in Folder "Missiles and Nuclear Weapons [1957'," Box 13, NSC Series, Briefing Notes Subseries, WHO, OSANSA, Records, 1952–61, DDEL; Elmer B. Staats memorandum to R. Hirsch, May 22, 1957, and memorandum captioned "Defense Suggestions Regarding New OCB Working Group on Publicity Re Advanced Weapons Systems and Related Matters," May 24, 1957, both in Folder "OCB 000.9 [Atomic Energy] (File #7) (3) [May–June 1957]," Box 11, OCB Central Files Series, WHO, NSC Staff Papers, 1948–61, DDEL; and Elmer B. Staats letter

to Alan T. Waterman, June 11, 1957, in Folder "OCB 000.9 [Atomic Energy] (File #7) (5) [May–June 1957]," Box 11, OCB Central Files Series, WHO, NSC Staff Papers, 1948–61, DDEL.

102. Oldfield retired from the Air Force without ever having been given another position. At that time, he was awarded a medal for *other* achievements promoting the Air Force's air defense activities. While Oldfield's efforts to publicize the Genie were not mentioned among his accomplishments in the paperwork justifying that medal, neither did they preclude the award. It is not clear if this demonstrates that his earlier transgression had been forgotten or was merely overlooked. See Kuter memorandum to Oldfield attached to "Memo from the Office of the Commander-in-Chief, CON[inental]A[ir]D[efense Command]," and Laurence S. Kuter memorandum captioned "Subject: "Recommendation for the Legion of Merit," July 19, 1962 in Oldfield Papers, Series 4, Box 30, Folder 10. The "Fact Sheet" accompanying the 1957 Genie deployment announcement noted that "[t]he yield of these weapons, their description and size, is security information and cannot be released at this time, nor can photographs be released or permitted." See "Fact Sheet; Nuclear Weapons for Air Defense," February 20, 1957, Department of Defense, Office of Public Information, in Folder "Nuclear Energy Matters (2) [Jan 1958]," Box 4, OCB Series, Subject Subseries, WHO, OSANSA, Records, 1952–61, DDEL.

103. For the cost of the Mk-74 and Mk-75 nuclear artillery shells, see "Restricted Data Classification Decisions, 1946 to the Present (RDD-8)," p. 96. In addition, in the 1990's the cost of the Advanced Cruise Missile's W-80 warhead was inadvertently disclosed. See Kevin O'Neill, "Building the Bomb," in Steven I. Schwartz, ed., *Atomic Audit: The Costs and Consequences of U.S. Nuclear Weapons Since 1940* (Washington: Brookings Institution, 1998), p. 94.

104. "Airpower's Greatest Showcase," *Air Force Magazine*, September 1957, pp. 48, 50.

105. "Presentation by Col. Sidney Bruce, Atomic Energy Division, North American Air Defense Command, Colorado Springs, Colorado, January 15, 1958, In St. Louis, Mo.," in Series 6 "Speeches, Addresses, 1950–1995, & Undated," Box 31, Folder 4, Oldfield Papers. Emphasis is in the original. The finding aid for the Oldfield Papers (p. 10) notes authorship.

106. "Atomic Rocket Ordered," *Washington Post and Times-Herald*, April 8, 1958, p. B8.

107. "Missiles in Stock Here," *New York Times*, February 6, 1958, p. 9.

108. Edward Teller and Albert L. Latter, "The Compelling Need for Nuclear Tests," *Life*, February 10, 1958, pp. 64–67, 70–71, 73; Edward Teller and Albert L. Latter, *Our Nuclear Future...Facts, Dangers, and Opportunities* (New York: Criterion Books, 1958), pp. 142–143. On the book's publication date, see "Books-Authors," *New York Times*, March 6, 1958, p. 24.

109. Edward Teller and Albert L. Latter, "The Compelling Need for Nuclear Tests," *Life*, p. 70.

110. Edward Teller and Albert L. Latter, "The Compelling Need for Nuclear Tests," *Life*, p. 70.
111. Edward Teller and Albert L. Latter, "The Compelling Need for Nuclear Tests," *Life*, p. 71.
112. See Ava Helen and Linus Pauling Papers, Oregon State University Special Collections, Box 401 ("Teller, Edward: Correspondence, Assorted Material, 1936–1961). For an additional critique of the Teller book from the left, see Lawrence S. Wittner, *Rebels Against War: The American Peace Movement, 1941–1960* (New York: Columbia University Press, 1969), pp. 241–242. For discussion of the publication within the Eisenhower administration, see F.M. Dearborn, Jr., memorandum to the president, February 14, 1958, in Folder "Chronological-Karl G. Harr, January–March 1958 (3)," Box 1, OCB Series, Administrative Subseries, WHO, OOSANSA, Records, 1952–61, DDEL. For Teller's assessment of the book and his relationship with Pauling, see Edward Teller with Judith L. Shoolery, *Memoirs: A Twentieth-Century Journey in Science and Politics* (Cambridge: Perseus Publishing, 2001) pp. 440–445. He writes, "Our book had little or no effect on public opinion." (p. 445).
113. Wittner, pp. 240–256, esp. pp. 246–247, 252. Quoted descriptions are Wittner's. See also Richard G. Hewlett and Jack M. Holl, *Atoms for Peace and War, 1953–61: Eisenhower and the Atomic Energy Commission* (Berkeley: University of California Press, 1989), pp. 483–484.
114. Charles O. Porter letter to Atomic Energy Commission, May 26, 1957, in Box 26, Folder 4, Hansen Collection. For background on subject test ("Pinion"), see Chuck Hansen, "Beware the Old Story," *Bulletin of Atomic Scientists* 57, no. 2 (March/April 2001): 52–55. For "liberal" identification, see "12 House Democrats Plan Long-Range Platform for Liberals," *Washington Post Times-Herald*, April 20, 1960, p. B6.
115. "Nuclear Protest Set," *New York Times*, April 19, 1958, p. 37; Warren Unna, "Congress' A-Tests Foe to Leave for Eniwetok," *Washington Post and Times-Herald*, April 27, 1958, p. A8.
116. *Air Force Magazine*, June 1958, pp. 26–27 (quotation); July 1959, p. 14; and *U.S. News and World Report*, August 31, 1959, p. 34.
117. Jack Raymond, "Air Defense Unit Has No Atom Curb," *New York Times*, October 7, 1958, p. 11.
118. Kenneth Schaffel, *The Emerging Shield: The Air Force and the Evolution of Continental Air Defense, 1945–1960* (Washington: Office of Air Force History, 1991), pp. 251–252.
119. Frederick W. Jandrey memorandum to Mr. [Robert D.?] Murphy, October 9, 1958, attached to Dwight J. Porter memorandum for Mr. Dale, October 13, 1958, Nuclear History document collection, item no. NH01343, National Security Archive.
120. Raymond, "Air Defense Unit Has No Atom Curb," *New York Times*, October 7, 1958.
121. Jack Raymond, "Swift Reprisal Set for Arctic Attack," *New York Times*, May 17, 1958, p. 1.

122. Frederick W. Jandrey memorandum to Mr. [Robert D.?] Murphy, October 9, 1958.
123. Dwight J. Porter memorandum for Mr. Dale, October 13, 1958; Maloney, pp. 418–420.
124. Quarles memorandum for the president.
125. Quarles memorandum for the president.
126. Peter Roman, remarks to the George Washington [University] Cold War Group, February 2, 2002 (notes in author's possession).
127. McMullen, pp. 198–204, 220, 223–224.
128. McMullen, pp. 189–196.
129. This figure is calculated based upon the chart "1962 Inspections of Nuclear Activities at Manned Interceptor Squadrons," in Ray, pp. 117–121. Elsewhere this source says there were "some 30" installations. (See, Ray, p. 24.)
130. Weitze, pp. 62–63. "Alert barns" owe their nickname to their resemblance to buildings in vernacular American agricultural architecture.
131. Thomas P. Hughes, *Rescuing Prometheus* (New York: Random House, 1998), pp. 43–44; McMullen, pp. 255–258; Ray, p. 31.
132. Ray, pp. 14, 27–28, 30–32; Telex from J[oint] C[hiefs] of S[taff] to C[hief of] S[taff] USAF [and] CINCONAD, March 28, 1960 (and attachment) in DDRS no. CK3100460560.
133. "Semiannual Historical Report; Headquarters, Field Command, The Armed Forces Special Weapons Project, Sandia Base, Albuquerque, New Mexico, Volume I, 1 July 1957–31 December 1957," pp. 207, 224; Hansen, *Swords of Armageddon*, pp. VII-87, VII-98 to VII-104; N.E. Bradbury letter to Brig. Gen. Alfred D. Starbird, October 11, 1956, Box 23, Folder 1; J.B. Macauley letter to Lewis Strauss, August 5, 1957, Box 24, Folder 4; W.F. Libby letter to Carl T. Durham, August 23, 1957, Box 24, Folder 4; all in Hansen Collection.
134. Quotation from Harold A. Knapp memorandum to Paul C. Fine, December 13, 1957, DOE/NV no. NV0103944. See also general manager [AEC] letter to Carl T. Durham, March 12, 1957, in Box 24, Folder 1, Hansen Collection; and Hansen, *Swords of Armageddon*, p. VII-96 and VII-97. The subsequent W-25 one-point test was conducted as "Project 57" during Plumbbob. Project 57 confirmed the plutonium dangers, but reduced the estimate of size of the area likely to be contaminated ("on the order of .01 square mile"), determined that "animal uptake" was "very slight," and concluded that decontamination could be conducted "rapidly and effectively" using "routine methods." See "Weekly Summary Report," Headquarters Air Force Special Weapons Center, Air Research and Development Command, December 19, 1958, in Box 28, Folder 4, Hansen Collection.
135. Scott D. Sagan, *The Limits of Safety: Organizations, Accidents, and Nuclear Weapons* (Princeton: Princeton University Press, 1993), pp. 95–97; Ray, pp. 28–29, 51–53.
136. "First Detailed Closeup of Genie Ground Handling," *Aviation Week*, November 10, 1958, p. 30; Ray, pp. 10, 19. At least one "inert" W-25 Genie was "lost" in a training or evaluation flight over the White Sands

Missile Range. This apparently was a rocket without a fissile core or high explosives, but with all the other components that comprised the nuclear version. "An organized search" was unsuccessful in locating it and it was therefore "considered lost." See Alfred D. Starbird letter to Carl T. Durham, November 19, 1958, Box 28, Folder 3, Hansen Collection.
137. Ray, pp. 29–30.
138. Ray, p. 32; "First Detailed Closeup of Genie Ground Handling," *Aviation Week*.
139. Ray, pp. 30, 33–34, 37–38; *History of Strategic Air and Ballistic Missile Defense: Volume II 1956–1972*, p. 313. Over course of two years, several practice rounds were released from F-89s as they landed, and one MB-1 fell a few inches from a stationary alert Scorpion onto a rocket trailer. Eventually it was determined that the fault rested with bolts meant to secure the arms to the pylons. All of the cases were considered equally serious because of the ramifications if the Genie-equipped planes ever flew, and because theoretically, even a small jolt could detonate high-explosive charges, which raised the risk of a one-point detonation. See "Semiannual Historical Report; Headquarters, Field Command, The Armed Forces Special Weapons Command, Sandia Base, Albuquerque, New Mexico, Volume II, 1 July 1956–31 December 1956," p. 279 (uncataloged collection, National Security Archive). The Genie rocket motor was designed to start when a lanyard connecting the MB-1 to the plane was torn out of place as the weapon dropped away from a pylon upon launch. If the nose gear was extended (as if the Scorpion was on the ground or preparing to land), this action was impossible. Such an arrangement prevented the rocket motor from igniting even if the weapon somehow fell from place accidentally. See e-mail to the author from a retired Air Force armament specialist, in author's possession.
140. Ray, pp. 54–55.
141. Ray, pp. 90–92.
142. Ray, p. 33.
143. Ray, p. 58; McMullen, pp. 220, 224.
144. Ray, pp. 92–101; Atkinson quotation, p. 94.
145. Rosson memorandum.
146. Weitze, p. 77.
147. Ray, p. 75.
148. Ray, p. 21.
149. Dorr, p. 41. This account is convincing, in part, because of its specificity (noting an exact number of weapons that were damaged, destroyed, or removed early from the inventory). However, the article's source documents cannot be located. See exchange of e-mail in author's possession.
150. M.S. Kennedy memorandum to W.C. Youngs, Jr., March 11, 1958, DOE/NV no. NV0970421; W.B. McCool memorandum to Atomic Energy Commission, November 6, 1958, p. 2, in Box 28, Folder 3, Hansen Collection; "x-unit" definition in Hansen, *U.S. Nuclear*

Weapons: The Secret History, p. 17. In early 1958, a "Quality Assurance Program" was instituted to ensure that the W-25, which was being shipped directly to the Air Force, met the necessary standards. In this case, "a randomly selected lot of weapons" was culled from the inventory and disassembled by military experts. Parts were tested (and some destroyed in the process). (See "Semiannual Historical Report; Headquarters, Field Command, The Armed Forces Special Weapons Project, Sandia Base, Albuquerque, New Mexico, Volume I, 1 July 1957–31 December 1957," pp. 383–384). As a result, the W-25 "arm/safe" switch was found to be "not entirely satisfactory." Addressing this situation may also account for program delays and possibly some of the destroyed weapons as previously noted. (See "Semiannual Historical Report; Headquarters, Field Command, The Armed Forces Special Weapons Project, Sandia Base, Albuquerque, New Mexico, Volume I, 1 January 1958–30 June 1958," p. 528 and preceding unmarked pages; "Semiannual Historical Report; Headquarters, Field Command, The Armed Forces Special Weapons Project, Sandia Base, Albuquerque, New Mexico, Volume II, 1 July 1958–31 December 1958," p. 426 in the uncataloged collection, National Security Archive.)

151. See remarks attached to Richard T. Coiner, Jr., memorandum to Chief, Armed Forces Special Weapons Project, June 4, 1957, p. 11.
152. Edward N. Parker memorandum to Commander-in-Chief, North American Air Defense Command, July 22, 1958 (and attachments) in Box 27, Folder 1, Hansen Collection.
153. Hansen, *Swords of Armageddon*, Table A-1, pp. 6, 11.

5 Nike-Hercules

1. "New Missile Unveiled at White Sands," *Las Cruces* (New Mexico) *Sun News*, February 26, 1957 (the "unveiling" was for members of the press, not public); "New Missile Undergoes Final Tests," *New York Times*, February 27, 1957, p. 12; News release, "Herculean Nike to Bolster Nation's Defense," Western Electric, March 1957, in Folder 20, Box 293, Desind Collection, Archives Division, National Air and Space Museum (hereafter Desind Collection); "Longer Range Nike Carries Atom Warhead," *Aviation Week* 66 (1957). For subsequent coverage, see, for example, "U.S. Tells Plans for Bay Missile Defense," *San Francisco Chronicle*, March 23, 1957.
2. "Military Power to Go on Display," *New York Times*, May 12, 1957, p. 12; "Giant Parade to Highlight AFD Activity," *Huntsville* (Alabama) *Times*, May 17, 1957, pp. 1, 7; "Thousands View Activities Of Military's Celebration," *Huntsville* (Alabama) *Times*, May 19, 1957, p. 1; "Nation's Armed Might Goes on Display," *Washington Post*, May 19, 1957, p. A19. Mary T. Cagle, *History of the Nike-Hercules Weapon System* (U.S. Army Missile Command: Redstone Arsenal, Alabama), 1973, pp. 19–27. Photographs from Redstone Arsenal in author's possession.
3. These evaluations were delayed, however, because of (an eventually discounted) concern about the possibility of a radar beam prematurely

detonating a test device. See "Operation Plumbbob, Project 6.5, Effects of Nuclear Detonations on Nike Hercules (U)," October 19, 1960, available from U.S. Department of Commerce, National Technical Information Service. For test dates and W-40 specifics, see Chuck Hansen, *Swords of Armageddon*, CD-ROM (1995), Table A-1, p. 10.

4. "Operation Plumbbob, Project 6.5;" Mary T. Cagle, *History of the Nike-Hercules Weapon System* (U.S. Army Missile Command: Redstone Arsenal, Alabama), 1973, pp. 79–80; Richard L. Miller, *Under the Cloud: The Decades of Nuclear Testing* (New York: The Free Press, 1986), p. 292; Mark Wolverton, "The Tube is Dead. Long Live the Tube," *Invention & Technology* (Fall 2002): 36.

5. "Memorandum for Dr. Libby," August 20, 1957, Box 24, Folder 4, Chuck Hansen Collection, National Security Archive (hereafter "Hansen Collection;" in this collection, most folders are unnamed but are arranged chronologically. Folder numbers are assigned for each box in ascending order from the oldest date to the most recent); and Hansen, pp. VII-196 and VII-197.

6. "Memorandum for Dr. Libby." There is some confusion about the danger posed by both a tritium-charged W-31 or a W-7 in the "retracted" state. Hansen reports that the W-31 tritium one-point test yielded a 300 *ton* nuclear explosion. He also reports Army concern about a "15% probability of a nuclear explosion resulting in as much as a 20-ton yield" in event of an accidental W-7 detonation. (See Hansen, p. VII-166 to VII-167. For the source document cited therein, see Box 24, Folder 3, Hansen Collection.) These are *relatively* low-order nuclear explosions, but significant nonetheless. There is no available evidence that this danger concerned officials. In the first case, it is possible that this is because the chance of a one-point detonation occurring with a tritium-charged warhead was remote since the gas had to be present at a precise moment. Concern about W-7 safety could have been minimized by the fact that only a very small number were to be deployed for a short period, or the one-point circumstances could have *spurred* the limited reliance on this warhead. It is also possible that the designs were altered after the results of the one-point tests became known. For warhead yield, see "Summary of Major Events and Problems of the [Army] Ordnance Corps, July 1955–June 1956," p. 44, call no. 40-2.1 AA 1956, in the collection of the U.S. Army Center of Military History (hereafter "USACMH").

7. Numbers calculated from information in Mark L. Morgan and Mark A. Berhow, *Rings of Supersonic Steel: Air Defenses of the United States Army, 1950–1979, An Introductory History and Site Guide* (San Pedro, California: Fort MacArthur Press, 2002).

8. For an engineering and institutional overview of the Nike-Hercules development, see Cagle, *Hercules*. Other treatments are Stephen P. Moeller, "Vigilant and Invincible," *ADA* (May–June 1995): 2–42; Tom Vanderbilt, *Survival City: Adventures Among the Ruins of Atomic America* (New York: Princeton Architectural Press, 2002), pp. 172–181. For discussion of the selection, construction, and operation of typical Nike-Ajax installations, see Cagel, *Ajax*, ppp. 181–194; Christopher John Bright, "Nike Defends

Washington: Antiaircraft Missiles in Fairfax County, Virginia During the Cold War, 1954–74," *Virginia Magazine of History and Biography* 105, no. 3 (Summer 1997): 317–346; Merle T. Cole, "W-25: The Davidsonville Site and Maryland Air Defense, 1950–1974," *Maryland Historical Magazine* 80, no. 2 (Fall 1985): 240–259; Christina M. Carlson and Robert Lyon, *Last Line of Defense: Nike Missile Sites in Illinois* (Denver: National Park Service, 1996); Anjanette U. Sivilich, "Wheeler/Portage Nike Missile Launch Site C-47: Historic Structure Report," M.A. thesis, Ball State University, 2000; Roger Hatheway, *Historical Cultural Resources Survey and Evaluation of the Nike Missile Sites in the Angeles National Forest, Los Angeles County, California* (San Diego: WESTEC Services, 1987); and John A. Martini and Stephen A. Haller, *What We Have We Shall Defend: An Interim History and Preservation Plan for Nike Site SF-88L, Fort Barry, California* (San Francisco: National Park Service Golden Gate National Recreation Area, 1998); and William C. Stark, "Cleveland Nike Bases—A Passing Phase," *Periodical Journal of the Council on America's Military Past* 14, no. 3 (September 1986): 35–46. These evaluations, of varying quality, also assess the arrival and operation of the Nike-Hercules at particular locations. For this, see also *Nike Hercules in Alaska* (n.p.: U.S. Army Corps of Enginners, Alaska District, n.d.); and John K. Hedstrom, "The Air Defenses of Minnesota During the Cold War, 1946–1989," M.A. thesis, Minnesota State University, Mankato, 2000.

9. See "Summary of Major Events and Problems of the [Army] Ordnance Corps, July 1956–June 1957," p. 40, call no. 40-2.1 AA 1957, USACMH; and and "Chronology of Significant Events and Decisions Relating to the U.S. Missile and Earth Satellite Development Programs, May 1942 through October 1957," p. 45.

10. Bright; Cole; Morgan and Berhow. Placing the batteries at some distance from the defended area increased the time available to engage attackers and permitted multiple engagements by one or more batteries. See Steven Malevich, "Nike Deployment," *The Military Engineer* 47, no. 320 (November–December 1955): 418–419. The separation of the parcels forming a single site was necessitated by the limitations of the missile tracking radar. It had to remain focused on the Nike-Ajax throughout its flight from before firing to the moment of interception. Because the missile accelerated from the launcher at a great speed, this required the large, heavy radar antenna to pivot skyward rapidly in order to maintain contact. Placing the radar at some distance to the Nike-Ajax lessened the speed and extent of the antenna's motion. Conversely, limitations in the transmission capacity of the cables that connected the electronics at the launch and control sites meant that the parcels could not be farther than six thousand yards apart. For this point, see Bright, pp. 324–325.

11. Mary T. Cagle, *Development, Production, and Deployment of the Nike Ajax Guided Missile System, 1945–1959* (Redstone Arsenal, Alabama: Army Guided Missile Agency), n.d., pp. 190–194; Bright.

12. Cagle, *Ajax*, pp. 190–194; Bright.

13. John A. Giles, "244 Revamped Nike Sites to Cost $200,000 Each," *Washington Evening Star*, March 20, 1957; Memorandum to Assistant Chief of Engineers for Military Construction from Chief, Missiles Branch, Engineering Division, July 18, 1957, in Box 33 "Anti-Ballistic Missile, Nike and Related Programs," Folder 3 "NIKE Const Progress"; and Memorandum to Chief of Engineers from DCSLOG, May 3, 1957 (and attachments) in Box 34, both at History Office, U.S. Army Corps of Engineers, Fort Belvoir, Virginia (hereafter USACE). Early construction to accommodate weapons with W-7 warheads may have required tritium detectors and alarms to warn if a concentration of the noxious gas leaked from a warhead. See Memorandum to Assistant Chief of Engineers for Military Construction from Chief, Missiles Branch, Engineering Division, July 18, 1957; Letter from M.F. Roy to Commander, Field Command, Armed Forces Special Weapons Project, March 23, 1956, in Box 22, Folder 2, Hansen Collection; and A.R. Luedecke memorandum to Chief of Staff, Department of Army [et al.], May 2, 1956, in Box 22, Folder 3, Hansen Collection.
14. The cities are listed in "Appendix "A" to Enclosure "A," attached to "Note by the Secretaries," August 25, 1958, *Declassified Documents Reference System* (hereafter *DDRS*) no. CK3100437104 Defense Secretary Charles Wilson objected to emplacing Nike-Hercules in the new locations on the basis that the required installations diverted funds better used elsewhere. See "Memorandum of Discussion at the 332nd Meeting of the National Security Council, Washington, July 25, 1957," in *Foreign Relation of the United States, 1955–1957*, vol. XIX, National Security Policy (Government Printing Office: Washington, 1990), p. 557 (hereafter identified as *FRUS* with year, volume, and page specified). The Joint Chiefs of Staff rejoinder is Maxwell D. Taylor memorandum for the Secretary of Defense, September 27, 1957, *DDRS* no. CK3100163315.
15. Memorandum to Assistant Chief of Engineers for Military Construction from Chief, Missiles Branch, Engineering Division, July 18, 1957.
16. "Guided Missile Station to Locate Here," *Dakota County* (Minnesota) *Tribune*, July 25, 1957, p. 1.
17. Fred Kaplan, *The Wizards of Armageddon* (Stanford: Stanford University Press, 1983), pp. 85–86, 92–93, 97–110, 117–121; Gregg Herken, *Counsels of War* (New York: Alfred A. Knopf, 1985), pp. 88–94; Lawrence Freedman, *The Evolution of Nuclear Strategy* (London: Macmillan Press, 1983), pp. 134–136. The RAND Corporation, the private think tank organized to assist the Air Force with such evaluations, studied SAC vulnerability periodically, starting in 1951. Among the solutions proffered was the construction of additional bomber bases to offer an attacker a greater number of more widely disbursed targets. For the Killian Committee, see "Meeting the Threat of Surprise Attack: Technological Capabilities Panel of the Science Advisory Committee," vol. II, February 14, 1955, p. 68, *DDRS* no. CK3100218088.
18. Almost all specifics about the TAPE group elude researchers. The "TAPE group" and Quarles are mentioned in Robert C. Sprague letter to Dillon Anderson, July 29, 1955, in Folder "Sprague Report [re continental

defense]," Box 18, Executive Secretary Subject File, White House Office [hereafter WHO], NSC Staff, Papers, 1948–61, Dwight D. Eisenhower Library [hereafter "DDEL"]. A vaguely defined "latest report from Robert Sprague," which, based upon timing (March 1956) and content, probably refers to the TAPE project, is mentioned in Richard M. Leighton, *Strategy, Money, and the New Look, 1953–1956: History of the Office of the Secretary of Defense, Vol. III* (Washington: Office of the Secretary of Defense, 2001), pp. 297–298 (quotation p. 297). Handwritten notes by Sprague from October 1955, which include a list of SAC bases and (bomber response?) times were declassified for this study. They may be notes taken in a TAPE-related briefing. See "Steven Committee Report," October 10, 1955, in Folder "Continental Defense, Study of-by Robert C. Sprague (1955) (9)," in Box 3, NSC Series, Subject Subseries, WHO, Office of Special Assistant for National Security Affairs [hereafter OSANSA], Records, 1952–61, DDEL.

19. John G. Norris, "Army Fights AF Missile Base Plans," *Washington Post and Times-Herald*, March 21, 1956, p. 1; Kenneth W. Condit, *History of the Joint Chiefs of Staff: The Joint Chiefs and National Policy, Vol. VI, 1955–1956* (Washington: Historical Office, Joint Staff, 1992), pp. 61–63. Talos warheads were tested at Teapot. See Hansen, Table A-1, pp. V-55 to V-56, VII-61, VII-64 to VII-65, VII-187 to VII-188; and "The Final Teapot Tests," March 23, 1955–May 15, 1955, DNA 6013F, p. 14, in the files of the Office of Corporate Historian, Sandia National Laboratories.

20. Eisenhower's belief that the Nike-Hercules and Talos were duplicative and the Defense secretary's response are in Dwight D. Eisenhower letter to Charles E. Wilson, July 8, 1957, *DDRS* no. CK3100252341; and Charles E. Wilson letter to Dwight D. Eisenhower, August 9, 1957, *DDRS* no. CK3100213013. Congressional attitudes addressed in Condit, pp. 64–65; and "Air Force Is Denied Bases for Missiles," *New York Times*, June 27, 1956, p. 62. For Talos cancellation, see "Summary of Major Events and Problems of the [Army] Ordnance Corps, July 1957–June 1958," p. 61, call no. 40-2.1 AA 1958, USACMH; and Robert J. Watson, *Into the Missile Age, 1956–1960: History of the Office of the Secretary of Defense, Vol. IV* (Washington: Office of the Secretary of Defense, 1997), p. 422. See also, Raymond H. Dawson, "Congressional Innovation and Intervention in Defense Policy: Legislative Authorization of Weapons Systems," *The American Political Science Review* 56 (1962): 42–57 (especially pp. 48–49).

21. For details on the four SAC bases that received the Nike-Ajax, see Morgan and Berhow. Note that one battery near Travis Air Force Base in California stored the missiles aboveground, in contrast to the arrangements elsewhere. (See Morgan and Berhow, p. 169.) The month after the last Nike-Ajax batteries at SAC installations became operational, the JCS received the results of a special Defense Department study of the nation's military forces, which they had requested in February. Among the items included in the report was an endorsement of the SAC defenses. The evaluation declared that if the Soviets launched the most optimally staged bomber attack under current or planned defensive arrangements, it was "highly

unlikely" that the United States could "achieve the objective of preventing high losses to the population." In light of the view that civilian casualties were nearly impossible to minimize, the study thus agreed with the decision to locate antiaircraft missile batteries at Strategic Air Command bases. Protection for the nation's retaliatory forces, rather than urban areas, was considered a worthwhile investment. See "Presentation by the Director, Weapons Systems Evaluation Group to the National Security Council on the Subject of Offensive and Defensive Weapons Systems," pp. 1, 7, 9–10, Nuclear History document collection, item no. NH00411, National Security Archive.
22. Watson, p. 422.
23. For a thorough treatment, see David L. Snead, *The Gaither Committee, Eisenhower, and the Cold War* (Columbus: Ohio State University Press, 1999) (quotation p. 47); and Valerie L. Adams, *Eisenhower's Fine Group of Fellows: Crafting a National Security Policy to Uphold the Great Equation* (Lanham, Maryland: Lexington Books, 2006). A slightly different interpretation is provided in Kaplan, pp. 125–154. A central aspect of Kaplan's account is the purported declaration by SAC commander Curtis LeMay of his intention to launch an unauthorized preemptive strike if he believed the Soviets were preparing an attack. This exchange is engaged in Richard K. Betts, "A Nuclear Golden Age? The Balance Before Parity," *International Security* 11, no. 3 (Winter 1986–1987): 19–20; and Peter Roman, "Ike's Hair-Trigger: U.S. Nuclear Predelegation, 1953–60," *Security Studies* 7, no. 4 (Summer 1998): 151–152 (note 88).
24. Snead, pp. 36, 47–52. The panel's work was conducted by four subcommittees, including one charged with evaluating "active defense and SAC vulnerability." (See Snead, p. 117.) This committee's work product is "Security Resources Panel, Volume I—Active Defense & SAC Vulnerability," November 27, 1957, *DDRS* no. CK3100525902. Robert Sprague's understanding of SAC vulnerability at the time is reflected in Richard D. Challener, interviewer, "A Transcript of a Recorded Interview with Robert Sprague," John Foster Dulles Oral History Project, Princeton University Library, 11 August 1964, pp. 17–19, 25–28, 32–33. The affect of RAND's analysis on Sprague is treated in Herken, p. 114; and Kaplan, p. 130.
25. Snead, pp. 46–48, 72–74, 91.
26. Snead, p. 91. The report is reproduced as "Deterrence and Survival in the Nuclear Age (The "Gaither Report" of 1957)," Joint Committee on Defense Production, United States Congress, 1976.
27. "Note by the Secretaries"; and Memorandum by the Director, Weapons Systems Evaluation Group, for the Joint Chiefs of Staff, December 23, 1957, *DDRS* no. CK3100437028 (quotation).
28. For numbers and locations, see Cagle, *Hercules*, p. 245.
29. Kaplan, pp. 203–219, especially 207; Freedman, p. 131–136.
30. Snead, pp. 79–89, 105–106. Snead believes Eisenhower was more receptive to the report than most other scholars suggest. See Snead, pp. 154–156. For a brief summary of Eisenhower's impression of the Gaither study and Secretary of State John Foster Dulles's concurrence

with the president, see "Memorandum of a Conversation Between the President and the Secretary of State, Washington, December 26, 1957," in *FRUS, 1955–1957*, vol. XIX, p. 712. In a 1964 oral interview, Robert Sprague expressed an unfavorable impression of Dulles's attitude and suggested a way to gauge American success in the Cold War: "[I]f Mr. Dulles had really understood our vulnerability to an air surprise attack by the Russians, he might not have taken as strong a position as he did in several cases [....] I would say that, if fifty years from now (or whatever time period), we get through this hazardous period we're now in [....] without a catastrophic nuclear attack [...] I think Mr. Dulles' policies will be vindicated [....] However, if some time in the next ten years, we are subject to an air nuclear attack, and tens of millions of Americans are killed, the fact that the situation wasn't clearly understood in the middle '50's [...] may have been the most serious mistake that was made." See Challener, pp. 23–25, 48–49 (quotation).
31. Quoted in David Alan Rosenberg, "The Origins of Overkill: Nuclear Weapons and American Strategy," in Norman A. Graebner, ed., *The National Security: Its Theory and Practice, 1945–1960* (New York: Oxford University Press, 1986), p. 157. Ike furthermore argued that "we have the capability of delivering the greater blow." (p. 157.)
32. Watson, p. 433.
33. Challener, p. 25.
34. James R. Killian, Jr., *Sputnik, Scientists, and Eisenhower: A Memoir of the First Special Assistant to the President for Science and Technology* (Cambridge: MIT Press, 1977), pp. 97–100.) The leak spurred Senator Lyndon Johnson unsuccessfully to seek copies of the Gaither report and the earlier product of the Killian panel. As a result of Johnson's request, Eisenhower asserted executive privilege after aides asked Sprague about the manner in which the report of the Technological Capabilities Panel had been handled. (See "Memorandum for the Files," by James S. Lay, Jr., December 9, 1957, in Folder "Sprague Report [re continental defense]," Box 18, Executive Secretary Subject File, WHO, NSC Staff, Papers, 1948–61, DDEL.)
35. Quoted in Adams, p. 186.
36. Killian, pp. 97–100; Adams, pp. 186–190.
37. Quoted in Adams, p. 188.
38. Adams, p. 188.
39. Quoted in Adams, p. 188. Sprague believed this additional group was necessary to examine the "most effective efforts" to be undertaken to protect the nation in the "very modest time" he believed was available before the defense situation became even more untenable. See Adams, p. 188.
40. John Prados, *Keepers of the Keys: A History of the National Security Council from Truman to Bush* (New York: William Morrow and Co., 1991), pp. 92–94; Challener, pp. 10–12.
41. John G. Norris, "New and Faster Nikes Replace Ajax in June," *Washington Post and Times-Herald*, January 29, 1958, p. A1 (first quotation); Jack Raymond, "New Atom Missiles Will Guard 4 Areas in Nation This June," *New York Times*, January 29, 1958, p. 1 (second quotation).

42. Norris.
43. "Hercules for Ajax," *Washington Post and Times-Herald*, February 3, 1958, p. A12.
44. *New York Times*, February 26, 1958, p. 17; *Washington Post and Times-Herald*, March 3, 1958, p. A15.
45. "Draft Statement of Policy Proposed by the National Security Council," [NSC 5408], February 11, 1954, *FRUS, 1952–1954*, vol. II, part 1, National Security Affairs (Government Printing Office: Washington, 1984), pp. 616, 617.
46. See "Memorandum of Discussion at the 288th Meeting of the National Security Council, Washington, June 15, 1956."
47. "U.S. Policy on Continental Defense, NSC 5802/1, February 19, 1958," *DDRS* no. CK3100418882.
48. "Discussion at the 355th Meeting of the National Security Council, Thursday, February 13, 1958," *DDRS* no. CK3100278852, pp. 4–5, 7 (quotations).
49. "Discussion at the 355th Meeting of the National Security Council," (quotations); Watson, pp. 127, 415–416.
50. Jeffrey T. Richelson, *American Espionage and the Soviet Target* (New York: William Morrow and Company, 1987), p. 177. An overflight of a nation conducted from space was not considered equally violative of national sovereignty as an aircraft overflight.
51. "Annex 'A,' Continental Defense Supplement to Department of Defense Report to National Security Council on Status of National Security Programs on June 30, 1958, NSC 5819, Part I," September 22, 1958, *DDRS* no. CK3100037841, p. A19.
52. "Status of National Security Programs on June 30, 1958, NSC 5819," September 9, 1958, Presidential Directives document collection, Part II, item no. PR0001, National Security Archive.
53. Cagle, *Ajax*, pp. 194–200, 283–293.
54. Edward Teller had another concern, to put it mildly. Although he was not necessarily confining his remarks to air defense weapons, he remarked in a November 1957 meeting of the AEC's General Advisory Committee about "an accidental detonation of an atomic weapon within the U.S." "His worry was," the meeting minutes report, "that such an accident might result in severe restrictions being placed in the use of atomic weapons." See "Minutes, Fifty-sixth Meeting of the General Advisory Committee to the United States Atomic Energy Commission, November 21, 22, and 23, 1957, Los Alamos, New Mexico," pp. 33–34, Department of Energy/Nevada Nuclear Testing Archive accession no. NV0073729 (hereafter "DOE/NV no.").
55. Cagle, *Ajax*, pp. 194–195 (footnote 22).
56. L. Edgar Prina, "Atom Mishap With Hercules is Discounted," *Washington Evening Star*, May 23, 1958.
57. The section below draws from "Middletown Nike: A Case Study in Army Public Relations," December 31, 1958 (call no. UZ410 U53 1959), a report in the collection of the U.S. Army Military History Institute, Carlisle Barracks, Pennsylvania.

58. "Residents Take Blast in Stride," *Red Bank* (New Jersey) *Register*, May 27, 1958 (reproduced in "Middletown Nike").
59. "Sympathy, Not Protest Marks Public Meeting on Nike Blast," *The* (Middletown, New Jersey) *Courier*, May 29, 1958 (reproduced in "Middletown Nike").
60. "Residents Take Blast in Stride."
61. Cagle, *Hercules*, pp. 57–66, 78–90, 95–98.
62. See, for example, memorandum on the Nike-Hercules missile booster progress, mentioned in "Staff Notes No. 313, February 27, 1958," *DDRS* no. CK3100309912.
63. Cagle, *Hercules*, pp. 99, 102, 132. "Pressure drop" could be related to the barometric device meant to arm the weapon once the proper high-altitude air pressure was detected. This source says two missiles were sent initially to the first batteries.
64. Cagle, *Hercules*, p. 240. Missiles were ordinarily placed twenty-five miles from the center of the defended area. In some cases (such as New York), the size of the region meant that missiles were located within municipal limits. In other situations, geography (such as Chicago's location on Lake Michigan) necessitated a deviation from the ideal and placed the Nike-Hercules in the midst of the urban zone. In connection with the number of missiles initially sent to each site, a June 30, 1958, photograph of the first Chicago site shows four Nike-Hercules erected on launchers. See photograph 9A02932 in "Nike Hercules (Ground Static)" in Desind Collection.
65. John G. Norris, "Defense Rockets Get Debut," *Washington Post and Times-Herald*, July 2, 1958, p. B4. This article inexplicably declares Davidsonville as the first Nike-Hercules site.
66. Hansen, p. VII-199.
67. L. Edgar Prina, "D.C. Area Rocket Sites Get Atomic Missiles," *Washington Evening Star*, July 1, 1958, p. A-10; and Gladwin Hill, "Hercules Tested in Army Display," *New York Times*, July 2, 1958, p. 11; Gladwin Hill, "Army Shows Off its Rocket Might," *New York Times*, July 1, 1958, p. 4 (quotation). The Nike-Hercules performed satisfactorily despite the fact that its recent problems had led some officials to urge that it not be included in Project Ammo. See Cagle, *Hercules*, p. 100.
68. Jeremi Suri, "America's Search for a Technological Solution to the Arms Race: The Surprise Attack Conference of 1958 and a Challenge for 'Eisenhower Revisionists,'" *Diplomatic History* 21, no. 3 (Summer 1997): 417–451 (quotation p. 426).
69. Watson, p. 433.
70. Suri, p. 426. Suri argues that the conference failed because of the Eisenhower's crabbed view of the conference's purpose. According to Suri, had the president been willing to become actively engaged in the proceedings and accede to force reductions advocated by the Soviet delegation, he would have demonstrated his managerial acumen while also tempering the Cold War. This analysis is contingent, of course, on the assumption that the Soviet position was sound and adopting it would have furthered American interests. For a discussion of a contrary approach

(engaging in an arms race as part of a strategy to prevail over the Soviet Union and ultimately reduce the number of nuclear weapons and lessen the danger of war) employed by the Reagan administration, see Paul Lettow, *Ronald Reagan and His Quest to Abolish Nuclear Weapons* (New York: Random House, 2005).
71. "Operation Alert Starts Quietly," *New York Times*, July 17, 1958, p. 13; Memorandum from Charles A. Sullivan to Heads of Executive Departments and Agencies, Subject: Relocation Operation Guides, April 15, 1958, *DDRS* no. CK3100048017; handwritten notes about Cabinet discussion of relocation process, [September 26, 1958?], *DDRS* no. CK31000214540.
72. Cagle, *Hercules*, p. 101; number of missiles to be fired is in Donald A. Quarles's letter to Lewis L. Strauss, February 28, 1958, DOE/NV no. NV0117801. In April 1958, the Philadelphia soldiers had won a competition among the Nike-Hercules units then in training to be the first regular (rather than test) battery to fire a Nike-Hercules. Their performance in this (otherwise unspecified "derby") may have led to their selection for the nuclear operation. See "Troops Fire Hercules," *ARADCOM Argus*, June 1, 1958. This is the newsletter of the Army Air Defense Command ("ARADCOM"). A complete run is available at the U.S. Army's Military History Institute, Carlisle Barracks, Pennsylvania.
73. Minutes of Executive Session of Meeting No. 1166, Atomic Energy Commission, January 24, 1956, p. 33, Box 22, Folder 1, Hansen Collection; K.E. Fields letter to Henry M. Jackson, February 24, 1956, DOE/NV no. NV0074039. See also chapter 4.
74. Albert D. Epley memorandum for record, November 9, 1956, p. 7, Box 23, Folder 6, Hansen Collection.
75. Albert D. Epley memorandum for record, November 9, 1956.
76. Alfred D. Starbird memorandum for the chairman, September 23, 1957, DOE/NV no. NV0108443.
77. Lewis L. Strauss letter to Herbert B. Loper, September 24, 1957, DOE/NV no. NV0108445. This letter is included twice in the Hansen Collection, once with an erroneous handwritten date ("September 21, 1957."). See Box 24, Folder 5, Hansen Collection. The Starbird memorandum cited above was used to craft this letter.
78. Quarles letter to Lewis L. Strauss, February 28, 1958. The Nike-Hercules was scheduled to undergo cold-weather tests at Fort Churchill in Manitoba, Canada. Quarles mentioned the possibility of conducting the nuclear missile tests at that time if a U.S. location was infeasible. He noted the topic had not yet been broached with the State Department, nor, presumably, with the Canadians. See Quarles letter.
79. W.B. McCool memorandum to the Atomic Energy Commission, AEC 977/3, April 9, 1958, Box 25, Folder 5, Hansen Collection. Two other objections are redacted.
80. Robert A. Divine, "Eisenhower, Dulles, and the Nuclear Test Ban Issue: Memorandum of a White House Conference, 24 March 958," *Diplomatic History* 2, no. 3 (Summer 1978): 321–330 (quotation 325–326). For a fuller treatment of the interplay of administration appointees on the topic

of a test ban, see Benjamin P. Greene, *Eisenhower, Science Advice, and the Nuclear Test Ban Debate, 1945–1963* (Stanford: Stanford University Press, 2007), pp. 134–164 (for discussion of March 24 meeting, see pp. 141–144). For the report of another colloquy between Strauss, Dulles, and others on the prospect of a nuclear test ban, see "Memorandum for the Files of Lewis L. Strauss," in Box 26A, Lewis L. Strauss Papers, Herbert Hoover Presidential Library. For more on this exchange, see Greene, pp. 151–153.

81. Cagle, *Hercules*, p. 100.
82. Cagle, *Hercules*, pp. 100–101; and [Alfred D.] Starbird telex to [K.F.] Hertford, et al., May 2, 1958, DOE/NV no. NV0123110. Warhead details are provided in Alfred D. Starbird telex to USAEC, ALOO [United States Atomic Energy Commission Albuquerque Operations Office] and LASL [Los Alamos Scientific Laboratory] July 24, 1958, Box 27, Folder 1, Hansen Collection; and V.H. Clabaugh memorandum entitled "Excerpts from the W-31 Production Sub-Committee Meeting Held August 13, 1958," August 20, 1958, DOE/NV no. NV0972108.
83. Starbird telex to Hertford, et al., May 2, 1958 also mentions need for four Genies: two to use and two for backup. Minutes of AEC-MLC conference attached to W.B. McCool memorandum for the Atomic Energy Commission, July 23, 1958, DOE/NV no. NV0072600. For code names, see George L. Trimble, Jr., letter to William B. Kieffer, July 5, 1958, DOE/NV no. NV0076948 ("Little David"); and Thomas W. Ray, *Nuclear Armament: Its Acquisition, Control, and Application to Manned Interceptors, 1951–1963*; A[ir] D[efense] C[ommand] Historical Study No. 20 (n.p.: Air Defense Command, n.d.), p. 8 ("Opera Hat").
84. Minutes of AEC-MLC conference attached to W.B. McCool memorandum for the Atomic Energy Commission, July 23, 1958.
85. Minutes of AEC-MLC conference attached to W.B. McCool memorandum for the Atomic Energy Commission, July 23, 1958; "History of the 1352nd Motion Picture Squadron (Lookout Mountain Air Force Station) 1 January 1958–30 June 1958," call no. K-SQ-MOT-1353-HI, Iris no. 426501, Air Force Historical Research Agency, Maxwell Air Force Base, Alabama, pp. 17–20; "Project Genie" film, 2 reels, nos. USAF 27976R1 and USAF 27976R2, National Archives and Records Administration [hereafter NARA].
86. Minutes of AEC-MLC conference attached to W.B. McCool memorandum for the Atomic Energy Commission, July 23, 1958; and SWPWT telex to CDR APOG [et al.], May 20, 1958, Box 26, Folder 3, Hansen Collection.
87. "Memorandum of Conference with the President, June 27, 1958—11:05 AM" June 30, 1958, in Folder "Atomic Weapons, Correspondence and Background for Presidential Approval and Instructions for Use of [1953–1960] (2)," Box 1, in NSC Series, Subject Subseries, WHO, OSANSA, Records, 1952–61, DDEL. (This memorandum was fully declassified in 2001 for National Security Archive analyst William Burr, in part, because the balance of the meeting addresses the pending predelegation instructions for weapons other than air defense arms. The

reference to nuclear tests over the Gulf of Mexico generated some press coverage when the document was released. See "Eisenhower Authorized Use of Nuclear Weapons over Mexico," Agence France Presse, May 19, 2001.) An earlier request for a meeting on this subject was rebuffed by Eisenhower aide Andrew Goodpaster "until after the principals concerned have been called together to discuss the matter." See Karl G. Harr, Jr., memorandum to General [Robert] Cutler and Mr. [Elmer] Staats, June 24, 1958, in Folder "Chronological-Karl G. Harr April–July 1958 (4)," Box 1, OCB Series, Administrative Subseries, WHO, OSANSA, Records, 1952–61, DDEL.

88. "Memorandum of Conference with the President, June 27, 1958—11:05 AM" June 30, 1958.
89. "Memorandum of Conference with the President, June 27, 1958—11:05 AM" June 30, 1958.
90. "Memorandum of Conference with the President, June 27, 1958—11:05 AM" June 30, 1958; Karl G. Harr memorandum for the record, June 27, 1958, in Folder "Chronological—Karl G. Harr April–July 1958 (4)," Box 1, OCB Series, Administrative Subseries, WHO, OSANSA, Records, 1952–61, DDEL. The latter memorandum was declassified for this project at the author's request.
91. Karl G. Harr, Jr. memorandum for the Sherman Adams, July 14, 1958, *DDRS* no. CK3100266226. This document also reports that the OCB's AEC representative also objected to the release of photographs (presumably of the weapons to be used) from the operation, further demonstrating the significance of the restriction of which Barney Oldfield later ran afoul.
92. George L. Trimble, Jr., letter to William B. Kieffer, July 5, 1958; W.B. Kieffer letter to W.M. Canterbury, July 3, 1958, DOE/NV no. NV0076947.
93. John R. McBride memorandum to Assistant Chief, and Acting Chief, Division of Radiological Health, July 25, 1958, DOE/NV no. NV0023334; Melvin W. Carter memorandum to James G. Terrill, Jr., August 6, 1958, DOE/NV no. NV0023332 (quotations).
94. Cagle, *Hercules*, pp. 102–103.
95. "Army Unit Fires Nike-Hercules," *Washington Post and Times-Herald*, July 15, 1958, p. A11.
96. Richard Pfau, *No Sacrifice Too Great: The Life of Lewis L. Strauss* (Charlottesville: University Press of Virginia, 1984), pp. 218–219.
97. Memorandum of Conference with the President, July 24, 1958, following NSC," July 24, 1958, in Folder "Staff Memos July 1958 (11)," Box 35, Dwight D. Eisenhower Diary Series, Dwight D. Eisenhower Papers as President, 1953–61, DDEL. Although this memorandum has long been declassified, at least two earlier scholars misunderstood its significance, probably because other information was not available about Snodgrass and Little David/Opera Hat at the time. Stephen Ambrose characterizes the discussions as related to "the ABM." See Stephen E. Ambrose, *Eisenhower: The President* (New York: Simon and Schuster, 1984), p. 477. Similarly, Robert Divine suggests the subject was "an

astonishing Pentagon proposal—to conduct tests of the experimental anti-missile missile, complete with an atomic warhead, over the Gulf of Mexico." See Robert A. Divine, *Blowing in the Wind: The Nuclear Test Ban Debate, 1954–1960* (New York: Oxford University Press, 1978), p. 220.

98. "Memorandum of Conference with the President, July 24, 1958, following NSC," July 24, 1958.
99. "Memorandum of Conference with the President, July 24, 1958, following NSC," July 24, 1958.
100. Divine, pp. 326, 327.
101. Alfred D. Starbird telex to USAEC, ALOO and LASL, Los Alamos, NM, September 24, 1958; and Donald A. Quarles memorandum for the Chairman, Joint Chiefs of Staff, July 25, 1958, attached to W.B. McCool "Note by the Secretary," August 7, 1958 (quotation); both in Box 27, Folder 1, Hansen Collection. For August 1 as date for first detonation, see George L. Trimble, Jr., letter to William B. Kieffer, July 5, 1958.
102. Melvin W. Carter memorandum to James G. Terrill, Jr., August 6, 1958.
103. "Quakers Meet Against A-Bomb," *Washington Post and Times-Herald*, August 6, 1958, p. B1.
104. Cagle, *Hercules*, p. 103; "Summary of Major Events and Problems of the [Army] Ordnance Corps, July 1958–June 1959," p. 64, call no. 40-2.1 AA 1959, USACMH.
105. Cagle, *Hercules*, p. 104; "Fact Sheet," October 1958, in "NIKE System" Folder, Army Air Defense Artillery Museum, Fort Bliss, Texas (hereafter "ADA Museum").
106. "Staff Notes No. 411, August 27, 1958," *DDRS* no. CK3100095673.
107. Ambrose, pp. 479–480. Gregg Herken, *Cardinal Choices: Presidential Science Advising from the Atom Bomb to SDI* (New York: Oxford University Press, 1992), pp. 107–114.
108. "Status of National Security Programs on June 30, 1958, NSC 5819," September 9, 1958, p. 122.
109. Watson, p. 423.
110. Quoted in James Meikle Eglin, *Air Defense in the Nuclear Age: The Post-War Development of American and Soviet Strategic Defense Systems* (New York: Garland Publishing, 1988), p. 192. The Eisenhower administration had "implied" the first point, but not the second.
111. Watson, p. 423.
112. "4th Region Begins New Sites," *ARADCOM Argus*, September 1, 1958, p. 1; "Rocket Shown Here Initially, Replaces Others," *Los Angeles Times*, August 30, 1958.
113. Photograph 9A02936 (and caption) in "Nike Hercules (Ground Static)" in Desind Collection.
114. Thomas B. Ross, "Air Force Seeks to Abolish Chicago Nike Installations," *Chicago Sun-Times*, September 1, 1958.
115. Cagle, *Hercules*, p. 146. Other Army reaction to the Chicago story is in "Army Denounces BOMARC Publicity," *New York Times*, September 5, 1958, p. 6.

116. "Army Unveils New Base for Atomic Air Defense," *Washington Evening Star*, September 4, 1958, p. A-12 (quotations); "'Absolute Denial' Of Invading Bombers Is Aim of Nike Hercules, Says Bn. C.O.," *Army Navy Air Force Journal*, September 13, 1958, p. 4; Jim Carberry, "Hercules Labors in Controversy," *Washington Post and Times-Herald*, September 5, 1958, p. D3; Western Electric Company press release, [September 4, 1958]; and U.S. Army Air Defense Command, "Fact Sheet on Nike Missiles, September 8, 1958; both in Folder 20, Box 293, Desind Collection.
117. "'Absolute Denial' of Invading Bombers Is Aim of Nike Hercules, Says Bn. C.O.," (first quotation); "Atomic Nike Defense Base," *New York Herald Tribune*, September 5, 1958 (second quotation).
118. See chapter 1. For another early reference to this capability, see "New Missiles Said to Void A-Bombs, *New York Times*, June 14, 1957, p. 16.
119. Robert S. Weiner, "At Ease," *American Heritage* 50, no. 2 (April 1999): 50.
120. "Army Unveils New Base for Atomic Air Defense," *Washington Evening Star*, September 4, 1958, p. A-12 (quotations); "'Absolute Denial' of Invading Bombers Is Aim of Nike Hercules, Says Bn. C.O.," *Army Navy Air Force Journal*, September 13, 1958, p. 4; Jim Carberry, "Hercules Labors in Controversy," *Washington Post and Times-Herald*, September 5, 1958, p. D3; Western Electric Company press release, [September 4, 1958]; and U.S. Army Air Defense Command, "Fact Sheet on Nike Missiles, September 8, 1958"; both in Folder 20, Box 293, Desind Collection.
121. John R. Thompson, "Test Reveals Nike Hercules Can Clear Sky; Could Wipe out Entire Attacking Fleet," *Chicago Tribune*, September 15, 1958.
122. *New York Times*, October 20, 1958, p. 33, and *Washington Post and Times-Herald*, October 20, 1958, p. A21.
123. Lillian Levy, "Women Important in Nike Work," *Washington Evening Star*, November 10, 1958.
124. "Women Important in Nike Work," *Washington Evening Star*.
125. Marvin Miles, "Make-Believe Air Force," *Air Force Magazine*, December 1958, pp. 114–118. This account argued that "reports from Russia indicate the extensive use of models in the Soviet educational system," but sought to reassure readers that "in the field of scale models, there is little doubt that the youth of America are far ahead."
126. Thomas Graham, *Remembering Revell Model Kits* (Atglen, Pennsylvania: Schiffer Publishing Company, 2002), p. 147.
127. Mat Irvine, *Creating Space: The Story of the Space Age Told Through Models* (Burlington, Ontario: Collector's Guide Publishing, Inc., 2002), pp. 185, 216, 229.
128. Box in author's possession.
129. Miles.
130. Revell president Lewis Glaser also "frequented some Marxist clubs" as a youth. See Graham, p. 29. On executive Henry Blankfort, see Graham and Robert Vaughn, *Only Victims: A Study of Show Business Blacklisting*

(New York: G.P. Putnam's Sons, 1972), pp. 145, 158, 166, 275, 280. Ten years after the HUAC hearings, Blankfort explained, "I pleaded the Fifth Amendment because of my strong belief in our country's Declaration of Independence, Constitution and Bill of Rights. And I felt that I never have to answer to anybody about my political beliefs except that I am patriotic to the American way of life." (Quoted in Dave Sheehan, "Toyland Tempest," *Evening Outlook*, July 14, 1961, p. 7; otherwise unidentified article in author's possession from Revell's corporate clipping service, provided courtesy of Professor Tom Graham, Flagler College.) There is much evidence that some CPUSA members earlier were engaged in espionage. See, for example, Harvey Klehr and John Earl Haynes, *Venona: Decoding Soviet Espionage in America* (New Haven: Yale University Press, 1999); and Allen Weinstein, *The Haunted Wood: Soviet Espionage in America—The Stalin Era* (New York: Random House, 1999).

131. See e-mail between Blankfort's son, Jeff, and the author, dated April 27, 2004, in author's possession.

132. Linda Hunt, *Secret Agenda: The United States Government, Nazi Scientists, and Project Paperclip, 1945–1990* (New York: St. Martin's Press, 1991), 196–216; Jeffrey T. Richelson, *A Century of Spies: Intelligence in the Twentieth Century* (Oxford: Oxford University Press, 1995), pp. 279–282; and "United States of America v. William Henry Whalen," copy of indictment, in author's possession, courtesy of Linda Hunt.

133. Memorandum captioned "ACSI-DSCC, Subject: Damage Assessment in the Case of Whalen (S)," c. April 1965, pp. 8 (quotation) and 11; and "Disposition Form" captioned "Subject: Damage Assessment of Classified Documents (U)," January 18, 1965; both in author's possession, courtesy of Jeffrey T. Richelson. It is possible that Whalen also provided information about Soviet missile telemetry data collected by the United States, thus allowing the USSR to have a good understanding of American knowledge of Soviet ICBM capabilities. (See Edward Jay Epstein, *Deception: The Invisible War Between the KGB and CIA* (New York: Simon and Schuster, 1989), pp. 162–173.) Similarly, another source suggests that Whalen provided other details about American estimates of Soviet ICBMs, encouraging Soviet efforts to exaggerate the threat their missiles posed. (See Victor Marchetti and John D. Marks, *The CIA and the Cult of Intelligence* (New York: Alfred A. Knopf, 1974), pp. 218–219.

134. Jack L. Stemper (Assistant to the Secretary of Defense, Legislative Affairs) letter to John T. Conway (Executive Director, Joint Committee on Atomic Energy, United States Congress), [c. 1966] in author's possession, courtesy of Linda Hunt.

135. Hunt, pp. 208 and 212. Details of the October 1959 background investigation, which involved a credit check and queries with local police departments about criminal records, are noted in document captioned "Agency Report," October 12, 1959, in author's possession, courtesy of Linda Hunt. Attention ultimately turned to Whalen after July 1962

because of information provided by Oleg Penkovskiy, a Soviet military officer spying for the Americans and British. To facilitate his efforts, Penkovskiy had asked for (and had been granted) access to a special library of U.S. documents maintained in the USSR that had been gathered as a result of Soviet espionage. When Soviet officials began to suspect Penkovskiy, he asked U.S. officials to help him falsify the reason he needed library privileges by helping him draft an article based on material held there drafted for publication in a Soviet military journal. Penkovskiy apparently suggested the Nike-Hercules as a subject, thus revealing the fact that the Soviets possessed classified information on the Army missiles. See Jerrold L. Schecter and Peter S. Deriabin, *The Spy Who Saved the World: How a Soviet Colonel Changed the Course of the Cold War* (New York: Charles Scribner and Sons, 1992), pp. 313–314.

136. Hunt, p. 197; "Ex-Officer Given 15-Year Term for Supplying Secrets to Soviet," *New York Times*, March 2, 1967. For tenure with Fairfax County Park Authority, see Robert Walters, "Ex-Colonel Is Indicted as Spy in Conspiracy with 2 Reds," *Washington Star*, July 13, 1966. There are two other known espionage cases that touch upon the Nike-Hercules. Between 1957 and 1959, a "disaffected" former Army sergeant became a guard at "missile sites" in California and Texas, and "purloined documents, photographs and...a sample of rocket fuel for the KGB." Since Nike-Ajax and Nike-Hercules were the only types of missiles deployed in either state during the period, the information gathered presumably related to these armaments. See Christopher Andrew and Vasili Mitrokhin, *The Sword and the Shield: The Mitrokhin Archive and the Secret History of the KGB* (New York: Basic Books, 1999), pp. 177–178. Also, in late 1960, a twenty-fiveyear-old Army private assigned to a Fort Bliss Nike-Hercules missile maintenance unit deserted to Mexico City and passed information to a Soviet official. W. Mark Felt, then the senior FBI agent in Kansas City and more than four decades away from gaining fame as the *Washington Post*'s Deep Throat during the Watergate scandal, took charge of the case when the soldier was arrested. Given the rank and duties involved, the security breach was likely modest, albeit troublesome. See "Giving Reds A-Data Charged to Deserter," *Washington Post*, March 17, 1962, p. A4.

137. Steven T. Usdin, *Engineering Communism: How Two Americans Spied for Stalin and Founded the Soviet Silicon Valley* (New Haven: Yale University Press, 2005); Ronald Radosh and Joyce Milton, *The Rosenberg File*, 2nd ed. (New Haven: Yale University Press, 1997), pp. xi–xiii. Barr left the United States with his lover, a neighbor's wife. In a 1992 television interview, Carol Dorothy recalled how their Soviet handler described the technological project on which Barr would be engaged upon their defection. "He said, 'One of the most frustrating things about the war was that when we shot at a plane, it had moved, and that we didn't know how to shoot so that we could hit the plane,' and so they very seldom hit them. He said, 'If you could invent something that will hit the plane, that would be what we need.'" See transcript of *ABC News Nightline* (Federal Document Clearing House, Inc.) June 15, 1992, p. 3.

138. "'Remarkable' Missile of Reds Seen Similar to Nike Ajax," *Washington Post and Times-Herald*, May 7, 1960, p. A7. Seven months before Powers was shot down, a National Intelligence Estimate proffered that "[i]n the surface-to-air missile category, a new system is being added to the defense of the Soviet industrial and population centers." The report suggested that the USSR was also considering nuclear warheads for this or a similar weapon, and for air-to-air armaments. See "NIE 11-5-59," November 3, 1959, in *FRUS, 1958–1960*, vol. III, National Security; Arms Control and Disarmament (Government Printing Office: Washington, 1996), p. 328.
139. Cagle, *Hercules*, pp. 101, 240; Morgan and Berhow, p. 138.
140. Cagle, *Hercules*, p. 240.
141. Hansen, p. VII-197. For production delays, see M.S. Kennedy memorandum to Walter C. [obscured], Manager, USAEC, April 10, 1959, DOE/NV no. NV0970433; and "Semiannual Historical Report; and (for quotation) Headquarters, Field Command, The Armed Forces Special Weapons Command, Sandia Base, Albuquerque, New Mexico, Volume II, 1 July 1958–31 December 1958," p. 359 (uncataloged collection, National Security Archive).
142. "Memorandum of Conference with the President, December 19, 1958—2:30 PM," December 19, 1958, from National Security Archive online predelegation document collection (in author's possession).
143. Neil McElroy memorandum to the president, January 12, 1959, *DDRS* no. CK3100399125. While this and other correspondence suggests the president was intimately familiar with air-defense nuclear weapons and their deployment arrangements, there is no evidence he ever visited an operational location. In a briefing on February 9, 1959, the JCS Chairman, General Nathan Twining "reviewed the concept of a trip by the president to SAC, to a Nike site, and to Cape Canaveral...." Eisenhower did not respond to this suggestion, and it appears to have not been implemented. See "Memorandum of Conference With President Eisenhower," February 9, 1959, in *FRUS, 1958–1960*, vol. III, p. 181.
144. Figures calculated from Cagle, Hercules, and Morgan and Berhow. Note that Alaska, Hawaii, and Greenland batteries are not included despite organizationally considered part of continental defenses. Furthermore, for the purposes of these calculations, Minneapolis-St. Paul is considered a single city, and Dallas and Forth Worth are considered separate.
145. In 1964, there were nine batteries in Alaska, six in Hawaii, twenty-four in Europe, eight in Okinawa, six in Korea, and four at Thule in Greenland. See document captioned "Army Has 2 Operational Surface-to-Air Missile Systems Deployed in U.S. and Overseas Areas," *DDRS* no. CK3100165859.
146. For a memorandum marked with Eisenhower's initials (indicating his review) noting the progress of deploying Nike-Hercules batteries to Alaska, see "Staff Notes No. 471, December 16, 1958," *DDRS* no. CK3100007217.

147. Watson, pp. 427–431, 433–434. Dawson, "Congressional Innovation and Intervention in Defense Policy: Legislative Authorization of Weapons Systems," pp. 51–55. A future president was outspoken on the topic. "In recent weeks some of our people in the Pentagon and the services have been more interested in a barrage of propaganda than they have been in barrages for the benefit of the air defense program," declared Michigan representative Gerald R. Ford. See Edward J. Kolodziej, *The Uncommon Defense and Congress, 1945–1963* (Columbus: Ohio State University Press, 1966), pp. 304–306 (quotation p. 305).
148. Orr Kelly, "Bay Defense Posts to Get Killer Rockets," *San Francisco Chronicle*, January 24, 1959.
149. "City Is Equipped for Hercules," *Milwaukee Journal*, March 21, 1959, p. 27.
150. "Granite Due Missile Unit," *Baltimore Sun*, April 2, 1959; "Equipment Due about Sept. 15 for 4 Nike Units," *St. Louis Post-Dispatch*, p. 8C.
151. Reva Cullen, "Nike Bases for Denver Called Nearly Certain," *Denver Post*, September 11, 1958, pp. 1, 35.
152. John C. Lonnquest, *To Defend and Deter: The Legacy of the United States Cold War Missile Program* (Rock Island, Illinois: Defense Publishing Service, 1996), p. 99.
153. "23rd Group Hercules Display Missile Familiar Sight to New York Citizens," *ARADCOM Argus*, September 1, 1959, p. 9; Morris Kaplan, "5th Avenue Parade with 16th Century Theme Marks Hudson's Voyage," *New York Times*, June 13, 1959, p. 1.
154. Elinor Lee, "Cookies Their Target," *Washington Post*, December 10, 1959, p. C4, and Elinor Lee, "Cookies Needed for Servicemen," *Washington Post*, December 6, 1959, p F14; "Office of the Mayor," proclamation dated April 12, 1960, in Folder "NIKE Site—Arlington Hts., Illinois," call no. AAA D96.38.1, ADA Museum.
155. See William J. Lawrence e-mail to the author, December 3, 2001, author's possession, about problems near Gary, Indiana. Also, see "Negro Crews of Nike Find Homes Scarce," *Washington Post and Times-Herald*, March 24, 1956, p. 1.
156. "Virginia Missilemen's Chorus," *ARADCOM Argus*, January 1, 1959.
157. "Nike-Hercules," U.S. Army Air Defense Command "Fact Sheet," May 1960; "A Brief Review of Nike Hercules," [Western Electric Company,] June 19, 1959; both in Folder 20, Box 293, Desind Collection.
158. "FACTS," *ARADCOM Argus*, November 1, 1959.
159. *The Nike-Hercules Story*, prod. by Herbert Kerkow, Inc. (for U.S. Army), c. 30 mins., 1958, videocassette (author's possession); Vanderbilt, p. 117.
160. Donald E. Baruch letter to Richard Flores, September 3, 1959, *Department of Defense Film Collection*, Georgetown University Special Collections (hereafter *DoD Film Collection*), Box 29, Folder 28. Baruch was the nephew of Bernard, the financier and Democratic stalwart. See Donald E. Baruch letter to Olin D. Johnston, December 3, 1957, *DoD Film Collection* Box 27, Folder 3. In another case, a producer was urged to delete the voice-over, "If they've forgotten anything, it's just too

bad," during a scene showing soldiers launching a missile. See "Nike vs. Bomber" script in Box 17, Folder 3, and suggested revisions and other correspondence in *DoD Film Collection*, Box 17, Folder 5.

161. Copy of trading card (in author's possession) courtesy of Robert Holden, Department of History, Old Dominion University, Norfolk, Virginia. While neither the Nike-Hercules nor the companion BOMARC card mentioned nuclear warheads, this was apparently not due to a reluctance to be specific with a presumably youthful cereal-eating audience. The "Sergeant" tactical missile card noted the weapon could "deliver a powerful nuclear blow deep behind enemy lines."

162. A.L. Singleton, "Nike Base Rolls Up Red Carpet; Now It's Fences, Sentries, Dog," *Washington Evening Star*, June 22, 1958.

163. Martini and Haller, pp. 49–50. For the recollections of an Army officer assigned to a Nike-Hercules battalion, see Wilfred O. Boettiger, *An Antiaircraft Artilleryman From 1939 to 1970* (n.p.: XLibris Corporation, 2005), pp. 177–181, 184–192.

164. "Summary of Major Events and Problems of the [Army] Ordnance Corps, July 1957–June 1958," p. 135.

165. Carlson and Lyon, p. 74. The president was technically informed about these arrangements, but it is unlikely he noted them in a routine, lengthy, and turgid Pentagon report. See "Annex 'A,' Continental Defense Supplement to Department of Defense Report...." p. A13.

166. Carlson and Lyon, pp. 70–71; Martini and Haller, pp. 25–26, 31–33. Although geographically outside the scope of this project, it is interesting to note that the location of the Alaska batteries allowed high-explosive training missiles to be fired from one of those sites. See "Nike-Hercules Shot Near Anchorage," *Washington Post and Times-Herald*, November 23, 1960, p. A6; Lonnquest, p. 300; Morgan and Berhow, pp. 44, 84.

167. One oral history purportedly recounts a time when code words were confused, leading to otherwise impermissible launching connections to be made. See Martini and Haller, pp. 26–28.

168. Martini and Haller, pp. 30–31, 125; Bright, p. 341; Cagle, *Hercules*, p. 80. In 1967 the Army objected to a recommendation that five nuclear Nike-Hercules missiles be replaced with the same number of conventional missiles at each battery in the United States. The Army sought to "retain the present stockpile of nuclear air defense rounds." While the ultimate configuration is not known, given the physical capacity of the missile boxes and other details, the Army's comments strongly suggest that batteries had four or fewer conventional missiles at the time. See "JCS Comments on Draft Presidential Memorandum on Nuclear Weapons Stockpile and Fissionable Materials Requirement," JCSM 558-67, October 18, 1967, in *U.S. Nuclear History: Nuclear Arms and Politics in the Missile Age, 1955–1968*, document collection, National Security Archive and ProQuest, item no. NH00082.

169. Martini and Haller, p. 34. Later electromechanical devices ("Permissive Action Links") were installed to physically prevent unauthorized activity. Determining the adequacy of personnel reliability and physical

security measures is difficult. In February 1971, four individuals formerly assigned to a Florida Nike-Hercules battery claimed there were security lapses there between December 1968 and August 1970. Among the allegations: Officers cheated on examinations intended to demonstrate their knowledge of Nike-Hercules handling, missiles were inadequately maintained, safes holding battle plans and launch material were left unlocked and/or not properly inventoried, and one of the officers was granted entry to a secure area without having his identification card checked. See Anthony Ripley, "Ex-Officers Accuse Army on Nuclear Base Security," *New York Times*, April 20, 1973, p. 3.

170. "Dogs Walk Nike Sentry Duty," *Denver Post*, October 12, 1958, p. 24A (quotation); Martini and Haller, p. 35. The establishment of the sentry program at Nike-Hercules sites saved the Army guard-dog initiative. A year before, budget concerns spurred a recommendation to end it. See "Army Plans to Drop Its Dog Sentry Corps," *New York Times*, February 20, 1957, p. 15.

171. "Sentry Dogs and Site Security," "Fact Sheet," U.S. Army Air Defense Command, Box 293, Folder 20, Desind Collection (quotation); "Sentry Course Developed for Missile Officers," *ARADCOM Argus*, May 1, 1959, p. 3.

172. "Security Dogs for Nike Sites," Army Information Digest, February 1960, in Folder "Nike System," ADA Museum.

173. Memorandum for Office of Chief of Information, D/Army, October 17, 1960, *DoD Film Collection*, Box 23, Folder 7.

174. "The Patriot" script, pp. 1, 20 in *DoD Film Collection*, Box 23, Folder 6. For approval, see William T. Ellington letter to Robert Golden, January 27, 1961, in *DoD Film Collection*, Box 23, Folder 7.

175. http://www.tvtome.com/tvtome/servlet/GuidePageServlet/showid-1110/epid-159742/

176. The final Nike-Ajax batteries were modified in October 1961. (See Cagle, *Hercules*, pp. 242–243.) However, during the Cuban Missile Crisis, mobile Nike-Hercules units were sent to southern Florida since air defense arrangements had not previously anticipated an attack from the south. After the crisis abated, permanent aboveground facilities were constructed to accommodate these missiles. These batteries are included in the total noted in the text, although they were not part of the original plans. (See Morgan and Berhow, pp. 95–97.)

177. "Table 5" included in an unidentified report, December 1, 1964, *DDRS* no. CK3100393973; and Memorandum for the President, December 3, 1964, in Folder "Memos to the President, Oct–Dec 1964," Box 44, Record Group 200, Robert McNamara papers, Strategic Forces, NARA (courtesy of William Burr).

178. This assumes fifty missiles allocated to Greenland and two hundred high-explosive warheads in the continental United States. By contrast, nuclear weapons researcher Chuck Hansen estimates "about 2550" W-31 Nike-Hercules warheads were manufactured. See Hansen, p. VII-197.

179. Author's calculations based upon varying box and capacity information in Cagle, Hercules, pp. 90, 240–245; and Morgan and Berhow.

6 BOMARC and Falcon

1. "AF Orders 4 Sites Built to Launch Its Bomarcs," *Washington Post and Times-Herald*, December 5, 1957, p. A2.
2. Richard F. McMullen, *History of Air Defense Weapons: 1946–1962* A[ir] D[efense] C[ommand] Historical Study 14 (n.p.: Air Defense Command, n.d.), pp. 276–277, 296.
3. For an overview of BOMARC, in addition to works cited elsewhere, see Mike Machat and Anthony Accurso, "Winged Missiles of the U.S. Air Force," *Airpower* (May 2004): 14–26, 54–62; Clayton K.S. Chun, "Winged Interceptor: Politics and Strategy in the Development of the Bomarc Missile," *Airpower History* (winter 1998): 44–59; Robert F. Dorr, "Missile Shielded U.S. from Atomic Attack," *Air Force Times*, February 24, 2003, pp. 44–45.
4. McMullen, *History of Air Defense Weapons*, pp. 87–89, 276–287. Other Falcon versions, which tracked targets by the heat emitted from their engines, also entered the inventory in the late 1950s. They, too, were trouble-prone, and the problems not addressed until early 1961. See McMullen, *History of Air Defense Weapons*.
5. McMullen, *History of Air Defense Weapons*, pp. 115–120, 207.
6. "Gallery of USAF Weapons," *Air Force Magazine* (August 1958): 56–57. "Falcon," in Bill Gunston, *The Illustrated Encyclopedia of Rockets and Missiles* (New York: Crescent Books, 1979), p. 224.
7. Thomas W. Ray, *Nuclear Armament: Its Acquisition, Control, and Application to Manned Interceptors, 1951–1963*; A[ir] D[efense] C[ommand] Historical Study No. 20 (n.p.: Air Defense Command, n.d.), p. 64.
8. McMullen, *History of Air Defense Weapons*, p. 135; "Armament System Specification F-106A Weapon System (U)," December 1957, in Chuck Hansen Collection, Box 25, Folder 2, National Security Archive (hereafter "Hansen Collection").
9. McMullen, *History of Air Defense Weapons*, pp. 212, 221.
10. Ray, *Nuclear Armament*, pp. 64–65.
11. Ray, *Nuclear Armament*, pp. 64–65. LeMay was the consummate "bomber general," a senior Air Force officer whose career trajectory was closely related to his success in leading strategic bombing raids during World War II and who was doctrinally committed to the concept of long-range air attack. Such individuals, who dominated the postwar Air Force senior ranks, were typically characterized as being skeptical about (if not hostile to) defensive measures, and were said to advocate maximum expenditures on forces for aerial (and later missile) bombardment. LeMay's visible patronage of the nuclear Falcon, which had only a defensive application, belies this stereotype.
12. "The Falcon Family: A History of Guided Aircraft Rocket Development," *Interavia* (no. 3, 1961): 354–355.
13. McMullen, *History of Air Defense Weapons*, pp. 296–297.
14. Chairman, Atomic Energy Commission [Lewis Strauss] memorandum to the President, June 12, 1958, Box 26, Folder 4 (quotation); and

Memorandum of Conference with the President, June 13, 1958, Box 26, Folder 5, both in Hansen Collection.
15. Document captioned "Atomic Energy Commission, Meeting 1357," p. 282, in Box 26, Folder 2, Hansen Collection; Chuck Hansen, *Swords of Armageddon*, CD-ROM (1995), pp. VII-114 to VII-115. The GAR-11 was previously known as the GAR-1Y. See "Semiannual Historical Report; Headquarters, Field Command, The Armed Forces Special Weapons Project, Sandia Base, Albuquerque, New Mexico, Volume II, 1 July 1958–31 December 1958," p. 250 (uncataloged collection, National Security Archive). Air Force naming conventions were confusing. "GAR" likely stood for "Guided Aerial Rocket," which is an unwieldy name for a projectile better known as a missile. The Genie designation (MB-1), by contrast, was probably a reference to a Missile with Ballistic (i.e., not maneuverable) characteristics (otherwise commonly referred to as a "rocket"). After 1963, the MB-1 was more commonsensically renamed the AIR-2A and the GAR-11 was redesignated as the AIM-26A. The letters stood for "Air Intercept Rocket" or "Air Intercept Missile." See the forward in Ray, *Nuclear Armament*.
16. Marvin Miles, "Hughes Will Build Nuclear Falcons for AF," *Los Angeles Times*, April 26, 1960, p. 4M.
17. Paul Ager memorandum to Alfred D. Starbird, November 24, 1958, in Box 28, Folder 3, Hansen Collection.
18. McMullen, *History of Air Defense Weapons*, p. 297 (date); Miles (yield); Hansen, pp. VII-118 (dimensions and lethal scope).
19. Jack Raymond, "U.S. to Build 4 Sites for BOMARC Missile," *New York Times*, December 5, 1957, p. 1; "AF Orders 4 Sites Built To Launch Its Bomarc," *Washington Post and Times-Herald*, December 5, 1957, p. A2; Fay, Spofford & Thorndike, Inc., press release captioned "BOMARC Missile to Guard New England," [December 5, 1957] in Folder "BOMARC Boeing (IM-99)," in the collection of the Air Force Association, Arlington, Virginia (hereafter AFA). For Armed Forces Day details, see Air Force News Service Release No. 984 captioned "AF shows Rascal, Bomarc Publicly for First Time," in collection of National Air and Space Museum archives, file no. OB-630000-02.
20. Richard F. McMullen, *Interceptor Missiles in Air Defense: 1944–1964*, A[ir] D[efense] C[ommand] Historical Study No. 30 (n.p.: Air Defense Command, n.d.), pp. 58–59, 64, in Box 1, Folder 9, Air Defense/Radar/Army Ground Training Collection (Record 343), National Security Archive.
21. "The BOMARC Weapon System," *BOMARC Service News* 1, no. 1 (April 1959): 7–9; Thomas W. Ray, *BOMARC and Nuclear Armament*, A[ir] D[efense] C[ommand] Historical Study No. 21 (n.p.: Air Defense Command, n.d.), pp. 10–12; Margaret C. Bagwell, *History of the BOMARC Weapon System: 1953 1957* (Wright-Patterson Air Force Base, [Ohio]: Air Materiel Command, 1959), pp 92–93. No information has been found to suggest why launch facilities were constructed in twenty-eight-unit increments or why the SAGE Ground to Air Transmitter (GAT) sites had to be physically distinct from the launch areas.

22. "Cape Hears about Bomarc Tonight," *Falmouth* (Massachusetts) *Enterprise*, December 13, 1957, p. 1; "Bomarc Shows Base Is on Cape to Stay," *Falmouth Enterprise*, December 17, 1957, pp. 1, 5 (quotations).
23. "Cape Hears About Bomarc Tonight," "Bomarc Shows Base Is on Cape to Stay."
24. "Bomarc Shows Base Is on Cape to Stay," p. 5.
25. "Missile Fever in Utah," *AMC Worldwide* 1, no. 7 (April 1958): 11; Helen Rice, *History of Ogden Air Materiel Area: Hill Air Force Base, Utah, 1934–1960* (n.p.: Air Force Logistics Command, n.d.), pp. 148, 152.
26. One source says the Revell kit was introduced in 1957 (Mat Irvine, *Creating Space: The Story of the Space Age Told Through Models* (Burlington, Ontario: Collector's Guide Publishing, Inc., 2002), p. 247). The kit's instructions bear a 1957 copyright, but make reference to a May 1957 Air Force decision, which places publication after that date. (Instructions in author's possession, courtesy of Allen B. Ury of Fantastic Plastic.) The definitive Revell history dates the kit to 1958. See Thomas Graham, *Remembering Revell Model Kits* (Atglen, PA: Schiffer Publishing Company, 2002), p. 147.
27. "Tactical Missile Coloration," *BOMARC Service News* 1, no. 1 (April 1959): 13.
28. Irvine, p. 185.
29. Carroll V. Glines, "Have Show…Will Travel," *Air Force Magazine* (December 1959): 47–50; Rice, pp. 151, 202.
30. McMullen, *Interceptor Missiles*, pp. 127–136. Despite the failures, there was one putatively beneficial aspect of an otherwise unsuccessful test flight. In May 1956, a BOMARC carried the cremated ashes of Margaret Wood McGrew, an Air Force engineering executive assigned to the program, to forty thousand feet. A malfunction caused the BOMARC to explode and scatter her remains in the heavens, just as McGrew had requested before she died of cancer. See Milton Bracker, "A Missile Pioneer Honored in Death," *New York Times*, August 31, 1958, p. 5.
31. "Presentation by the Director, Weapons Systems Evaluation Group to the National Security Council on the Subject of Offensive and Defensive Weapons Systems," pp. 5–6, 10, 14, Nuclear History document collection, item no. NH00411, National Security Archive.
32. "Discussion at the 382nd (Special) Meeting of the National Security Council, Monday, October 13, 1958," October 14, 1958, *Declassified Documents Reference System* (hereafter *DDRS*) no. CK3100102432.
33. Gordon Gray letter to Nathan F. Twining, October 30, 1958, *DDRS* no. CK3100447261. A referenced attachment is J.R. Killian, Jr., memorandum to Gordon Gray, October 29, 1958, *DDRS* no. CK3100107229. Additional background on this memorandum is provided in B. McMillan memorandum to J.R. Killian, October 29, 1958, *DDRS* no. CK3100319341.
34. Gray letter to Nathan F. Twining, October 30, 1958 (emphasis in original).
35. Robert J. Watson, *Into the Missile Age, 1956–1960: History of the Office of the Secretary of Defense, Vol. IV* (Washington: Office of the Secretary of Defense, 1997), pp. 423, 426–427.

36. Watson, p. 422. In July 1959, Admiral Arthur Radford, who had been recalled from retirement to active duty to serve temporarily as JCS chairman while an ill Twining recovered, suggested that this arrangement be revisited. In a meeting with the president, Radford raised the possibility that the Air Force assume the total air defense mission and said both affected service chiefs were receptive to this idea. Nothing came of it. See "Memorandum of Conference with President Eisenhower," July 14, 1959, in *Foreign Relation of the United States, 1958–1960*, vol. III, National Security Policy; Arms Control and Disarmament (Government Printing Office: Washington, 1996), pp. 253–254 (hereafter identified as *FRUS* with year, volume, and page specified).
37. Donald A. Quarles memorandum to Gordon Gray, February 13, 1959, DDRS no. CK3100082163; and "Memorandum of Meeting with the President (Monday, February 16, 1959, at 10:00 a.m.)," in Folder "Meetings with the President—1959 (6)," Box 4, Special Assistant Series, Presidential Subseries, White House Office [hereafter "WHO"], Office of the Special Assistant for National Security Affairs [hereafter "OSANSA"], Records, 1952–61, Dwight D. Eisenhower Library (hereafter "DDEL"); Watson, p. 423.
38. Watson, pp. 423–427; "Nike-Hercules Defense Hit By Sen. Jackson," *Seattle Post-Intelligencer*, May 25, 1959, p. 9.
39. See, for example, Elton C. Fay, "Army Warns Nike-Hercules Cutback Would Menace Security of Nation," *Washington Post and Times-Herald*, May 23, 1959, p. A1; "Army Puts Fire in Missiles Feud," *New York Times*, June 3, 1959, p. 14 (favorable to Nike-Hercules); and "Boeing Man Cites Bomarc Capabilities," *Seattle Times*, May 26, 1959, p. 3; and "Nike Missile Reported 8% Effective," *Seattle Post-Intelligencer*, May 27, 1959, p. 3 (favorable to BOMARC). An internal memorandum circulated by the Chief of Naval Operations, the head of a service that was not a party to the dispute, offered some observations of the dispute. "The Army position is clear. It is fighting to stay in the surface to air missile business. The Air Force push for Bomarc is not so clear, except that it is supporting an Air Force devised missile." See "CNO Personal No. 49," June 4, 1959, in author's possession courtesy of William Burr.
40. "Discussion at the 408th Meeting of the National Security Council, Thursday, May 28, 1959," p. 13, DDRS no. CK3100282048.
41. "Memorandum of Meeting with the President (Monday, 1 June 1959 at 10:00 a.m.)," June 5, 1959, p. 2, DDRS no. CK3100212209.
42. Watson, pp. 427–429; Richard F. McMullen, *The Aerospace Defense Command and Antibomber Defense, 1946–1972*, A[ir] D[efense] C[ommand] Historical Study no. 39 (n.p.: Air Defense Command, 1973), p. 97.
43. "Memorandum of Conference with the President, June 9, 1959," June 10, 1959, DDRS no. CK3100364339. Despite the number and extent of briefings that Eisenhower received about BOMARC over the course of several years and his demonstrable familiarity with the weapon, he had a peculiar exchange with General Twining in November 1959. At that time, after the JCS chairman briefed the president and NSC on the status

of various defense programs, the minutes of the meeting report that Eisenhower inquired about "the characteristics" of the Air Force's surface-to-air missile and "whether the BOMARC was a completely defensive weapon." Such a fundamental query about an armament that had occupied much of the president's time in the past year is difficult to reconcile with the balance of the record. Of course, it is possible that the president misspoke or the meeting minutes misstate the inquiry. See "Discussion at the 425th Meeting of the National Security Council, Wednesday, November 25, 1959," p. 10, *DDRS* no. CK3100321291.

44. "Editorial Note," in *FRUS, 1958–1960*, vol. III, National Security Policy; Arms Control and Disarmament, pp. 215–216.

45. "Memorandum of Conference with the President, February 12, 1959—10:40 AM (After NSC)," February 12, 1959, pp. 2, 3, *DDRS* no. CK3100455984. When the President expressed his support "for small weapons in air defense and missile defense," Andrew Goodpaster's notes also indicate that Ike "pointed out that the three scientists who had visited him the day before...had shown less enthusiasm that he has heard at other times in this area." This was almost certainly a reference to Eisenhower's meeting on February 10 with three members of the president's Science Advisory Committee (Edwin Land and James Killian) and Harvard physicist and Nobel laureate Edward M. Purcell. Goodpaster's notes from that discussion reflect a wide-ranging conversation about ballistic missiles, including velocities and launch-warning technology, and reconnaissance matters. There is no indication that the group discussed missile defense at all, much less reflected pessimistically on the topic. This may indicate a flaw in the note taking. Goodpaster set forth his recollection of the February 10 meeting on February 13, three days after the meeting and one day after a follow-on meeting in which the President referenced it. See "Memorandum of Conference with the President, February 10, 1959," February 13, 1959, *DDRS* no. CK3100092480. For background on the PSAC, see Benjamin P. Greene, *Eisenhower, Science Advice, and the Nuclear Test Ban Debate, 1945–1963* (Stanford: Stanford University Press, 2007), pp. 147–148.

46. Raid Test Today to Cover Nation," *New York Times*, April 17, 1959, p. 1.

47. Philip Benjamin, "Radio and TV Blacked Out Over U.S.," *New York Times*, April 18, 1959, p. 1; "Raid Test Today to Cover Nation." Civilians in Washington largely ignored the drill. Eisenhower was vacationing away from the city and did not take part. See "Radio and TV Blacked Out Over U.S.," "Raid Test Today to Cover Nation." and Wendell P. Bradley, "Alert Goes Ignored by Civilians," *Washington Post*, April 18, 1959, p. D1.

48. Watson, pp. 429–430.

49. John G. Norris, "Boeing Ad Is Criticized As Lobbying," *Washington Post and Times-Herald*, June 12, 1959, p. A2; and "Boeing Defends Its Ad Backing Bomarc Missile," *Washington Star*, June 12, 1959. Both articles cite a May 27 Boeing ad that, curiously, cannot be located in editions of that paper that survive. It is possible it ran in only certain editions.

50. Another ad which Boeing cited as forming part of its series (*New York Times*, January 7, 1959, p. 40) sought engineers and scientists for the IM-99 program. The map can be found in *New York Times*, April 8, 1959, p. 22. The other referenced ad is in the *Washington Post and Times-Herald*, March 25, 1959, p. B6. It also appeared in *Air Force Magazine*, May 1959, p. 1.
51. *Newsweek*, February 2, 1959. This also appeared in *Air Force Magazine*, February 1959, p. 4.
52. Norman G. Cornish, "Probers Charge Boeing Tried to Sway Public for Bomarc," *Washington Post and Times-Herald*, August 7, 1959, p. A18.
53. "House Probers Told Army Suggested Contractor Advertise Nike-Hercules," *Washington Post and Times-Herald*, August 13, 1959, p. A19. The relevant Western Electric ad is in *New York Times*, May 18, 1959, p. 23.
54. Drew Pearson, "Lobby Not a Lobby, Hebert Learns," *Washington Post and Times-Herald*, August 18, 1959, p. B19.
55. "House Probers Told Army Suggested Contractor Advertise Nike-Hercules."
56. "Army Explains Role in Nike Missile Ads," *Washington Star*, August 19, 1959; Norman G. Cornish, "Army Admits It Urged Stepup in Ads on Nike," *Washington Post and Times-Herald*, August 20, 1959, p. A13.
57. Drew Pearson, "Defense 'Partnerships' Criticized," *Washington Post and Times-Herald*, August 17, 1959, p. B19.
58. C.P. Trussell, "Ex-Officers Face Defense-Job Curb," *New York Times*, January 18, 1960, p. 1; C.P. Trussell, "House Votes Bill to Curb Officers," *New York Times*, April 8, 1960, p. 18.
59. Frank E. Snyder and Brian H. Guss, *The District: A History of the Philadelphia District, U.S. Army Corps of Engineers, 1866–1971* (Philadelphia: U.S. Army Engineer District, 1974), p. 152; Frank Rosen, "Air Base in N.J. Gets Missile Launchers to Bolster Area Defense," *Philadelphia Inquirer*, November 21, 1958; Robert C. Toth, "What Bomarc Missile Is and How It's Operated," *New York Herald Tribune*, June 8, 1960; Ray, *BOMARC and Nuclear Armament*, p. 10.
60. Snyder and Guss; McMullen, *Interceptor Missiles*, pp. 54–55. For a general overview of site preparation requirements, see Margaret C. Bagwell, *History of the BOMARC Weapon System, 1953–1957* (Wright-Patterson Air Force Base, [Ohio]: Air Materiel Command, 1959), pp. 93–96.
61. McMullen, *Interceptor Missiles*, pp. 83–84.
62. McMullen, *Interceptor Missiles*, pp. 83–84; Byron Porterfield, "L.I. BOMARC Base is Taking Shape," *New York Times*, April 26, 1959, p. 34.
63. McMullen, *Interceptor Missiles*, p. 81.
64. McMullen, *Interceptor Missiles*, p. 54.
65. Ray, *BOMARC and Nuclear Armament*, pp. 13–14; McMullen, *History of Air Defense Weapons*, p. 330.
66. Toth, "What Bomarc Missile Is."
67. "Report of the Ad Hoc Panel on Continental Defense," c. September 1959, *DDRS* no. CK3100326059.

68. See *DDRS* no. CK3100322637; "Memorandum For: Members and Consultants, Continental Air Defense Panel, January 18, 1960," *DDRS* no. CK3100326007l; Watson, p. 357; and various papers in Box 4, WHO, Office of Special Assistant for Science and Technology [hereafter "OSAST"], Records, 1957–61, DDEL. This study also indirectly influenced the English language. A front-page *New York Times* article about Air Force complaints about a recommendation to "drop plans" for the BOMARC B described the missile as "a 'follow-on' air defense weapon" that was based on an earlier version. Editors of the Random House dictionary took note of this phraseology. Apparently, it was the first time that "follow-on" had been used as an adjective, and the company's reference book was altered accordingly. See Jack Raymond, "Air Force Balks at Spending Cuts," *New York Times*, November 8, 1959, p. 1; and William Safire, "Maid Service," *New York Times*, September 4, 1994, p. F18.
69. McMullen, *History of Air Defense Weapons*, p. 103.
70. "N[ational] I[ntelligence] E[stimate] 11-8-59," in *FRUS, 1958–1960*, vol. III, National Security Policy; Arms Control and Disarmament, p. 378.
71. Watson, pp. 357, 434; "Memorandum for General Persons," March 12, 1960, *DDRS* no. CK3100466160; John W. Finney, "Air Force Planning Bomarc Missile Cut," *New York Times*, March 25, 1960.
72. McMullen, *History of Air Defense Weapons*, pp. 185–187.
73. Richard F. McMullen, *Air Defense and National Policy; 1958–1964* A[ir] D[efense] C[ommand] Historical Study 26 (n.p.: Air Defense Command, n.d.), p. 12.
74. McMullen, *History of Air Defense Weapons*, pp. 187–188.
75. McMullen, *History of Air Defense Weapons*, pp. 181–186.
76. McMullen, *Air Defense and National Policy*, pp. 25–27; Marquis Childs, "Death of Bomarc May Stir Debate," *Washington Post*, April 13, 1960; May 1997 report by researcher Mark Morgan in author's possession.
77. McMullen, *Air Defense and National Policy*, p. 27
78. McMullen, *History of Air Defense Weapons*, p. 352.
79. Stephen E. Ambrose, *Eisenhower: The President* (New York: Simon and Schuster, 1984), pp. 571–572; Michael R. Beschloss, *Mayday; Eisenhower, Khrushchev and the U-2 Affair* (New York: Harper & Row, 1986), p. 45.
80. Information is drawn from the website http://www.conelrad.com, based upon research at DDEL and John F. Kennedy Library, and several telephone interviews undertaken by individuals associated with that website. Printouts of Conelrad.com information in author's possession.
81. Ray, *BOMARC and Nuclear Armament*, p. 22; McMullen, *History of Air Defense Weapons*, p. 330.
82. McMullen, *History of Air Defense Weapons*, pp. 330–332.
83. McMullen, *History of Air Defense Weapons*, pp. 330–332; Ray, *BOMARC and Nuclear Armament*, p. 36; Philip Dodd, "Helium Bottle Burst Blamed in Bomarc Fire," *Chicago Tribune*, June 24, 1960.
84. Memorandum captioned "Report of Special Weapons Incident [deleted], Bomarc Site, McGuire AFB, New Jersey," June 13, 1960, in Box 30, Folder 5, Hansen Collection.

85. "A-Missile Burns Up in N.J.," *Washington Post and Times-Herald*, June 8, 1960, p. A1.
86. Leonard Katz and Edward Kosner, "Bomarc Fire," *New York Post*, June 8, 1960, p. 9; "Disaster News," *New York Post*, June 8, 1960, p. 9; Robert C. Toth, "Jersey C.D. and Air Force Wrangle over Handling of Atom Missile Fire," *New York Herald Tribune*, June 9, 1960; "Scare Is Laid to Sergeant," *Baltimore Sun*, June 9, 1960.
87. "Disaster News."
88. Toth, "Jersey C.D. and Air Force Wrangle"; "Scare is Laid to Sergeant"; George Cable Wright, "U.S. Studies Fire in Atom Missile," *New York Times*, June 9, 1960. The overseas press was less inhibited in touting news of a nuclear disaster. In London, the *Daily Herald*'s headline proclaimed "A-Rocket Blows Up—Death-Dust Danger Panics New York." Other papers trumpeted an "A-Burst Mystery" and an "Atomic Warhead on Fire at U.S. Base." See Thomas P. Ronan, "Papers in Britain Give Big Play to U.S. Missile Fire in Jersey," *New York Times*, June 9, 1960.
89. "4-Way Probe opens in Fire of A-Missile," *Philadelphia Inquirer*, June 9, 1960; "Report of Special Weapons Incident"; memorandum captioned "File no. Cooperation 3 Air Force," June 8, 1960, in Box 30, File 5, Hansen Collection.
90. "Report of Special Weapons Incident"; "Scare is Laid to Sergeant."
91. Memorandum attached to memorandum captioned "Radiological Decontamination," June 26, 1961, Box 31, Folder 2, Hansen Collection.
92. "Report of Special Weapons Incident"; "Airmunitions Letter," September 8, 1960, Box 31, Folder 1; and "Point Paper on 1960 Bomarc Nuclear Weapon Accident," July 10, 1985, Box 30, Folder 5, both in Hansen Collection.
93. Frank Borsky, "Assails General's Report on A-Alarm," *New York Journal American*, June 9, 1960; McMullen, *History of Air Defense Weapons*, p. 330.
94. Ray, *BOMARC and Nuclear Armament*, p. 35.
95. After the facility closed in 1972, however, civic sensibilities changed and doubts arose about the accident and the dangers it posed to the nearby area. An extensive investigation of the site conducted by the U.S. Department of Health and Human Services nearly forty years after the fire found that individuals involved in fighting the blaze or securing the area were not likely to have been harmed, even assuming "worst case exposure level[s]," for which there was no evidence. In addition, the assessment reported that "the BOMARC site poses no threat to public health," provided that the concrete and asphalt cap remains in place. (See "Public Health Assessment, Boeing Michigan Aeronautical Research Center/McGuire Missile, New Egypt, Ocean County, New Jersey," U.S. Department of Health and Human Services, Agency of Toxic Substances and Disease Registry, in author's possession.) Nonetheless, in response to community concerns, the Air Force excavated the contaminated pavement and soil and shipped it to a waste storage facility in Utah in 2004.

(See Bob Vosseller, "Soil Transfer at Plumsted Bomarc Site Complete," *New Egypt* (New Jersey) *Press*, June 18, 2004).
96. Ray, *BOMARC and Nuclear Armament*, pp. 36–37; and McMullen, *Interceptor Missiles*, p. 103.
97. "Memorandum of Conference with the President, July 13, 1959," July 14, 1959, DDRS no. CK3100085312; "Memorandum of Conversation," August 13, 1959, *FRUS, 1958–1960*, vol. III, National Security Policy; Arms Control and Disarmament, pp. 770–772; "Report, Ad Hoc Panel on Nuclear Test Requirements," August 18, 1959, pp. 1, 3–5, DDRS no. CK3100114618; Robert N. Thorn and Donald R. Westervelt, "Hydronuclear Experiments," Los Alamos National Laboratory, February 1987, LA-10902-MS.
98. Hansen, pp. VI-24, VII-202 to VII-203; and document hand-captioned "B. United States Weapon Progr[am]," c. June 1956, Box 22, Folder 4, Hansen Collection.
99. "Memorandum of Conference with the President, July 13, 1959."
100. "Memorandum of Conversation," November 17, 1959, *FRUS, 1958–1960*, vol. III, National Security Policy; Arms Control and Disarmament, pp. 801–802.
101. "Memorandum of Conference with the President, March 11, 1960," March 14, 1960, Box 30, Folder 4, Hansen Collection; Thorn and Westervelt, pp. 3–5; and "DARHT Conducts Fully Contained Hydrotest," *NNSA News*, National Nuclear Security Administration, Washington, DC, July 2007, p. 7.
102. Thorn and Westervelt; George B. Kistiakowsky, *A Scientist at the White House: The Private Diary of President Eisenhower's Special Assistant for Science and Technology* (Cambridge: Harvard University Press, 1976).
103. Hansen, p. VII-202; and Thorn and Westervelt, p. 5.
104. "Memorandum of Conference with the President, July 13, 1959."
105. Ray, *BOMARC and Nuclear Armament*, pp. 21, 23–24. For coverage of the installation in French River, Minnesota, see Hal Quarforth, "Duluth Bomarc Base is Completed," *Minneapolis Morning Tribune*, November 1, 1960, p. 8; William Johnson, "'Turkey Farmers' Keep Missile's Eye on Sky," *Minneapolis Sunday Tribune*, March 12, 1961, p. 1B.
106. Richard F. McMullen, *Air Defense and National Policy; 1958–1964* A[ir] D[efense] C[ommand] Historical Study no. 26 (n.p.: Air Defense Command, n.d.), p. 45; Ray, *BOMARC and Nuclear Armament*, pp. 25–26.
107. Andrew Merey, "Beau-Marks: Champions of Canadian Rock 'n' Roll," May 28, 2010, on the Web site of the Metroland Durham (Ontario) Region Media Group, in author's possession. There were significant events surrounding Canada's acquisition of the BOMARC, including the downfall of a government and distress in the nation's industrial sector because the missiles replaced an indigenously designed interceptor then in the late stages of development. These circumstances are outside the scope of this project. See, for example, John Clearwater, *Canadian Nuclear Weapons: The Untold Story of Canada's Cold War Arsenal* (Toronto: Dundurn Press, 1998); Watson pp. 42–421, 434–435, and

Palmiro Campagna, *Storms of Controversy: The Secret Avro Arrow Files Revealed* (Toronto: Stoddart Publishing, 1997).
108. McMullen, *History of Air Defense Weapons*, pp. 182–187.
109. McMullen, *Interceptor Missiles*, p. 122; McMullen, *History of Air Defense Weapons*, p. 187.
110. McMullen, *History of Air Defense Weapons*, pp. 182–187. In January 1962, a routine safety survey at Langley also identified a potential security problem affecting all BOMARCs. It was determined that an individual with access to the IM-99's computerized controls and knowledge of the system's operation could potentially insert a programming tape that would cause the missile to fire without proper authorization. As a result, various security changes were implemented, including imposition of the "two-man" rule in the control facilities. See Ray, *BOMARC and Nuclear Armament*, p. 16.
111. U.S. Army, *History of Strategic Air and Ballistic Missile Defense: Volume II, 1956–1972* (Washington: Center of Military History, c. 1975), p. 153.
112. McMullen, *Interceptor Missiles*, p. 41.
113. Ray, *BOMARC and Nuclear Armament*, p. 48.
114. Roger A. Mola, "This Is Only a Test," *Air and Space Smithsonian* (February/March 2002): 50–55.
115. Mola.
116. Mola.
117. Ray, *Nuclear Armament*, p. 63.
118. McMullen, *History of Air Defense Weapons*, pp. 297–298; Ray, *Nuclear Armament*, pp. 69–71; Hansen, pp. VII-116 and VII-117.
119. Hansen, p. VII-117 and VII-118 and Table A-1, p. 22.
120. McMullen, *History of Air Defense Weapons*, p. 300; Ray, *Nuclear Armament*, pp. 72–73; Hansen, p. VII-118.
121. Miles; Max B. Cook, "New Guided Rocket to Join Defense Unit," *New York World-Telegram and Sun*, May 24, 1961 (quotations).
122. "Air Force to Get New Nuclear Missile," *Washington Post, Times-Herald*, April 26, 1960, p. A8; *Air Force Magazine*, June 1960, p. 29; *Aviation Week*, May 16, 1960, p. 88; *Ordnance* (July–August 1960), p. 106.
123. *Air Force Magazine*, September 1960, pp. 196–197.
124. Ray, *Nuclear Armament*, p. 65. The number produced is in "Fact Sheet, The Falcon Family of Air-to-Air Guided Missiles," Hughes Aircraft press release, [circa 1963], in Folder OF-060000-01, Archives Division, National Air and Space Museum.
125. Ray, *Nuclear Armament*, pp. 75, 78–80.

Conclusion

1. "Inaugural Ceremony—1961" film, ARC Identifier 83354; and "Inauguration Day Activities—1961," film ARC Identifier 83302, both from Record Group 428: General Records of the Department of the Navy, 1941–1981, National Archives and Records Administration.

2. Chuck Hansen, *U.S. Nuclear Weapons: The Secret History* (Arlington, TX: Aerofax, 1988), p. 177; Air Force Association information on "AIR-2 Genie" in author's possession.
3. Mary T. Cagle, *History of the Nike Hercules Weapon System* (U.S. Army Missile Command: Redstone Arsenal, Alabama), 1973, pp. 242–243.
4. Richard F. McMullen, *Air Defense and National Policy, 1958–1964* A[ir] D[efense] C[ommand] Historical Study 26 (n.p.: Air Defense Command, n.d.), p. 45; Thomas W. Ray, *BOMARC and Nuclear Armament*, A[ir] D[efense] C[ommand] Historical Study No. 21 (n.p.: Air Defense Command, n.d.), pp. 25–26.
5. Richard F. McMullen, *History of Air Defense Weapons, 1946–1962* A[ir] D[efense] C[ommand] Historical Study 14 (n.p.: Air Defense Command, n.d.), p. 300; Chuck Hansen, *Swords of Armageddon*, CD-ROM (1995), p. VII-118.
6. Thomas W. Ray, *Nuclear Armament: Its Acquisition, Control, and Application to Manned Interceptors, 1951–1963*; A[ir] D[efense] C[ommand] Historical Study No. 20 (n.p.: Air Defense Command, n.d.), pp. 9–10; James E. Reeves memorandum to Brig. General A.W. Watts, January 10, 1962, Department of Energy/Nevada Nuclear Testing Archive accession no. NV0308980.
7. Extent information about Blue Straw suggests at least one operational component involved placing radiation and blast measurement equipment in airspace near an airborne nuclear weapon detonation. It is possible that such diagnostic activities were also planned to take place amid a Genie and/or GAR-11 airburst. See "Sandia Corporation Monthy Reports 1958–1963," available from Office of Science and Technology (OSTI), U.S. Department of Energy, p. 10, in author's possession.
8. Raymond L. Garthoff, *Reflections on the Cuban Missile Crisis* (Washington: Brookings Institution, 1987), Garthoff, p. 66, note 101; Aleksandr Fursenko and Timothy Naftali, *"One Hell of a Gamble": Khrushchev, Castro, and Kennedy, 1958–1964* (New York: W.W. Norton and Company, 1997), p. 210. Anatoli I. Gribkov and William Y. Smith, *Operation ANADYR; U.S. and Soviet Generals Recount the Cuban Missile Crisis* (Chicago: Edition Q, Inc., 1994), pp. 4, 27.
9. Samuel B. Frankel memorandum to Steuart Pittman, November 1, 1962, Cuban Missile Crisis document collection, item no. CC1805, National Security Archive [hereafter "CMC document no."]; Ernest R. May and Philip D. Zelikow, *The Kennedy Tapes: Inside the White House During the Cuban Missile Crisis* (Cambridge: Belknap Press, 1997), pp. 69–70, 88–89, 131–133, 196; and David G. Coleman, "The Missiles of November, December, January, February...The Problem of Acceptable Risk in the Cuban Missile Crisis Settlement," *Journal of Cold War Studies* 9, no. 3 (Summer 2007): 16, 21, 24–25, 27, 41. When the NSC's Executive Committee first convened on October 16, Secretary of Defense Robert McNamara declared: "If there are nuclear warheads associated with the [missile] launchers, you must assume there will be nuclear warheads associated with aircraft." (See May and Zelikow, p. 60.) Although the USSR had sent a half dozen six- to eight-kiloton nuclear bombs to Cuba as the

potential payload for several specially configured Beagles, this fact did not become known until decades later. See Michael Dobbs, *One Minute to Midnight: Kennedy, Khrushchev, and Castro on the Brink of Nuclear War* (New York: Alfred A. Knopf, 2008), pp. 246–248; Fursenko and Naftali, p. 210; and Gribkov and Smith, p. 4, 27.

10. Scott D. Sagan, *The Limits of Safety: Organizations, Accidents, and Nuclear Weapons* (Princeton: Princeton University Press, 1993), pp. 95–98, 135.
11. Sagan, pp. 95–98, 135. For a slightly different interpretation of the advent of the Genie (quoting one veteran calling it "the dumbest weapons system ever purchased") and the dangers of interceptor dispersal, see Dobbs, pp. 39–40, 47, and 48–49.
12. Memorandum for General Parker, Admiral Sharp, General Burchinal, General Hayes, December 21, 1962, CMC document no. CC02780. Emphasis added. See also, Sagan, pp. 100–102.
13. Sagan, pp. 98–102, 136–140, 153 (quotations, p. 101); See also Dobbs 132–134; 264–265.
14. "The Air Defense Command in the Cuban Crisis," December 1962, CMC document no CC02654, p. 69.
15. See, for example, Alaska batteries discussed in "The Cuban Crisis," December 1962, CMC document no. CC02656, pp. 388–90.
16. Ray, *BOMARC and Nuclear Armament*, pp. 36–37.
17. Richard F. McMullen, *Interceptor Missiles in Air Defense, 1944–1964*, A[ir] D[efense] C[ommand] Historical Study No. 30 (n.p.: Air Defense Command, n.d.), p. 111, in Box 1, Folder 9, Air Defense/Radar/Army Ground Training Collection (Record 343), National Security Archive.
18. Memorandum for General Parker, et al.; May and Zelikow, p. 60; and Dino Brugioni, *Eyeball to Eyeball* (New York: Random House, 1991), pp. 290–291.
19. John C. Lonnquest, *To Defend and Deter: The Legacy of the United States Cold War Missile Program* (Rock Island, Illinois: Defense Publishing Service, 1996), pp. 329–330; War Room Journal, October 24, 1962, CMC document no. CC01120, items 13 and handwritten 33. Rail transit is noted in "Status of ADA units being deployed to SE US" attachment to War Room Journal, October 31, 1962, CMC document no. CC01773; and in Brugioni, p. 371. The date is shown as October 23 in Memorandum for General Parker et al., p. 38. The Air Defense Command History reports the date as October 27. (See "The Air Defense Command in the Cuban Crisis," p. 282.)
20. The Nike-Hercules unit that was moved was the 2/52nd Air Defense Battalion. It was short one battery because the forth was on Johnson Atoll in the Pacific. Its absence worried Army leaders who ordered it returned to the United States to bring the parent unit to full strength. (See CINCSTRIKE telex to AIG 930, October 24, 1962, CMC document no. CC01201; and JCS memorandum to Secretary of State, October 25, 1962, CMC document no. CC01325.)
21. Cable from General John Gerhart to Joint Chiefs of Staff, CINCNORAD message 262345Z, October 27, 1962, in Chief of Naval Operations Cuba

history files, Boxes 58–72, Operational Archives, U.S. Navy Historical Center, Washington, DC, in author's possession, provided by very special courtesy of Michael Dobbs; Dobbs, p. 248.

22. Memorandum for General Parker et al., p. 50.
23. War Room Journal, October 31, 1962, CMC document no. CC01773, item 29. A "General Parker" is referenced in the documents from the National Security Archive. General Theodore Parker is also discussed in Brugioni. It is presumed that the disparate references are to the same individual, based upon rank, service, and responsibilities.
24. War Room Journal, October 31, 1962, CMC document no. CC01773, item 29; War Room Journal, October 24, 1962, CMC document no. CC01120, item 16 (and copy of journal pages included therein) and item 19; and War Room Journal, October 25, 1962, CMC document no. CC1320, items 31, 35, 43.
25. Nelson Rockefeller plucked Parker from this assignment to work with him. See Cary Reich, *The Life of Nelson A. Rockefeller: Worlds to Conquer, 1908–1958* (New York: Doubleday, 1996).
26. Laurence Martin, *Arms and Strategy: An International Survey of Modern Defence* (London: Weidenfeld and Nicolson, 1973), p. 132.
27. Lonnquest, p. 330; Bill Dupriest, "Army Missilemen Move to New Home," *Miami Herald*, March 4, 1965; Steve Hatch, *Cold War in South Florida Historic Resource Study* (Atlanta, Georgia: National Park Service, 2004), pp. 75–86.
28. Howard Van Smith, "People Behind Our Missiles," *Miami News*, c. 1966, in author's possession.
29. McMullen, *Interceptor Missiles*, pp. 119–120.
30. McMullen, *Interceptor Missiles*, pp. 117–118, 123–124.
31. McMullen, *Interceptor Missiles*, pp. 122–123.
32. Lloyd Mallan, *Peace is a Three-Edged Sword* (Englewood Cliffs, NJ: Prentice-Hall, 1964), pp. 68–69.
33. Joseph Califano memorandum to President Johnson, November 18, 1965, *Declassified Documents Reference System* (hereafter *DDRS*), no. CK3100098951; John M. Steadman memorandum to Joseph Califano, November 13, 1965, *DDRS* no. CK 3100471394.
34. Mark L. Morgan and Mark A. Berhow, *Rings of Supersonic Steel: Air Defenses of the United States Army, 1950–1979: An Introductory History and Site Guide* (San Pedro, California: Fort MacArthur Press, 2002). South Dakota's Ellsworth Air Force Base also had a Nike-Hercules battery between 1958 and 1961, at which time the equipment was moved to Hartford, Connecticut. This is probably because by this point the base became the headquarters of an ICBM unit. Since in the event of war, the associated missiles would presumably have been launched by the time the field could have come under attack by planes, it did not require antibomber defenses. See Morgan and Berhow, pp. 82–83. In addition, the conventional Nike-Ajax was considered outmoded almost immediately after the introduction of its successor missile. All Ajax sites were shut down between 1961 and 1964. See Morgan and Berhow.
35. Morgan and Berhow.

36. "Jets are Shifted to the Air Guard," *New York Times*, March 26, 1972, p. 4.
37. "Canada to Close Out Missiles over American Objections," *Washington Post*, August 25, 1971, p. A17.
38. Morgan and Berhow, p. 26.
39. Hansen, *Swords of Armageddon*, p. VII-118.
40. Michael Getler, "Big Cut Set in U.S. Air Defense Force," *Washington Post*, October 7, 1973, p. A2.
41. Bill Keller, "A Venerable Line of Defense Is about to Get a Facelift," *New York Times*, January 27, 1985, p. E3.
42. Getler.
43. Morgan and Berhow.
44. "Nike Sentry Dogs Looking for Jobs," *Army Times*, February 20, 1974, p. 3.
45. Getler; "Stateside Rotation Base on for Overseas Missilemen," *Army Times*, February 20, 1974, p. 3.
46. Morgan and Berhow, pp. 45, 96–97.
47. John W. Finney, "U.S. May Tighten Atomic Control," *New York Times*, March 19, 1976, p. 69.
48. Walter Pincus, "Nuclear Missile Has Navy in a Quandary," *Washington Post*, January 14, 1984, p. A10.
49. Thomas B. Cochran, William M. Arkin, and Milton M. Hoenig, *Nuclear Weapons Databook*, vol. 1, "U.S. Nuclear Forces and Capabilities" (Cambridge: Ballinger, 1984), p. 41.
50. Hansen, *Swords of Armageddon*, p. VII-105; Air Force Association information on "AIR-2 Genie."
51. Lloyd Mallan, *Peace is a Three-Edged Sword* (Englewood Cliffs, NJ: Prentice-Hall, 1964), p. 50.
52. Steven J. Zaloga, *Target America: The Soviet Union and the Strategic Arms Race, 1945–1964* (Novato, CA: Presidio Press, 1993), pp. 63–88; David Holloway, *Stalin and the Bomb* (New Haven: Yale University Press, 1994), pp. 242–245, 322–324.
53. Quoted in Holloway, p. 322.

Bibliography

Archives and Repositories

Air Force Association.
Air Force Historical Research Agency.
California State Archives.
Dwight D. Eisenhower Presidential Library.
Georgetown University Library, Special Collections Division.
Herbert Hoover Presidential Library.
History Office, U.S. Army Corps of Engineers.
National Air and Space Museum.
National Archives and Records Administration.
National Security Archive.
Nebraska State Historical Society.
Office of Corporate Historian, Sandia National Laboratories.
Oregon State University Special Collections.
U.S. Army. Air Defense Artillery Museum.
U.S. Army. Center of Military History.
U.S. Army. Military History Institute.
U.S. Department of Energy. Nevada Nuclear Testing Archive.

Government Histories and Reports

Bagwell, Margaret C. *History of the BOMARC Weapon System; 1953–1957.* Wright-Patterson Air Force Base [Ohio]: Air Materiel Command, 1959.

Barlow, E.J. *Active Air Defense of the United States; 1954–1960*, R-250 (abridged). Santa Monica, CA: Rand Corporation, 1953.

Barnard, Roy S. *The History of ARADCOM; Volume 1, the Gun Era: 1950–1955.* U.S. Army, n.d.

Cagle, Mary T. *Development, Production, and Deployment of the Nike Ajax Guided Missile System; 1945–1959.* Redstone Arsenal, Alabama: Army Guided Missile Agency, n.d.

———. *History of the Nike Hercules Weapon System.* U.S. Army Missile Command: Redstone Arsenal, Alabama, 1973.

Carlson, Christina M. and Robert Lyon. *Last Line of Defense: Nike Missile Sites in Illinois.* Denver: National Park Service, 1996.

Condit, Doris M. *History of the Office of the Secretary of Defense; Vol. II; The Test of War, 1950–1953.* Washington: Historical Office, Office of the Secretary of Defense, 1988.

Condit, Kenneth W. *History of the Joint Chiefs of Staff; The Joint Chiefs and National Policy, Vol. VI; 1955–1956.* Washington: Historical Office, Joint Staff, 1992.

Defense's Nuclear Agency; 1947–1997. Washington: Defense Threat Reduction Agency, 2002.

Goodpaster, Andrew. "Cold War Overflights: A View from the White House" in *Early Cold War Overflights; Symposium Proceedings, Volume I: Memoirs.* Washington: National Reconnaissance Office, 2003.

Hatch, Steve. *Cold War in South Florida Historic Resource Study.* Atlanta: National Park Service, 2004.

Hatheway, Roger. *Historical Cultural Resources Survey and Evaluation of the Nike Missile Sites in the Angeles National Forest, Los Angeles County, California.* San Diego: WESTEC Services, 1987.

History of Strategic Air and Ballistic Missile Defense: Volume I 1945–1955 and *Volume II 1956–1972.* Washington: Center of Military History, c. 1975.

Leighton, Richard M. *Strategy, Money, and the New Look, 1953–1956; History of the Office of the Secretary of Defense, Vol. III.* Washington: Office of the Secretary of Defense, 2001.

Lonnquest, John C. *To Defend and Deter: the Legacy of the United States Cold War Missile Program.* Rock Island, IL: Defense Publishing Service, 1996.

Malik, John. "The Yields of the Hiroshima and Nagasaki Nuclear Explosions." Los Alamos National Laboratory. September 1985.

Martini, John A. and Stephen A. Haller. *What We Have We Shall Defend: An Interim History and Preservation Plan for Nike Site SF-88L, Fort Barry, California.* San Francisco: National Park Service Golden Gate National Recreation Area, 1998.

McMullen, Richard F. *History of Air Defense Weapons; 1946–1962.* A[ir] D[efense] C[ommand] Historical Study no. 14. n.p., n.d.

———. *Air Defense and National Policy; 1958–1964.* A[ir] D[efense] C[ommand] Historical Study no. 26. n.p., n.d.

———. *Interceptor Missiles in Air Defense; 1944–1964.* A[ir] D[efense] C[ommand] Historical Study no. 30. n.p., 1965.

———. *The Aerospace Defense Command and Antibomber Defense; 1946–1972.* A[ir] D[efense] C[ommand] Historical Study NO. 39. n.p., 1973.

National Research Council. *Film Badge Dosimetry in Atmospheric Nuclear Tests.* Washington: National Academy Press, 1989.

Nike Hercules in Alaska. n.p., n.d.

Nuclear Weapons in the Air Defense System; Special Historical Study no. 2. n.p. [September 1953?] (Known otherwise as Volan, Denys. *The Use of Nuclear Weapons in Air Defense, 1952–1953.* A[ir] D[efense] C[ommand] Historical Study no. 2. n.p., n.d.).

Pedlow, Gregory W. and Donald E. Welzenbach. *The CIA and the U-2 Program, 1954–1974.* Washington: Central Intelligence Agency, 1988.

"Public Health Assessment, Boeing Michigan Aeronautical Research Center/ McGuire Missile, New Egypt, Ocean County, New Jersey." U.S. Department of Health and Human Services, Agency of Toxic Substances and Disease Registry. n.d.

Ray, Thomas W. *Nuclear Armament; Its Acquisition, Control, and Application to Manned Interceptors, 1951–1963.* A[ir] D[efense] C[ommand] Historical Study no. 20. n.p., n.d.

———. *BOMARC and Nuclear Armament.* A[ir] D[efense] C[ommand] Historical Study no. 21. n.p., n.d.

Recollections for Tomorrow; 1949–1989. Sandia National Laboratories, 1989.

"Restricted Data Classification Decisions, 1946 to the Present (RDD-8)." U.S. Department of Energy. January 1, 2002.

Rice, Helen. *History of Ogden Air Materiel Area: Hill Air Force Base, Utah, 1934–1960.* n.p., n.d.

Schaffel, Kenneth. *The Emerging Shield; the Air Force and the Evolution of Continental Air Defense; 1945–1960.* Washington: Office of Air Force History, 1991.

Thorn Robert N. and Donald R. Westervelt. "Hydronuclear Experiments." Los Alamos National Laboratory February 1987.

Watson, Robert J. *History of the Joint Chiefs of Staff; The Joint Chiefs and National Policy, Vol. V; 1953–1954.* Washington: Historical Division, Joint Chiefs of Staff, 1986.

———. *Into the Missile Age; 1956–1960; History of the Office of the Secretary of Defense, Vol. IV.* Washington: Office of the Secretary of Defense, 1997.

Weitze, Karen J. *Cold War Infrastructure for Air Defense: The Fighter and Command Missions.* Langley Air Force Base, Virginia: Air Combat Command, 1999.

Unpublished Theses and Dissertations

Hedstrom, John K. "The Air Defenses of Minnesota During the Cold War, 1946–1989." Minnesota State University, Mankato, 2000.

Jockel, Joseph T. "The United States and Canadian Efforts at Continental Air Defense; 1945–1957." Johns Hopkins University, 1978.

Larkins, James Randall. "The International Aspects of Air Defense of the United States Against Attack by Hostile Aircraft." Georgetown University, 1959.

Silverman, Michael Joshua. "No Immediate Risk: Environmental Safety in Nuclear Weapons Production, 1942–1985." Carnegie Mellon University, 2000.

Sivilich, Anjanette U. "Wheeler/Portage Nike Missile Launch Site C-47: Historic Structure Report." Ball State University, 2000.

Published Document Collections

The Cuban Missile Crisis, 1962.
Declassified Documents Reference System.
Foreign Relations of the United States, 1952–1954, vol. II, part 1, National Security Affairs. Washington: Government Printing Office, 1984.
Foreign Relations of the United States, 1955–1957, vol. XIX, National Security Policy. Washington: Government Printing Office, 1990.

Foreign Relations of the United States, 1958–1960, vol. III, National Security; Arms Control and Disarmament. Washington: Government Printing Office, 1996.
U.S. Nuclear History: Nuclear Arms and Politics in the Missile Age, 1955–1968.

Periodicals

Air Force Magazine.
Air Force Times.
ARADCOM Argus.
Army Navy Air Force Journal.
Army Times.
Aviation Week.
Baltimore Sun.
BOMARC Service News.
Boston Globe.
Chicago Sun-Times.
Chicago Tribune.
Dakota County (Minnesota) Tribune.
Denver Post.
Evening Outlook.
Falmouth (Massachusetts) Enterprise.
Huntsville (Alabama) Times.
Los Angeles Examiner.
Las Cruces (New Mexico) Sun News.
Los Angeles Times.
Miami Herald.
Miami News.
Milwaukee Journal.
Minneapolis Tribune.
New Egypt (New Jersey) Press.
New York Herald Tribune.
New York Post.
New York Times.
New York World-Telegram and Sun.
Norfolk Virginian-Pilot.
Ordnance.
Philadelphia Inquirer.
Red Bank (New Jersey) Register.
Salt Lake Tribune.
San Francisco Chronicle.
Santa Fe New Mexican.
Seattle Post-Intelligencer.
Seattle Times.
St. Louis Post-Dispatch.
U.S. News & World Report.
Washington Evening Star.
Washington Post.

Electronic Media and Miscellanea

The Atomic Filmmakers; Behind the Scenes. Produced and directed by Peter Kuran. Visual Concept Entertainment. Videocassette, 1997.
Atomic Veterans History Project (www.aracnet.com/~pdxavets).
Challener, Richard D. "A Transcript of a Recorded Interview with Robert Sprague." John Foster Dulles Oral History Project. Princeton University Library.
Conelrad (www.Conelrad.com).
Hansen, Chuck. *Swords of Armageddon.* CD-ROM, 1995.
Metroland Durham (Ontario, Canada) Region Media Group Web site (http://www.newsdurhamregion.com/).
The Nike-Hercules Story. Produced by Herbert Kerkow, Inc. Videocassette, c. 1958.
Oldfield, Barney and Vada Web site (www.oldfields.org/home.html).
Presidential Papers of Dwight David Eisenhower (www.eisenhowermemorial.org/presidential-papers).
Transcript of *ABC News Nightline.* Federal Document Clearing House, Inc., June 15, 1992.

Books

Adams, Valerie L. *Eisenhower's Fine Group of Fellows; Crafting a National Security Policy to Uphold the Great Equation.* Lanham, MD: Lexington Books, 2006.
Ambrose, Stephen E. *Eisenhower: The President.* New York: Simon and Schuster, 1984.
Andrew, Christopher and Vasili Mitrokhin. *The Sword and the Shield: The Mitrokhin Archive and the Secret History of the KGB.* New York: Basic Books, 1999.
Balzer, Gerald and Mike Darrio. *Northrop F-89 Scorpion.* Arlington Texas: Aerofax, 1993.
Baucom, Donald R. *The Origins of SDI: 1944–1983.* Lawrence: University Press of Kansas, 1992.
Beschloss, Michael R. *Mayday; Eisenhower, Khrushchev and the U-2 Affair.* New York: Harper & Row, 1986.
Boettiger, Wilfred O. *An Antiaircraft Artilleryman from 1939 to 1970.* n.p.: XLibris Corporation, 2005.
Bowie, Robert R. Bowie and Richard H. Immerman. *Waging Peace; How Eisenhower Shaped an Enduring Cold War Strategy.* Oxford: Oxford University Press, 1998.
Bruce-Biggs, B. *The Shield of Faith; a Chronicle of Strategic Defense from Zepplins to Star Wars.* New York: Simon and Schuster, 1988.
Brugioni, Dino. *Eyeball to Eyeball.* New York: Random House, 1991.
Bundy, McGeorge. *Danger and Survival; Choices about the Bomb in the First Fifty Years.* New York: Random House, 1988.
Call, Steve. *Selling Air Power: Military Aviation and American Popular Culture after World War II.* College Station: Texas A&M University Press, 2009.

BIBLIOGRAPHY

Campagna, Palmiro. *Storms of Controversy; the Secret Avro Arrow Files Revealed.* Toronto: Stoddart Publishing, 1997.
Ceruzzi, Paul. *Internet Alley: High Technology in Tysons Corner, 1945–2005.* Cambridge, MA: MIT Press, 2008.
Clearwater, John. *Canadian Nuclear Weapons; the Untold Story of Canada's Cold War Arsenal.* Toronto: The Dundurn Press, 1998.
———. *U. S. Nuclear Weapons in Canada.* Toronto: Dundurn Press, 1999.
Cline, Ray S. *Secrets, Spies, and Scholars; Blueprint of the Essential CIA.* Washington: Acropolis Books, 1976.
Cochran, Thomas, B., William M. Arkin, and Milton M. Hoenig. *Nuclear Weapons Databook*, vol. 1, "U.S. Nuclear Forces and Capabilities." Cambridge, MA: Ballinger, 1984.
Cutler, Robert. *No Time for Rest.* Boston: Little, Brown, 1966.
Dalzell, Frederick. *Engineering Invention: Frank J. Sprague and the U.S. Electrical Industry.* Cambridge, MA: MIT Press, 2010.
Davis, Larry Davis and Dave Menard. *F-89 Scorpion in Action.* Carrollton, TX: Squadron/Signal Publications, 1990.
Divine, Robert A. *Blowing in the Wind: the Nuclear Test Ban Debate, 1954–1960.* New York: Oxford University Press, 1978.
Dobbs, Michael. *One Minute to Midnight: Kennedy, Khrushchev, and Castro on the Brink of Nuclear War.* New York: Alfred A. Knopf, 2008.
Drew, S. Nelson, ed. (with analysis by Paul H. Nitze). *NSC-68; Forging the Strategy of Containment.* Washington: National Defense University Press, 1994.
Dupuy, Trevor N. *The Evolution of Weapons and Warfare.* New York: Da Capo Press, 1984.
Eglin, James Meikle. *Air Defense in the Nuclear Age; the Post-War Development of American and Soviet Strategic Defense Systems.* New York: Garland Publishing, 1988.
Eliot, Marc. *Jimmy Stewart: A Biography.* New York: Harmony Books. 2006.
Epstein, Edward Jay. *Deception: The Invisible War between the KGB and CIA.* New York: Simon and Schuster, 1989.
Fagan, M.D., ed. *A History of Engineering and Science in the Bell System; National Service in War and Peace (1925–1975)*, vol. 2. New York: Bell Telephone Laboratories, 1975.
Freedman, Lawrence. *US Intelligence and the Soviet Strategic Threat.* Princeton: Princeton University Press, 1986.
Fursenko, Aleksandr and Timothy Naftali. *"One Hell of a Gamble"; Khrushchev, Castro, and Kennedy 1958–1964.* New York: W.W. Norton and Company, 1997.
Garthoff, Raymond L. *Assessing the Adversary; Estimates by the Eisenhower Administration of Soviet Intentions and Capabilities.* Washington: Brookings Institution, 1991.
———. *Reflections on the Cuban Missile Crisis.* Washington: Brookings Institution, 1987.
Graham, Thomas. *Remembering Revell Model Kits.* Atglen, Pennsylvania: Schiffer Publishing Company, 2002.

Green, Benjamin P. *Eisenhower, Science Advice, and the Nuclear Test Ban Debate, 1945–1963*. Stanford: Stanford University Press, 2007.
Gribkov, Anatoli I. and William Y. Smith. *Operation ANADYR; U.S. and Soviet Generals Recount the Cuban Missile Crisis*. Chicago: Edition q, inc., 1994.
Gunston, Bill. *The Illustrated Encyclopedia of Rockets and Missiles*. New York: Crescent Books, 1979.
Furman, Necah Stewart. *Sandia National Laboratories: The Postwar Decade*. University of New Mexico Press, 1990.
Hansen, Chuck. *U.S. Nuclear Weapons; the Secret History*. Arlington, Texas: Aerofax, 1988.
Herken, Gregg. *Counsels of War*. New York: Alfred A. Knopf, 1985.
———. *Cardinal Choices: Presidential Science Advising from the Atomic Bomb to SDI*. New York: Oxford University Press, 1992.
Hewlett, Richard G. and Jack M. Holl. *Atoms for Peace and War, 1953–61; Eisenhower and the Atomic Energy Commission*. Berkeley: University of California Press, 1989.
Hewlett, Richard G. and Oscar E. Anderson, Jr. *Atomic Shield; a History of the United States Atomic Energy Commission, Vol. II, 1947–1952*. Berkeley: University of California Press, 1990.
Holloway, David. *Stalin and the Bomb*. New Haven: Yale University Press, 1994.
Hughes, Thomas P. *Rescuing Prometheus*. New York: Random House, 1998.
Hunt, Linda. *Secret Agenda: The United States Government Nazi Scientists, and Project Paperclip, 1945–1990*. New York: St. Martin's Press, 1991.
Huntington, Samuel P. *The Common Defense, Strategic Programs in National Politics*. New York: Columbia University Press, 1966.
Irvine, Mat. *Creating Space: The Story of the Space Age Told through Models*. Burlington, ON: Collector's Guide Publishing, Inc., 2002.
Jackson, Henry M., ed. *The National Security Council; Jackson Subcommittee Papers on Policy-Making at the Presidential Level*. New York: Frederick A. Praeger, 1965.
Kaplan, Fred. *The Wizards of Armageddon*. Stanford: Stanford University Press, 1983.
Killian, James R., Jr. *Sputnik, Scientists, and Eisenhower; a Memoir of the First Special Assistant to the President for Science and Technology*. Cambridge, MA: MIT Press, 1977.
Kingseed, Cole C. *Eisenhower and the Suez Crisis of 1956*. Baton Rouge: Louisiana State University Press, 1995.
Kistiakowsky, George B. *A Scientist at the White House: the Private Diary of President Eisenhower's Special Assistant for Science and Technology*. Cambridge, MA: Harvard University Press, 1976.
Klass, Philip J. *Secret Sentries in Space*. New York: Random House, 1971.
Klehr, Harvey and John Earl Haynes. *Venona; Decoding Soviet Espionage in America*. New Haven: Yale University Press, 1999.
Kolodziej, Edward J. *The Uncommon Defense and Congress, 1945–1963*. Columbus: Ohio State University Press, 1966.
Krugler, David F. *This is Only a Test: How Washington, D.C. Prepared for Nuclear War*. New York: Palgrave Macmillan, 2006.

Mallan, Lloyd. *Peace Is a Three-Edged Sword.* Englewood Cliffs, NJ: Prentice-Hall, 1964.

Maloney, Sean M. *Learning to Love the Bomb: Canada's Nuclear Weapons during the Cold War.* Washington: Potomac Books, 2007.

Marchetti, Victor John D. Marks. *The CIA and the Cult of Intelligence.* New York: Alfred A. Knopf, 1974.

Martin, Laurence. *Arms and Strategy; an International Survey of Modern Defence.* London: Weidenfeld and Nicolson, 1973.

May, Ernest R. and Philip D. Zelikow. *The Kennedy Tapes; Inside the White House during the Cuban Missile Crisis.* Cambridge, MA: Belknap Press, 1997.

Miller, Richard L. *Under the Cloud; the Decades of Nuclear Testing.* New York: Free Press, 1986.

Morgan, Mark L. and Mark A. Berhow. *Rings of Supersonic Steel: Air Defenses of the United States Army 1950–1979, an Introductory History and Site Guide.* San Pedro, CA: Fort MacArthur Press, 2002.

Needell, Allan A. *Science, Cold War, and the American State; Lloyd V. Berkner and the Balance of Professional Ideals.* Amsterdam: Harwood Academic Publishers, 2000.

Oakes, Guy. *The Imaginary War; Civil Defense and American Cold War Culture.* New York: Oxford University Press, 1994.

Oldfield, Barney. *Never a Shot in Anger.* New York: Duell, Sloan and Pearce, 1956.

Passer, Harold C. *The Electrical Manufacturers, 1875–1900; Study in Competition, Entrepreneurship, Technical Change, and Economic Growth.* Cambridge, MA: Harvard University Press, 1953.

Pfau, Richard. *No Sacrifice Too Great: the Life of Lewis L. Strauss.* Charlottesville: University Press of Virginia, 1984.

Poole, Walter S. *History of the Joint Chiefs of Staff; the Joint Chiefs and National Policy, Vol. IV; 1950–1952.* Wilmington, DE: Michael Glazier, Inc., 1980.

Prados, John. *The Soviet Estimate; U.S. Intelligence Analysis and Soviet Strategic Forces.* Princeton: Princeton University Press, 1986.

———. *Keepers of the Keys; a History of the National Security Council from Truman to Bush.* New York: William Morrow and Co., 1991.

Radosh, Ronald and Joyce Milton. *The Rosenberg File.* New Haven: Yale University Press, 1997.

Reich, Cary. *The Life of Nelson A. Rockefeller; Worlds to Conquer 1908–1958.* New York: Doubleday, 1996.

Richelson, Jeffrey T. *American Espionage and the Soviet Target.* New York: William Morrow and Company, 1987.

———. *A Century of Spies: Intelligence in the Twentieth Century.* Oxford: Oxford University Press, 1995.

Rosenberg, Howard L. *Atomic Soldiers; American Victims of Nuclear Experiments.* Boston: Beacon Press, 1980.

Rostow, W.W. *Open Skies; Eisenhower's Proposal of July 21, 1955.* Austin: University of Texas Press, 1982.

Sagan, Scott D. *The Limits of Safety; Organizations, Accidents, and Nuclear Weapons.* Princeton: Princeton University Press, 1993.

Saunders, Frances Stonor. *The Cultural Cold War; the CIA and the World of Arts and Letters.* New York: The New Press, 1999.

Schecter, Jerrold L. and Peter S. Deriabin. *The Spy Who Saved the World; How a Soviet Colonel Changed the Course of the Cold War.* New York: Charles Scribner and Sons, 1992.

Schwartz, Stephen I. *Atomic Audit; the Costs and Consequences of U.S. Nuclear Weapons since 1940.* Washington: Brookings Institution Press, 1998.

Shelton, Frank H. *Reflections of a Nuclear Weaponeer.* Colorado Springs: Shelton Enterprises, 1988.

Smith, Starr. *Jimmy Stewart, Bomber Pilot.* St. Paul, Minnesota: Zenith Press, 2005.

Snead, David L. *The Gaither Committee, Eisenhower, and the Cold War.* Columbus: Ohio State University Press, 1999.

Snyder, Frank E. and Brian H. Guss. *The District; A History of the Philadelphia District, U.S. Army Corps of Engineers, 1866–1971.* Philadelphia: U.S. Army Engineer District, 1974.

Suid, Lawrence H. *Guts and Glory; the Making of the American Military Image in Film.* Lexington: University Press of Kentucky, 2002.

Teller, Edward and Albert L. Latter. *Our Nuclear Future...Facts, Dangers and Opportunities.* New York: Criterion Books, 1958.

Teller, Edward with Judith L. Shoolery. *Memoirs; a Twentieth Century Journey in Science and Politics.* Cambridge, MA: Perseus Publishing, 2001.

Titus, A. Constandina. *Bombs in the Backyard; Atomic Testing and American Politics.* Reno and Las Vegas: University of Nevada Press, 2001.

Ulanoff, Stanley. *Illustrated Guide to U.S. Missiles and Rockets.* Garden City, NY: Doubleday & Company, 1959.

Usdin, Steven T. *Engineering Communism: How Two Americans Spied for Stalin and Founded the Soviet Silicon Valley.* New Haven: Yale University Press, 2005.

Vanderbilt, Tom. *Survival City: Adventures among the Ruins of Atomic America.* New York: Princeton Architectural Press, 2002.

Vaughn, Robert. *Only Victims; a Study of Show Business Blacklisting.* New York: G.P. Putnam's Sons, 1972.

Weinstein, Allen. *The Haunted Wood: Soviet Espionage in America—the Stalin Era.* New York: Random House, 1999.

Wenger, Andreas Wenger. *Living with Peril: Eisenhower, Kennedy, and Nuclear Weapons.* Lanham, MD: Rowman & Littlefield, 1997.

Witter, Lawrence S. *Rebels Against War; the American Peace Movement, 1941–1960.* New York: Columbia University Press, 1969.

Zaloga, Steven J. *Target America; the Soviet Union and the Strategic Arms Race, 1945–1964.* Novato, CA: Presidio Press, 1993.

Articles and Chapters

Aronsen, Lawrence. "Seeing Red: US Air Force Assessments of the Soviet Union, 1945–1949. *Intelligence and National Security* 2 (Summer 2001): 103–132.

Berkner, Lloyd V. "Continental Defense." *Current History* 26 (May 1954): 257–262.

Betts, Richard K. "A Nuclear Golden Age? The Balance before Parity." *International Security* 11 (Winter 1986–1987).
Billman, O.H. "Basic Instinct." *Air and Space Smithsonian* (August/September 2004).
Bouchard, Joseph F. "Guarding the Cold War Ramparts; the U.S. Navy's Role in Continental Air Defense." *Navy War College Review* 52 (Summer 1999).
Boyne, Walter J. "The Dawn of Discipline: A B-47 Pilot Remembers When an Airplane—And Curtis LeMay—Stiffened the Spine of the Strategic Air Command." *Air and Space Smithsonian* (July 2009).
Bright, Christopher John. "Nike Defends Washington; Antiaircraft Missiles in Fairfax County, Virginia during the Cold War, 1954–74." *Virginia Magazine of History and Biography* 105 (Summer 1997): 317–346.
Chun, Clayton K.S. "Winged Interceptor: Politics and Strategy in the Development of the Bomarc Missile." *Airpower History* (Winter 1998): 44–59.
Cole, Merle T. "W-25: The Davidsonville Site and Maryland Air Defense, 1950–1974." *Maryland Historical Magazine* 2 (Fall 1985): 240–259.
Coleman, David G. "The Missiles of November, December, January, February…the Problem of Acceptable Risk in the Cuban Missile Crisis Settlement." *Journal of Cold War Studies* 9, no. 3 (Summer 2007): 5–48.
Damms, Richard B. "James Killian, the Technological Capabilities Panel, and the Emergence of President Eisenhower's 'Scientific-Technological Elite'." *Diplomatic History* 24 (Winter 2000).
Dawson, Raymond H. "Congressional Innovation and Intervention in Defense Policy: Legislative Authorization of Weapons Systems." *The American Political Science Review* 56 (1962): 42–57.
Divine, Robert A. "Eisenhower, Dulles, and the Nuclear Test Ban Issue: Memorandum of a White House Conference, 24 March 958." *Diplomatic History* 2 (Summer 1978): 321–330.
Engel, Jeffrey A. "The Surly Bonds: American Cold War Constraints on British Aviation." *Enterprise & Society: the International Journal of Business History* 6 (March 2005): 1–44.
Gray, Colin S. "'Gap' Prediction and America's Defense: Arms Race Behavior in the Eisenhower Years." *Orbis* 16 (Spring 1972): 257–274.
Gup, Ted. "Doomesday Hideaway." *TIME* (December 9, 1991): 26–29.
Hall, R. Cargill. "The Truth about Overflights." *MHQ; the Quarterly Journal of Military History* 9 (Spring 1997): 25–39.
Hansen, Chuck. "Beware the Old Story." *Bulletin of Atomic Scientists* 57 (March/April 2001): 52–55.
Hardesy, Von. "Made in the U.S.S.R." *Air and Space Smithsonian* (February/March 2001): 68–79.
Jervis, Robert. "The Military History of the Cold War." *Diplomatic History* 15 (Winter 1991): 91–113.
Killian, James R. and A.G. Hill. "For a Continental Defense." *Atlantic* 192 (November 1953): 37–41.
Lamont, James. "The Atomic Cannon; It Was Fired Once, But it Helped End a War." *Invention & Technology* 21 (Summer 2005).
Machat, Mike and Anthony Accurso. "Winged Missiles of the U.S. Air Force." *Airpower* (May 2004): 14–26, 54–62.

Malevich, Steven. "Nike Deployment." *The Military Engineer* 47 (November–December 1955): 418–419.

Miller, Jay. "The Scorpion; a Pictorial Report." *Air University Review* 31 (July–August 1980).

Moeller, Stephen P. "Vigilant and Invincible." *ADA* (May–June 1995): 2–42.

Mola, Roger A. "This is only a Test." *Air and Space Smithsonian* (February/March 2002): 50–55.

Murphy, Charles J.V. "The U.S. as a Bombing Target." *Fortune* 9 (November 1953): 118–120, 219–228.

Posey, Carl. "The Thin Aluminum Line: Supersonic Airplanes and a Screen of Radar Stood Ready during the Cold War to Avert the End of the World." *Air and Space Smithsonian* (December 2006/January 2007): 60–67.

Roman, Peter. "Ike's Hair-Trigger; U.S. Nuclear Predelegation, 1953–60." *Security Studies* 7 (Summer 1998): 121–64.

Rosenberg, David Alan. "The Origins of Overkill: Nuclear Weapons and American Strategy," in Norman A. Graebner, ed., *The National Security; Its Theory and Practice, 1945–1960*. New York: Oxford University Press, 1986.

Shuchman, Daniel. "Nuclear Strategy and the Problem of Command and Control." *Survival* 29.

Stark, William C. "Cleveland Nike Bases—A Passing Phase." *Periodical Journal of the Council on America's Military Past* 14 (September 1986): 35–46.

Suri, Jeremi. "America's Search for a Technological Solution to the Arms Race: The Surprise Attack Conference of 1958 and a Challenge for 'Eisenhower Revisionists'." *Diplomatic History* 21 (Summer 1997): 417–451.

Vann, Walter M. Vann. "Antiaircraft Defense." *Military Review* 37 (January 1958).

Weiner, Robert S. "At Ease." *American Heritage* 50 (April 1999).

Wells, Samuel F., Jr. "The Origins of Massive Retaliation." *Political Science Quarterly* 96 (Spring 1981).

Wolverton, Mark. "The Tube Is Dead. Long Live the Tube." *Invention & Technology* (Fall 2002).

Index

1352nd Motion Picture
Squadron,
213–14n87

Acheson, Dean, 12
Aerojet General Company,
204n18
Agan, Arthur C., 157
Air Defense Command
(ADC), 6–9, 18,
20, 36, 67, 73, 78,
80, 85, 91–2, 128,
145, 157, 178n40,
213–14n87
Agan, Arthur C. and, 157
Atkinson, Joseph H and,
73–4, 81, 92
Air Defense Master Plan,
135–8, 140
Air Force Association, 83,
164n21, 214n87
Air Force Special Weapons
Center, 8
AIR-2 Genie rocket, see Genie
rocket (MB-1)
Alert barns, 90, 218n30
Ambrose, Stephen E.,
231n97
Anderson, Dillon, 47–8, 52,
189n42
Anderson, Sherman,
212–13n79
Antiaircraft defenses, tactics,
procedures and
need for, 6, 13,
24, 36, 44, 54,
101, 103–4,
235n137
See also civil defense and
continuity of
government,
facilities and
planning for, and
Nuclear weapons,
antiaircraft,
theories, policies
and requirements
for use of
Armed Forces Day, 95, 130,
241n19
Armed Forces Special
Weapons Project
(AFSWP), 93–4,
112, 206n33
Parker, Edward N.
and, 112
Atkinson, Joseph H., 73–4,
81, 92
"atomic," use of the term, 4
Atomic Energy Commission
(AEC), 1, 9–11,
19, 21, 28–9,
31–3, 35, 41–5,
48–51, 58, 61, 63,
66–70, 129,
194n80, 214n91
See also Strauss, Lewis
Division of Military
Application of, 71
Field, Kenneth, and, 70
Floberg, John F. and,
111–12
Graves, Alvin C. and,
72, 74
McCone, John and, 114,
145–6
Rowen, W. H. and, 43
Starbird, Alfred Dodd,
and, 72, 208n47
Aurora, 118, 133

B-52 bomber, 45, 188n27
See also Bomber aircraft
Ball, Frank, 85
Balloon reconnaissance
project, 59,
199n129
See also Reconnaissance
and intelligence
collection, U.S.
efforts of
Barbee, Cliff, 82
Barr, Joel (Joseph Berg), 119
Baruch, Donald E.,
237–8n160
Baxter III, James Phinney,
14, 37, 169n68
Beagle bomber, 152,
250–1n9
See also Bomber aircraft
Beau Marks, 147
Bell Telephone Laboratories,
10, 13, 33
Bellboy project, 19, 65–6
See also F-89
Berg, Joseph (Joel Barr), 119
Bird Dog project, 172n99
Bison bomber (M-4), 27–8,
30, 34, 37–8, 45,
59, 176n30
See also Bomber aircraft
Black and Veatch, 67
Blankfort, Henry, 118,
233–4n130,
234n131
Blue Straw test, 152,
250n7
Bodinger, Norman, 77,
211n71
BOAR, see Bombardment
Aircraft Rocket

INDEX

Boeing Company, 8, 135, 138–9, 142, 244n49, 245n50
BOMARC missile (IM 99), 1, 8–11, 14, 17–21, 26, 36–8, 57, 115–16, 127–48, 151, 154–60, 161n2, 171n96, 178n40, 242n30, 243–4n43, 247n95, 248–9n107, 249n110
  Armed Forces Day and, 130, 241n19
  characteristics and specifications of, 8, 130
  cultural references, and Beau Marks, 147
  Miss BOMARC, 131, 132
  models, plastic kits of, 131–3
  deployment reductions related to ICBM threat, 140–2
  Eglin Air Force Base, testing at, 154
  Eisenhower, Dwight D. opinion on, 134–5
  JCAE briefed on, 37
  launch site characteristics and naming convention, 130, 139, 147
  locations of, 127, 130, 139–41, 146–7, 156, 158, 161n2
    Canada and, 147, 158, 248–9n107
    Cape Cod, Massachusetts deployment near, 130–1, 146
    Eglin Air Force Base considered for, 155–6
    Langley Air Force Base, Virginia deployment near, 146–7
    McGuire Air Force Base, New Jersey deployment near, 139, 143–5, 147, 158, 161n2
      accident at, 143–5
      first operational site, 139
    Niagara Falls deployment at, 141, 147, 151, 156, 158
    Otis Air Force Base, Massachusetts deployment near, 130, 147, 161n2, 212n76
    Suffolk Air Force Base, New York deployment at, 140, 142, 147, 156, 161n2
    Westhampton Beach, New York deployment near, 140
  Nike-Hercules missile, competition with, 115–16, 120–1, 134–6
  nomenclature of, 8
  nuclear warhead proposed for, 9–10, 14. *See also* Nuclear weapons, warheads of (W-40)
  numbers of, 147, 161n2
  performance shortcomings and criticism of, 133–5, 139–40, 156, 249n110
  public relations activities related to, 130–1, 138
  Semi-Autonomous Ground Environment (SAGE) system and, 130, 241n21
  television reception, no interference with, 131
  versions, 130, 147, 154, 156, 158
  Wedemeyer panel briefed on, 36
  withdrawal from inventory, 156, 158
  See also Nuclear weapons, warheads of (W-40)
Bombardment Aircraft Rocket (BOAR), 19, 171n96, 178n40
Bomber aircraft:
  B-52, 45, 188n27
  Bear (TU-95), 45, 59, 160, 188n27
  Beagle bomber (IL-28), 152, 250–1n9
  Bison (M-4), 27–8, 30, 34, 37–8, 45, 59, 176n30
  Bull (Tu-4), 6, 27, 30, 163n7
  See also USSR
Bowie, Robert R., 167–8n53
Bowring, Eva, 32
Brodie, Bernard, 35
Bronson, Charles, 81
Bruce, Sidney, 84–5
Bull, Harold "Pinky," 13–14, 18, 25, 30, 168n59
Bundy, McGeorge, 54

Califano, Joseph, 158
Canada, 6, 39, 48, 52, 61, 71, 80, 87–8, 137, 147–8, 158, 161–2n4, 195–6n87, 201n148, 220n78, 248n107
  See also Royal Canadian Air Force
Cape Cod, Massachusetts, 130–1, 146
Castle test series, 27, 42, 176n28
Chicago, Illinois, 106–7, 116, 121, 228n64
Civil Defense and preparations for air attack:
  Distant Early Warning (DEW) line, 6–7
  Ground Observer Corps, 6
  Hoegh, Leo A., and Civil Defense and Defense Mobilization, Office of, 137

INDEX 269

Gaither Committee and, 99–100
Operation Alert (1955), 45–6 (1956), 58 (1957), 69 (1960), 142
Sky Shield, 147–8
See also Office of Defense Mobilization *and* continuity of government, facilities and planning for
Cole, W. Sterling, 25, 35, 164n21
See also United States Congress, Joint Committee on Atomic Energy (JCAE)
Committee on Non-Violent Action, 86
"continental defense," defined, 6
Continental Air Defense Command (CONAD), 43, 73, 76, 90
Partridge, Earle E. and, 73–4, 79–80, 83, 87–90, 148, 213n84
Continuity of Government, facilities and planning for
Emergency Action Designees, 142
"High Point" White House relocation facility, 46, 69, 142
"Raven Rock" facility, 46
relocation arc, 108
Cousins, Norman, 77, 87, 211n71
Cuba *see* Cuban Missile Crisis *and* Nuclear weapons and warheads, tests of, (Snodgrass/Little David/Opera Hat)
Cuban Missile Crisis, 152–9
air attack, possibility of and concern about, 152, 154, 250–1n9

BOMARC testing suspended, 154
Nike-Hercules and alert procedures, 153–4
Florida defended by, 154, 239n176
nuclear antiaircraft arms, airborne permitted by Air Force, 84, 91, 152–3, 251n11
Parker, Theodore W. and, 155, 252n23, 252n25
Rules of Engagement, 154–5
Cutler, Robert, 16, 24–38, 41–3, 47, 102, 170n87, 178n35, 179n43, 184n81, 189n42

Daley, Richard, 121
Davidsonville, Maryland, 106, 116–17, 123, 228n65
Day, Dorothy, 137
Dean, Gordon, 35
Defense Department, budget of, 15, 17, 34, 67–8, 103
Defense Contractors, criticism of, 135–6, 138–9
Defense Mobilization, Office of:
Flemming, Arthur S. and, 17
Ding Dong project, 19, 50, 66, 70
See also Genie rocket
Distant Early Warning (DEW) line, *see* Civil Defense and preparations for air attack
Divine, Robert, 231–2n97
Donaldson, Sam, 117
Doolittle, James H., 37, 184n79
Dorothy, Carol, 235n137
Douglas, Jr., Donald, 117, 139
Douglas Aircraft Corporation, 10, 19, 35, 66, 87, 92,
95, 102, 105, 116–17, 139
See also Genie rocket, Nike-Ajax missile, *and* Nike-Hercules missile
Dulles, Allen, 14, 31, 134, 136–7, 142, 182n66
Dulles, John Foster, 51–2, 102, 109–10, 112, 114, 188n32, 225–6n30

Edemski, Sergei, 118
Edwards, Idwall H., 13, 168n56
Eglin Air Force Base, 109–15, 117, 155–6
Eisenhower, Dwight D.:
Air Defense Master Plan assent to, 137
Anderson, Clinton P. and, 182n71
on balloon reconnaissance project, 199n129
BOMARC and, 69, 134–5, 243–4n43
Cutler, Robert and, 31, 34, 177–8n35, 179n43
Dulles, John Foster and, 109–10, 112
executive privilege and, 35, 226n34
foreign policy of, 184n79, 207n42, 214n87
Gaither study and, 99–102, 225–6n30
Genie rocket and, 65, 69, 78, 109–15
Hardtack test series and, 129
Killian Committee, and, 37, 38
Knight, Goodwin J. and, 78–9, 212–13n79
McCone, John and, 145–6
Nike-Hercules and, 69, 95, 105, 109–10, 120, 125, 224n20, 236n146

INDEX

Eisenhower, Dwight D.
—*Continued*
  NSC and, 12–17, 29–31,
    34, 36, 40–2, 47,
    51–2, 58, 134–5,
    179–80n43
  nuclear air defense
    weapons,
    comments about,
    16, 17, 29, 33–4,
    53–4, 55, 69, 137,
    244n45
  nuclear testing and, 55–6,
    68–9, 109–15,
    146–7
  Open Skies initiative and,
    58, 199n128
  Operation Alert (1955)
    and, 45–6
  Operation Alert (1956)
    and, 58
  Operation Alert (1957)
    and, 69
  Operation Alert (1960)
    and, 142
  Plumbbob test series
    and, 71
  Snodgrass/Little David/
    Opera Hat test
    and, 109–15
  Sprague, Robert and,
    23–33, 36, 40,
    47–8, 101–2,
    173n1, 189n43
  Strauss, Lewis and, 41,
    110, 112, 177–
    8n34, 182–3n71
  Surprise Attack
    Conference and,
    107–8
  U-2 and, 38, 199n128
  USSR and, 3, 16, 27–9,
    37, 53–4, 58, 104,
    107, 136–7, 142,
    160, 199n128,
    228–9n70
  Wedemeyer report and, 37
Eisenhower, Mamie, 16, 46
Eniwetok Proving Grounds,
    56, 87, 108–9,
    112, 114,
    129, 152
Espionage, activities
    associated with
  Barr, Joel (Joseph Berg)
    and, 119

Berg, Joseph (Joel Barr)
    and, 119
  Nike-Ajax and Nike-
    Hercules,
    accusations related
    to, 235n136
  Edemski, Sergei
    and, 118
  Felt, W. Mark, and,
    235n136
  Whalen, William H.
    and, 118–19,
    234n133,
    234–5n135
  Rosenberg, Julius
    and, 119
  Sarant, Alfred (Philip
    Staros) and, 119
  Staros, Philip (Alfred
    Sarant) and, 119

F-89 "Scorpion" interceptor,
    7, 18–19, 21,
    65–6, 70, 72, 77,
    81, 84, 90–3, 111,
    127–8, 164n20,
    209–10n64,
    210n66, 219n139
  Bellboy project and, 19,
    65–6
  Minneapolis-St. Paul,
    Minnesota,
    deployment to, 21
  See also interceptor aircraft
F-101B "Voodoo"
    interceptor, 84–5,
    90, 92, 111, 115,
    128
  See also interceptor aircraft
F-102 "Delta Dagger"
    interceptor,
    127–8, 148–50,
    153, 158, 178n40
  See also interceptor aircraft
F-106 "Delta Dart"
    interceptor, 90–2,
    128, 153, 158–9
  See also interceptor aircraft
Fairfax County, Virginia,
    economic
    development of,
    174n7
Falcon missile (GAR-11), 1,
    125, 127–30,
    148–50, 158, 160,
    240n11, 250n7

Blue Straw test proposal
    for, 152, 250n7
  dimensions and
    characteristics
    of, 129
  LeMay, Curtis and,
    128–9, 240n11
  handling, storage, and
    alert procedures
    and, 150
  high-explosive warhead,
    version equipped
    with, 7, 18, 26,
    127–9, 240n4
  need for and origins of,
    128–9
  nomenclature of, 129,
    241n15
  numbers of, 150, 151,
    161n2
  production delays, 148
  publicity about, 148, 150
  withdrawal from inventory
    of, 158
  See also Hughes Aircraft
    Corporation and
    Nuclear weapons,
    warheads of
    (W-54)
Felt, W. Mark, 235n136
Field, Kenneth, 70
Films and television, 2
  Baruch, Donald E.,
    237–8n160
  Bronson, Charles, 81
  Donaldson, Sam and, 117
  Joseph M. Schenck
    Enterprises, 80–1,
    83, 214n87
  Lassie (television series),
    124–5, 150, 159
  Nike-Hercules Story, 122
  Stewart, Jimmy, 81, 150,
    213–14n87,
    214–15n92
  Strategic Air Command,
    81
  Telefon, 81–2
  Television reception and
    BOMARC, 131
  "Weaponeer, The"
    (television
    series), 81–2,
    213–14n87
Flemming, Arthur S., 17
Floberg, John F., 111–12

INDEX 271

Folding Fin Air-to-Air
 Rockets (FFAR),
 7, 18–21, 26, 31,
 127, 164n20
Frost, Frances, 131

Gaither, Jr., H. Rowan, 99
 See also Gaither
  Committee
Gaither Committee, 99–102,
 174–5n13,
 225n30, 226n34
 establishment, leadership,
  and mandate of,
  99–100
 report of, 99–100
Sprague, Robert, and,
 101–2
GAR-11, *see* Falcon missile
 (GAR-11)
Genie rocket (MB-1), 19,
 65–94, 115, 128,
 153, 159, 161n2,
 172n99, 211n68,
 211n69, 219n139,
 251n11
 Bellboy project and, 19,
  65–6
 Bird Dog name
  erroneously
  attributed to,
  172n99
 deployment of
  locations, 65, 67, 90,
  100, 195n87
 shipment method, 66,
  78–9, 212n77
 description,
  characteristics,
  and cost of, 19,
  81, 82–83
 Ding Dong name
  given to, 19, 50,
  66, 70
 handling and storage
  facilities and
  procedures,
  49–50, 67, 69–70,
  78, 90–2, 204n18
 construction related to,
  67, 69–70
 interception techniques
  and associated
  equipment and,
  66, 76, 90, 93
 JCAE briefed on, 37

Kennedy, John F. in
 inaugural parade
 of, 150
Killian Committee,
 endorsement
 of, 38
 manufacture of, 66, 151
 National Security
  Council, briefing
  and action on,
  31–5, 69
 nomenclature of, 19,
  241n15
 number of, 92–3, 159,
  161n1
 Oralloy version, "Fleegle"
  considered, 49, 91
 origins of, 18–19, 171n94
 publicity about, 80, 84–5
  advertisements, 87
 Oldfield, Barney role
  in, 79
 tactics for use of, 74, 90–1
 Wedemeyer panel briefed
  on, 36
 withdrawal from
  inventory, 159
 See also Nuclear weapons
  and warheads,
  tests of, (Blue
  Straw, Plumbbob
  and Snodgrass/
  Little David/
  Opera Hat) *and*
  Nuclear weapons,
  warheads of
  (W-25)
Gerhart, John, 154
Goodpaster, Andrew J., 62,
 78, 89, 114, 137,
 142, 189n43,
 200n130, 207n42,
 230–1n87,
 244n45
Goose Bay Air Base,
 195n87
Graves, Alvin C., 72, 74
Gray, Gordon, 134–6, 142
Greenland, 125, 195n87,
 212n77, 214n87,
 236n144–5,
 239n178
Ground Observer Corps, 6
 See also Civil Defense and
  preparations for
  air attack

Gulf of Mexico, 109,
 111–12, 230–1n87,
 231–2n97

Hansen, Chuck, 146, 221n6,
 239n178
Hardtack test series, 109,
 112, 129
Harriman, Averell, 12
Heavenbound, *see* Nuclear
 weapons,
 organizations,
 studies, and
 activities
 associated with
 the development
 of
Hebert, F. Edward, 139
Hercules missile, *see* Nike-
 Hercules missile
Herter, Christian, 112–13
Hoegh, Leo A., 137
Hughes Aircraft
 Corporation, 7,
 127, 129, 148, 150
 See also Falcon missile
Humphrey, George, 31, 68,
 204n24
Hutchison, Cliff
 "Hutch," 82

ICBMs, Soviet, 136, 141,
 150–1, 157–8,
 160, 234n133,
 252n34
IM-99, *see* BOMARC missile
 (IM-99)
Intelligence, *see*
 Reconnaissance
 and intelligence
 collection, U.S.
 efforts of
Interceptor aircraft
 See also numeric
  designation
  of specific
  interceptor
 alert barns for, 90, 218n30
 Electronic
  Countermeasures
  (ECM) and, 18
 Semi-Autonomous
  Ground
  Environment
  (SAGE) system
  and, 24

INDEX

Intercontinental Ballistic Missiles, *see* ICBMs

Jackson, Henry M., 102, 135, 137, 142
Johnson, Lyndon, 54, 157, 226n34
Joint Chiefs of Staff (JCS), 10, 13–19, 28–9, 33–4, 37, 47–8, 50–1, 71, 100, 109, 114, 134–6, 153–5, 180–1n51, 190n46, 193n69, 211n69, 224n21
  See also Radford, Arthur; Twining, Nathan
Joint Air Defense Board (JADB), 10, 18, 165n35
Joint Committee on Atomic Energy (JCAE), *see* United States Congress
Joseph M. Schenck Enterprises, 80–1, 83, 214n87

Kefauver, Estes, 24–5
Kelly, Mervin, 13, 168n59
Kennedy, John F., 150–2
Khrushchev, Nikita, 107, 142, 160
Killian, Jr., James R., 37–43, 47–8, 50–1, 54–5, 59, 63, 75, 93, 98–9, 101–8, 140, 184n79, 184n81, 186–7n12, 190n46, 244n45
  See also Killian Committee
Killian Committee, 226n34
  Baxter III, James Phinney and, 37
  Eisenhower, Dwight D. briefed on, 38
  Land, Edwin H. and, 37–8, 59
  membership, meetings, and mandate of, 37
  nuclear antiaircraft arms and
    advocacy of, 38–9, 55
    predelegated use, advocacy of, 39

public disclosures, recommended for, 39, 42–3
origins of, 37, 183–4n76
Sprague, Robert role in, 38
U-2 and, 38
Kistiakowsky, George, 140, 142, 146
Korean War, 6, 80, 186n8, 195n83
Kyes, Roger M., 25–6

Land, Edwin H., 37–8, 59, 244n45
Lassie (television series), 124–5, 150, 159
Latter, Albert L., 85
Lay, James, 51, 189n43
LeMay, Curtis, 128–9, 211n68, 225n23, 240n11
Lemnitzer, Lyman, 136
Letterkenny Ordnance Depot, Pennsylvania, 123, 125
Lindbergh, Charles, 35
Little David test, *see* Nuclear weapons and warheads, tests of, (Snodgrass/Little David/Opera Hat)
Loper, Herbert, 60–2
Los Alamos Scientific Laboratory, 19, 72, 129, 172n104
Lovett, Robert, 12

Manhattan Project, 23, 25, 191n58
Master Plan for Air Defense, *see* Air Defense Master Plan
MB-1 Genie rocket, *see* Genie rocket (MB-1)
McCone, John, 114, 145–6
McDonnell Aircraft, 84–5
  See also interceptor aircraft
McElroy, Neil, 103, 110, 120, 135–8
McGuire Air Force Base, New Jersey, 139–43, 145, 147, 158, 161n2
  See also BOMARC missile

McNamara, Robert, 159–60, 250n9
Mexico, 112–14, 235n136
Minneapolis-St. Paul, Minnesota, 21
Miss BOMARC, 131–3
  See also BOMARC missile
"Missile" defined, 7
Model kits and collectables:
  Aurora, 118, 133
  cereal trading cards, 123
  Revell, Inc., 117–18, 131–3, 233–4n130, 242n26
  Blankfort, Henry and, 118, 233–4n130, 234n131
Montrose Beach, Chicago, Illinois, 106–7, 116, 228n64
  See also Nike-Hercules

National Committee for a Sane Nuclear Policy, 77
National Security Council, 1, 12–17, 27–43, 46–54, 57–8, 69, 78, 100, 103–4, 133–6, 148, 158
  Anderson, Dillon and, 47–8, 52, 189n42
  Baxter III, James Phinney and, 14
  Bowie, Robert R and, 167–8n53
  Bull, Harold "Pinky" and, 13–14, 18, 25, 30, 168n59
  Cutler, Robert and, 16, 24–38, 41–3, 47, 102, 170n87, 178n35, 179n43, 184n81, 189n42
  Eisenhower, Dwight D., participation in meetings and impressions of, 179–80n43
  Edwards, Idwall H. and, 13, 168n56
  Gray, Gordon and, 134–6, 142
  Harriman, Averell and, 12
  Humphrey, George and, 31, 68, 204n24

INDEX

Kyes, Roger M. and, 25–6
Lay, James and, 51, 189n43
Lovett, Robert and, 12
meeting locations and typical attendance of, 31, 46–7, 179n43
Net Capabilities Evaluation Subcommittee of, 30, 32, 92, 66, 182n66
Operations Coordinating Board (OCB) of, 42–3, 61–2, 71, 78, 83, 113, 186–7n12, 231n91
role in approving public announcements related to nuclear arms
antiaircraft weapons, deployment of, 61, 62
Redwing test series, 57–8
Snodgrass/Little David/Opera Hat, 113
Teapot test series, 41–2
Planning Board of, 13–14, 52, 168n59
records accurately reflect discussions of, 167–8n53
Stassen, Harold E., 33–4
National Security Council reports
See also Robert Sprague
paper number system, 18, 170n85
papers:
NSC 68, 6, 163n5
NSC 140/1, 13, 168n56
NSC 149/2, 12
NSC 159, 14–15, 170n87
NSC 159/3, 14–15
NSC 159/4, 15–17
NSC 159/5, 17–18
NSC 162, 15, 17, 20, 50, 167n51, 169n74, 173n109

NSC 162/2, 50
nuclear weapons use articulated in, 15–16, 20–1, 50
NSC 1706, 83, 113
NSC 5408, 18, 27, 29–30, 34–6, 46–7, 103, 170n82, 170n85, 170n87
NSC 5422, 33–5, 50, 181n54
NSC 5422/2, 35
NSC 5522, 48, 190n46
NSC 5606, 103
NSC 5802, 103–4
Net Capabilities Evaluation Subcommittee, 30, 32, 92, 182n66
Nevada Test Site (NTS), 41–3, 71–2, 75–6, 86, 94, 108–9, 113, 148, 191n57, 205n27, 209n63, 210n66
News Nob, 73, 78
Niagara Falls, 141, 147, 151, 156, 158
See also BOMARC missile
Nike-Ajax missile, 13, 26, 31, 239n176
Bell Telephone Laboratories and, 10
characteristics and description of system, 9, 96–7, 221–2n8, 222n10
explosion at Leonardo, New Jersey of, 104–5, 115–16
locations of, 9, 96, 99, 195–6n87, 224n21, 235n136, 252n34
nomenclature of, 9–10
nuclear warhead contemplated for, 10, 190n46
Nike-Hercules missile, 1
advent of, 10, 221–2n8
Armed Forces Day and, 95
BOMARC missile, competition with,

115–16, 120–1, 134–6
characteristics of, 10–11
construction or modification of launching sites for, 98, 116, 151, 223n13
Eisenhower and, 120
espionage related to, 118–19, 234–5n135–6
Huntsville, Alabama and, 95
ICBMs, ineffective against, 157–9
JCAE briefed on, 37
Killian Committee endorsement of, 38
launch sites of, 98, 100, 102, 106, 107, 119–21, 224n21, 252n34
Chicago, Illinois, 106–7, 116, 121, 228n64
community relations around, 121–2
Davidsonville, Maryland, 106, 116–17, 123, 228n65
description and designation of, 98, 106, 124
Florida, 155, 159
guard dogs and, 124, 159, 239n170
manufacturing and testing of, 105–6, 117
National Security Council, discussion of, 30–1, 69
numbers of, 125, 161n2
operational procedures for, 123–4
popular culture and:
cereal trading cards, 123
Lassie and, 124–5
Jimmy Stewart visit to launching site, 213–14n87
models, plastic kits of, 117–18

INDEX

Nike-Hercules missile
—*Continued*
performance problems
of, 105–6,
228n62,
228n67
publicity about, 56–7,
60–1, 95, 102,
105, 114, 116–17,
121, 138–9
Project AMMO (Army
Mobile Missile
Orientation) and,
106, 113–14,
228n67
Project TRUTH, 116
storage at:
Letterkenny Ordnance
Depot,
Pennsylvania,
123, 125
Pueblo Ordnance
Depot, Colorado,
123, 125, 155
Talos missile, competition
with, 56–7,
224n20
warhead nuclear,
design and
development for,
10, 14, 56,
166n45, 171n96,
190n46
warhead, nuclear and
conventional ratio,
124, 154, 155,
238n168
withdrawal from
inventory, 157–9
See also Nuclear weapons
and warheads,
tests of,
(Snodgrass/Little
David/Opera Hat)
and Nuclear
weapons, warheads
of (W-7, W-31,
W-37)
Nixon, Richard M., 31
North American Aerospace
Defense
Command
(NORAD), *see*
United States Air
Force
North Korea, 6

Northrop F-89 "Scorpion"
interceptor, *see*
F-89 "Scorpion"
Nougat test, 148
"nuclear," use of the term, 4
Nuclear weapons, *see also*
name of various
armaments
Nuclear weapons, antiaircraft
announcement of, public,
60–4
cost of, 82–3, 216n103
in popular culture, 2
theories, policies and
requirements for
use of, 1–9,
11–12, 20, 26–8,
37–8, 41, 43–4,
45, 48, 54–5, 57,
74–5, 81, 85–6,
93, 116, 151, 155,
157, 159–60,
172n103, 190n46
See also Eisenhower,
Dwight D. *and*
Strauss, Lewis *and*
Films and
television *and*
specific weapons
Nuclear weapons,
organizations and
individual
opposed to:
antiaircraft arms, absence
of objections to, 86
Committee on Non-
Violent Action, 86
Cousins, Norman and, 77,
87, 211n71
Day, Dorothy, 137
National Committee for a
Sane Nuclear
Policy, 77
Pauling, Linus, 86, 94,
217n112
Porter, Charles O., 86–7
Quakers, 115
Nuclear weapons,
organizations,
studies, and
activities
associated with
the development
of:
Air Force Special Weapons
Center, 8

Armed Forces Special
Weapons Project
(AFSWP), 93–4,
112, 165n35,
206n33
Atomic Energy
Commission
(AEC), 1, 9–11,
19, 21, 28–9,
31–3, 35, 41–5,
48–51, 58, 61,
63, 66–70, 129,
194n80,
214n91
Development assignments,
U.S. military
services, 5, 9, 99
Los Alamos Scientific
Laboratory, 19,
72, 129, 172n104
Plutonium facility,
192n60
Project Heavenbound, 8,
18, 165n24
Rand Corporation,
18–20, 100,
171n94, 171n96,
183n76, 223n17,
225n24
Sandia Corporation, 10,
33, 49, 56, 66,
72–3
Sugar (Burlington plant),
66, 203n12
Nuclear weapons,
predelegated
authority to
use, 50
Canadian role considered,
52–4
implementing instructions
for, 195n85
Killian Committee
and, 39
Loper, Herbert and, 60–2
New York Times, revealed
in, 87–8
Partridge, Earle and, 80,
87–90
rescindment of, 159
Roman, Peter and, 53, 89,
173n109
Rules of Engagement,
related
development of,
52–3

INDEX 275

U.S. News and World Report, revealed in, 80
Nuclear weapons, safety and surety of, 120, 221n6, 227n54
One Point, tests to ensure, 48–51, 91, 96, 191n57, 192n60
Permissive Action Links, 238–9n169
pressure drop problem, 106, 228n63
nuclear weapons, strategy for:
counterforce, 101
offense and defense balance between, 11, 16, 68, 103, 157–8, 190n46, 223n14
Nuclear weapons and warheads, tests of, 55–6, 68–9, 109–15, 146–7
Blue Straw, 152, 250n7
Castle, 27, 42, 176n28
Eniwetok Proving Grounds, 56, 87, 108–9, 112, 114, 129, 152
Hardtack, 109, 112, 129
Nevada Test Site (NTS) and, 41–3, 71–2, 75–6, 86, 94, 108–9, 113, 148, 191n57, 205n27, 209n63, 210n66
News Nob at, 73, 78
Nougat, 148
Plumbbob, 71–6, 81, 83, 85–6, 94–6, 112, 207n41, 210n67, 211n73, 218n134
announcement of, 71–2
Eisenhower, approval of, 71
Nike-Hercules, and, 95–6
Shot John of, 73, 75–83, 85–7, 93–5, 108–9, 111–13, 210n66, 211n68, 214–15n92

1352nd Motion Picture Squadron and, 111, 213–14n87
aircraft used in, disposition of, 81
Atkinson, Joseph H and, 73–4, 81, 92
Ball, Frank and, 85
Barbee, Cliff and, 82
Bodinger, Norman and, 77, 211n71
Bruce, Sidney and, 84–5
Canadian observers and, 74
Division of Military Applications, AEC, and, 71
Graves, Alvin and, 74
Hutchison, Cliff "Hutch" and, 82
Joint Committee on Atomic Energy, and 70
News Nob, 73, 78
Oldfield, Arthur B. "Barney" and, 73, 76–7, 79–84, 111, 150, 159–60, 208–9n54, 211n69, 213n83–4, 213–14n87, 214–15n92, 215n95, 216n102, 231n91
See also Oldfield, Barney
Our Nuclear Future and, 85
participants, recognition of, 83
Partridge, Earle E. and, 73–4, 79–80, 83
proposal, initial for, 70–1
radiation exposure from, 71–7, 85–6, 210n66–7, 214n91
safety considerations for, 73–5, 77, 112
Yoshitake, George and, 211n69, 212n74

Strauss, publicity objections to, 71
U.S. Public Health Service and, 71
Redwing, 56–8, 123n199
announcement of, 57
warhead test, W-25, for Genie, 56
warhead test, W-37, for Nike-Hercules missile, 56
warhead test, W-40, for BOMARC missile, 57
Snodgrass/Little David/Opera Hat, 111–17, 231n97
1352nd Motion Picture Squadron and, 111
AEC and, 109, 110, 111–12
Eisenhower, Dwight and, 112–15
description of, 110–11, 113–14, 115
diplomatic activities associated with, 113, 114
Dulles, John Foster, and, 109–10, 112
Nike-Hercules unit selected for, 110, 229n72
origins of, 108
Parker, Edward N. and, 112
proposed location of, 108–9, 111–12, 229n78, 230–1n87, 231–2n97
publicity about, 111, 113, 114, 117
safety planning and preparations for, 112, 113
scholarly references to, 231n97
Strauss, Lewis and, 108–9, 110, 112
United States Public Health Service and, 113, 114–15
Teapot, 41–5, 48, 56–7, 63, 66, 73,

INDEX

Nuclear weapons and warheads —*Continued*
   186n7–8, 187n23, 198n111, 224n19
   "high altitude" test in, 41, 44, 73
   Nike-Hercules warhead test, W-31, for, 44–5
   press coverage of, 44, 45
   publicity plans for, 42–3, 44
   United States Public Health Service role in, 42
   Upshot-Knothole, 186n8
   Wigwam, 70, 110, 206–7n37
Nuclear weapons, radiation exposure from, 11–12, 27, 39, 42–4, 63, 71–7, 85–6, 96, 122, 144–6, 210n66, 210n67, 214n91, 250n7
Nuclear weapons, warheads of:
   boosting, 44, 96
   EC-25, 48, 72, 120
   numbers built, 67, 203n15
   purpose for, 48, 66–7
   supplier, components of, 203n13
   withdrawal from inventory of, 69–70, 206n33
   See also W-25
   emergency capability (EC) defined, 48
   "high kill" probability and, 14, 32, 36, 122
Hiroshima, Japan, kilotonage of warhead used against, 11, 198n118
Hydro-dynamic test, 146
implosion weapon, 10, 11, 48
in-flight insertion in, 11, 56, 166n44

kilotonage defined, 10
Oralloy (Oak Ridge alloy) in, 49, 91, 191n58
plutonium and, 10–11, 49, 55, 90–1, 94, 105, 113, 144–5, 150, 191n57, 192n60, 218n134
sealed pit design, 19–20, 44
"Sugar" manufacturing facility for, 66
tritium, 96
W-7:
   BOAR, considered for, 18
   description and characteristics, 10, 11, 56, 166–7n45, 221n6
   Nike-Hercules, emergency capability provided to, 10–11, 21, 96, 106, 120
   nomenclature of, 10
   pressure drop problem of, 106, 228n63
W-12:
   BOAR considered for, 18, 21, 30, 36
   BOMARC considered for, 10
   characteristics of, 10
W-25, 20, 31, 51, 69, 84, 204n18, 208n51
   dimensions, 19
   kilotonage, 19
   one point test of, 49, 51, 91, 191n54, 218n134
   "Oralloy" version, "Fleegle," considered, 49
   production of, 93, 191n54, 203n12, 219–20n150
   Redwing, tested at, 56
   sealed pit design, 19–20
   training version lost, 218–19n136
   X-unit problem in, 93
   W-54, compared to, 129
   See also EC-25 *and* Genie rocket

   (MB-1) and Nuclear weapons and warheads, tests of, (Plumbbob and Snodgrass/Little David/Opera Hat)
W-31, 110–11, 124–5
   characteristics of, 56, 107, 166–7n45, 197–8n108, 221n6
   Nike-Hercules, designed for, 56
   one point test and, 96
   production difficulties of, 119
   ratio of W-31-Y1 and W-31-Y-2 warheads, 124
   Redwing test and, 56
   Y-2 version, 56, 96, 197–8n108
   Teapot test and, 44–5, 56, 187n23
W-37, 56
   See also W-31-Y-2 version
W-40, 57, 96, 140, 143, 145–6, 198n118
   BOMARC missile selected for, 57
   dimensions of, 57
   kilotonage of, 57
   Plumbbob test, 96
   problems of, 140, 142, 145–6
   Redwing test, 57
W-54, 129, 148–9
   characteristics of, 129, 149
   kilontonage of, 129
   Nougat test and, 148
   production problems, 148
   W-25 compared to, 129
   XW-31 warhead, 187n23
   See also W-31

Oldfield, Arthur B.
   "Barney," 73, 76–7, 79–84, 111, 150, 159–60, 208–9n54, 211n69, 213n83–4, 213–14n87,

INDEX

214–15n92,
215n95, 216n102,
231n91
admonished for Genie
revelations, 83
background of, 79–80
Partridge, Earle E. and,
73–4, 79–80, 83,
87–90, 148,
213n84
Reagan, Ronald and, 79,
213n83
One Point, tests, 48–51, 91,
191n57, 192n60
Open Skies initiative, 58,
199n128
Suri, Jeremi and,
228–9n70
Opera Hat, *see* Nuclear
weapons and
warheads, tests of
(Snodgrass/Little
David/Opera Hat)
Operation Alert, *see* Civil
Defense
Operation Snodgrass, *see*
Nuclear weapons
and warheads,
tests of
(Snodgrass/Little
David/Opera Hat)
Operations Coordinating
Board (OCB), *see*
National Security
Council
Oralloy (Oak Ridge alloy),
191n58
Otis Air Force Base,
Massachusetts,
130, 147, 161n2,
212n76
See also BOMARC missile
Our Nuclear Future
(book), 85

Parker, Edward N., 112
Parker, Theodore W., 155,
252n23, 252n25
Partridge, Earle E., 73–4,
79–80, 83, 87–90,
148, 213n84
predelegated nuclear use
and, 80, 87–90
Pauling, Linus, 86, 94,
217n112
Pearl Harbor, attack on, 6

Penkovskiy, Oleg, 234–
5n135
Permissive Action Links, *see*
nuclear weapons,
safety and surety
of
Planning Board, *see* National
Security Council
Plumbbob test series, *see*
Nuclear weapons
and warheads,
tests of
Plutonium, *see* Nuclear
weapons,
warheads of
Porter, Charles O., 86–7
Powers, Francis Gary, 59,
119, 236n138
Predelegation, *see* nuclear
weapons,
predelegated
use of
Project 56, *see* Nuclear
weapons, safety
and surety of
Project AMMO (Army
Mobile Missile
Orientation), 106,
113, 228n67
Project Heavenbound, *see*
Nuclear weapons,
organizations,
studies, and
activities associated
with the
development of
Project TRUTH, 116
Pueblo Ordnance Depot,
Colorado, 123,
125, 155

Quarles, Donald A., 31–3,
88–9, 98, 109,
114, 134, 137,
180n44, 180n48,
180–1n51,
223n18, 229n78
Quesada, Elwood "Pete,"
26, 35

Radford, Arthur W., 15–16,
18, 28–9, 31,
52–5, 69, 103,
182n66, 196n94,
204–5n24,
243n36

Radiation exposure, *see*
Nuclear weapons,
radiation exposure
from
Rand Corporation, 18–20,
100, 171n94,
171n96, 183n76,
223n17, 225n24
Raven Rock, 46
Reagan, Ronald, 79, 213n83,
228–9n70
Reconnaissance and
intelligence
collection, U.S.
efforts of:
Balloon project, 59,
199n129
May Day, (1954), 27,
(1955), 45
Open Skies initiative, 58,
199n128
Suri, Jeremi and
interpretation of,
228–9n70
overflights of USSR,
RB-47, 27, 53,
58–9, 62,
176–7n30,
188n27, 195n87,
196n91, 200n130,
201n148, 227n50
Penkovskiy, Oleg,
234–5n135
Powers, Francis Gary, 59,
119, 236n138
U-2, 38, 59–60, 101, 104,
119, 142, 152–3,
199n128
See also USSR
Redwing test series, *see*
Nuclear weapons
and warheads,
tests of
Relocation arc, 108
See also Continuity of
Government,
facilities and
planning for
rem (Roentgen Equivalent
Man), 210n66
Revell, Inc., 117–18, 131–3,
233–4n130,
242n26
"Rocket" defined, 7
Roman, Peter, 53, 89,
173n109

INDEX

Rosenberg, Julius, 119
Rowen, W. H., 43
Royal Canadian Air Force, 54, 74–5

Saltonstall, Leverett, 24–30, 35–6, 40, 175n20
Sandia Corporation, 10, 33, 49, 56, 66, 72–3
Sarant, Alfred (Philip Staros), 119
Security Resources Panel, see Gaither Committee
Schenck, Joseph M., 214n87
   See also Joseph M. Schenck Enterprises
Schenck, Nicholas, 214n87
Schlesinger, James, 158–9
Science Advisory Committee, 37, 141, 183–4n76, 244n45
Scorpion, see F-89
Semi-Autonomous Ground Environment (SAGE) system, 7, 24, 130, 141, 154, 174n7, 241n21
   See also interceptor aircraft
Shot John nuclear test, see Nuclear weapons and warheads, tests of
Sky Shield, 147–8
Snodgrass, John T., 115
   See also Nuclear weapons and warheads, tests of (Snodgrass/Little David/Opera Hat)
South Korea, 6, 120, 195n87
Soviet Union, see USSR
Sprague, Frank J., 23
Sprague, Robert, 3, 23–40, 47, 55, 65, 68, 90, 98–102, 173n1, 173–4n6, 174–5n13, 178n35, 178n40, 179n42, 180–1n51, 189n43, 204–5n24, 225–6n30, 225n24, 226n39

Joint Committee on Atomic Energy and:
   briefing to 25–6, 28
   briefing to Eisenhower about, 26
   supplemental study for, 28
Eisenhower, Dwight D. and, 23–33, 36, 40, 47–8, 101–2, 173n1, 189n43
Gaither Committee and, 99, 101–2
Killian Committee and, 38, 98
National Security Council, appointment as consultant to, 29–30
nickname, 23
nuclear weapons, antiaircraft, advocacy of, 26, 31–3, 35, 65
personal and family history of, 23
Senate Armed Services, U.S. Committee of, study for, 24–5
Saltonstall, Leverett, relationship with, 24
Sprague Electric Company and, 23
Strategic Air Command and vulnerability of, 98–9, 157–8
TAPE group and, 98–9
Undersecretary of Air Force, selection as, 24
Sprague Electric Company, 23
Sputnik, 130
Starbird, Alfred Dodd, 72, 208n47
Staros, Philip (Alfred Sarant), 119
Stassen, Harold E., 33–4
Stennis, John C., 135
Stevenson, Adlai, 55
Stewart, Jimmy, 81, 150, 213–14n87, 214–15n92

Strategic Air Command, 81
Strauss, Lewis, 28–9, 31, 35, 41–2, 51–2, 57–8, 60–2, 71, 108–12, 114, 177–8n34, 182–3n71, 185n4, 197n98, 199n124
   nuclear air defense weapons, advocacy of, 29, 69
Streibert, Theodore C., 57, 123n199
Suffolk Air Force Base, New York, 140, 142, 147, 156, 161n2
Sugar (Burlington plant), 66, 203n12
Surprise Attack Conference, 107–8

Talos missiles, 56, 62, 99, 135, 198n111, 224n19–20
TAPE group, 98–9, 223–4n18
Teapot test series, 41–5, 48, 56–7, 63, 66, 73, 186n7–8, 187n23, 198n111, 224n19
Technological Capabilities Panel (TCP), see Killian Committee
Telefon (film), 81–2
Teller, Edward, 85–6, 217n112, 227n54
Television, see Films and Television
Tests, see Nuclear weapons and warheads, tests of
Thule Air Force Base, 185n87, 195–6n87, 214n87, 236n145
Toys, see models and collectables
Travis Air Force Base, 224n21
Truman, Harry, 1, 6, 11–13, 46, 99, 168n59
Tu-4 Bull bomber, 6, 27, 30, 163n7
Tu-95 Bear bomber, 45, 59, 160, 188n27
Twining, Nathan, 17, 27, 103, 134, 170n82,

236n143, 243n36, 243–4n43

U-2, see Reconnaissance and intelligence collection, U.S. efforts of
United States Air Force
1352nd Motion Picture Squadron, 213–14n87
Air Defense Command (ADC), 6–9, 18, 20, 36, 67, 73, 78, 80, 85, 91–2, 128, 145, 157, 178n40, 213–14n87
Air Force Special Weapons Center, 8
Agan, Arthur C., 157
Atkinson, Joseph H., 73–4, 81, 92
Continental Air Defense Command (CONAD), 43, 73, 76, 90
Gerhart, John, 154
LeMay, Curtis, 128–9, 211n68, 225n23, 240n11
North American Aerospace Defense Command (NORAD), 80–1, 87–90, 148, 154, 159
Partridge, Earle E., 73–4, 79–80, 83, 87–90, 148, 213n84
Strategic Air Command, 11–12, 56, 68, 90, 98–101, 131, 183–4n76
United States Congress:
House of Representatives: Armed Services Committee of, 36–7, 138–9
Hebert, F. Edward, 139
Joint Committee on Atomic Energy (JCAE), 25–6, 35, 37, 62, 70, 108, 183n74, 211n69
Brodie, Bernard and, 35

Cole, W. Sterling and, 25, 35, 164n21
Eisenhower and objections to studies by, 35
Lindbergh, Charles and, 35
Plumbbob test series and, 70
Quesada, Elwood "Pete" and, 26, 35
Sprague and, 25–6, 28
Strauss and, 35
Wedemeyer report and, 35–7
York, Herbert and, 35
Senate:
Armed Services, Committee
Air Defense Master Plan presented to, 137
Jackson, Henry M., 102, 135, 137, 142
Johnson, Lyndon, 54, 157, 226n34
Kefauver, Estes and, 24–5
Saltonstall, Leverett, 24–30, 35–6, 40, 175n20
Stennis, John C., 135
United States Information Agency, 57
United States Public Health Service, 42, 71, 113–15
Upshot-Knothole, 186n8
USSR:
antiaircraft missiles, similar to Nike-Ajax, 119, 236n138
Bear (Tu-95) bomber of, 45, 59, 160, 188n27
Bison (M-4) bomber of, 27–8, 30, 34, 37–8, 45, 59, 176n30
bombers, U.S. estimates of numbers possessed by, 101, 134, 135–7, 140–1

Bull (Tu-4) bomber of, 6, 27, 30, 163n7
Eisenhower and, 3, 16, 27–9, 37, 53–4, 58, 104, 107, 136–7, 142, 160, 199n128, 228–9n70
ICBMs of, 136, 141, 150–1, 157–8, 160, 234n133, 252n34
Khrushchev, Nikita, 107, 142, 160
May Day (1954), 27, (1955), 45
nuclear antiaircraft arms, U.S. as deterrent to, 82, 159–160
nuclear arsenal, U.S. estimates of 6, 30, 34
Open Skies initiative, 58, 199n128
See also Khrushchev, Nikita and Reconnaissance and intelligence collection, U.S. efforts of

Warheads, see nuclear weapons, warheads of
"Weaponeer, The" (television show), 81–2, 213–4n87
Weapons Systems Evaluation Group (WSEG), 190n46
Wedemeyer, Albert C., 35–7
Western Electric Company, 105, 116, 122, 138–9
Westhampton Beach, New York, 140
See also BOMARC missile
Whalen, William H., see Espionage, activities associated with
White House Relocation Site, 46

INDEX

White Sands Proving Ground, New Mexico, 106, 108, 218n136
White, Thomas D., 136
Whitman, Ann C., 31, 179–80n43
Wilson, Charles E., 15, 28–32, 35–6, 50–2, 60, 62–3, 69, 103, 178n35, 223n14
Wurtsmith Air Force Base, Michigan, 65–7, 70, 78, 203–4n16
See also Genie rocket
Hamilton Air Force Base, California, 65–7, 70, 78, 203–4n16
See also Genie rocket

York, Herbert, 35
Yoshitake, George, 211n69, 212n74

Zanuck, Darryl, 213–14n87